C

D1246199

The views expressed in this book are those of the
individual authors and not necessarily those of the
World Bank or the Institute of Development Studies.

Edited by Ian Bowen and Brian J. Svikhart

REDISTRIBUTION
WITH GROWTH

Policies to improve income distribution in developing countries
in the context of economic growth—
a joint study by the
World Bank's Development Research Center and the
Institute of Development Studies at the University of Sussex

by

HOLLIS CHENERY
MONTEK S. AHLUWALIA
C.L.G. BELL
JOHN H. DULOY
RICHARD JOLLY

Published for the
WORLD BANK

and the

INSTITUTE OF DEVELOPMENT STUDIES
University of Sussex

OXFORD UNIVERSITY PRESS

Oxford University Press

NEW YORK OXFORD LONDON GLASGOW
TORONTO MELBOURNE WELLINGTON HONG KONG
TOKYO KUALA LUMPUR SINGAPORE JAKARTA
DELHI BOMBAY CALCUTTA MADRAS KARACHI
NAIROBI DAR ES SALAAM CAPE TOWN

ISBN 0 19 920070 X
paperback edition
First printing   August 1974
Second printing   July 1975
Third printing   March 1979

PREFACE

This report has its origins in discussions between members of the Institute of Development Studies (University of Sussex) and the Development Research Center of the World Bank over the past several years. Our point of departure was the notable inconsistency between the general perception of income distribution and employment as major problems for developing countries on the one hand, and the analytical tools available to policy-makers on the other. In order to focus the attention of both policy-makers and researchers on the approaches to this problem that are now available, we commissioned a set of papers covering the "state of the art" in the design of policies in this field. These papers were discussed at a workshop convened at the Rockefeller Foundation Conference Center in Bellagio in April 1973.

A first draft of this Report was prepared by five of the participants on the basis of the workshop discussion and the contributed papers. This document was widely circulated and discussed at a seminar held at the Institute of Development Studies in Sussex. This conference brought together most of the original participants plus a number of analysts and policy-makers from both industrial countries and the Third World. In these discussions we tried to translate the general approach proposed in the first Report into a concrete set of proposals for action that more fully reflect the variety of conditions in developing countries.

The present document attempts to produce a synthesis of the initial ideas and to develop them in a more solid analytical form. This process has been helped by a series of seminars on the theoretical and practical aspects of the problems of poverty in the World Bank, the Institute of Development Studies, and the Center for International Affairs at Harvard University. While acknowledging gratefully the many contributions from our colleagues, they clearly cannot be implicated in the final result. Similarly, while we have all reacted at length to each other's drafts, the individual chapters of this report remain the responsibility of their authors. Although we agree on the major themes advanced, we have not tried to produce a "committee report" that would reconcile all our differences. Such an attempt seems inappropriate in a document that tries to bring together the perceptions of policy-makers as to the nature of economic and political problems and the suggestions of researchers as to how to solve them.

We are grateful to the Rockefeller Foundation for inviting us to use their facilities at the Villa Serbelloni for our initial discussions. We also owe a particular debt to Professor Dudley Seers of the Institute of Development Studies, who took the initiative in proposing this collaborative effort but whose subsequent participation was unfortunately limited by illness. A special word of thanks is due D.C. Rao of the World Bank for his notable contribution to our analysis of urban poverty and to the six authors of the country analyses included in the Annex.

Finally, we are indebted to Hans Singer, who first developed the theme of redistribution with growth in a paper prepared for the report of the International Labour Office's Employment Mission to Kenya (*Employment, Incomes and Equality,* ILO, 1972), organized in connection with the World Employment Programme of the ILO.

HOLLIS CHENERY
MONTEK S. AHLUWALIA
C.L.G. BELL
JOHN H. DULOY
RICHARD JOLLY

TABLE OF CONTENTS

Participants in the Conference on Redistribution with Growth, Institute of Development Studies, University of Sussex (September 1973) were:

*Irma Adelman	University of Maryland
Ponniah Arudsothy	University of Malaysia
*Montek S. Ahluwalia	Development Research Center, World Bank
*Pranab Bardhan	Delhi School of Economics
*C.L.G. Bell	Institute of Development Studies
*Charles Blitzer	Development Research Center, World Bank
Gordon Bridger	Economic Planning Staff, ODA, London
*Jorge Causs	Development Research Center, World Bank
Hikmet Cetin	Economics Department, Planning Organisation, Ankara
*Hollis Chenery	World Bank
*Peter Clark	Development Research Center, World Bank
*John H. Duloy	Development Research Center, World Bank
I. J. Ebong	Ministry of Economic Development and Reconstruction, Lagos
Charles Elliot	Overseas Development Group, University of East Anglia
H. A. Fell	Economic Planning Staff, ODA, London
Alejandro Foxley	Centro de Estudios de Planificación, Santiago
Charles Frank	The Brookings Institution, Washington, D.C.
*Reginald Green	The Treasury, Dar es Salaam
Ravi Gulhati	Development Economics Department, World Bank
Mahbub ul Haq	Policy Planning and Program Review Department, World Bank
Geoffrey Heal	University of Sussex
John Healey	International Economics Division, ODA, London
Lal Jayawardena	Ministry of Planning and Economic Affairs, Colombo
*Richard Jolly	Institute of Development Studies
*Leonard Joy	Institute of Development Studies
*Geoffrey Lamb	Institute of Development Studies
Donald McGranahan	U.N. Research Institute for Social Development, Geneva
Festus Mogae	Ministry of Finance and Development Planning, Gaborone
Ahmed el Morshidy	Ministry of Planning, Cairo
Jacob Mwanza	University of Zambia
Yung Chul Park	Korea Development Institute, Seoul
Felix Paukert	Employment Planning and Promotion Department, ILO, Geneva

*Members of the Bellagio Workshop (April 1973), which also included Henk Bos (Netherlands School of Economics), Albert Fishlow (University of California), Ralph Hofmeister (World Bank), and Norman Uphoff (Cornell University).

Anibal Pinto   U.N. Economic Commission for Latin America
Stanley Please   Eastern Africa Region, World Bank
Graham Pyatt   University of Warwick
Gustav Ranis   Economic Growth Center, Yale University
*Dudley Seers   Institute of Development Studies
Hans Singer   Institute of Development Studies
T. N. Srinivasan   Indian Statistical Institute
*Lance Taylor   University of Brasilia; Harvard University
Erik Thorbecke   Employment Planning and Promotion Department, ILO, Geneva
Miguel Urrutia   Banco de la República, Bogota
Flavio Versiani   University of Brasilia
Tsunehiko Watanabe   University of Osaka
Larry Westphal   Northwestern University
Ponna Wignaraja   Asian Institute for Economic Development and Planning, Bangkok
Jon Wilmshurst   Economic Planning Staff, ODA, London
Francis Wilson   University of Cape Town
Charles Young   Economic Planning Staff, ODA, London

INTRODUCTION
HOLLIS CHENERY

IT IS NOW clear that more than a decade of rapid growth in under-developed countries has been of little or no benefit to perhaps a third of their population. Although the average per capita income of the Third World has increased by 50 percent since 1960, this growth has been very unequally distributed among countries, regions within countries, and socio-economic groups. Paradoxically, while growth policies have succeeded beyond the expectations of the first development decade, the very idea of aggregate growth as a social objective has increasingly been called into question.

As the evidence of growing inequality in the Third World has come to light over the past five years, it has produced varied reactions among politicians, policy-makers, and economists. In many countries the rhetoric of income redistribution has been used as a political substitute for the design of policies that might help to bring it about. While some economists have started proclaiming the necessity to sacrifice growth in order to achieve better distribution, others contend that it is only through an increase in GNP that there will be anything significant to distribute.

The conference that provided the starting point for this report was designed to assess the relations between growth and distribution in representative countries and to suggest an analytical framework within which a more fruitful approach to policy-making could take place. These discussions have led us to reexamine the problems of distribution and growth as a necessary preliminary to reformulating the techniques of economic planning.

From our examination of both the experience of development and the conceptual underpinnings of policy, we have reached several conclusions which, though still preliminary in form, differ markedly from traditional approaches to development policy:

- On the empirical side, the new conventional wisdom seems to be almost as misleading as the old. While in some growing economies the poor receive little or no benefit, in others the opposite is true: even the relative share of the poverty groups has increased in several notable cases. This diversity of experience provides a basis for identifying different approaches to policy and for evaluating their effects on poverty.

- On the theoretical side, it is necessary to discard the conceptual separation between optimum growth and distribution policies that lies at the heart of traditional welfare economics. For the poorer countries, at least, it should be replaced by the notion of a development strategy having growth implications for different groups in society that can be modified by fiscal measures only within fairly narrow limits.

As explained in the Preface, this study is intended as a progress report on work on this agenda in the World Bank and the Institute of Development Studies over the past two or three years. It grows out of dissatisfaction with the inadequate responses of policy-makers to the growing problems of relative poverty and underemployment, and a desire to provide them with analytical tools that are relevant to these problems. While a comprehensive and adequately tested formulation of the ideas advanced here is probably several years in the future, we do not feel that it is necessary to wait for the results of further research to begin the reorientation of policy that is so badly needed.

Our report consists of a set of interrelated essays that start with an empirical diagnosis of the dimensions of poverty and brief discussions of the economic and political framework within which they should be analyzed. These introductory statements are followed by discussions of the policy instruments available to governments, the differences among strategies needed to reach the several rural and urban poverty groups, and the implications of our analysis for international policies. Taken together, the eight chapters in Part I offer a fairly compact and nontechnical statement of our proposed reorientation of development policy.

Implementation of this approach by planners and academic researchers requires discussion at a more technical level. Our proposed shift in the focus of planning does not imply that balance of payments or savings constraints are less important than was previously thought—on the contrary, they are critical aspects of any attempt to reformulate planning methods. In Part II we therefore survey the elements of existing planning models that can be combined with new forms of analysis of asset distribution and the ways in which the incomes of different groups are generated. We also stress the statistical requirements for further progress in this area and indicate some promising lines of research.

The report, which is written by five authors in varying combinations, provides a systematic development of these themes. The principal elements of the analysis are summarized here as a guide to the reader, so that he can get an idea of the main thrust of the argument before becoming immersed in its details.

Diagnosis

Recent evidence confirms earlier speculations that in the early stages of development the distribution of income tends to become more concentrated. Increases in output come disproportionately from relatively small modern sectors of primary production and industry, which absorb a high proportion of total investment and have relatively high rates of productivity growth. This pattern of concentrated growth is perpetuated by limited access to land, credit, education, and modern-sector employment, and is often reinforced, unintentionally or otherwise, by the government's fiscal and trade policies as well as the distribution of public expenditures.

As growth continues, its benefits are more widely spread, but there are a number of obstacles that limit the share received by the poor. The rapid growth of population of the past fifteen or twenty years has led to an excess supply of unskilled labor in most developing countries, including almost all the larger ones. Since they cannot be absorbed in wage employment, the bulk of the poor are self-employed small farmers, rural artisans, and members of the rapidly growing urban "informal" sector. For these poverty groups, income growth is limited by lack of access to land, capital, and other public facilities, often by outright discrimination. To some extent they are outside the organized market economy and have only weak links with it.

While these factors help to explain the tendency for the benefits of growth to be concentrated in the early stages and to spread only slowly thereafter, the experience of countries with income levels above $200 per capita demonstrates that further increases in concentration are by no means inevitable. In several countries, access to modern-sector employment has been improved through education and the rapid growth of demand for labor, while in others land has been redistributed and public investment redirected to offset the initial disadvantages of the poor. While generalizations as to the relative effectiveness of different policies are not yet possible, the bulk of the developing countries in which the poor have shared equitably in income growth — Israel, Yugoslavia, Taiwan, Korea, Sri Lanka, Costa Rica, Tanzania — consists of countries that have taken positive action to this end.

This diagnosis has several important policy implications. (i) The poor are prevented from sharing equitably in a general increase in output by a number of specific disabilities that can be summed up as *lack of physical and human capital* and *lack of access*. Policies designed to offset these handicaps must take account of the particular socio-economic characteristics of given *target groups*. (ii) Although growth tends initially to be concentrated in a few sectors of the economy, with little effect on major poverty groups, a number of countries have devised policies for offsetting this tendency so that the benefits of growth can be shared more equally.

Social Objectives

Our diagnosis of the causes and dimensions of poverty calls into serious question the accepted approaches to policy-making. To deal with the problems of poverty groups, we need to design overall programs or "policy packages" rather than a set of isolated projects. The choice among alternative programs for using public and private resources requires a statement of social objectives against which they can be evaluated, which is currently lacking in planning procedures.

Although the gross national product was not designed as a measure of social welfare, it is the index most widely used for that purpose. Its deficiencies become clear if we start from the increase in incomes of different socio-economic groups — however defined — and then aggregate them into a single index of social welfare. Considered in these terms, the growth of GNP is a special case in which weights are proportional to the group's existing share in the national product. In the typical developing countries, this means that a weight of 75 percent is given to the growth of the top 40 percent of income recipients, but only 12 percent to the growth of the bottom 40 percent, whom we identify as the poverty groups. Even if the investment of public funds to remove the disabilities of the poverty groups is highly successful, the resulting increase in output is likely to take longer to materialize than a project in the modern sector, and the project will therefore appear less "productive" unless we allow for the distribution of its benefits.

To remedy this lack of a usable index of economic and social performance, we have proposed that the income growth of different groups in society be given weights either in proportion to their numbers ("one man, one vote") or inversely proportional to their initial income levels ("poverty weights"). The equal weights imply that an increase of $10 in a family having an income of $1000 would be valued equally with an increase of $1 to a family with an income of $100, since each produces a one-percent advance. The methodology is politically neutral, since the weights can be chosen to fit the preferences of a given society. In these terms, the conflict between "equity" and "efficiency" disappears, since the most efficient program is the one which maximizes the welfare measure selected.

Applications of this measure in Chapter II to all countries having time series of income distributions show that it provides a useful synthesis of distribution and growth considerations. Slower-growing countries with improving distribution are evaluated more favorably than by the growth of GNP, while fast-growing countries in which the poor have not shared proportionately are evaluated less favorably. For planning purposes, the welfare index can be used to evaluate the effects of proposed development programs, as illustrated in Chapter XI.

Policy Instruments and Political Constraints

Our analysis assumes the existence of political and administrative conditions that are typical of developing countries, not the simplified premises of economic theory. We have attempted to introduce elements of realism into the analysis in several ways—by considering a number of actual cases (of which six are reviewed in the Annex), by assuming limitations to the use of policy instruments (e.g., tax levels), and by introducing political considerations in the statement of objectives and design of development strategies.

While few countries are likely to accept the full implications of the poverty-oriented measure of social welfare and economic performance just outlined, such measures can have a considerable impact on policy-making in most developing countries. However, the requirements of governments to secure and maintain political support from diverse groups must also be taken into account in any statement of objectives. This requirement leads policy-makers to design strategies that may be less effective in purely distributional terms but will provide some benefits to a broader range of socio-economic groups.

The bulk of developing countries have mixed economic systems combining elements of public and private ownership as well as mixed political systems combining democratic and authoritarian features. These conditions limit the range of application of the laissez faire instruments of taxation and price policy as well as the socialist instruments of state ownership and direct intervention. Our diagnosis of the available administrative and political options leads us to conclude that elements of both systems are needed.

The assessment of the effectiveness of different policy instruments in Chapter IV has important implications for the choice of development strategies. The design of a poverty-oriented strategy requires the selection of a mix of policy instruments that can reach the target groups that have been identified. While we advocate maximum use of instruments that operate through factor and product markets, often they will not be sufficient for this purpose. We have therefore given particular attention to a range of direct measures, such as land reform, the distribution of education, and other public services, and measures to redistribute assets towards the poverty groups. Without such a redistribution of at least the increments of capital formation, other distributive measures are not likely to have a lasting impact on the poverty problem.

Since our main concern is with the more typical countries of the Third World, we have not attempted to assess the experience of either the socialist countries or the earlier policies of the now advanced Western countries, although there is much to be learned from both. Some brief observations on the Cuban experience with socialism are given in the Annex, since it represents one of the more extreme examples of the effects of policies in which a clear preference is given to equal distribution of income rather than growth.

Poverty-focused Strategies

Our diagnosis of the nature of poverty in developing countries and of the inadequacy of conventional measures of social progress leads us to propose a fundamental redirection of development strategy. Before this can be undertaken, the general diagnosis must first be refined to fit the conditions of each country. This requires a specific analysis of the characteristics of the principal poverty groups, which vary greatly between rural and urban areas and according to their response to different policies.

The recognition that 80 percent or more of the low-end poverty group are employed in some fashion has shifted the focus of policy from increasing the quantity to improving the quality of employment. While the tools for analyzing the sectors that employ most of the poor — small-scale agriculture and the urban "informal" sector — are primitive, the available studies suggest that there is considerable scope for expanding the productive use of resources in these activities. Since many governments currently discriminate against them in favor of more capital-intensive alternatives, a widespread reconsideration of these impediments is indicated.

This approach needs to be adapted to the different characteristics of the rural and urban poverty groups. The former tend to benefit less from linkages to the modern sectors of the economy and hence from a general expansion of output. Our rural strategy therefore focuses on increasing the productivity of the small farmer and the self-employed through better access to land, water, credit markets, and other facilities.

The urban poor require a more diversified strategy. In the first place, it is desirable to restructure the modern sector to make it more responsive to the opportunity costs of labor and capital, which implies a shift toward more labor-intensive products and processes. However, even with optimal policies, the modern sector cannot provide employment for the bulk of the rapidly growing urban labor force. A second range of policies designed to reach the self-employed and to make small-scale producers more efficient is therefore necessary. This direct approach focuses on improved access to inputs, the redirection of public investment, and the removal of discrimination against small producers, and therefore has much in common with the direct approach to rural poverty problems.

Planning Techniques

A reorientation of policy requires a reorientation of planning methods. The term "reorientation" is used advisedly, since poverty-focused planning does not imply the abandonment of growth as an objective. It implies instead redistribution of the benefits of growth.

The major change needed in the design of planning models is the addition of a new dimension: the identification of socio-economic groups of asset holders and income recipients, including the principal target groups on whom specific policies are focused. The main purpose of this grouping by types of income recipients is to trace the effects of a given policy on different groups and to incorporate indirect benefits to the poverty groups through their linkage to the rest of the economy. Without an attempt to treat these aspects of interdependence systematically, there is a danger that policy-making will veer too far from exclusive reliance on indirect (trickle down) benefits to ignoring their importance entirely.

Since no suitable models of this sort have yet been tried out for a given country, we have designed a prototype of such a model that is illustrated in Chapter XI. It has the limited objectives of (i) incorporating asset formation and accumulation by different groups into the analysis; (ii) tracing the effects of wage linkages between poverty groups and the rest of the economy; and (iii) comparing in broad terms our preferred strategy of "investment redistribution" to other approaches to the problem of poverty. One by-product of this analysis is to give a more precise content to the general concept of a trade-off between growth and distribution, suggesting that in the investment redistribution strategy the trade-off is likely to take the form of a longer gestation period for investment in assets held by the poor rather than a permanent reduction in GNP.

Since three-quarters of the poor are located in rural areas, agriculture and rural development must be a major concern of poverty-oriented planning. Models focusing on the agricultural sector can be used to trace out the farmers' supply response to pricing policy and how it changes with the availability of new technology. More aggregate models, at the level of the sector, can quantify some of the trade-offs between farmers and consumers, which are particularly marked in a sector with low elasticities of demand and supply. They can also provide guidelines as to the allocation of investment in agriculture and its impact on employment and on farmers' incomes and simulate the responsiveness of the sector to a wide range of policies.

Data and Research

The reorientation of policy and of planning requires a parallel reorientation of priorities for the collection of data. These new information requirements are discussed in Chapter XII. They involve, in particular, far more attention to the collection of data to describe the socio-economic characteristics of the poor, and the tabulation of existing data in ways which permit an analysis of the distributional aspects of policy measures.

How government budget resources are generated and how they are allocated are basic questions for any distribution policy. Government budgets typically are not disaggregated by categories relevant for distribution purposes although the information to do so is generally available. For example, household consumption surveys provide information on the consumption patterns of different income groups, which can be used to evaluate the incidence of different patterns of indirect taxation. However crude, these estimates provide a basis for a more selective approach to raising government revenues.

We give our views on some fruitful directions for research in Chapter XIII. Because of the lack of an adequate theory of income distribution, we do not put high priority upon the construction of more elaborate general-purpose models. Instead, the development of more limited models directed at particular problems appears more promising, when combined with attempts to link these analyses into a more comprehensive analysis.

However far we may be from a theory of distribution relevant to the problems of the Third World, and from quantitative models based on it, it is evident that a great deal can be done by adapting existing and proven methods of analysis. The major obstacle to a better sharing of the benefits of growth is not the availability of data nor of quantitative analytical techniques. It is, instead, the determination of developing countries to redefine the objectives of development, to reorient their policies, and to implement them.

The International Setting

As this report is being completed, the international economy is in a state of economic disequilibrium and institutional disarray not seen since the early postwar years. While the ultimate outcome of the structural changes precipitated by the sudden rise in energy prices can be only dimly perceived at this point, the adjustment processes will almost inevitably exacerbate the problems with which we are concerned here. This prospect makes it even more urgent to try to safeguard the interests of the poor in designing the mechanisms by which adjustments in the international economy are to be brought about.

The producers of oil and other primary products who are currently benefiting from changes in relative prices constitute less than a quarter of the population of the Third World. Apart from Indonesia and Nigeria, the bulk of the world's poor live in countries whose continued growth is seriously threatened by the rise in petroleum prices and its repercussions on export markets and the supply of fertilizers and foodstuffs.

To offset the large increases in the cost of their imports, many countries will have to change their development priorities in the direction of import substitution, development of indigenous energy sources, and export expansion. This redirection will be accomplished by a once-and-for-all reduction in income levels, but it does not necessarily require a slackening of growth nor a worsening of internal income distribution. Both are likely to occur, however, unless adequate provision is made to prevent them. Detailed prescriptions for these problems are outside the scope of this report, and they are only treated very briefly in Chapter VIII. However, the need to cope with a serious balance of payments disequilibrium should not be made an excuse for adopting measures that exacerbate the already serious problems of income distribution and employment.

PART ONE: REORIENTATION OF POLICY

CHAPTER I

INCOME INEQUALITY: SOME DIMENSIONS
OF THE PROBLEM
Montek S. Ahluwalia

Recent discussions of economic development reflect an increasing concern with widespread poverty in underdeveloped countries. The fact of poverty is not new: it was always self-evident to those familiar with economic realities. What *is* new is the suspicion that economic growth by itself may not solve or even alleviate the problem within any "reasonable" time period. Indeed it is often argued that the mechanisms which promote economic growth also promote economic concentration, and a worsening of the relative and perhaps even absolute position of the lower-income groups. This pessimistic view has led to some questioning of growth-oriented development strategies which assume that the poverty problem would be solved without much difficulty if growth could be accelerated.

The empirical evidence underlying the new pessimism is limited but persuasive. Detailed studies of the nature and extent of poverty in particular countries show that the problem is of truly gigantic proportions. A study of poverty in India estimated that, in 1960, about 38 percent of the rural population and 50 percent of the urban population lived below a poverty level defined by consumption yielding 2,250 calories.[1] A recent study of Brazil showed that, also in 1960, about 30 percent of the total population lived below a poverty level defined by the minimum wage in northeast Brazil (the poorest region).[2] More importantly, both studies argued that the situation had worsened over the sixties, at least in terms of relative equality. Similarly pessimistic results on changes in relative equality over time were reported in a study of Argentina, Mexico, and Puerto Rico.[3] In addition to these case studies there is some evidence from cross-country analysis of distribution patterns which can be interpreted as showing that economic growth is associated with a worsening in the distribution of income, at least in the initial stages of development.

These studies raise important questions relevant to policy formulation. What is the extent of relative and absolute poverty in underdeveloped countries and does it vary systematically with the level of development? What evidence is there on the relationship between growth and inequality and how far can this relationship be affected by policy? What are the economic characteristics of the poor and what do they imply for distributional strategies?

I am grateful to Robert Cassen and Dudley Seers for their vigilant concern about the dangers of using "garbage data" which served to strengthen my own considerable reservations on this subject. Acknowledgements are also due Shail Jain and Julio Kipnis, who provided computational assistance.

[1]Dandekar and Rath (1971). See also Bardhan (1970) and (1973a).
[2]Fishlow (1972).
[3]Weisskoff (1970).

In this chapter we will attempt to sift the available evidence to provide qualitative answers to some of these questions. But first a general caveat is necessary. Analysis of income distribution problems is severely limited by the quality and reliability of the available data and a brief digression on this subject is desirable.

LIMITATIONS OF THE DATA

The primary sources of information on patterns of income distribution are sample surveys which provide data on income (and in some cases only consumption) and other socio-economic characteristics of the units sampled. Until recently, data of this type were available for only a few underdeveloped countries and generalizations about patterns of distribution were therefore based on very limited information. For example, Kuznets's (1963) study of cross-country patterns of income distribution included only eleven underdeveloped countries. The situation has changed considerably since then. A large number of surveys have been carried out in underdeveloped countries and results from these surveys are increasingly being used in analyses of income distribution problems.

Unfortunately, the increase in data availability has not been accompanied by an adequate improvement in statistical quality. In many cases the growing interest in the subject has simply led to the proliferation of crude estimates of income distribution for various countries, based on data sources which may be "the best available" but are simply not good enough. An exhaustive review of these problems is beyond the scope of this chapter, but some indication of their importance can be obtained by considering three major sources of error in this field.

First, the income concept used in many surveys falls far short of the comprehensive definition needed. For purposes of welfare measurement, the income concept should refer to "permanent income" and should include income from all sources whether accruing in the form of money income or income in kind (including production for own consumption and investment).[4] Furthermore, if it is to be a measure of welfare, the income concept should be adjusted for tax incidence and transfer payments. In practice, available surveys measure income over a short period—usually a month or at most a year. Frequently they cover only money income, and sometimes only wage income, giving a distorted picture of the true distribution of income in the economy.

Second, even if the income concept is properly defined, it may be difficult to measure in practice. Very different problems arise at the two ends of the income scale. In the highest income groups there is the ever present likelihood of deliberate understatement of income for fear of incurring a tax liability. At the other end of the income scale there is a genuine difficulty in valuing

---

[4]Permanent income takes account of variations over the lifetime of the individual arising from both the age profile of income and random fluctuations around this profile. Income differences due to age are an important element of observed inequality in most samples of individuals at different stages in their working life.

production for own consumption or investment in the subsistence sectors of the economy.[5] Closely related to the measurement problem is the difficulty in using relative money incomes as a measure of relative real incomes, given the wide variation in prices facing different consumers. Rural prices of some goods are typically much lower than urban prices, so that comparisons of urban-rural money incomes typically understate rural real income levels.

Third, there is the problem of accuracy in estimating the distribution of income in the population from the observed distribution in sample surveys. The accuracy of sample estimates depends upon a number of factors relating to the size of the sample and its representativeness. Many available estimates of income distribution are derived from samples that are statistically inadequate in these respects with the result that sample estimates are both biased and have a large variance. In several cases the samples from which data are available were never originally intended to be representative of the population as a whole.[6] In other cases, despite an attempt at ensuring representativeness, the difficulties of sample design or implementation may have proved overwhelming. For example, no adequate sampling frame may exist from which to select a sample ensuring proportional coverage of different income groups. The existence of nomadic populations or inaccessible regions presents the most extreme form of this problem.

Because of these problems, available estimates of income distribution in most underdeveloped countries are, at best, approximations of the underlying distribution we wish to measure. Inaccuracy of measurement is not, of course, unique to income distribution; national accounts data are also subject to such errors. But the data limitations for income distribution are usually regarded as more serious. National accounts data are at least collected on a systematic basis and are therefore much more comparable over time and (although to a lesser extent) between countries. No such comparability can be claimed for data on income distribution. Estimates for different countries, and even for the same country at different points of time, are typically based on noncomparable data sources, making intercountry and intertemporal comparisons very hazardous.

These limitations present a familiar dilemma in empirical analysis. The data are very weak, but they are also the only data we have. An extreme response to the problem is to reject any use of most of the available data for analytical purposes. The approach adopted in this chapter is less puristic. We assume that until better data become available, cautious use of existing data—with all its limitations—provides some perspective on the nature of

---

[5]Even if the consumption items can be quantified in physical terms, there is the problem of determining the appropriate prices to use in obtaining a "money value" for this consumption. Producer prices (farm gate prices) differ from retail prices, especially in different seasons. The problem of valuing production for direct investment (i.e., various types of labor using farm improvements) is even more complex since there is typically no market for the capital good produced.

[6]This is true, for example, of labor force surveys directed at determining the structure of wages, urban household surveys aimed at constructing cost-of-living indexes for particular socio-economic sections of the population and, of course, tax data which cover only a very small percentage of the population.

the problem. In common with Kuznets (1955), our excuse "for building an elaborate structure on such a shaky foundation" is the view that "speculation is an effective way of presenting a broad view of the field and . . . so long as it is recognized as a collection of hunches calling for further investigation, rather than a set of fully tested conclusions, little harm and much good may result."

The Extent of Inequality: Relative and Absolute Poverty

The first step in defining the dimensions of the problem with which this volume is concerned is to consider the extent of inequality in developed and underdeveloped countries. Cross-section data are particularly useful for this purpose because they reveal possible "uniform patterns" which characterize the problem in different countries. Identifying such uniformities helps to establish "averages" with which levels of inequality observed in particular countries can be compared. They also serve to determine reasonable "benchmarks" in terms of which targets and prospects for improvement can be defined. We distinguish for this purpose between two different approaches to income distribution. The first is concerned with the degree of relative inequality within a country and the second with the degree of absolute poverty. Both aspects of the problem are relevant for policy but in particular countries or situations greater emphasis may be placed on one or the other.

Relative Inequality

The conventional approach to income inequality is to define the problem in purely relative terms. A familiar technique for this purpose is to measure inequality by the extent to which the income share of groups of individuals or households differs from their population share. In this section, we will examine the problem in terms of income shares of the lowest 40 percent, the middle 40 percent, and the top 20 percent of households ordinally ranked by income.[7] For some countries, distribution estimates are available only for individuals in the workforce. We have included these estimates in our data set as the best available approximation to household income distribution.

The choice of income shares instead of one of the various conventional indexes of inequality calls for some explanation.[8] The conventional indexes are designed to provide summary measures of inequality over the entire range of the population and as such may be insensitive to the degree of inequality in

---

[7] The choice of households rather than individuals as the basic income unit reflects the assumption that income within a household is equally distributed. Even so there are problems arising from variations in household size and age structure. An alternative is to rank the population according to household per capita income, but data on this basis are available only for a few countries.

[8] The best known of the various indexes is the Gini coefficient, which is based on the Lorenz curve. Others include the variance of income, the variance of logarithms of income, the coefficient of variation, and also entropy measures borrowed from information theory such as the index developed by Theil (1967). Atkinson (1970) proposes a new measure of inequality which is explicitly related to an underlying social welfare function and therefore provides a more meaningful basis for comparing or ranking alternative distributions.

particular ranges. Our treatment in terms of the income shares of ordinally ranked income groups enables us to concentrate on inequality at the lower end of the income range which may be of special interest for policy.

Table I.1 presents income share data for sixty-six countries cross-classified according to different levels of overall inequality and per capita income levels.[9] The table distinguishes between three inequality levels defined as high, moderate, and low (according to specified ranges of the share of the lowest 40 percent) and three income groupings defined as high, middle, and low (according to specified ranges of per capita GNP). The extent of inequality varies widely among countries but the following broad patterns can be identified.

The *socialist countries* have the highest degree of overall equality in the distribution of income. This is as we would expect, since income from the ownership of capital does not accrue as income to individuals.[10] The observed inequality in these countries is due mainly to inequality in wages between sectors and skill classes. Since the structural factors operating towards equality are the strongest in these countries, their average income share of the lowest 40 percent—amounting to about 25 percent of total income—may be taken as an upper limit for the target income share to which policy-makers in underdeveloped countries can aspire.

The *developed countries* are evenly distributed between the categories of low and moderate inequality. The average income share of the bottom 40 percent amounts to about 16 percent, which is lower than the average for socialist countries but better than most of the underdeveloped countries. A major problem in comparing income distribution data between developed and underdeveloped countries is that pretax data does not reflect the equalizing impact of progressive taxes combined with welfare-oriented public transfer mechanisms. These fiscal corrections are generally more substantial and more egalitarian in developed countries. If this factor is taken into account, developed countries may be somewhat more egalitarian than appears from Table I.1.

Most of the *underdeveloped countries* show markedly greater relative inequality than the developed countries. About half of the underdeveloped countries fall in the high inequality range with another third displaying moderate inequality. The average income share for the lowest 40 percent in all underdeveloped countries as a group amounts to about 12.5 percent, but there is considerable variation around this average. Those of the underdeveloped countries classified in the low inequality category have income shares for the lowest 40 percent averaging 18 percent, as is the case with the most egalitarian of the developed countries. Against this, however, half the underdeveloped countries show income shares of the lowest 40 percent, averaging only 9 percent.

---

[9]The data are taken from Jain and Tiemann (1974). The original sources for each country as reported in that document are listed in the Appendix to Chapter I.

[10]Income distribution data for these countries may overstate income equality since they frequently refer to "workers," which may exclude workers outside the state system who are usually in the lower income ranges.

Table I.1: Cross-classification of Countries by Income Level and Equality

HIGH INEQUALITY
Share of Lowest 40% less than 12%

Country (year)	Per Capita GNP US$	Lowest 40%	Middle 40%	Top 20%
Income up to U.S. $300				
Kenya (1969)	136	10.0	22.0	68.0
Sierra Leone (1968)	159	9.6	22.4	68.0
Iraq (1956)	200	6.8	25.2	68.0
Philippines(1971)	239	11.6	34.6	53.8
Senegal (1960)	245	10.0	26.0	64.0
Ivory Coast (1970)	247	10.8	32.1	57.1
Rhodesia (1968)	252	8.2	22.8	69.0
Tunisia (1970)	255	11.4	33.6	55.0
Honduras (1968)	265	6.5	28.5	65.0
Ecuador (1970)	277	6.5	20.0	73.5
Turkey (1968)	282	9.3	29.9	60.8
El Salvador (1969)	295	11.2	36.4	52.4
Income U.S. $300-$750				
Malaysia (1970)	330	11.6	32.4	56.0
Colombia (1970)	358	9.0	30.0	61.0
Brazil (1970)	390	10.0	28.4	61.6
Peru (1971)	480	6.5	33.5	60.0
Gabon (1968)	497	8.8	23.7	67.5
Jamaica (1958)	510	8.2	30.3	61.5
Costa Rica (1971)	521	11.5	30.0	58.5
Mexico (1969)	645	10.5	25.5	64.0
South Africa (1965)	669	6.2	35.8	58.0
Panama (1969)	692	9.4	31.2	59.4

MODERATE INEQUALITY
Share of Lowest 40% between 12% and 17%

Country (year)	Per Capita GNP US$	Lowest 40%	Middle 40%	Top 20%
Burma (1958)	82	16.5	38.7	44.8
Dahomey (1959)	87	15.5	34.5	50.0
Tanzania (1967)	89	13.0	26.0	61.0
India (1964)	99	16.0	32.0	52.0
Madagascar (1960)	120	13.5	25.5	61.0
Zambia (1959)	230	14.5	28.5	57.0
Dominican Republic (1969)	323	12.2	30.3	57.5
Iran (1968)	332	12.5	33.0	54.5
Guyana (1956)	550	14.0	40.3	45.7
Lebanon (1960)	508	13.0	26.0	61.0
Uruguay (1968)	618	16.5	35.5	48.0
Chile (1968)	744	13.0	30.2	56.8

LOW INEQUALITY
Share of Lowest 40%, 17% and above

Country (year)	Per Capita GNP US$	Lowest 40%	Middle 40%	Top 20%
Chad (1958)	78	18.0	39.0	43.0
Sri Lanka (1969)	95	17.0	37.0	46.0
Niger (1960)	97	18.0	40.0	42.0
Pakistan (1964)	100	17.5	37.5	45.0
Uganda (1970)	126	17.1	35.8	47.1
Thailand (1970)	180	17.0	37.5	45.5
Korea (1970)	235	18.0	37.0	45.0
Taiwan (1964)	241	20.4	39.5	40.1
Surinam (1962)	394	21.7	35.7	42.6
Greece (1957)	500	21.0	29.5	49.5
Yugoslavia (1968)	529	18.5	40.0	41.5
Bulgaria (1962)	530	26.8	40.0	33.2
Spain (1965)	750	17.6	36.7	45.7

Country	Per capita GNP			
Venezuela (1970)	1004	7.9	27.1	65.0
Finland (1962)	1599	11.1	39.6	49.3
France (1962)	1913	9.5	36.8	53.7
Argentina (1970)	1079	16.5	36.1	47.4
Puerto Rico (1963)	1100	13.7	35.7	50.6
Netherlands (1967)	1990	13.6	37.9	48.5
Norway (1968)	2010	16.6	42.9	40.5
Germany, Fed. Rep. (1964)	2144	15.4	31.7	52.9
Denmark (1968)	2563	13.6	38.8	47.6
New Zealand (1969)	2859	15.5	42.5	42.0
Sweden (1963)	2949	14.0	42.0	44.0
Poland (1964)	850	23.4	40.6	36.0
Japan (1963)	950	20.7	39.3	40.0
United Kingdom (1968)	2015	18.8	42.2	39.0
Hungary (1969)	1140	24.0	42.5	33.5
Czechoslovakia (1964)	1150	27.6	41.4	31.0
Australia (1968)	2509	20.0	41.2	38.8
Canada (1965)	2920	20.0	39.8	40.2
United States (1970)	4850	19.7	41.5	38.8

Income Above U.S. $750

Note: Sources for these data are listed in the Appendix to Chapter I. The income shares of each percentile group were read off a free-hand Lorenz curve fitted to observed points in the cumulative distribution. The distributions are for pretax income. Per capita GNP figures are taken from the World Bank data files and refer to GNP at factor cost for the year indicated in constant 1971 U.S. dollars.

It is worth noting that overall income inequality in the underdeveloped countries is not particularly associated with relatively low income shares for the middle-income group rather than the poorest group. This view was originally put forward by Kuznets (1963) on the basis of data for eighteen countries in which it was observed that the shares of the lowest-income groups in underdeveloped countries were comparable with those in developed countries but the shares of upper-income groups were markedly larger. Kuznets suggested that higher income inequality in underdeveloped countries may be due to greater inequality between the top and middle group and speculated that the equalizing impact of development was perhaps based on a rising share of the middle. Table I.1 suggests that this generalization is not valid when the sample is widened to include other countries. There are many underdeveloped countries which show high inequality in terms of low income shares for both the middle and the poorest group.

Absolute Poverty

The extent of relative inequality in underdeveloped countries is an important dimension of the problem of income distribution, but it tells us little about the extent of absolute poverty. Yet much of the current interest in income distribution is not simply due to a concern with relative inequality. It is more often a concern with absolute standards of living in terms of calorie intake and nutrition levels, clothing, sanitation, health, education, and so on. For this we need a measurement of poverty which reflects deficiencies in these essential requirements. To the extent to which these deficiencies are reflected in income levels, such a measure can be approximated by comparing absolute levels of income or consumption of different sections of the population with "minimum levels" somehow defined.

The incidence of poverty in underdeveloped countries defined in absolute terms has powerful appeal for dramatizing the need for policy action in both domestic and international spheres. Estimates of this type have been attempted for some countries using arbitrary poverty lines for each country to measure population below these levels.[11] Similar estimates can be derived for the underdeveloped countries in Table I.1 by combining income share data with total income estimates obtained from the national accounts. For each country we have estimated the population living below two arbitrary "poverty lines" of annual per capita incomes of U.S. $50 and U.S. $75 (in 1971 prices).[12] Such estimates are obviously extremely crude from a statistical point of view. They also suffer from conceptual problems involved in defin-

---

[11]See, for example, Dandekar and Rath (1971), Fishlow (1972), and Anand (1974). These studies use available survey data and apply minimum levels defined in terms of income or consumption. This "head count" approach to the measurement of poverty ignores the degree of poverty below the poverty line. For a better measure, see Sen (1973b).

[12]The population below any poverty line can be read off the Lorenz curve at the point where the slope of the curve equals the ratio of the poverty income level to per capita income. The relevant income concept for these calculations is personal income but data on personal income are not available in most countries. We have therefore arbitrarily taken 85 percent of GNP per capita at factor cost (1971 U.S. dollars) as a measure of personal income.

ing a minimum real income level to be applied across all countries. To be socially meaningful, minimum levels cannot be defined according to some absolute biological standards but must necessarily vary with the general level of economic, social, and political development.[13] Despite these limitations it is instructive to consider the resulting estimates of incidence of absolute poverty presented in Table I.2.

The countries included in the table account for about 60 percent of the total population of the developing countries excluding China. About a third of this population falls below the poverty line defined by U.S. $50 per capita and about half falls below U.S. $75 per capita. Much of this is clearly due to the low levels of per capita income of many countries rather than to highly skewed income distribution patterns. India, Pakistan, Bangladesh, and Sri Lanka with 55 percent of the total population together account for about 75 percent of the population living below U.S. $50. These countries are all characterized by low to moderate inequality. More interestingly, the table shows that a high per capita income does not ensure that there is no "absolute poverty" problem. Differences in the patterns of income distribution between countries mean that the poverty problem may be equally serious in countries with very different per capita income levels. Both Ecuador and Sri Lanka have about a third of the population below the U.S. $50 poverty line even though Ecuador's per capita income is three times as high. Similarly, Peru and the Philippines both have a quarter of the population below the poverty line, although the per capita income of Peru is twice that of the Philippines.

These estimates provide some indication of the scale of absolute poverty in underdeveloped countries and its relationship to per capita GNP and the distribution of income. Much of the poverty problem is a direct reflection of low levels of per capita income, but skewed distribution patterns are also important. Observed differences in the degree of inequality are such as to offset per capita incomes which are two or three times higher. It follows that development strategies which succeed in raising the level of per capita income may not have much impact on the poverty problem if they are accompanied by a deterioration in relative income shares.

Growth and the Lowest 40 Percent

The above discussion of distributional patterns (in terms of both the relative and absolute income approaches) has been limited to describing existing conditions. We have not considered whether these conditions are improving or deteriorating over time. Yet it is precisely these questions that are most often raised in evaluating performance and designing policy.

Measuring changes in distributional conditions can be done in terms of either relative income shares or absolute incomes. The limitations of a purely relative approach are self-evident: changes in relative equality tell us little about changes in income levels of the poor unless we also know what has

---

[13]Even a biological standard does not lead to the same level of minimum real income. Variations in climate are a well-known factor affecting minimum requirements of both food and housing for the same level of welfare.

Table I.2: Estimates of Population below Poverty Line in 1969

Country	1969 GNP Per Capita	1969 Population (millions)	Population below $50		Population below $75	
			Millions	% of Total Population	Millions	% of Total Population
LATIN AMERICA						
Ecuador	264	5.9	2.2	37.0	3.5	58.5
Honduras	265	2.5	.7	28.0	1.0	38.0
El Salvador	295	3.4	.5	13.5	.6	18.4
Dominican Republic	323	4.2	.5	11.0	.7	15.9
Colombia	347	20.6	3.2	15.4	5.6	27.0
Brazil	347	90.8	12.7	14.0	18.2	20.0
Jamaica	640	2.0	.2	10.0	.3	15.4
Guyana	390	.7	.1	9.0	.1	15.1
Peru	480	13.1	2.5	18.9	3.3	25.5
Costa Rica	512	1.7	..	2.3	.1	8.5
Mexico	645	48.9	3.8	7.8	8.7	17.8
Uruguay	649	2.9	.1	2.5	.2	5.5
Panama	692	1.4	.1	3.5	.2	11.0
Chile	751	9.6	..	..	..	..
Venezuela	974	10.0	..	..	..	..
Argentina	1054	24.0	..	..	..	..
Puerto Rico	1600	2.8	..	..	..	..
Total	545	244.5	26.6	10.8	42.5	17.4
ASIA						
Burma	72	27.0	14.5	53.6	19.2	71.0
Sri Lanka	95	12.2	4.0	33.0	7.8	63.5
India	100	537.0	239.0	44.5	359.3	66.9
Pakistan (E&W)	100	111.8	36.3	32.5	64.7	57.9
Thailand	173	34.7	9.3	26.8	15.4	44.3
Korea	224	31.0	1.7	5.5	5.3	17.0
Philippines	233	37.2	4.8	13.0	11.2	30.0
Turkey	290	34.5	4.1	12.0	8.2	23.7
Iraq	316	9.4	2.3	24.0	3.1	33.3
Taiwan	317	13.8	1.5	10.7	2.0	14.3
Malaysia	323	10.6	1.2	11.0	1.6	15.5
Iran	350	27.9	2.3	8.5	4.2	15.0
Lebanon	570	2.9	..	1.0	.1	5.0
Total	132	889.7	321.0	36.1	502.1	56.4
AFRICA						
Chad	75	3.5	1.5	43.1	2.7	77.5
Dahomey	90	2.6	1.1	41.6	2.3	90.1
Tanzania	92	12.8	7.4	57.9	9.3	72.9
Niger	94	3.9	1.3	33.0	2.3	59.9
Madagascar	119	6.7	3.6	53.8	4.7	69.6
Uganda	128	8.3	1.8	21.3	4.1	49.8
Sierra Leone	165	2.5	1.1	43.5	1.5	61.5
Senegal	229	3.8	.9	22.3	1.3	35.3
Ivory Coast	237	4.8	.3	7.0	1.4	28.5
Tunisia	241	4.9	1.1	22.5	1.6	32.1
Rhodesia	274	5.1	.9	17.4	1.9	37.4
Zambia	340	4.2	.3	6.3	.3	7.5
Gabon	547	.5	.1	15.7	.1	23.0
South Africa	729	20.2	2.4	12.0	3.1	15.5
Total	303	83.8	23.8	28.4	36.6	43.6
Grand Total	228	1218.0	371.4	30.5	583.2	47.9

Note: .. = negligible

happened to total income. An alternative approach which places greater emphasis on absolute income levels of the poor is to consider whether the levels of living of the poor have improved over time.

Systematic examination of such trends calls for time series data on both the distribution of income and the growth of income. Unfortunately time series data on the distribution of income are not available even for most developed countries. At most, we have a collection of countries for which distribution data are available for two points in time. These data can be combined with national accounts data to give us rough estimates of the income accruing to the lowest 40 percent at two points in time.[14] Figure I.1 plots the estimated annual growth rate of income of the lowest 40 percent against the rate of growth of GNP for eighteen countries. Changes in relative equality can be inferred for each country by considering its position with respect to the 45° line. Countries above the 45° line are countries in which the income share of the lowest 40 percent increased over the period so that their estimated rate of growth of income for this group is higher than for the economy as a whole. Countries below the 45° line are countries in which the relative income shares of the lowest 40 percent declined.

The scatter suggests considerable diversity of country experience in terms of changes in relative equality. Several countries show a deterioration in relative equality but there are others showing improvement. These changes have an important impact on the estimated growth of income of the lowest 40 percent. Both Peru and Sri Lanka, for example, experienced the same rate of GNP growth over the respective periods reported, but income of the lowest 40 percent grew over 8 percent per annum in Sri Lanka—compared to only 3 percent in Peru—because of improvements in relative income shares. In other cases, a high rate of growth of GNP offsets a deterioration in relative income shares to produce substantial increases in income of the poor. Mexico and Brazil, for example, experienced an increase in inequality in terms of relative income shares but income of the lowest 40 percent grew by about 6 percent per annum in both cases.

Since individual observations are subject to substantial error, it is perhaps more important to look for patterns in the data.[15] Figure I.2 suggests that there is no strong pattern relating changes in the distribution of income to the rate of growth of GNP. In both high-growth and low-growth countries there are some which have experienced improvements and others that have experienced deteriorations in relative equality. The absence of any marked relationship between income growth and changes in income shares is important for policy purposes. It suggests there is little firm empirical basis for the view that higher rates of growth inevitably generate greater inequality. This

---

[14]We apply the available income shares to the total GNP at each point in time and calculate the rate of growth of income of each percentile group. The use of GNP instead of personal income is an approximation but since we are interested in rates of growth it does not matter as long as the proportion of personal income to GNP is the same in the two years for each country.

[15]Each country observation is affected by the error in estimated income shares at each end of the period and these errors are additive.

Figure I.1: Growth and the Lowest 40 Percent

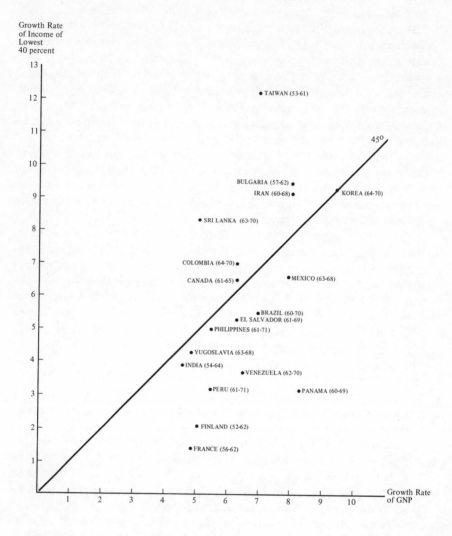

Figure I.2: Variations in Income Shares

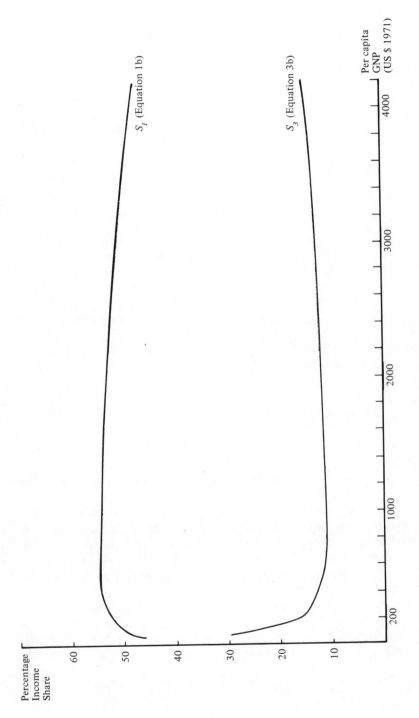

* The curves correspond to predicted values for S_1 and S_3 at different per capita GNP levels as estimated from Equations 1b and 3b respectively holding other variables at mean values for the sample (with both Dummies set at zero).

may have happened in particular cases but an explanation for this must be sought in the circumstances of each particular case and not in terms of a generalized relationship.

The above review of available data has been concerned with identifying broad dimensions of the problem in terms of both relative inequality and absolute poverty. By itself this is of little interest to policy-makers since it serves only to describe observed patterns. For purposes of policy it is more important to consider what determines the patterns of concentration in income and to what extent they can be influenced through government policy. This calls for an analysis of the determinants of income distribution distinguishing between structural variables over which the government has no control and other variables that can be influenced by policy. Some of the problems in developing such an analysis are discussed in the next two sections.

THE DETERMINANTS OF INEQUALITY

Ideally the determination of relative income shares should be analyzed in the context of a fully developed theory of the size distribution of income. Such a theory should take into account not only the economic factors affecting the distribution of income, but also the political and institutional context in which these factors operate. Needless to say, we are far from having such a comprehensive theory. There are however several partial hypotheses about particular factors affecting the distribution of income which provide some of the elements of a comprehensive theory.[16] As a first step in the analysis we need to study the empirical validity of these hypotheses using available data.

In the absence of time series data, such tests must rely heavily on cross-country data of the type discussed above. Cross-country differences in income inequality can be explained in terms of various "explanatory variables" reflecting different influences on distribution patterns. Associative relationships of this type cannot, of course, be presented as proof of causality, but they help to indicate relationships which deserve further study. Results along these lines have been reported by Adelman and Morris (1973) and Chenery and Syrquin (forthcoming). Further work is currently underway in the World Bank's Development Research Center parallel with attempts to improve the data base. In this section we present preliminary results using multiple regression to estimate equations "explaining" variations in the income share of the top 20 percent (S_1), the middle 40 percent (S_2), and the lowest 40 percent (S_3). A detailed account of the estimated equations is given in the Appendix to Chapter I.

The results of our cross-section analysis may be summarized as follows:

(i) The explanatory variables used included both structural variables such as the level of per capita income and the share of agriculture in GDP and other variables which can be influenced by policy such as the

---

[16]These hypotheses are "partial" in the sense that the hypothesized relationship is not derived from a general theory of the determination of income distribution. As a result the various interactions underlying particular relationships are not explicitly stated.

rate of growth of the economy, the rates of enrollment in primary and secondary schooling, and the rate of growth of population. The variables explain about half of the observed variation in income shares across countries. The large proportion of variation unexplained is not surprising. We have not considered a number of potential explanatory variables which can be identified a priori. The most important of these is the concentration of wealth (including agricultural land) and mechanisms perpetuating this concentration pattern. Other economic factors that may be relevant are various institutional and market mechanisms that discriminate against low-income groups. The influence of these factors could not be examined due to lack of data and the difficulty in specifying an appropriate explanatory variable.

(ii) There is some confirmation of the hypothesis that income inequality first increases and then decreases with development.[17] Figure I.2 plots the predicted behavior of S_1 and S_3 against per capita GNP obtained from equations [1b] and [3b] (see Appendix). The predicted share of the lowest 40 percent declines sharply up to per capita income levels of $400 and then flattens out rising steadily after per capita GNP crosses $1,200. This movement is paralleled by an offsetting movement in the share of the top 20 percent. Interestingly, the share of the middle 40 percent does not appear to be significantly related to income levels.

(iii) Education is positively related to equality in terms of income shares of the lowest and middle group. We have tested for the influence of primary schooling and secondary schooling separately and it is worth noting that the primary school enrollment rate is more significant in explaining S_3 while the secondary school enrollment rate is more significant in explaining S_2.

(iv) The growth of population is positively related to inequality as measured by the income share of the lowest 40 percent. The size of the estimated coefficient suggests that this effect is quantitatively substantial: a one percentage point difference in the rate of growth of population being associated with a 1.6 percentage point difference in S_3.

(v) The cross-section evidence does not support the view that a high rate of economic growth has an adverse effect upon relative equality. Quite the contrary, the rate of growth of GDP in our sample was positively related to the share of the lowest 40 percent, suggesting that the objectives of growth and equity may not be in conflict.

The policy implications of these results are difficult to evaluate given the limitations of both the data and the methodology. Perhaps the most important finding is that income shares are related not only to structural factors such as per capita income levels but also to variables which can be influenced

---

[17]This hypothesis can be traced to Kuznets's (1955) study of historical data for the developed countries in which he observed that whereas the degree of inequality in these countries had declined steadily during this century, this was not true of the early stages of their growth when inequality probably increased. More recently, it has been presented as a characteristic of the development process affecting underdeveloped countries. See for example Oshima (1962).

by policy. The level of education and the rate of growth of population are particularly important in this context since they indicate areas in which government action can improve distribution patterns. As stated above, our results do not constitute proof of causality—indeed the causal relationship may well run in the opposite direction—but the observed association clearly calls for further investigation.

In general, however, the cross-section results do not provide any firm basis for policy formulation. One reason for this is that the specification of the underlying relationship is too simplistic. For one thing, we have ignored such obvious determinants of distribution patterns as the concentration of wealth. We have also ignored the effect of various socio-political and institutional factors which may influence patterns of distribution in particular countries. But the problem is not simply one of allowing for additional explanatory variables. A large number of potential "explanatory" variables have been examined by other researchers but without much concrete pay-off in terms of policy directions.[18] The problem lies in the highly aggregative character of the comparisons involved in cross-section analysis.

Income share data provide a useful summary picture of the degrees of inequality in a country but they do not tell us about the underlying economic structures causing this inequality. These structures may vary widely between countries and yet produce the same overall degree of inequality. Since the impact of particular factors on the distribution of income will depend upon the nature of these underlying structures, there is no simple relationship between income shares and various determinants of inequality which is valid for all countries. The impact of education on income inequality, for example, cannot be determined independently of whether the structural characteristics of the economy are such as to encourage the absorption of skilled labor into high-wage employment. Broad cross-country comparisons can hardly capture the complex nature of these interactions.

Because of these limitations it may be more useful to adopt a disaggregated approach to analyzing the determinants of income distribution. Rather than trace direct relationships between broad measures of the distribution of income (such as income shares of percentile groups) and various economic factors, we can treat the problem in two stages. The first stage consists of identifying the composition of the low income population—the lowest 40 percent, for example—in terms of homogeneous socio-economic groups with particular economic characteristics. The second stage of the analysis examines the determinants of income of these groups and its growth over time. In the next section we consider the first or purely diagnostic stage of this exercise.

---

[18]Adelman and Morris (1973) use an analysis of variance technique to examine the relationship between income shares and thirty-one socio-economic variables. They find that the level of per capita income is less important than such indicators as the rate of improvement of human resources, the natural resource base, the rate of government activity, the extent of dualism and the degree of political participation. It should be noted that only the rate of improvement of human resources and the rate of government activity are "policy variables" in the sense used above.

Economic Characteristics of Poverty Groups

The need for detailed "profiles of poverty" highlighting the economic characteristics of poverty groups has been widely emphasized in recent literature.[19] Indeed, it can be argued that the overwhelming need for data on income distribution is not so much for better data on income shares as for better data on the sectoral distribution of the poor, their occupational characteristics and educational levels, their ownership of productive assets, and their access to key production inputs. These characteristics determine the processes of income generation in poverty groups and the constraints on these processes. In this section we will examine the data for several countries to identify some broad economic characteristics of poverty groups that have a direct relevance for policy formulation. For these purposes we will assume that the poverty groups can be defined in relative terms as the lowest 40 percent of the population.

Sectoral Characteristics: Rural-Urban Balance

The sector in which poverty groups are located is a key element in the profile of poverty, since governments frequently intervene in various ways to influence the sectoral balance of the economy. Such interventions have a direct impact on income distribution and can be designed to achieve distributional objectives.

The basic fact that the poor are disproportionately located in the rural areas and are engaged in agriculture or allied rural occupations is well established in conventional wisdom and easily verified. Table I.3 presents data for three countries showing the distribution of income recipients in different percentile groups across broadly defined economic sectors. While the percentage breakdown is different for different countries, in all cases the poorest group corresponds to the lowest 40 percent to 50 percent of the population. About two-thirds of this group earn their livelihood from agriculture and can be assumed to be small farmers and farm workers. The remaining third are distributed among other sectors. Since some of those not engaged in agriculture, such as artisans and small traders, are undoubtedly located in rural areas, we conclude that at least 70 percent of the poverty group in these countries live in the rural areas. Furthermore, since the countries included in Table I.3 are among the more developed of the underdeveloped countries, the percentage is likely to be even higher in countries with lower per capita income.

Given the scale of the problem and the limited capacity of other sectors to expand productive employment, it follows that a viable strategy for raising incomes of the lowest 40 percent of the population must necessarily focus on the agricultural sector. But it is important to recognize that a mere shift in sectoral emphasis towards promoting agriculture and allocating resources to rural development is not enough. The impact of government policies on

---

[19]See for example ECAFE (1971), Fishlow (1972), ILO (1972), and Visaria and Visaria (1973).

Table I.3: Sectoral Distribution of Income Groups
(Figures in each row are percentage distribution across sectors)

	Percentile Groups	Agriculture	Mining and Industry	Construction	Transport and Commerce	Services	Other	Total
I. Mexico (1963)	Richest 6	19.0	23.0	2.0	19	37.0	—	100.0
	17	30.0	19.0	2.0	18	30.0	1.0	100.0
	30	29.0	24.0	5.0	16	25.0	1.0	100.0
	Poorest 47	63.0	9.0	6.0	8	14.0	—	100.0
	Total 100	45.0	16.0	5.0	13	21.0	—	100.0
II. Malaysia (1970)	Richest 5	9.0	14.0	3.0	25	47.0	2.0	100.0
	46	33.0	13.0	4.1	24	24.0	2.0	100.0
	Poorest 49	71.0	7.0	2.0	12	7.0	1.0	100.0
	Total 100	50.0	10.0	3.0	18	17.0	2.0	100.0
III. Chile (1968)	Richest 5	33.0	16.0	9.0	18	19.0	5.0	100.0
	19	51.0	13.0	5.0	13	14.0	4.0	100.0
	37	57.0	14.0	8.0	8	6.0	7.0	100.0
	Poorest 39	70.0	7.0	5.0	5	2.0	11.0	100.0
	Total 100	56.0	10.0	6.0	10	8.0	10.0	100.0

Note: These tables are computed from data reported in Banco de Mexico (1966), Anand (1974), and Direccion General de Estadistica y Censos (1969).

the target population will also depend upon the distributional incidence of these policies within the agricultural sector. General support schemes (which may involve significant direct and indirect resource costs) may prove inefficient for our purposes if the incidence of their benefits is sharply skewed in favor of upper-income groups in the rural areas.

This problem is often ignored in policy formulation, but its importance can be appreciated by examining income inequality within the rural sector and inferring from the existing degree of inequality the distributional incidence of general policies aimed at the agricultural sector. The assumption that increases in sectoral income will be distributed along the same lines as total income is arbitrary but quite persuasive. Income distribution in agriculture is determined largely by structural factors, such as the distribution of land, and it is reasonable to suppose that the distribution of additional income generated will be similarly determined. Table I.4 presents data on the degree of inequality in the rural sector for ten countries and compares it with inequality in the urban sector. In most countries the rural sector is more equal than the urban but the degree of inequality in the rural sector is nevertheless considerable. Even if we define the target beneficiaries as the lowest 80 percent of the rural population, this group receives only about 50 percent of total income; the rest is appropriated by the upper 20 percent, who do not form part of the target population.

Table I.4: Rural and Urban Inequality

Country	Share of Top 20%		Share of Lowest 80%	
	Rural	Urban	Rural	Urban
1 Chile (1968)	48.3	50.2	51.7	49.8
2 Colombia (1970)	50.7	58.2	49.3	41.8
3 Honduras (1968)	55.0	55.8	45.0	44.2
4 India (1964)	43.0	57.0	57.0	43.9
5 Mexico (1963)	54.0	56.2	46.0	43.8
6 Pakistan (E&W) (1964)	42.5	52.0	57.0	49.0
7 Panama (1968)	46.0	45.3	54.0	54.7
8 Thailand (1970)	51.0	45.5	49.0	54.5
9 Tunisia (1961)	50.0	50.0	50.0	50.0
10 Venezuela (1962)	50.0	50.0	50.0	50.0

Note: See Appendix to Chapter I for data sources.

Policies of general support to a particular sector, therefore, are likely to involve substantial leakage of benefits beyond the intended beneficiaries. Given the high resource costs of most sector-promotion strategies, there is a clear need to design these policies to ensure that such leakages are minimized. These designs must be based on the specific socio-economic characteristics of poverty groups.

Employment Status: The Importance of Wage Labor

Along with the sectoral characteristics discussed above, we need better information on the employment status of poverty groups in terms of broad categories such as "employer," "employee," "self-employed," "unemployed," and so forth. Differentiation along these lines is useful for policy purposes because the determinants of income generation in each group are different and the policy intervention needed to help each group will differ accordingly.

Particularly relevant in designing suitable policies is the relative importance of wage employment as the primary source of income for the poor. Discussion of distributional problems in underdeveloped countries is frequently conducted in terms of factors affecting the level of employment and the share of labor. These associations are deeply ingrained in ways of thinking, if only because economic theory as propounded by both classical and neoclassical economists has treated distributional problems in these terms. But the available data suggest that this classification may not be very illuminating in underdeveloped countries. A substantial proportion of the poor in these countries are not engaged in wage labor, nor can they be described as currently unemployed and searching for employment. They are engaged in production as "independent" workers, i.e., they are self-employed but suffer from very low income levels.

Some indication of the size of this category is given by Table 1.5. In the case of Malaysia and Brazil, half of the poorest group are engaged in self-employment while only 40 percent are engaged in wage employment. By contrast, Chile, which is relatively more developed, has a somewhat different profile of poverty with three-fourths of the poorest group consisting of workers and salary earners. Data along these lines are not available for a large number of countries, but the patterns observed in Malaysia and Brazil probably reflect the situation in most underdeveloped countries where the bulk of the poor are self-employed farmers (including both owner-cultivators and tenant farmers) whose incomes are not directly affected by conditions of the labor market.

The existence of self-employment in the poverty group has immediate implications for both theoretical analysis and policy formulation. In countries where the poverty group is essentially a part of the labor market, distribution policies must rely heavily upon expanding employment to absorb the unemployed and upgrading the structure of demand for labor to generate high-wage employment for those currently employed at low wages. But if the bulk of the poverty group is engaged in self-employment, this approach may not be sufficient. Expanding employment is undoubtedly one way of absorbing the population engaged in low-income activity, but we also need to consider the alternative of raising production levels in existing occupations. An operational plan along these lines requires a detailed identification of the different types of self-employment in which the poor are engaged, the constraints on production in these occupations, and the extent to which these constraints can be relaxed by policy action.

Table I.5: Distribution of Percentile Groups by Employment Status

(Figures in Each Row are Percentage Distribution across Occupation)

Percentile Group		Employer	Self-Employed	Employee	Housewife/Houseworker	Unemployed	Total
I. Malaysia (1970)	Richest 5	11.5	12.8	72.6	0.8	2.3	100.0
	46	4.0	29.1	59.8	3.2	3.9	100.0
	Poorest 49	0.5	51.8	41.8	2.3	3.6	100.0
	Total	2.7	39.3	51.8	2.6	3.6	100.0

Percentile Group		Employer	Self-Employed	Employee Private Sector	Employee Public Sector	Sharecropper	Total
II. Brazil (1960)	Richest 69	4	45	38	9	4	100.0
	Poorest 31	0.5	51	37	3	8	100.0
	Total	2.8	47.0	38.0	7.0	5.2	100.0

Percentile Group		Employer	Self-Employed	Salary Earners	Workers	Total
III. Chile (1968)	Richest 6	13.0	26.0	54.0	7.0	100.0
	18	3.0	24.0	57.0	16.0	100.0
	30	1.0	21.0	33.0	45.0	100.0
	Poorest 46	0.0	24.0	5.0	71.0	100.0
	Total	2.0	23.0	26.0	49.0	100.0

Note: This table is based on data reported in Anand (1974), Fishlow (1972), and Foxley and Munoz (1973).

Ownership and Availability of Capital

Another characteristic of poverty groups that is relevant for the diagnosis of distribution problems is the lack of capital as measured by ownership of productive assets. Comprehensive data on the distribution of wealth are not available for any underdeveloped country, but there can be little doubt that the distribution of total productive wealth in these economies is even more unequal than the distribution of income.[20] This inequality is an underlying cause of income inequality since concentration of productive assets produces greater concentration in income.

The most important productive asset for our purposes is agricultural land, which is a critical constraint on income of small farmers. Data on the distribution of land by size of holding are available for most countries and indicate severe concentration patterns with the bulk of operational holdings being of very small size and accounting for a small proportion of total crop land. Estimates based on the 1960 world census for agriculture suggest that today there are more than 100 million smallholders in the developing countries, operating farms of less than five hectares. About half of these holdings are less than one hectare. The problem of poverty in this socio-economic group is therefore inseparably linked to the availability of land, or at least to the availability of capital needed to improve the quality of land. Similar arguments apply to the self-employed urban poor who suffer from constraints in terms of supply of capital.

The skewed distribution of land—or other productive assets—presents a static picture of the problem of lack of capital in poverty groups. Behind this static picture are a number of forces which tend to generate and perpetuate this concentration pattern over time. A systematic analysis of these forces is beyond the scope of this chapter, but we can point to three broad directions which need to be explored in this context.

First, the demographic characteristics of poverty groups may operate systematically in favor of capital concentration. If population growth in poverty groups is faster than for the rest of the economy, there is a tendency toward greater dilution of owned capital in these groups. In the case of agriculture this would lead to progressively diminishing holdings, or larger families supported by the same holding, and also to a steady migration of landless poor to the cities. Better evidence on these demographic characteristics would help us to understand these forces more clearly.

Second, differences in rates of saving by income class perpetuate patterns of capital concentration over time. The evidence for such savings differentials is somewhat firmer than for demographic behavior. A large number of household budget surveys show that average savings rates are much lower for lower income groups. The data presented in Table I.6 give some indication of the observed spread with the lowest income group in the sample,

---

[20]Data on the distribution of net wealth is not available for any country. Instead we have data on the distribution of particular components of wealth, e.g., agricultural land and different types of livestock. Ownership of corporate stock can be safely attributed to the top one percent in most countries.

Table I.6: Variations in Household Savings by Income Groups

India (Urban) 1960			India (Rural) 1963			Mexico 1956			Korea (Urban) 1971	
Income Class (Rs per year)	Percentile Group	Savings Rate Percentage	Income Class (Rs per year)	Percentile Group	Savings Rate Percentage	Income Class (Pesos per month)	Percentile Group	Savings Rate Percentage	Income Class (Won)	Savings
Under 1000	42	−20.6	Up to 720	33	− 5.1	0 – 300	36.0	−14.8	0 – 2000	−19.7
1000 – 1999	32.5	− 6.0	721 – 1200	30	− 0.4	301 – 500	21.0	.8	2001 – 3000	− 6.3
2000 – 2999	10.7	− 1.0	1201 – 2400	27	+ 3.9	501 – 750	18.0	8.7	3001 – 4000	+ 0.2
3000 – 3999	5.8	0.4	2401 – 4800	8	+ 9.1	751 – 1000	9.0	11.6	4001 – 6000	+ 5.9
4000 – 5999	4.6	9.7	4801 and over	2	+17.2	1001 – 2000	11.0	17.1	6001 and Over	+11.1
6000 – 9999	2.4	11.4				2001 – 3000	3.0	28.1		
10,000 and over	1.5	38.1				Over 3000	2.0	38.1		
All Households	100	3.3	All Households	100	4.7	All Households		14.6	All Households	n.a.

Note: This table is based on data reported in NCAER (1962), NCAER (1965), Navarette (1960), and Economic Planning Board (1972).

usually showing negative savings rates. There are many reasons why the observed savings rates in the low-income groups are likely to be underestimates, so that the observed variation in savings rates probably exaggerates the true variation.[21] But even when allowance is made for these factors it is likely that different income classes (and also socio-economic classes) do save different proportions of income and thus have very different ability for generating internally the supply of capital needed to raise incomes.

Finally there is the problem of access to capital. The constraints on production in the poverty groups are not solely due to the lack of internal generation of capital. They are also a reflection of a limited access to capital due to market fragmentation, institutional rigidities, and other forms of nonmarket allocation mechanism. Limitations of access cover a broad range including tenancy rights, access to financial markets, and access to public infrastructure, all of which impose constraints on the ability to raise production in the poorer groups. These limitations are probably as important as the observed concentration in ownership of capital.

These factors perpetuating inequality all relate to the availability of physical capital in poverty groups. Equally important from the point of view of income distribution is the limited availability of human capital. As we would expect, the many economic disadvantages of the poor are also reflected in a lack of schooling. Low levels of education and other labor skills may be an important constraint on the ability to absorb the low-income population into an expanding modern sector.

The economic characteristics discussed above are obviously not a comprehensive list for analyzing problems of income distribution in underdeveloped countries. They serve only to translate the general concern about low-income groups—the lowest 40 percent—into a concern about specific groups with defined socio-economic characteristics. As stated at the outset, this is only the first stage of the analysis of distributional problems. These characteristics together with the characteristics of the rest of the economy interact to determine the distribution of income between groups. The scope for government intervention is then determined by the extent to which we can affect these interactions through policy. It is to these questions that the subsequent chapters in this volume are addressed.

---

[21]The most well-known of these is the fact that low-income units observed in any given sample have a disproportionate concentration of individuals or families suffering from "transitory" low incomes, while their consumption is geared to a higher permanent income level. Sample estimates therefore understate savings in low-income groups and correspondingly overstate savings in high-income groups. Added to this problem is the underestimation of savings in low-income groups (especially farmers) due to the fact that much of the "savings" may be in the form of direct on-farm investment. Such investment usually involves direct application of labor and the output is never reflected in the income accounts, understating both income and savings.

The data presented in Chapter I represent the first stage output of an on-going program of work in the World Bank's Development Research Center on the compilation, evaluation, and analysis of available data on the distribution of income. Detailed evaluations of these data are not yet available and any analytical results should therefore be treated as preliminary. The cross-section results described below are presented in this spirit.

Cross-section Results

The variation in the income share of the top 20 percent (S_1), the middle 40 percent (S_2), and the lowest 40 percent (S_3) was explained by fitting the following equation to cross-country data:

$S_i = a_0 + a_1$ [log per capita GNP] $+ a_2$ [log per capita GNP]$^2 +$
$\quad a_3$ [Growth of GNP] $+$
$\quad a_4$ [Primary-school Enrollment] $+ a_5$ [Secondary-school Enrollment] $+$
$\quad a_6$ [Rate of Growth of Population] $+ a_7$ [Share of Agriculture] $+$
$\quad a_8$ [Dummy: Developed Countries] $+ a_9$ [Dummy: Socialist Countries].

The form of the equation is not derived from any explicit model in which interactions between different economic variables have been systematically spelled out. It is arbitrarily specified to reflect certain relationships about which economists have speculated at various times.

The estimated equations for each income share are presented in Table I.7. The particular relationships tested and our findings in each case are summarized below. Throughout this discussion we use the term *significant* to refer to coefficients where the sign on the coefficient is significant at the 5-percent level for a one-tail test.[22]

(i) The relationship between the *level of development* and the distribution of income is perhaps the most familiar of the various hypotheses tested. Underlying this relationship are several different influences sometimes operating in opposite directions. On the one hand, the process of development gives economic impetus to the modern high-income sectors and dislocates traditional low-income sectors, thus promoting relative inequality and perhaps even absolute impoverishment. On the other hand, development also promotes the demand for skilled labor, raising real wages and employment levels in the modern sector, thus enabling low-income groups to share in the benefits of growth. Under some optimistic assumptions about the trend in wage share, this may lead to a reduction in relative inequality. These conflicting influences are usually reconciled by treating them as sequential, i.e., income inequality increases in the early stages of development but then declines as development continues.

We have tested this hypothesis by taking the logarithm of per capita GNP at factor cost (in constant 1971 U.S. dollars) as a measure of the

---

[22]The corresponding *t* value for our sample is 1.7.

Table I.7: Estimated Equations

Dependent Variable	Constant	Log Per Capita Income	(Log Per Capita Income)²	Primary School Enrollment Rate	Secondary School Enrollment Rate	Rate of Growth of Population	Rate of Growth of GNP	Share of Agriculture in GDP	Dummy 1 Developed Countries	Dummy 2 Socialist Countries	$\bar{R}^2$	SEE	F
Share of Top 20 Percent													
equation [1a]	−57.35 (0.9)	81.51 (1.8)	−13.07 (1.6)	−.11 (1.4)	−.15 (1.7)	1.29 (0.7)	−.77 (1.22)	.25 (0.9)	−3.53 (0.6)	−18.33 (3.1)	.50	6.6	6.1
equation [1b]	−10.2 (0.2)	52.4 (1.7)	−9.29 (1.6)		−22.6 (3.2)					−16.7 (3.6)	.50	7.1	12.3
Share of Middle 40 Percent													
equation [2a]	56.45 (1.3)	−21.86 (0.7)	+34.53 (0.6)	.06 (1.1)	.10 (1.9)	.15 (0.1)	.25 (0.6)	−0.05 (0.3)	3.57 (0.9)	8.25 (2.1)	.41	4.4	4.5
equation [2b]	54.24 (2.0)	−19.85 (1.0)	3.69 (1.0)		.14 (3.0)					6.54 (2.2)	.44	4.5	10.1
Share of Lowest 40 Percent													
equation [3a]	100.90 (3.5)	−59.65 (3.0)	9.62 (2.7)	.06 (1.7)	.04 (1.0)	−1.44 (1.7)	.52 (1.9)	−.19 (1.7)	−.04 (0.0)	10.08 (3.9)	.56	2.8	7.5
equation [3b]	103.3 (3.8)	−63.09 (3.6)	10.54 (3.6)	.07 (2.1)		−1.62 (2.3)	.63 (2.6)	−.18 (1.7)		10.13 (4.4)	.57	2.9	9.6

Note: The figures in parentheses are *t* ratios.

level of development and introducing this variable in quadratic form in the estimated equations. This form indicates a U-shaped or inverted U-shaped relationship when the coefficients on the two income variables are both significant and of opposite signs. Our results confirm the existence of a U-shaped relationship in the case of S_3 and an inverted U-shaped relationship in the case of S_1. It should be noted that this finding is weaker in the case of S_1 since the coefficient on the squared term is not significant at the level indicated above. The income share of the middle 40 percent does not appear to be significantly related to per capita GNP.

(ii) The relationship between distribution and per capita income levels as discussed above reflects the secular influence of growth over very long periods. Policy-makers are, however, less concerned about secular trends than about the short term impact of *economic growth* on patterns of distribution. A pessimistic view of this relationship is that a high rate of economic growth generates an increase in relative inequality, implying that growth and distribution may be somewhat inconsistent as twin objectives of development strategy.

To test this hypothesis we included the average growth rate of GDP (in the five years preceding that for which distribution was measured as an explanatory variable in the regression equations). The coefficient on this variable can be interpreted as measuring the short-term relationship between distribution and growth at given levels of per capita income. In both equations [3a] and [3b], the variable has a significant positive influence on the shares of the lowest 40 percent. These results suggest definite rejection of the hypothesis that high rates of economic growth have an adverse impact on relative equality.

(iii) *Education* is frequently presented as an important determinant of distribution patterns, and one that can be manipulated by government policy. It operates on the skill level of the labor force to generate higher productivity and higher labor incomes.

In the absence of data on the educational and skill characteristics of the labor force, we have taken primary- and secondary-school enrollment rates (percentage of school-aged population enrolled) as reflecting these factors.[23] The estimated equations show a significantly positive relationship between education and income equality as measured by S_2 and S_3. When both variables are included, a significant coefficient is obtained on only one, although either variable by itself yields a significant coefficient. It is worth noting that the primary-school enrollment rate is more significant in explaining S_3 while the secondary-school enrollment rate is more significant in explaining S_2.

---

[23]This is admittedly an unsatisfactory approximation since educational attainments of the working-aged population—which is the relevant group—are determined not by current school enrollment rates but by school enrollment rates in the past. Lack of data on enrollment rates over time prevents any use of a lagged specification.

(iv) The importance of *population growth* is extensively discussed in the context of poverty because of its immediate impact on per capita income levels. But its relationship to relative income shares has not yet been systematically studied. There are, however, several plausible arguments suggesting that higher rates of growth of population may have an adverse effect on the income shares of the lower groups. A high rate of population growth may perpetuate a labor surplus situation, holding back a rise in real wages that might otherwise occur. Alternatively, high rates of population growth may reflect differential rates of growth of population in which low-income groups grow faster than others with adverse effects on income shares of the lower percentile groups (see Chapters V and XI).

These effects are tested by including the annual growth rate of population over the preceding decade as an explanatory variable. We find a significant inverse relationship between the share of the lowest 40 percent and the rate of growth of population. Interestingly, the coefficient on this population variable is not significant in the equations for S_1 and S_2, indicating that there is no clear pattern as to whether the poor benefit at the expense of the rich or middle.

(v) The *production structure* of the economy in terms of the importance of traditional sectors is sometimes treated as a potential determinant of distribution patterns. We have tested this relationship by including the share of agriculture in total GDP as an explanatory variable in each equation. A barely significant negative coefficient is obtained in the case of S_3, indicating that a larger share of agriculture is associated with a smaller income share of the lowest 40 percent.

(vi) Finally, we test for differences between underdeveloped countries on the one hand and the *developed countries* and *socialist countries* on the other. This is done by including two dummy variables, one for the developed countries and another for the socialist countries. The dummy variable for developed countries is insignificant in all equations, suggesting that the determinants of income shares in these countries are similar to those in underdeveloped countries. By contrast, the dummy variable for socialist countries indicates that the share of the lowest 40 percent and the middle 40 percent is significantly higher than would be accounted for by the influence of other variables. Note that the size of the coefficients is very large, indicating substantially higher equality.

Data Sources

The sources for the data presented in this chapter are listed below. In several cases, estimates have been taken from unpublished documents and are identified as such.

ARGENTINA   1970   Argentina, Consejo Nacional de Desarrollo Conade. "Encuesta de Empleo y Desempleo." Encuesta de Hogares de Propósitos Múltiples. Buenos Aires, 1970.

AUSTRALIA   1968   Podder, N. "Distribution of Household Income in
                             Australia." *Economic Record* 48 (June 1972):181-
                             200.

BRAZIL   1960, 1970   Langoni, C. G. *Distribucão de Renda e Desenvolvi-
                             mento Econômico do Brasil.* Rio de Janeiro: Edi-
                             tora Expressão e Cultura, 1973.

BULGARIA   1957, 1962   United Nations, Economic Commission for Europe.
                             *Incomes in Postwar Europe: A Study of Policies,
                             Growth and Distribution.* Economic Survey of
                             Europe in 1965, Part 2 (E/ECE/613/ADD.1),
                             Geneva, 1967, Chapter 8, p. 71.

BURMA   1958   Computed from Burma Central Statistical and Eco-
                             nomics Department Report on the 1958 *Survey of
                             Household Expenditure in Rangoon,* pp. 18, 30.

CANADA   1967, 1965   Computed from *Canadian Statistical Review* 44
                             (August 1969), from Canada, Dominion Bureau of
                             Statistics, *Income Distribution, Income of Non-
                             families and Individuals in Canada, 1961, 1965.*
                             Ottawa. 1966 [?].

CHAD   1958   Morrisson, C. *La Repartition des Revenus dans les
                             Pays du Tiers Monde.* Paris: Editions Cujas, 1969.

CHILE   1968   Chile, Dirección General de Estadística y Censos.
                             Encuesta Nacional Sobre Ingresos Familiares, Serie
                             de Investigaciones Muestrales. Santiago, 1969.

COLOMBIA   1964   Urrutia, M. and Sandoval, C. E. "La Distribución
                             de Ingresos entre los Perceptores de Renta en Co-
                             lombia, 1964." *Revista del Banco de la República*
                             43 (July 1970):987-1006.

                   1970   Colombia, Departamento Administrativo Nacional
                             de Estadística. "Encuesta de Hogares, 1970." En-
                             cuesta de Hogares de Própositos Múltiples. Bogotá,
                             1971. Also, DANE, "Encuesta de Hogares, 1970:
                             Análisis de Ingresos." Bogotá, 1971.

COSTA RICA   1961   United Nations, Economic Commission for Latin
                             America. *Economic Survey of Latin America, 1968,
                             Part One: Some Aspects of the Latin American
                             Economy towards the End of the Nineteen-Sixties.*
                             (E/CN.12/825), Santiago, 1968, p. 13.

                   1971   Universidad de Costa Rica, Institute de Investiga-
                             ciones. *Costa Rica: La Distribución del Ingreso y el
                             Consume de Algunos Alimentos, 1971.* Universidad
                             Serie Economía y Estadística, no. 45. San José,
                             1973.

CZECHOSLOVAKIA   1964   United Nations, Economic Commission for Europe.
                             *Incomes in Postwar Europe: A Study of Policies,
                             Growth and Distribution.* Economic Survey of
                             Europe in 1965, Part 2 (E/ECE/613/ADD.1),
                             Geneva, 1967, Chapter 8, p. 71.

DAHOMEY   1959   Morrisson, C. *La Repartition des Revenus dans les
                             Pays du Tiers Monde.* Paris: Editions Cujas, 1969.

DENMARK	1968	Computed from *Statistik Tiars o Versigt, 1971*.

DOMINICAN REP. 1969 Banco Central de la Republica Domincana, Oficina Nacional de Estadística, and Agencia Internacional para del Desarrollo [USAID]. *Estudio Sobre Presupuestos Familiares. I: Ingresos de la familia en la Cuidad de Santo Domingo, 1969*. Santo Domingo, 1971. p. 128.

ECUADOR 1970 El Segundo Decenio de las Naciones Unidas para el Desarrollo. *El Desarrollo Agricola en America Latina*. (E/CN.12/829). Santiago, 1969 [?]. Cited in Ecuador. Junta Nacional de Planificación y Coordinación Económica, Secretaría General de Planeación Económica. *El Desarrollo de Ecuador, 1970-73*.

EL SALVADOR 1961 United Nations, Economic Commission for Latin America. *Economic Survey of Latin America, 1968, Part One: Some Aspects of the Latin American Economy towards the End of the Nineteen-Sixties*. (E/CN.12/825), Santiago, 1968, p. 13.

1969 de Vries, J. "La Distribución del Ingreso en los Paises Centro Americanos." Restricted distribution mimeograph. San Salvador [?]: Grafica, 1970.

FINLAND 1952, 1962 United Nations, Economic Comission for Europe. *Incomes in Postwar Europe: A Study of Policies, Growth and Distribution*. Economic Survey of Europe in 1965, Part 2 (E/ECE/613/ADD.1), Geneva, 1967, Chapter 6, p. 15.

FRANCE 1956, 1962 United Nations, Economic Commission for Europe. *Incomes in Postwar Europe: A Study of Policies, Growth and Distribution*. Economic Survey of Europe in 1965, Part 2 (E/ECE/613/ADD.1), Geneva, 1967, Chapter 6, p. 15.

GABON 1968 Morrison, C. "Gabon." Paper prepared for the Development Research Center, World Bank. Mimeographed. Washington, D.C., 1972.

F. R. GERMANY 1964 United Nations, Economic Commission for Europe. *Incomes in Postwar Europe: A Study of Policies, Growth and Distribution*. Economic Survey of Europe in 1965, Part 2 (E/ECE/613/ADD.1), Geneva, 1967, Chapter 6, p. 15.

GREECE 1957 Crockett, J. *Consumer Expenditures and Incomes in Greece*. Athens: University of Pennsylvania and Center of Planning and Economic Research, 1967.

GUYANA 1956 Computed from Guyana, Ministry of Labour, Health and Housing, *Survey of Family Expenditure, 1956*, Georgetown, 1957.

HONDURAS 1968 Honduras, Secretaría de Economía y Hacienda Dirección de Estadística y Censos. "Encuesta de Ingresos y Gastos." Encuesta de Ingresos y Gastos Familiares, 1967-68. Tegucigalpa, 1970.

HUNGARY | 1969 | Computed from Mod, Margaret, "Manpower Balances in Socio-Economic Statistical Systems." Paper presented to the International Association for Resources in Income and Wealth, Ronneby, Sweden, August 30-September 4, 1971.

INDIA | 1954, 1964 | Ojha, P. D. and Bhatt, V. V. "Patterns of Income Distribution in India: 1953-55 to 1963-65." Paper prepared for the Economic Development Institute, World Bank. Mimeographed. Washington, D.C., 1974.

IRAN | 1959, 1968 | Bank Markazi, Economic Statistics Department. "Urban Household Budget Survey in Iran, 134 (March 21, 1967-March 20, 1968)." Quoted in Jaffe, A. J., "Notes on Family Income Distribution in Developing Countries in Relation to Population and Economic Changes."

IRAQ | 1956 | Morrisson, C. *La Repartition des Revenus dans les Pays du Tiers Monde.* Paris: Editions Cujas, 1969.

IVORY COAST | 1970 | Morrisson, C. "Ivory Coast." Paper prepared for the Development Research Center, World Bank. Mimeographed. Washington, D.C., 1972.

JAMAICA | 1958 | Ahiram, A. "Income Distribution in Jamaica, 1958." *Social and Economic Studies* [University of the West Indies, Institute of Social and Economic Research] 13 (September 1964):337.

JAPAN | 1963 | Oshima, H. T. "Income Inequality and Economic Growth: The Postwar Experience of Asian Counties." East-West Technology and Development Center reprint no. 3. Honolulu: East-West Center, n.d.

REP. KOREA | 1964 | International Labour Organization. *Household and Expenditure Statistics, 1950-64, 1967.* Geneva, 1967. pp. 44-45.

 | 1970 | Morrisson, C. "Income Distribution in Korea." Paper prepared for the Development Research Center, World Bank. Mimeographed. Washington, D.C., 1972.

KENYA | 1969 | Morrisson, C. "Income Distribution in Kenya." Paper prepared for the Development Research Center, World Bank. Mimeographed. Washington, D.C., 1972.

LEBANON | 1955, 1960 | Morrisson, C. *La Repartition des Revenus dans les Pays du Tiers Monde.* Paris: Editions Cujas, 1969.

LIBYA | 1962 | Computed from Libya, Ministry of National Economy, Central Statistics Office, *Family Budget Survey in Tripoli Town.* Tripoli, 1962.

MALAGASY REP. | 1960 | Morrisson, C. *La Repartition des Revenus dans les Pays du Tiers Monde.* Paris: Editions Cujas, 1969.

MEXICO   1963, 1969   Navarrete, I. M. "La Distribución del Ingreso en
                               Mexico, Tendencias y 'Perspectivas.' " In *El Perfil
                               de Mexico en 1980,* vol. 1, pp. 15-72. Mexico City:
                               Instituto de Investigaciones Sociales, Universidad
                               Nacional Autonoma de Mexico, 1970.

NETHERLANDS   1967   Computed from Netherlands, Central Bureau voor
                               de Statistiek, *Statistical Yearbook of the Nether-
                               lands, 1971.* The Hague, 1971. p. 285.

NEW ZEALAND   1968, 1969   Computed from New Zealand, Department of Sta-
                               tistics, *Income and Income Tax to 1968-69 in New
                               Zealand,* Wellington, 1970. p. 7.

NIGER   1960   Morrisson, C. *La Repartition des Revenus dans les
                               Pays du Tiers Monde.* Paris: Editions Cujas, 1969.

NORWAY   1963   United Nations, Economic Commission for Europe.
                               *Incomes in Postwar Europe: A Study of Policies,
                               Growth and Distribution.* Economic Survey of
                               Europe in 1965, Part 2 (E/ECE/613/ADD.1),
                               Geneva, 1967, Chapter 6, p. 15.

PAKISTAN   1964   Bergan, A. "Personal Income Distribution and Per-
                               sonal Savings in Pakistan." *The Pakistan Develop-
                               ment Review* 7 (Summer 1967):196-198.

PANAMA   1960   United Nations, Economic Commission for Latin
                               America. *Economic Survey of Latin America, 1968.
                               Part One: Some Aspects of the Latin American
                               Economy towards the End of the Nineteen-Sixties.*
                               (E/CN.12/825), p. 13.

                 1968   Computed from Estadística Panamena, Dirección
                               de Estadística y Censos, "Estadísticas del Trabajo,
                               1968." Encuesta de Hogares de Propósitos Múlti-
                               ples. Año XXIX, Serie "o," n.p., 1970.

                 1969   McLure, C. E., Jr. "The Distribution of Income
                               and Tax Incidence in Panama, 1969." Rice Uni-
                               versity Program of Development Studies Working
                               Paper no. 36. Mimeographed. Houston, n.d.

PERU   1961   Cha, D. "Income Distribution, 1961." Private
                               communication of the Instituto Nacional de Plani-
                               fication. Lima, n.d.

                 1971   Servicio del Empleo y Recursos Humanos. "Encues-
                               ta Nacional de Hogares de Propósitos Múltiples
                               de 1970." Lima, 1971.

PHILIPPINES   1961   Morrisson, C. "Income Distribution in the Philip-
                               pines." Paper prepared for the Development
                               Research Center, World Bank. Mimeographed.
                               Washington, D.C., 1972.

POLAND   1964   United Nations, Economic Commission for Europe.
                               *Incomes in Postwar Europe: A Study of Policies,
                               Growth and Distribution.* Economic Survey of
                               Europe in 1965, Part 2 (E/ECE/613/ADD.1),
                               Geneva, 1967, Chapter 8, p. 71.

PUERTO RICO   1963   Weisskoff, R. "Income Distribution and Economic Growth in Puerto Rico, Argentina and Mexico." *The Review of Income and Wealth,* Series 16, no. 4 (1970):303-332.

RHODESIA   1968   Morrisson, C. "Income Distribution in Rhodesia." Paper prepared for the Development Research Center, World Bank. Mimeographed. Washington, D.C., 1972.

SENEGAL   1960   Morrisson, C. *La Repartition des Revenus dans les Pays du Tiers Monde.* Paris: Editions Cujas, 1969.

SIERRA LEONE   1968   Computed from "Sierra Leone Household Survey," *Africa Research Bulletin* 5, no. 1 (February 28, 1968):917.

SOUTH AFRICA   1965   Compiled from data cited in the following, using *Demographic Yearbook* data for population distribution (all rural income was assumed to be distributed as in the Cape Peninsula): Republic of South Africa, Bureau of Statistics, *Survey of Family Expenditure: Ten Principal Urban Areas and the Urban Areas of the Vaal and the Orange Free State Gold Fields* (Report no. 11-06-03), Pretoria, 1966; Feldmann-Laschin, G. R., Radel, F. E., and DeConing, C., *Income and Expenditure Patterns of Coloured Households, Cape Peninsula,* Pretoria: University of South Africa Bureau of Market Research, 1965; United Nations, *Yearbook of National Accounts Statistics,* various years; and United Nations, *Demographic Yearbook,* various years.

SPAIN   1964, 1965   Computed from Spain, Instituto Nacional de Estadística, *Encuesta de Presupuestos Familiares, Marzo 1964-Marzo 1965,* Madrid, 1965.

SRI LANKA   1963   Central Bank of Ceylon, Department of Economic Research. *Survey of Ceylon's Consumer Finances, 1963.* Colombo, 1964.

                     1970   International Labour Organization. *Matching Employment Opportunities and Expectations: A Program of Action for Ceylon.* ILO Ceylon Mission Technical Papers, p. 62. Geneva, 1971.

SURINAM   1962   Surinam, Algemeen Bureau voor de Statistiek. "Surinam in Figures," no. 44, Paramaribo, 1967.

SWEDEN   1963   United Nations, Economic Commission for Europe. *Incomes in Postwar Europe: A Study of Policies, Growth and Distribution.* Economic Survey of Europe in 1965, Part 2 (E/ECE/613/ADD.1), Geneva, 1967, Chapter 6, p. 15.

TAIWAN   1953, 1961   Chang, K., ed. *Economic Development in Taiwan.* Taipei: Cheng Chung, 1968; idem., "Report on the Pilot Study of Personal Income and Consumption in Taiwan." Paper prepared under the sponsorship of the Working Group of National Income

Statistics Directorate, General of the Budget, Account and Statistics, The Executive Yuan. Taipei [?], 1963.

1964   Oshima, H. T. "Income Inequality and Economic Growth: The Postwar Experience of Asian Countries." East-West Technology and Development Center reprint no. 3. Honolulu: East-West Center, n.d.

TANZANIA   1968, 1969   Morrisson, C. "Income Distribution in Tanzania." Paper prepared for the Development Research Center, World Bank. Mimeographed. Washington, D.C., 1972.

THAILAND   1970   United Nations, Economic Commission for Asia and the Far East. *Economic Survey of Asia and the Far East, 1971* (E/CN.11/1047), Bangkok, 1972, p. 59.

TUNISIA   1970   Morrisson, C. "Income Distribution in Tunisia." Paper prepared for the Development Research Center, World Bank. Mimeographed. Washington, D.C., 1972.

TURKEY   1968   Bulutay, T., Timur, S., and Ersel, H. *Turkiye'de Gelir Dagilimi, 1968.* Ankara: Sevinc Matbaasi, 1971.

UGANDA   1970   Computed from "Employment and Income Distribution in Uganda," University of East Anglia Development Studies Discussion Paper, Tables d and t(iii). Norwich, 1970.

UNITED KINGDOM   1968   Computed from United Kingdom, Central Statistical Office [?], *Family Expenditure Surveys, 1960 and 1968, United Kingdom Distribution of Households by Household Income.* London: Her Majesty's Stationery Office, 1969.

UNITED STATES   1960, 1966   United States, Bureau of the Census. *Statistical Abstract of the United States.* 89th Edition. Washington, D.C.: U.S. Government Printing Office, 1968.

1970   Computed from United States, Bureau of the Census, *Current Population Reports, Consumer Income,* Tables A and 1, Washington, D.C., n.d.

URUGUAY   1968   Uruguay, Ministerio de Hacienda, Dirección General de Estadística y Censos. *Ocupación y Desocupación.* Encuesta de Hogares, October-December 1968. Montivideo, 1971.

VENEZUELA   1962   United Nations, Economic Commission for Latin America. *Economic Survey of Latin America, 1968, Part One: Some Aspects of the Latin American Economy towards the End of the Nineteen-Sixties.* (E/CN.12/825), Santiago, 1968, p. 13.

1970   Computed from preliminary worksheets based on 1970 census preliminary figures, subject to revision.

YUGOSLAVIA   1963   International Labour Organization. *Household and Expenditure Statistics, 1950-64, 1967.* Geneva, 1967. Table ii, p. 76.

1968   Computed from Yugoslavia, Federal Institute of Statistics, *Household Budget Survey of 1968.* Belgrade, n.d.

ZAMBIA   1959   Baldwin, R. F. *Economic Development and Export Growth: A Study of Northern Rhodesia, 1920-60.* Berkeley and Los Angeles: University of California, 1966.

Chapter II

THE ECONOMIC FRAMEWORK

MONTEK S. AHLUWALIA AND HOLLIS CHENERY

THE MAGNITUDE and persistence of income inequalities demonstrated in Chapter I argue for a revision in the way development policy is formulated. It is not sufficient that we should pay more attention to distribution or to the incomes of the poor within the existing framework of policy analysis. Rather, it is necessary to reformulate the framework itself so as to incorporate an explicit analysis of the processes by which the incomes of the poor are generated and the policy instruments by which these processes can be affected.

The first step in this reformulation is a statement of social objectives that can encompass varying social preferences as well as realistic constraints on policy. In this context the conventional treatment of income distribution in terms of relative income shares obscures the nature of the choice between growth and income distribution objectives. A concern with income distribution is not simply a concern with income shares but rather with the level and growth of income in lower-income groups. Distributional objectives therefore cannot be viewed independently of growth objectives. Instead they should be expressed dynamically in terms of desired rates of growth of income of different groups.

In this chapter we present a framework for the economic analysis of growth and distribution policies that takes account of these problems. This framework reflects the basic approach to strategy reorientation adopted in this volume and various aspects are elaborated in other chapters.[1] Here we focus on three main aspects:

(i) A statement of objectives that combines growth and distribution in a single measure of social welfare. The use of this index is illustrated by data for the past decade.

(ii) A growth-*cum*-distribution theory that brings out the linkages between the growth of different economic groups and defines the scope for policy intervention.

(iii) A summary comparison of some alternative strategies of distribution and growth, such as maximal growth of GNP, redirection of investment to raise incomes of the poor, and redistribution of consumption.

REDEFINING OBJECTIVES: GROWTH AND DISTRIBUTION

So long as economists were willing to assume the possibility of unrestricted transfers among income groups, they found no conflict in principle between the objectives of distribution and growth.[2] Once it is

---

[1] Particularly in Chapters V and XI.

[2] Perhaps for this reason there has been relatively little discussion of this problem in the theoretical literature of welfare economics.

recognized that large-scale transfers of income are politically unlikely in developing countries, however, it becomes necessary to evaluate the results of any development policy in terms of the benefits it produces for different socio-economic groups. While this idea has been accepted in the recent literature of project evaluation,[3] it has found little reflection in the methodology of macroeconomic planning and policy formulation.

An index of economic performance reflecting these objectives can be developed as follows. Assume a division of society into N socio-economic groups, defined by their assets, income levels, and economic functions. For purposes of policy analysis, it is necessary to distinguish several poverty groups such as small farmers, landless laborers, urban under-employed, and others according to the similarity of their responses to policy measures (see Chapter V). In order to illustrate the problem of evaluation, we will classify merely by income size into ordinally ranked percentile groups.

Assuming a division by income level into quintiles, the rate of growth of income of each group, g_i, can be taken to measure the increase of its social welfare over the specified period. The rate of increase in welfare of the society as a whole can therefore be defined as a weighted sum of the growth of income of all groups:

$$G = w_1 g_1 + w_2 g_2 + w_3 g_3 + w_4 g_4 + w_5 g_5 \qquad [1]$$

where G is an index of the growth of total social welfare and w_i is the weight assigned to group i.[4]

A summary measure of this type enables us to set development targets and monitor development performance not simply in terms of growth of GNP but in terms of the distributional pattern of income growth. The weights for each income class reflect the social premium on generating growth at each income level; they may be set according to the degree of distributional emphasis desired. As the weight on a particular quintile is raised, our index of the increase in social welfare reflects to a greater extent the growth of income in that group. Thus if we were only concerned with the poorest quintile we would set $w_5 = 1$ and all other $w_i = 0$, so that growth in welfare would be measured only by g_5. This approach is closely related to the more formal approach to welfare choices using explicit social welfare functions to measure improvements in welfare (see Appendix to Chapter II).

In these terms the commonly used index of performance — the growth of GNP — is a special case in which the weights on the growth of income

---

[3]See Chapter X, in which the relations between the present approach and the project evaluation methodologies of OECD, UNIDO, and others are summarized.

[4]This measure can be applied either to the income or the consumption of each group. When applied to income, the weight assigned should take account of the contribution made by each group to the financing of investment and government expenditure. For long run simulations of policy (as in Chapter XI), an index based on consumption only is preferable.

of each quintile are simply the income share of each quintile in total income. The shortcomings of such an index can be seen from the following income shares for the different quintiles, which are typical for underdeveloped countries (see Table I.1 above).

Quintiles	1	2	3	4	5	Total
Share in Total Income	53%	22%	13%	7%	5%	100%

The combined share of the top 40 percent of the population amounts to about three-quarters of the total GNP. Thus the rate of growth of GNP measures essentially the income growth of the upper 40 percent and is not much affected by what happens to the income of the remaining 60 percent of the population.

An alternative welfare principle that has considerable appeal is to give equal social value to a one-percent increase in income for any member of society. On this principle, the weights in equation [1] should be proportional to the number of people in each group and would therefore be equal for each quintile.[5] Thus a one-percent increase in income in the lowest quintile would have the same weight in the overall performance measure as a one-percent increase in income for any other quintile, even though the absolute increment involved is much smaller for the lowest quintile than for the others.

When we use the growth of GNP as an index of performance, we implicitly assume that a dollar of additional income creates the same additional social welfare regardless of the income level of the recipient.[6] Given the typical income shares of the different quintiles, it follows that a one-percent growth in income in the top quintile is given almost eleven times the weight of a one-percent growth in the lowest quintile (in the preceding example) because it requires an absolute increment which is eleven times as great. In contrast to the GNP measure, the equal weights index gives the same weight to a one-percent increase in income in the lowest quintile as it does to a one-percent increase in the highest quintile. In this case a dollar of additional income in the lowest quintile is valued at eleven times a dollar of additional income in the highest quintile.

Many individuals (and some countries) may wish to define social objectives almost exclusively in terms of income growth of the lowest groups, placing little value upon growth in the upper-income groups beyond its contribution to national savings and investment. The welfare implications of such a "poverty weighted" index are stronger than those underlying

---

[5]See the Appendix to Chapter II for the form of social welfare function consistent with this weighting system.

[6]This statement has to be qualified to allow for the higher savings of the upper income recipients and their greater contribution to future growth. In a more complete analysis, the increase in social welfare can be measured by the weighted growth of consumption rather than income, as is done in Chapter XI.

either the rate of growth of GNP or the "equal weights" index, since it would be a welfare function based primarily on the lower-income groups.[7]

Weighted indexes of the sort discussed above provide a very different evaluation of performance in many countries than is obtained from conventional measures. This can be illustrated using data presented in Chapter I for the fourteen developing countries for which we have observations at two points in time. The numerical results presented here are subject to the limitations of the data and are essentially "illustrative" to show the potential usefulness of weighted growth indexes in evaluating performance. They are not presented as definitive assessments of country experience.

Table II.1 shows the difference in estimates of welfare increments based on three different weighting systems: shares of each quintile in GNP (giving the rate of growth of GNP); equal weights for each quintile; and "poverty weights" of 0.6 for the lowest 40 percent, 0.3 for the next 40 percent, and 0.1 for the top 20 percent.[8] The following differences can be observed among the countries when comparing GNP growth with the other two indexes.

(i) In four countries (Panama, Brazil, Mexico, and Venezuela), performance is worse when measured by weighted indexes. In these countries the data show that relative income distribution worsened over the period considered, i.e., growth was disproportionately concentrated in the upper-income groups. The indexes giving greater weight to the growth of income in lower-income groups are therefore lower than the rate of growth of GNP.

(ii) In four countries (Colombia, El Salvador, Sri Lanka, and Taiwan), the weighted indexes are higher than GNP growth. In these countries the data show that distribution improved over the period, i.e., the growth of incomes in lower-income groups was faster than that in higher-income groups.

(iii) In five countries (Korea, the Philippines, Yugoslavia, Peru, and India) the use of weighted indexes does not alter the GNP measurement of growth to any great extent. In these cases the data show that distribution remained largely unchanged and all income classes grew at about the same rate.

In general the extent to which a weighted index of growth diverges from the growth rate of GNP and the direction of divergence are measures of the extent and direction in which growth is distributionally biased.

It is important to note that the proposed index is a measure of the *increase* in welfare rather than of total welfare. Increasing equality is indicated by a weighted growth rate in excess of GNP growth and increasing

---

[7]The "equal weight" scheme and various poverty weight schemes are derivable from a social utility function of semilogarithm form as shown in the Appendix to Chapter II.

[8]In terms of weights for unit increments, these weights imply that a dollar of income accruing to the bottom 40 percent is worth 33 times a dollar accruing to the top 20 percent, instead of 11 times as with equal weights.

Table II.1: Income Distribution and Growth

Country	Period	I. Income Growth Upper 20%	Middle 40%	Lowest 40%	II. Annual Increase in Welfare (A) GNP Weights	(B) Equal Weights	(C) Poverty Weights	III. Initial Gini Coefficient
Korea	1964-70	10.6	7.8	9.3	9.3	9.0	9.0	.34
Panama	1960-69	8.8	9.2	3.2	8.2	6.7	5.6	.48
Brazil	1960-70	8.4	4.8	5.2	6.9	5.7	5.4	.56
Mexico	1963-69	8.0	7.0	6.6	7.6	7.0	6.9	.56
Taiwan	1953-61	4.5	9.1	12.1	6.8	9.4	10.4	.55
Venezuela	1962-70	7.9	4.1	3.7	6.4	4.7	4.2	.52
Colombia	1964-70	5.6	7.3	7.0	6.2	6.8	7.0	.57
El Salvador	1961-69	4.1	10.5	5.3	6.2	7.1	6.7	.53
Philippines	1961-71	4.9	6.4	5.0	5.4	5.5	5.4	.50
Peru	1961-71	4.7	7.5	3.2	5.4	5.2	4.6	.59
Sri Lanka	1963-70	3.1	6.2	8.3	5.0	6.4	7.2	.45
Yugoslavia	1963-68	4.9	5.0	4.3	4.8	4.7	4.6	.33
India	1954-64	5.1	3.9	3.9	4.5	4.1	4.0	.40

Note: The rates of growth of income in each income group were calculated as follows: income shares were applied to GNP (constant prices) to obtain the income of each group in each year. The growth rate is the annual compound growth rate estimated from the two endpoint income estimates for each income group. Sources of income share data for each country are identified in Chapter I. GNP series are from the World Bank data files. Equal weights imply a weight of 0.2, 0.4, and 0.4 for the three income groups while poverty weights are calculated by giving weights of 0.1, 0.3, and 0.6 respectively.

inequality by the opposite difference. The measure cannot be used to compare performance among countries without allowing for their initial distribution of income. For example, Table II.1 shows inequality increasing in both Brazil and India, but in India the starting point was a relatively equal distribution in 1954 while in Brazil distribution was already quite unequal in 1960.

We recognize that the use of such indexes for evaluation of performance will be severely limited by the initial lack of accurate data. For the present they are perhaps more valuable as analytical devices to be used in redefining the objectives of development strategy. They help to clarify both the statement of distributional objectives and the limits of acceptable trade-offs between growth and income distribution. In particular, the use of welfare indexes emphasizes the importance of increasing the rates of growth of income in the poverty groups instead of focusing on the static picture of income inequality.

TOWARD A THEORY OF DISTRIBUTION AND GROWTH

The preceding section suggests that the objective of distributive justice is more usefully conceived of as accelerating the development of the poorer groups in society rather than in terms of relative shares of income. As a way of implementing this approach, we can visualize the role of the state as using available policy instruments (including the allocation of investment in physical and human capital) so as to maximize a welfare function of the type just described. State intervention of this sort requires both an analysis of the determinants of income in poverty groups and of the linkages between the incomes of different groups. The fact of income linkages is crucial for any analysis of distributional problems since they impose important constraints on policy. Thus tax-financed transfers from the rich to the poor may raise the income of the poor but, if they reduce savings and capital accumulation by the rich, they may in time lead to lower income in the poorer groups. An analysis of these interactions requires an integration of growth and distribution theory. In this section we present the main elements of the integration proposed in the volume. A simulation model reflecting this integration is presented in Chapter XI.

Distribution of Income and Capital

Existing theories of income distribution are of only limited value in establishing an analytical framework for comprehensive governmental action because they are somewhat narrowly focused on the functional distribution of income between labor and capital. Most theories conceive the central problem of income distribution as the determination of the levels of employment and remuneration of the factors of production, usually grouped into capital and labor. They differ mainly in their assumptions about market behavior and the way in which wages and product prices are determined. Neoclassical theory assumes competitive equilibrium in all markets and thus derives factor returns from pure production relationships and demand patterns, given factor supply conditions. At the other extreme, the classical and Marxist wage theory that forms the basis for most dual economy models assumes relatively fixed real wages with all surplus value appropriated by the owners of capital.

The inadequacy of existing theories for our purposes arises less from the lack of consensus as to the determinants of the functional division of income than from the omission of other aspects of the problem. The available evidence on the nature of poverty in underdeveloped countries shows that half of the poor are self-employed and do not enter the wage economy. Most wage-earners are already in the middle-income groups, so that policies affecting the split between wages and profits mainly concern the upper end of the distribution.

The principal element that is missing from existing theories is an explicit treatment of the distribution of the various forms of assets.[9] A more general statement would recognize that the income of any household is derived from a variety of assets: land, privately owned capital, access to public capital goods, and human capital embodying varying degrees of skills. A grouping of households according to the type and productivity of

---

[9]Recognition of the importance of asset distribution is common to neoclassical theorists as well as to Marxists, but it has not been incorporated in empirical models.

their assets provides more insight into the nature of income determination among the lower-income groups than does a narrower focus on the determinants of wages for different types of labor.

There is considerable evidence that the distribution of assets is more concentrated than the distribution of incomes, and in many cases government action serves to increase rather than reduce this concentration. Although definitive statistical analyses are lacking, it is quite plausible to associate much of the variation in income at the lower levels with a lack of human skills, as well as lack of ownership of physical capital and access to complementary assets and other inputs.[10] Whatever the shares of labor and capital as determined in the factor markets, greater equality of personal incomes could be achieved if ownership of private capital and access to public facilities were more equally distributed.

Recognition of the role of asset distribution in explaining the pattern of personal income distribution has important implications for development strategy. Policy should operate on a wider front than solely on the functional distribution of income, in favor of those factors of production that are owned by the lower-income groups. Policy should also attempt to alter over time the underlying pattern of concentration of both physical and human capital. In practice most policy discussions have tended to concentrate upon the former type of instrument. Distributional objectives are commonly sought through policies aimed at promotion of employment, which would raise the total wage bill (and possibly wage share), thus benefiting lower-income groups. Such policies are important when the scope for substitution in both production and demand is fairly large, and they are discussed in some detail in Chapter IV. Equally important, in our view, are policies aimed at altering the pattern of concentration of productive assets over time and reducing barriers to entry into more profitable types of production. Reallocation of public investment is an effective instrument to achieve this change in asset concentration patterns.

The precise form of public investment depends upon the particular characteristics of the target groups to be helped. In the rural areas the target groups are landless laborers deriving their income mainly from unskilled labor and small farmers relying on a combination of family labor and small amounts of land. They also include self-employed craftsmen, artisans, and those engaged in services in the villages. In the urban areas the target groups include unskilled workers and also the unemployed at all but the highest skill levels.[11] Also included in the urban target groups is

---

[10]See, for example, Fishlow's analysis for Brazil (1972, 1973a).

[11]Excluding the highest skilled levels from the target groups is simply a reflection of the fact that a substantial part of the urban unemployment may exist in the middle-income educated work force. While these individuals may earn no income, they may still be above the low-income target groups in terms of household incomes. This is not to suggest that the problem of urban unemployed belonging to middle (and even upper) income households is not important. Given the political strength of this group, this may be an overwhelming problem requiring immediate attention. See, for example, the ILO report on Sri Lanka (1971a).

the large body of underemployed labor currently engaged in low productivity self-employment in the so-called informal sector.[12]

The importance of direct action on the asset side can be illustrated by considering the situation of peasant households in the rural sector—the largest component of the total target population. Output of these households is the result of a joint application of family labor and owned physical assets (land and a few primitive implements). Family income is basically constrained by the availability of complementary physical inputs—including land, capital improvements on land, working capital, fertilizers—and by the prices received for their output. Since the scope for manipulating farm prices or providing wage employment for these households in the rest of the economy is limited, government policy must attempt to provide access to an appropriate mix of physical and financial inputs (and technical know-how) in order to raise incomes in this sector. This is unlikely to be achieved solely through changes in relative prices, although they facilitate the productive use of existing assets. An effective strategy also requires action on a large scale to make available both the complementary public assets (infrastructure) and the privately owned assets (in particular, land) needed to increase production.

This emphasis on asset accumulation is further reinforced if we treat human capital as a productive income-earning asset and consider that the poor have very little of this asset. It may be argued that the scope for productive use of labor (and hence income-earning employment) depends very much on the availability of a skilled labor force. That is to say, the scope for substituting labor for capital is much greater if we are operating in an environment where the supply of skills is plentiful. On this view the scope for expanding the employment of unskilled labor and thus increasing total wage earnings is probably extremely limited. The real hope lies mainly in upgrading skills of the labor force, thus increasing both productivity and earnings. If this is true, acting on the pattern of concentration of human capital is almost a precondition for the success of strategies aiming at greater labor absorption in the modern sector.

Linkages and Relative Growth Rates

The design of policy cannot focus on the poverty groups in isolation from the rest of the economy. Because of the income linkages between groups, it is necessary to consider the effect of policy on the growth rates of different economic groups in society and the ways in which these growth rates are interrelated. For this purpose we need an analysis of eco-

---

[12]As pointed out in the ILO report on Kenya (1972), this sector is not a marginal or temporary phenomenon. It includes a large proportion of the work force engaged in a wide variety of production activities which are "economically efficient and profit-making though small in scale and limited by simple technologies, little capital, and lack of links with the other ('formal') sector." Statistical information on this sector is scarce, but rough estimates for Kenya suggested that the informal sector provides about 25 percent to 30 percent of total urban employment.

nomic growth that is sufficiently disaggregated to determine some of the linkages between the growth of income in the poverty groups and the growth of the rest of the economy.

The poverty groups, being composed largely of peasant farmers and urban self-employed, tend to have fewer links to the rest of the economy than do the middle- and upper-income groups. But it is a mistake to ignore income linkages through employment and commodity markets. To analyze the dependence of poverty groups on growth in the rest of the economy, we use a modified version of the surplus labor dual economy models proposed by Lewis (1954) and Fei and Ranis (1964). Following these models we recognize that labor is available from the traditional (subsistence) sector for employment in the capitalist sector. The resulting flow of wage income from capital owned by richer groups is an important component of the income of lower-income groups.

Instead of the simple distinction between the modern and traditional sector in familiar surplus labor models, we distinguish small-scale capitalists — farmers and small businessmen — from larger-scale producers using more capital and modern technology. From a distributional standpoint this distinction is quite important. Small-scale employers tend to use production techniques that are more labor-intensive and can more readily employ the less-educated labor from the poverty groups. Furthermore, income from their capital goes largely to the middle-income group and should be given more weight in social policy than the higher incomes of the large employers.

The resulting wage linkages among the three groups in our model are summarized in Table XI.1. It shows the incomes of the poverty groups as being determined by (i) wages from the modern (high-income) sector; (ii) wages from small-scale producers; (iii) self-employment income, based on their own stock of physical and human capital; and (iv) net transfers from the rich via the fiscal system. It is the combined effect of policy on all these elements that determines the net effect upon the incomes of the poorer groups.

This formulation of income linkages enables us to take into account the adverse effects of reduced growth in the upper-income groups on the income of poorer groups. The costs of transfer programs proposed for the poverty groups can be included as reductions from the investable resources of the other groups. A lower rate of capital accumulation by the rich is ultimately reflected in lower wage incomes for the poor with adverse effects on income growth in the target groups. Conversely, the benefits of such programs can also be stated more broadly by tracing them to the different income groups and evaluating their total impact in terms of the welfare function proposed earlier in this chapter.

The Need for Investment in the Poor

The above statement of the relations between distribution and growth and the importance of asset concentrations leads to a basic change in the terms in which development objectives are formulated. For one thing, the allocation of investment cannot be separated from the distribution of its product. They should be thought of as different dimensions of a single development strategy. In addition to the allocation of investment according to sectors of production, we also need to think of the allocation of investment among the capital stocks of different socio-economic groups. The need to direct public investment to support incomes of poorer groups by building up their ownership of and access to physical and human resources is a common theme running through this volume.

Without some increase in the investment in capital stocks owned or controlled by the poor—above what can be provided from their own savings—it seems almost inevitable that their per capita income will grow more slowly than that of higher-income groups, at least for a considerable period. In the face of high population growth in rural areas and plentiful supplies of unskilled labor, the poor will only benefit from the growth of other sectors through an increase in their employment but not through increases in wages.[13] In the absence of investment in the subsistence sector—or more broadly in the physical and human capital of the poor—this form of wage linkage is not likely to produce growth in per capita income at rates comparable to those of the rest of the economy, particularly when the net effects of population growth are considered.[14]

Some redirection of the investment of the economy toward the poverty groups can modify this process substantially over one or two decades. If it is provided in an appropriate mix of education, public facilities, access to credit, land reform, and so forth, investment in the poor can produce benefits in the form of higher productivity and wages in the organized sectors as well as greater output and income for the self-employed poor. In the short run, there may be a reduction in the growth of other groups through this redirection of investment toward the poor, although this is by no means necessary. In the longer run, however, it can be argued that the transformation of poverty groups into more productive members of society is likely to raise the incomes of all. On this view the trade-off between distribution and growth—if it exists in a given country—may well be an intermediate phenomenon limited to the period that is required to make the investment in the poor productive. Much of this report is devoted to applying this concept to different poverty groups and translating it into more operational terms.

ALTERNATIVE STRATEGIES

The analytical framework described above cannot as yet be translated into an operational planning model because of the statistical limitations

---

[13]As pointed out in Chapter IV, there are some possibilities for increases in both output and employment from "getting the prices right," which would benefit all groups.

[14]In his original article on surplus labor, Lewis (1954) emphasized the fact that lack of productivity growth in subsistence agriculture would also affect wages in the capitalist sector and worsen income distribution.

described in the previous chapter. Nevertheless it provides a basis for identifying and evaluating alternative distributional strategies. We distinguish four basic approaches to the problem of raising the welfare of the low-income groups: (i) *Maximizing GNP growth* through raising savings and allocating resources more efficiently, with benefits to all groups in society. (ii) *Redirecting investment* to poverty groups in the form of education, access to credit, public facilities, and so on. (iii) *Redistributing income* (or consumption) to poverty groups through the fiscal system or through direct allocation of consumer goods. (iv) *A transfer of existing assets* to poverty groups, as in land reform. In most countries some elements of each of these approaches will be applicable, depending on the initial economic and social structure.

The advantages and limitations of each strategy will vary with the circumstances of each country, and an assessment of these considerations is necessarily a matter of detailed study. Nevertheless, it is useful to consider some broad characteristics of each strategy in a relatively pure form.[15] The general conclusions from the analysis in this volume can be summarized as follows:

(i) Maximizing the growth of GNP involves some measures that benefit all groups, as well as others—such as favoring high-savings groups through lower income taxes or wage-restraint policies—in which there is a conflict with distributional objectives. Because of the relatively weak income linkages between the poverty groups and the rest of the economy, their growth tends to lag until the expansion of employment creates a shortage of unskilled labor and hence an upward pressure on wage rates. Although—as suggested by Table II.1—the poor may be better off even in this case than with slower GNP growth, the welfare effects of a maximal growth strategy can almost always be improved by adding transfers.

(ii) As compared to maximal growth of GNP, increased investment in the physical and human assets of the poverty groups is likely to require some sacrifice of output in the short run because returns on investment in human capital take longer to develop. Even so, the welfare index will be higher because these investments lead to income growth in target groups which have higher welfare weights. While this strategy has a short-run cost to the upper-income groups, in the longer run they may even benefit from the "trickle up" effects of greater productivity and purchasing power of the poor.

(iii) General transfers of income in support of consumption can also raise the weighted welfare index in the short run, but they have too high a cost in terms of foregone investment to be viable on a large scale over an extended period.[16] Nevertheless, some direct con-

---

[15]In Chapter XI we simulate the effects of each of the first three strategies over a forty-year period for a hypothetical economy.

[16]The cost in reduced income growth and employment of the food subsidies in Sri Lanka illustrate this point, as discussed in ILO (1971*a*) and the Sri Lanka Country Study in the Annex.

sumption supplements for specific target groups (child nutrition, maternal health services) are a necessary supplement to an investment-oriented strategy, since they are the only way to alleviate some types of absolute poverty.

(iv) Political resistance to policies of asset redistribution makes this approach unlikely to succeed on any large scale in most countries. However, in areas such as land ownership and security of tenure, some degree of asset redistribution is an essential part of any program to make the rural poor more productive (see Chapter VI). Beyond this essential minimum, a vigorous policy of investment reallocation in a rapidly growing economy may well be a more effective way of increasing the productive capacity of the poor than redistribution from the existing stock of assets, which is likely to have a high cost in social and political disruption.

(v) In the longer term, population policy can have an important influence on both the distribution of incomes and the level of consumption in the poverty groups. Our simulations show a tendency of income distribution to worsen with population growth above 2.5 percent per year, while with more optimistic assumptions it tends to improve. There is considerable demographic evidence that investments in the health, education, and economic growth of the poverty groups may also contribute to a reduction of fertility and hence indirectly to better income distribution.

Particular emphasis is given in this volume to directing public investment to raise the productive capacity and incomes of the poor. There is a strong analogy between this strategy and an international strategy of assisting investment in poor countries. In both cases transfers of resources which increase productive capacity and lead to greater self-support in the future are both more efficient and more attractive to donors than continuing subsidies for consumption. In both cases it should be possible to get greater political support for the more developmental approach.

APPENDIX TO CHAPTER II

The weighting schemes described in the chapter can be formally derived as indexes of welfare improvement from a social utility function of the semi-logarithmic type.

$$U = \Sigma \beta_j \log y_j, \qquad\qquad\qquad [1]$$

where y_j is the income of jth individual. If all individuals in the ith income class are identical, then $y_{ji} = Y_i$ and $\beta_{ji} = \beta_i$ for each individual j in the ith income class. Equation [1] can then be written:

$$U = \Sigma n_i \beta_i \log Y_i \qquad\qquad\qquad [1']$$

where n_i = number of individuals in each income class

Both the equal weights index and the poverty weights index can be shown to be approximations of increases in welfare measured by a utility function of this type with appropriate parameters shown below.

(i) Equal Weights

The equal weights index can be shown to be a measure of the increase in welfare if we assume that the utility function is symmetric, i.e., all $\beta_i = \beta$. Differentiating [1'] we have:

$$dU = \Sigma n_i \beta \cdot \left(\frac{dY_i}{Y_i} \right). \qquad\qquad\qquad [2]$$

Note that $\Sigma n_i \beta = \beta N$, where N is total population. Dividing equation [2] through by βN, we have

$$\frac{dU}{\beta N} = \Sigma \frac{n_i}{N} \cdot \left(\frac{dY_i}{Y_i} \right).$$

Thus the equal weights index, weighting the growth rate of income in each income class by its share in population, approximates the increment in welfare dU up to a scalar multiple given by $\dfrac{1}{\beta N}$.[17]

(ii) Poverty Weights

The poverty weights index provides a measure of welfare improvement consistent with the more general form of the utility function when the β_i are different for different income classes. Differentiating [1'] and dividing throughout by $\Sigma n_i \beta_i$, we have:

$$\frac{dU}{\Sigma n_i \beta_i} = \Sigma \frac{n_i \beta_i}{\Sigma n_i \beta_i} \cdot \left(\frac{dY_i}{Y_i} \right) \qquad\qquad\qquad [3]$$

---

[17]It is an approximation because we are dealing with discrete instead of infinitesimal changes in Y_i.

This is in effect the poverty weights scheme with the weights w_i given by

$$w_i = \frac{n_i\beta_i}{\Sigma n_i\beta_i}$$

The weighted growth rate measures the utility increment up to a scalar transformation given by $1/\Sigma n_i\beta_i$. The weights sum up to unity and are proportional to the parameters β_i of the utility function for income classes with the same population shares. The parameters β_l and β_t which yield the poverty weights 0.6 and 0.1 for the lowest 40 percent and the top 20 percent as assumed in the chapter can be derived as follows:

$$\frac{w_l}{w_t} = \frac{n_l\beta_l}{n_t\beta_t} = 6.$$

Since $\dfrac{n_l}{n_t} = 2$ the poverty weights used imply $\dfrac{\beta_l}{\beta_t} = 3$.

The utility function defined above can obviously be applied either in economy-wide planning to obtain social utility streams from income streams for different classes or to project decisions to derive "project weights" for income accruing at different income levels. The weight a_l on a unit increment of income accruing to individual l at income level y_l which makes it comparable, in terms of social utility, to a unit increment accruing to individual t at income level y_t can be written:

$$a_l = \frac{U_l}{U_t} = \frac{\beta_l y_t}{\beta_t y_l} \tag{4}$$

If $\beta_l = \beta_t = \beta$, as in the equal weights case, this implies project weights are inversely proportional to income size. If the parameters of the utility function correspond to the poverty weights case, then project weights are even higher.

In the above discussion we have assumed the social utility function to be defined in terms of incomes of individuals in society. For intertemporal analysis it is theoretically more appropriate to use consumption rather than income. This presents several problems in project analysis, but these are distinct from the problem of distributional weighting. The use of social utility indexes based on consumption streams for an economy-wide application is illustrated in Chapter XI.

Chapter III
THE POLITICAL FRAMEWORK
C.L.G. BELL

A STRATEGY involving the annual transfer of some 2 percent of GNP from the rich to the poor for one or two decades would not be accepted readily by the rich. Its adoption would threaten to telescope into a comparatively short historical period—by gradualist standards, at least—a major redistribution of income and wealth, and hence of power, status, and prestige. Whether measures necessary to effect such a transfer are implemented by a government is primarily a question of who wields political power, what they perceive their interests to be, and how free they are to maneuver. Governments are not "above" the political process, in the sense of needing merely to muster the "will" to do what is just or desirable. Irrespective of political system, they have to further the interests of those groups on which they are dependent for support, interests that may well require the maintenance of the status quo.

The chances of there arising a durable coalition of interests able to bring off such a reshaping of policy as a whole depend on a number of factors. First, there is the nature of the regime and whom it represents, both of which reflect the existing distribution of assets and power. Second, there is the strength and disposition of the domestic and foreign groups who stand to lose or gain most. Third, there is the degree to which potential losers and gainers are homogeneous among themselves and how far their political behavior is determined simply by an economic "balance sheet" criterion. A fourth consideration is whether or not there exists more than one set of measures capable of transferring the (large) bundle of resources involved; to the extent that the distributive ("tax") incidence of each set varies, there may be a number of plausible coalitions. As will often be the case, where the initial redirection of policy is less than radical and the associated measures are essentially piecemeal, the "style" of politics, the structure and ethos of the administration, and the scope for the policy analyst in government to play a political role assume considerable importance.

These are the static considerations. In the event that such a reformist coalition comes to power, the nature of its attempts to initiate and carry through the strategy will have an impact on the chances of a successful continuation. Under certain conditions, including the kinds of policies adopted, the ruling alliance will gain in strength and freedom to

An earlier version of this chapter drew heavily on papers presented at Bellagio by Lamb, Seers, and Uphoff; their influence is still visible. Comments on that version from Bela Balassa, Roger Norton, Dudley Seers, T. N. Srinivasan, Ernest Stern, and John White—and on a subsequent draft from Mariluz Cortez and Geoff Lamb—wrought many improvements in the one presented here. I owe an especially heavy debt to David Lehmann and Bernard Schaffer for constant encouragement and discussions throughout the drafting process. All of the aforementioned are hereby granted absolution from surviving errors of analysis. The opinions and the ideology underlying them, of course, are necessarily my own.

maneuver, while the opposition falls into disarray. Even if the poor themselves are not heavily involved at first, early successes and a visibly fluid political situation may stir them into active support of the regime. Here, what a mildly reformist regime intends as essentially palliative measures may open Pandora's box. Alternatively, what began as drastic redistributive interventions may, after some early dislocation and violence, lead to a more quiescent society as the poor's initial gains are consolidated. The other, perhaps more proximate possibility is that the coalition will itself splinter or be bundled out by a coup, perhaps with foreign backing. But whatever the case, it is plain that static and partial approaches to analyzing the political "feasibility" of changes in policy may come severely adrift.

So much for the preamble; some of these issues are analyzed in the sections which follow. First, the basis of political behavior among potential gainers and losers, some possible alliances, and political "style" are taken together. Next, the thematic transfer of resources to the poor and a number of the major policy interventions to effect it—which are examined in the remainder of Part I—are assessed in the light of the foregoing discussion. Then, the associated issues of the mobilization of the poor, decentralization, and the nature and influence of administrative structures are considered. Finally, we focus on the planner as a political actor.

THE POLITICS OF REDISTRIBUTION

One way of answering the question, "who are the poor?" is to list their ostensible socio-economic characteristics (Fishlow, 1973). But there is an immediate difficulty: do categories like "landless," "jobless," "sharecropper," and so forth define groups in ways which are consistent with existing or plausible political alignments? A simple class structure has considerable merit: feudal landlords, rich peasants, tenants, and landless in the countryside; national bourgeoisie, lower middle class, proletariat, and underemployed marginals in the towns; and perhaps foreign capital in both. Yet, although those at the bottom of the pile thus defined should match closely the poverty "target groups," they do not form a single class having a clear perception of its common interests and of how to act in order to secure them. Of course, there may be a strong economic basis for a class alliance among small farmers, tenants, landless, jobless, and urban marginals. But working alliances of this kind tend to be rare, which is one major reason why the poor remain poor. By the same token, rich and privileged groups do not form a "class" either. Unlike the poor, however, they are organized, often in alliance, to extract benefits from the political system.

Class categories (or plausible alliances) and political groupings are often imperfectly matched because there are bases of association other than economic loss or gain which mould individuals' perceptions of their interests, but which cross-cut class distinctions. The most obvious and persuasive examples are caste, tribe, race, region, religion, and town and country. Whether one of these or class forms the actual basis on which people are politically organized is not a simple empirical question, but a matter of consciousness. For example, a landless laborer may see caste as defining the boundaries of solidarity and division. Simply to label such perceptions of reality as "false consciousness" is unhelpful so long as people continue to see the structure of their world in such ways, though it remains true that a change in the awareness of the poor may have to precede the growth of their political power.

If, to begin with, the poor are politically weak (their numbers notwithstanding) and the rich strong, on what grounds will the latter choose to transfer a stream of resources to the former over a lengthy period? The first possibility is that the elite — or some sections of it — will make concessions to the poor out of enlightened self-interest. It may fear, rightly or otherwise, that the revolutionary potential of the poor will be realized unless the burden of their poverty is eased. The rich who subscribe to this view may be prepared to give up something so as not to lose all in a total revolution. More positively, certain kinds of investments in the poor, such as education and health, may lead to long term pay-offs to the rich, who need productive workers to operate their capital (see *infra* and Chapters II and XI). Even if elite opinion is not unanimous on these matters, the fact of disagreement holds out some prospects for reformers of all kinds.[1]

The second possibility is that the different constituent groups of the elite will have conflicts serious enough for them to seek a measure of support from among other groups of the polity,[2] thereby increasing the effective representation of the latter in the political system. For example, it can be argued that, in some circumstances, a rising industrial bourgeoisie and the dominant rural groups (be they feudal landlords or rich peasants) will eventually fall out over the setting of the prices of agricultural products relative to those of industrial goods. As all urban groups have an interest in cheap food, urban capitalists may attempt to enlist the support of organized workers in order to break the power of the landed interests now opposed to them. With the same end in view, they may also side with peasants' demands for a distributist land reform if the resulting smallholder system promises a better economic and political accommodation. Such potential cleavages among ruling groups provide reformers and others representing sections of the poor with opportunities to exploit, which, if seized, may provide further openings through an improvement in the "representativeness" of the political system.

However, in some countries the alliance of privileged groups is robust and the basis for the division of spoils stable. If its constituent groups dominate government and the apparatus of the state, including the means

---

[1] For a persuasive and intelligent "reform-monger's" approach to these issues, see Hirschman (1963), Chapter 5.

[2] In nineteenth-century Britain, landed interests supported the reformers over the issue of industrial working conditions, and the capitalists fought successfully to have the Corn Laws repealed.

of repression, then the best hope for the poor lies in "trickle down" benefits from rapid growth in aggregate output. Under certain circumstances, such authoritarian regimes are able to engineer large increases in GNP over longish periods, and their very success may dispose them to introduce limited measures to supplement "trickle down" with the object of receiving wider support—or at least grumbling acquiescence. But if output remains sluggish, the prospects for the poor are bleak. Nor are they likely to be improved if national elites are allied with substantial foreign capital interests. While military intervention by metropolitan countries may be less common over the next decade than in the fifties and sixties—though South East Asia remains vulnerable—that is in part because economic sanctions and financial support to key groups can serve the same purpose.

The above considerations rest on rather general principles, which may be less than evident, at first glance, in the political process. In those less developed countries which have a limited degree of social and economic integration, exemplified by the coexistence of "modern" and "traditional" forms of production in many sectors, political life is likely to be strongly fragmented and, from the viewpoint of simple class categories, confused. Ethnic or communal groups are rallied to the support of leaders who claim access to state resources on a regional or communal basis. A different sort of geographical or regional distribution is implied by the demands of political groups having their interests predominately in rural or urban areas, populist movements being one characteristic form. Again, there will be identifiable or emerging class interests—for example, in the demands of urban workers or entrepreneurs, or in the social and political power of landlords or "progressive" farmers.

The sheer number and diversity of these class categories and political groupings leads to a "style" of politics which emphasizes bargaining, mercenary loyalties, and endless maneuver, and which is epitomized in the institutionalization of factionalism and patronage. Potitical leaders tend to build coalitions of quite disparate groups and maintain their allegiance by delivering benefits (or perhaps by seeming to do so) to a wide variety of clients. There are thus very heavy demands on the decision-making process, which must cope with shifting political groups and with demands which may themselves be the result of politicians trying, largely without success, to cope with mutually inconsistent pressures. Decision *outcomes,* to put it mildly, may be very difficult to evaluate as planning *goals.*

In summary, the political process may provide relatively poor answers to the kinds of questions the policy analyst needs to ask about "what is to be done." It is subject also—and thereby subjects the policy making process—to a series of ad hoc revisions and pragmatic adjustments to particularist pressures which reflect the constellation of factions and interest groups operating at various levels in the political system.[3]

---

[3]It goes without saying that this conclusion applies as forcibly to developed as to less-developed countries. In the former, it is usually only during periods of what the whole nation sees to be an "emergency" (particularly in the face of a perceived external threat) that the decision-making process is focused on a few "national" objectives which are well defined.

The configuration of social forces and the nature of the political process are closely connected with the system of economic organization, which exerts particular influences on the pattern of distribution and the scope for changing it. The end points of the range of systems are defined by ideal types: the *laissez faire economy,* in which all allocations are determined by the market and the *command economy,* in which they are set by central fiat. Virtually all real economies lie somewhere in between, with varying degrees of reliance on nonmarket forms of allocation, and varying degrees of private ownership and control over the means of production.

Most less-developed countries can be described as being somewhere near the center of this hypothetical span, though the intragroup variance is certainly large. The state intervenes over a wide range of economic activity and the public sector is substantial; against this, private property rights are much in evidence and private capital plays a major role. Where urbanization is well advanced, an "interventionist" style coupled with a good deal of public ownership (though not workers' control) is likely to reflect the demands of the comparatively numerous middle class fretting about the position of yet more privileged elites. In more agrarian settings, such a style may result from an uneasy, but solid, alliance between the urban lower middle class and rich peasants (Raj, 1973). An ambiguous attitude towards foreign capital—regulation but not outright prohibition—may hold sway in both. In these "intermediate regimes," which rest on finely balanced coalitions of interest, the use of policy instruments requires a careful scrutiny of their impact as a whole on the support base.

Forms of Policy Intervention

In the previous chapter, strategies for increasing the income and welfare of the poor were classified in economic terms as follows: maximize aggregate growth, reallocate investment, reallocate consumption, and transfer existing assets. However, in espousing the general principle of redistributing the benefits of growth, an essentially political judgment was made, which is thematic to the volume as a whole. This is that intervention which alters the distribution of the *increment* to the overall capital stock and income will arouse less hostility from the rich than transfers which bite into their existing assets and incomes.[4] The preferred strategy—to divert a proportion of the annual investment resources of the rich (amounting to 2 percent or 3 percent of GNP) towards the poor—is given a detailed examination in Chapter XI in the light of both equity and time considerations.

Our concern here is to analyze, against the background of the section above, which forms of intervention will make the strategic option of incremental redistribution politically plausible. In assessing whether or not the rich are likely to agree to such a "contract" for several decades, one further—and essentially "economic"—consideration must be brought into the reckoning: the overall weight of the burden on the rich and how

[4]That is to say, an evolutionary rather than a revolutionary, approach is being examined.

it is shared among them. If the transfer is effected from the investment resources of the rich (as is the case in Chapter XI), then its short-term impact depends on three factors: the size of the transfer expressed as a fraction of GNP (τ), the share of the rich in national income (σ_1), and their average propensity to save (s_1). The proportion of the savings of the rich siphoned off will rise with the first, but will fall with increases in the second and third. As shown in detail in Chapter XI, the greater the fraction of the rich's investment resources diverted to the poor, the more slowly will their incomes grow in the near future—though they may benefit later on as a result of the poor accumulating extra assets.

To illustrate this point, consider three numerical examples with the transfer set at 2 percent of GNP. No allowances are made for indirect benefits accruing to the rich through income linkages, so that the figures indicate an outside estimate of the burden of the transfer.[5]

(i) Fairly high inequality with fairly abstemious rich.

$\sigma_1 = 0.6$, $s_1 = 0.2$, implying that only one-sixth (0.02/0.6 x 0.2) of the rich's savings are diverted. (This case corresponds to strategies I and II of Chapter XI.) If the productivity of their capital and their share in its output stream are unaffected, then the total income of the rich will grow at a rate only one-sixth below what they would have enjoyed in the absence of the transfer—scarcely an overwhelming sacrifice.

(ii) Fairly high inequality with profligate rich.

$\sigma_1 = 0.6$, $s_1 = 0.1$, implying that one-third of the investment resources of the rich are diverted, and hence the growth rate of their incomes reduced in the same proportion.

(iii) Low inequality with profligate rich.

$\sigma_1 = 0.4$, $s_1 = 0.1$, implying a savings diversion of fully 50 percent. If the natural increase of the rich were 2 percent per annum and their incomes would otherwise have grown at 4 percent a year, then so long as the transfer lasted, their per capita income level would be frozen.

These examples make the intuitively obvious point that to achieve a given level of resource transfer, the sacrifice exacted of the rich varies inversely with their share in total income.[6] The second conclusion to emerge is more subtle: that the closer the rich approach to the idealized Protestant ethic by refraining from consumption, the slighter will be the adverse effects of the transfer upon them.

Be that as it may, the chances are that the rich would attempt to find ways of displacing some part of the "tax" side of the transfer onto the middle 40 percent.[7] Alternatively, some groups in the top quintile or so

---

[5]Let Y and Y_1 denote GNP and the total income of the rich, respectively. Then the volume of savings transferred is τY, which equals τ/σ_1. Y_1 The total savings of the rich are $s_1 Y_1$, so that the fraction diverted to the poor is $\tau/s_1\sigma_1$.

[6]This follows a fortiori from diminishing marginal utility considerations if comparisons are made among countries with similar levels of average income per capita, assuming similar utility functions, of course.

[7]Here, we are concerned solely with political behavior, not with the effects of different allocations of the tax burden on equity, incentives and efficiency.

would seek an opportunity to derive a positive advantage from the situation by pressing for a pattern of "burden-sharing" which would erode the economic and political power of their rivals. The fact that the size distribution of incomes does not correspond perfectly to a classification of households by their socio-economic characteristics means that prescriptions for taxes and transfers on an income ranking basis may imply sharp changes in distribution within income classes. Landowners and capitalists may dominate the top quintile but, in the long run, their interests may also be fundamentally opposed. In brief, the policy substance of the notional x percent transfer must be specified fairly precisely if useful conclusions are to be drawn about likely coalitions and conflicts.[8] A good case in point is the transfer of resources from affluent to backward regions within a country. In Brazil, for example, the allocations to the Northeast have certainly amounted to something of the order of 2 percent of GNP annually in recent years. But whether the relatively numerous poor people living there have shared in the transfers on something approaching a "one man, one dollar" basis is to be doubted. This sort of distribution rarely happens because the political structures within the recipient regions are usually dominated by comparatively privileged groups, which determine the fate of funds from the central budget. Moreover, in the circumstances of most less developed countries the intraregional multiplier effects of such expenditures are likely to be strongly attenuated by Keynesian leakages in the form of demands for imports from the more advanced regions. Small wonder, then, that "regional" policy should be politically attractive, for rich people in poor regions are usually well placed to appropriate a very large share of the transfers, with privileged groups in the richer regions benefiting also through interregional trade. Nevertheless, there are other circumstances in which regional policies' distributive efficiency would be relatively high.

Where linkages are concerned, benefits accruing to the poor will provide an indirect pay-off for the rich. One such possibility, explored in Chapter XI, is that as the poor become better educated and fed, they will operate more efficiently the capital owned by the well-off. Such gains may lie far off in the future, but they need not necessarily do so. In any case, when they do arise they will reduce the burden of resource transfer on the rich below the levels indicated by the illustrative examples set out above.

Before examining particular forms of policy intervention, two general remarks are in order. First, the chances of a specific intervention coming off successfully depend significantly on whether or not the situation affected is perceived as an essentially zero-sum game, with one party losing what the other wins.[9] This is the essence of a distributist land reform

---

[8]Uphoff (1973) provides some useful insights into the distributive effects of choosing particular instruments, but his analysis is essentially partial.

[9]An interesting and readable approach, based on game theoretic ideas, to analyzing the politics of pushing through reform may be found in Hirschman (1963).

without compensation in which each acre gained by a landless laborer is one acre lost by a rich peasant, feudal landlord, or foreign corporation. However, there is a fair range of circumstances in which all groups could, in principle, gain from correct intervention, an obvious example being the removal of distortions in factor and product markets leading to an improved allocation of resources. In practice, of course, there is almost bound to be some group or other which would lose as a result—unless they were to receive compensation from the rest. The trick here is to choose interventions which would cause the poor to gain, and then to devise specific means whereby rich—and politically powerful—losers could be *actually* compensated, while leaving the poor better off than before. Here, the resulting changes in the positions of richer groups relative to one another may require further action. For example, organized urban workers are unlikely to moderate their money wage demands in the cause of "getting the prices right" if the main effect is to boost capitalists' post-tax profit.

Second, one must be wary of introducing a sort of Marshallian partial equilibrium method into political analysis. Although none of the forms of policy intervention discussed here and in Chapters IV through VII is able to reach the intended target groups without imposing costs on support groups, it is the *total* impact of all policies which ultimately counts. For example, those farmers who would lose part of their holdings in a land reform might acquiesce more readily if there were also a general prospect of a program to create new rural infrastructure, from which they would benefit heavily. The strategy's implementation will require the deployment of many policy instruments, and there will be more than one set of interventions capable of realizing it. All this points to a greater freedom of maneuver in bargaining and accommodation than a separate consideration of each instrument might suggest.

The first two interventions to be discussed—land reform and nationalization—affect existing assets, but they need not entail cuts in the stock of capital owned by the rich if they are carried out gradually. Asset confiscation is not relevant to the provision of education, infrastructure, and consumption transfers.

Land Reform

In Chapters V and VI, great emphasis is placed on the necessity for a sharp move toward an egalitarian distribution of land ownership, both to relieve poverty directly by a redistribution of productive assets and to ensure that the benefits of other redistributive interventions go overwhelmingly to the target groups. But who, apart from impoverished tenants, marginal farmers, and the landless, will press for it? Scarcely the feudal landlords or rich peasants who would lose thereby, unless they were to be handsomely compensated. If the redistributive impact of the policy were to be preserved, the bill for compensation would have to involve some group other than the land reform beneficiaries. However, the urban bourgeoisie might see some advantage in such a reform if its alliance with landed interests were a fragile one.[10] In particular, where much potentially productive land in the hands of big landowners lies uncultivated, there may be widespread support for measures to turn it over to small farmers without a hint of an attack on rights to property. Moreover, if the country is fairly urbanized and claimants to land are not too numerous, the bill for compensation will not be too onerous. More generally, dealing with a diffuse mass of smallholders might prove to be an easier task than reaching an accommodation with highly organized landlords or rich farmers, as is now recognized in certain industrialist circles, for example.[11] Besides, the post-reform agrarian structure could promise a mass market for industrial consumer goods; the marketed surplus—to feed urban workers, satisfy industrial demand for agricultural raw materials, and earn foreign exchange—might still be extracted on terms favorable to urban interests. On the other hand, should the alliance be more durable, then urban interests would have to bear some part of the costs of confiscation, the fraction to be determined by bilateral bargaining. In Peru, for example, landlords are paid a higher fraction of the value of their expropriated lands if they elect to invest the proceeds, together with a matching sum from other sources, straightaway in industry.

In societies where land accounts for a major part of all tangible wealth, an egalitarian distributist land reform may entail a rate of asset transfer well in excess of the equivalent of 2 percent of GNP per year. This is not a statement about arithmetic, but about the dynamics of the process once started. As the reform gets under way, the timetable may seem too slow for many would-be beneficiaries. Encouraged by the sight of some progress, they may begin to encroach on expropriable land before the legal details are settled, as in Bolivia in the early fifties and (to a lesser extent) in Allende's Chile. A sort of "landgrab" epidemic may result, accompanied by a good deal of dislocation and perhaps violence. This is precisely the fear which haunts many urban interests (and even enlightened landowners), for the ensuing upheaval would threaten revolutionary repercussions in the towns and call private rights to property into question more generally.

However, it is by no means clear that the process is likely to take the above course. First, as Hobsbawm emphasizes, there is the peasantry's "sense of its weakness and inferiority . . . as illiterates against the educated, [and its] lack of effective armed force."[12] Allied to this, communication among rural communities is often poor, both politically and

---

[10]The classic treatment of this issue is Moore's (1966). For alternative analyses of the urban middle class-rich peasant alliance in the context of Indian land reforms, see the chapters by Bell, Byres and Lipton in Lehmann (1974).

[11]The Venezuelan land reform of the late fifties involved a deal in which landowners were compensated with funds from oil revenues and USAID. For general reviews of experience throughout the Third World, see the various issues of *The Spring Review of Land Reform* (USAID, 1970a and 1970b).

[12]Hobsbawn (1973), p. 12.

physically. More importantly, there is the general thesis that once the peasantry's immediate demands for land are met, it will become a conservative force, a bulwark of the [new] status quo.[13] Provided the process is controlled, therefore, a land reform in a setting where land ownership is initially highly concentrated can do much to alleviate the lot of the poor without tearing apart the fabric of society. In many less developed countries, the necessary legislation is in the statute book; what remains is for a ruling coalition of interests to perceive that they will gain much and lose little by implementing it. In this, foreign interests may exercise a decisive influence, either against the reform by making tacit threats, or in support of it by offering financial and technical assistance.

Nationalization

Moves against "big business," especially where it has close foreign connections, usually have strong popular appeal. But in itself, nationalization may do little to promote—and may actually set back—a redistribution of incomes and effective claims on assets towards the poor. The trouble is that, in the absence of complementary policies, the main beneficiaries are likely to be, not the poor, but the bureaucrats and organized workers who run—and sometimes run down—the enterprises after the takeover. Even private-sector firms buying their outputs at what are effectively subsidized prices would have no cause for dismay.

There are, however, several cases where the immediate distributive consequences of nationalization are likely to be favorable. First, the nationalization of plantations, even if not followed up by the large-scale creation of peasant holdings, should lead to an improvement in the conditions of low-paid estate workers, as happened in Tanzania.[14] Second, some nationalized firms may generate substantial surpluses which are appropriated, not by their employees, but by the exchequer, and then earmarked for projects designed to benefit the poor. Third, there will be welfare gains if the enterprises taken over produce mass consumption goods (or inputs used intensively in their production), the pricing of which was formerly influenced by a significant degree of monopoly. (A likely candidate falling into the indirect category is chemical fertilizers.) Even where the firms nationalized had no monopoly power before, they could still charge lower prices for basic necessities after the event provided any associated losses were made up from taxes bearing on the rich. A related case is the crea-

---

[13]This was Lenin's conclusion on analyzing Stolypin's (partially implemented) agrarian policy. From the other end of the political spectrum, Huntington (1968), a devotee of political "order," quotes Lenin approvingly. Some radical opinion is more agnostic concerning the stabilizing effects of land reforms—see, for example, Lehmann (1971)—despite the success of "conservative" reforms in Japan, South Korea, and Taiwan during the immediate postwar period. In Italy, Iran, Colombia, and Mexico, the extent of redistribution was far more limited.

[14]The problem in Ceylon is less tractable owing to racial differences between plantation workers and the rest of the population (ILO, 1971a). The conditions of estate workers in parts of Central America require no further comment here.

tion of entirely new state-owned enterprises producing mass consumption goods, as is occurring in the Indian textiles industry, which may meet with less opposition from established interests than moves to nationalize existing assets. In the third case, it should be added that there are, in principle, other means of achieving the same results, namely, antitrust regulation and direct subsidies, respectively.

Although the immediate distributive effects of state takeover may prove disappointing, in a wider setting a program of selective nationalization may be used to establish a number of key areas of control in economic and political life. Once again Peru provides an interesting example. Before 1968, there was hardly a state machine to speak of. Now, what is essentially state capitalism has brought new influences to bear on class structure and created a powerful technocratic elite which enjoys the support of the military — and the whole based on the creation of big state enterprises (Zaldivar, 1974). Such a structure would certainly be capable of underpinning a resource transfer of the magnitude discussed in this volume. The important part played by nationalization in directing resources to the poor in Israel and Yugoslavia is evidence enough on that point — though nationalization did not feature prominently in South Korea or Taiwan.

The general conclusion to be drawn is that nationalization requires supporting, complementary measures in the short run. Over a longer period, however, it can play a key role in redistribution through the control it confers on some central areas of economic life. Whether it is a necessary or a sufficient condition for a successful redistributive strategy in a reformist framework is a more difficult proposition to establish.

Education

Unlike land reform and nationalization, which affect the ownership of existing assets, the extension of education to the poor results in the creation of new [human] capital. This is one reason why the rich are likely to look on it more kindly than partial asset confiscation, even though the implementation of the general strategy may mean that they have to bear the major part of the direct costs through increases in taxation. In short, the financial costs to the losers are less "visible." Whether or not the direct gains to the poor will be large is problematical (see Chapter IV). But there may be appreciable long-run gains to those owning physical capital, for all societies attempting to modernize need ample supplies of literate and disciplined workers with the right skills. In this connection, it should be recalled that universal elementary education was introduced early in most of the now industrialized economies, not primarily because of popular demand, but to further the interests of ruling elites concerned with accelerating industrialization by increasing the supply of relevant skills.

As far as today's dominant groups are concerned, the main political returns to education may be in its legitimizing the social system.[15] If the

[15]On education, literacy, and political attitudes among India's landless, however, see Zagoria (1972).

view that everyone has equal chances through education is widely held, wide differences in incomes and occupational status are more likely to be acceptable. There is ample evidence, of course, to show that in most societies, even those with equal education do not have equal access to work opportunities and incomes, nor in fact does everyone have equal access to education. The fact that middle-class children generally have a better chance of moving up the ladder of education and thus on to better rewarded jobs is enough, it seems, to encourage these sections of the population to work within the system rather than against it. As yet, the rest seem not to have revised their expectations.

In most countries, the prospects of lucrative rewards, however remote for most of the population, have set up virtually irresistable pressures for the expansion of education in order to provide more chances of moving up the top rungs of the ladder. Such pressures have often led to the expansion of secondary or higher education at the expense of the primary level, where opportunities are far more relevant to the poor. Moreover, these developments have often had disastrous effects on the content and nature of the education provided, encouraging the worst forms of examination-oriented, white-collar book learning because this is the sort which best appears to meet middle- and lower middle-class demands.

In terms of reform, therefore, the structure of private rewards to different types of education must be changed, a move which entails altering the structure of earnings. If the latter continues to be highly unequal, present pressures for a simple expansion of the existing system will continue, and attempts at reforming course curricula, content, and values in appropriate directions will not find much support among, let alone initiative from, children and parents.

Infrastructure and Public Goods

Public goods are politically attractive in that governments which dispense them satisfy the groups they represent and, by stressing equal opportunity of access, appear simultaneously magnanimous to all. In reality, of course, most goods of this sort are not in a strict sense equally accessible to all; a road connects some communities but not others; a school serves a particular village, piped water supplies specific urban areas, and so on. Even when services are near at hand, the information possessed by different groups and their ability to take advantage of it vary widely. Still, within the groups or communities thus provided, most, if not all, households will have at least some share in the benefits, whatever their income levels. In the language of Chapter VI, there will be "leakages" to non-target groups. As already noted, this fact may make the "efficiency" of the policy measure low, but it will increase the likelihood of intervention, perhaps considerably.

Generally speaking, the more egalitarian the distribution of public goods and privately-held assets, the lower the "leakages" of intervention—that is why the provision of infrastructure to villages and land reform are strongly complementary. To take a specific example, the construction of drainage systems with the object of giving seasonal employment to landless laborers and improving output on small farms will usually be good for contractors' profits and big farmers' production at the same time. Such projects are bound to be politically popular, although they would have to be legion to contribute in a major way to the goal of a *net* transfer to the poor of 2 percent of GNP per year.

Consumption Transfers

The issue of asset versus consumption transfers is a strategic one (see Chapter XI for a detailed analysis). The aim of providing the poor with assets is to give them adequate and self-sustaining levels of income over the longer run, whereas consumption transfers will have a big immediate impact but must be sustained indefinitely if the poor do not accumulate also sufficient means of production. In practice, however, the income levels of the poor are so low that any increase in their consumption standards will make them more productive. This fact makes the line between asset and consumption transfers difficult to draw. For example, clean water supplies (a public good) will improve health and nutrition, but so will extra food intake—all the more so, it must be admitted, if there is clean water to go with it. For this reason alone, it cannot be said, pejoratively, that consumption support treats only the symptoms of poverty.

Of course, attitudes to the giving and receiving of doles to increase private consumption are another matter. In many countries, the rich are likely to view a dole system as an encouragement to the poor to be lazy, and may prefer the asset transfer strategy, which at least promises to end some day. For their part, the poor may see doles as a device to prevent them from gaining independence, self-respect, and a stake in the society at large. Alternately, and this is a more plausible response in less developed countries where the poor's awareness has not been aroused so acutely, consumption transfers may be strongly preferred. Not only are the immediate effects larger (the poor's discount rate is high), but the poor are bound to see major uncertainties surrounding the productivity of such assets as they do receive. All these perceptions will be heavily influenced by society's culture, and no general conclusions are possible.[16]

Nevertheless, there might be attractions in a selective approach. Some categories of wage goods—especially food—could be supplied at subsidized prices through a system of "fair price" shops, provided only the poor have access to them. Such a move would also have the advantage of mollifying powerful urban groups, whose anger is easily aroused by increases in the prices of necessities. A related possibility, which has a substantial human-investment component, is to mount selective school feeding programs.

---

[16]The heavy administrative demands made by a comprehensive dole system should not be forgotten either. For this reason, it is probably an impractical form of intervention except in urbanized, semideveloped economies.

Full-scale intervention to secure a desired distribution of basic consumer goods through rationing has little to recommend it, except in the conditions of a grave emergency. It would be impossible to implement in a noncollectivist agrarian society. In more urbanized settings, it would probably lead to a proliferation of black markets and extensive queues — with the likely result that a frustrated public would vent its ire on the government, even though the equity of distribution had changed for the better.

MOBILIZING SUPPORT

In the previous sections, our primary concern was with the constraints on choosing and implementing a policy strategy in favor of the poor. Fortunately, these have a [potential] obverse: the mass, organized support of the poor constitutes a political resource, which can be put to use in carrying through programs to their advantage. Indeed, a strategy which seeks to remove poverty may prove empty or impossible to implement unless the poor develop sufficient consciousness and organization to provide support from below to maintain the momentum of the poverty-alleviation program over a period of many years. They possess the local knowledge which can supply some of that detail which selective projects and intervention require, both technically and in the sense of articulating needs. Released from fear and distrust of official authority, as embodied in the administration at least, they are well placed to bring pressure to bear on the agencies charged with implementation. And given a measure of organization and help, they can do much to help themselves, often more flexibly and efficiently than intervention from above could manage.

Where is the initiative for mobilization to come from if the poor are not politically organized, on the basis of their shared poverty at least, especially if they are prevented, in part, from perceiving the causes of their condition by notions fostered in them by dominant groups? Here, the adoption of a poverty-focused strategy, backed by preliminary action as an earnest of good intent, can itself serve as an instrument of mobilization. First, by encouraging those in poverty to see themselves primarily as "poor" rather than as people of region X or caste Y, for example, the "message" of the strategy and its implementation can provide a counterideology to appeals based on regional or caste identity. Thus, if a successful start is made (and it is a big *if*), the strategy will begin to erode existing political alignments. Second, and this is a closely related point, by holding out the prospects of benefits distributed with the backing of authority, the "plan" can provide just the stimulus for the poor to convert perceptions of shared interests into organized political action in pursuit of their economic well-being. This stimulus is likely to be especially strong in situations where the issue is that of defending gains already realized, or gains apparently to be realized in the near future. Vague promises, which are often accompanied by enjoinders to work hard and bear austerity in the cause of "national unity and development," will more likely than not have a limited effect.

More specifically, in view of the often limited communication among the poor, one very useful form of intervention from above would take the form of financial and logistic support from government for the creation of "trade unions" for the underprivileged, especially in rural areas (see Chapter VI). These would provide focal points for the organization of tenants and landless in the countryside, and for urban "marginals" in the towns. Whether or not such moves to mobilize the poor would promote political "order," with which many political scientists—not to speak of regimes—are now preoccupied, is a moot point.[17] Certainly, mobilization must take place within some sort of institutional framework—even in the case of protest—if the poor are to use their power purposefully.

Once the poor are mobilized, there remains the issue of how much independent initiative they can exercise in decision-making. This is partly a matter of how they came to be organized, and partly a matter of institutional decentralization. Clearly, if the poor's solidarity and organization sprang from their own awareness and capacity, they would not be easily led or manipulated by government agencies. But the extent of devolution in decision-making power towards local agencies and communities still places limits on the scope for the poor to play an active role in determining how resources are allocated. Moreover, in itself, decentralization in an institutional sense—for example, the creation of a federal from a previously unitary system of government, or the granting of special discretionary powers to a district administrator—need not involve the poor at all. Although it is commonly held that a strong measure of decentralization of decision-making and political power is a necessary condition for a reduction in inequality, this is only so if the underprivileged are *already* organized to take advantage of the opportunities thus offered. If they are not, decentralization may actually worsen the position by giving dominant local groups an occasion to capture institutions and lines of access, which will then be placed to subvert to their own advantage many kinds of intervention from above. A well-documented example of exactly this process is provided by the failure of the Community Development Program in India, which was undertaken without any prior attempt to change the pre-existing social structures at the local level.[18] More generally, the rather romantic earlier involvement of some sociologists with the concept of "grassroots" (Selznick, 1949) and the analysis flowing from it have been subjected to a strong critique (Martin, 1956).

The power relationship between central and local decision-making units involves more general issues. For example, whether or not a radical redistribution of income can be combined with a fast rate of growth in the absence of iron central control over key sectors is very much an open question and one which the Chinese experience has not settled decisively.

[17]For an incisive account of those political scientists' disenchantment with democracy as an ideal, see Cruise O'Brien (1972).

[18]For critique of the Community Development approach in relation to issues of development, administration, and copious references of a more general kind, see Schaffer (1969), p. 203ff.

The fact that the combination may not be possible implies that in any situation where fast growth is imperative, an associated and unavoidable degree of centralization has somehow to be reconciled with the concept of "democracy" embodied in blanket prescriptions to decentralize. "Key" sectors apart, however, the case that decentralization in political life and decision-making must be accompanied by the decentralization of production demands close consideration.[19]

The tension, even contradiction, between these two views of local versus central control is real enough, but it is overstated by the above account. If decentralization is not, after all, a self-evident good, then the question becomes not so much how far it ought to go, as what form it should take. The simplistic notion that all will be well if power and initiative are devolved to the local level is based on the faulty diagnosis that the essential problem lies in center—periphery relations. By contrast, the argument here is that local power structures and their national linkages exercise a dominant influence over the balance and effects, intended and otherwise, of policy measures. Thus the nature and timing of decentralization initiatives must be chosen with care so as to counteract rather than bolster the existing configuration of social structures at the local level, which is typically inimical to the interest of the poor.

THE ADMINISTRATIVE SYSTEM

The workings of existing administrative systems and the training of the personnel who man them are the subjects of an extensive literature to which little can be usefully added here.[20] Suffice it to say that profound changes in the composition and emphasis of policy as a whole raise a number of important issues. Today's boundaries of responsibility and function between departments and agencies may be entirely inappropriate. Indeed, wholly new institutions may well be necessary. Of greater weight still is the implicit demand for continuing innovation in the way decisions are made. Yet innovation runs directly against the primacy of precedent in bureaucratic behavior. At a more general level, because the administrative function has discretionary elements, the administration is not merely an instrument in the hands of the politicians. The administration has a political lifeforce all of its own. Administrative style and ethos, by exerting a strong influence on what kinds of decisions can be made and implemented, are more critical than capacity in the sense of how much can be done.[21] Thus the problem is not purely, or even primarily in many cases, one of the availability, the integrity, and the efficiency of trained manpower.

What can be done to circumvent or overcome these difficulties, apart from rebuilding the system from scratch? We consider two courses of ac-

---

[19] The Yugoslav experience is highly relevant here.

[20] See especially Riggs (1964) and Schaffer (1969).

[21] For an analysis of the bureaucratic style and its distributive consequences, see Schaffer (1969), p. 192ff.

tion, neither of which remotely suffices by itself, but which taken together should produce a discernible impact. The first is to fashion the system's incentives, sanctions, and criteria for evaluating performance in a way consistent with the priorities implicit in a poverty focused strategy. The second is to create entirely new institutions and agencies which will serve the poor exclusively.

On the first point, it is almost invariably the case that the able, diligent, or well-connected civil servant will spend much of his career in the company of his peers and politicians, with the "occasional" diversion of meetings with foreigners. When he is posted to outlying towns or rural areas, usually early in his service, he may well regard the period spent there as necessary time-serving or as a punishment for falling out of favor, and chafe constantly to get back to the center. Thus, the active business of administration which is intimately bound up with implementing the strategy—agricultural and industrial extension, land reform, public works, and the like—is probably conducted by officers who are less gifted or disaffected or both. For in most countries, such work carries comparatively little prestige, and there is rarely any offsetting financial compensation—if anything, the reverse. Changes in the structure of incentives and sanctions—money, moral, and prestige—are essential if the administration of policy towards the poor is to be in the hands of the best cadres.

Even within those activities central to the implementation of the strategy, there may be problems stemming from the inappropriate criteria by which performance is assessed. Suppose, for example, that a block officer is given a blanket target of 10,000 acres of high-yielding wheat. Perhaps his only way to meet that target will be to concentrate his and his staff's efforts on rich peasants who might grow ten to twenty acres each rather than on ten to twenty times that number of small farmers, all reluctant to try a new technology. A more disturbing example still is provided by the dilemmas often confronting District Magistrates in India arising out of their "law and order" role. Should they attempt to implement land reform law, perhaps following a "land grab" by the landless, the ensuing flare-up will demand that "order" be imposed forthwith and "law" quietly forgotten (Bandopadhyay, 1972).

On the second course of action, the fact that privileged groups have got special, sometimes virtually exclusive, access to government extension, input and credit agencies—in part by virtue of their social and political connections with the cadres who administer such services—is well documented. This fact suggests that wholly new institutions endowed with ample resources and the best cadres, which cater solely to the needs of the poor, may be required to complement the mobilization initiatives discussed above. For perhaps the only way of equalizing access to existing institutions is to break the power of the groups which have captured them. In rural areas, that almost certainly means a land reform.

In this connection, a set of detailed and specific proposals for the establishment of "Agencies for Small Farmers" is laid out in Chapter VI. Here, the experience gained from the Indian Small Farmer's Development Agency (SFDA) program is highly illuminating. These district-level institutions are supposed to coordinate the actions of other government agencies supplying inputs—credit, fertilizer, seeds, irrigation, and so on—so that resources will be channeled freely to registered small farmers. However, the day-to-day work is under the direction of an officer who is of the same rank as those he is charged to coordinate. As the SFDAs are registered charities and enjoy no *de jure* status within the administrative structure, their directors cannot command, but must plead, that small farmers be given good treatment by the agencies which control the goods. While predictably disappointing under these circumstances, the results do not imply that the basic concept of the SFDAs is mistaken. But fundamental questions about authority—and priority—remain, questions which must be addressed directly if initiatives of this kind are to succeed.

THE PLANNER AS A POLITICAL ACTOR

It has been argued above that, more often than not, the political process will fail to generate a well-defined social welfare function. Where this is so, there will tend to be a good deal of latitude for policy analysts and administrators involved in the planning process to impress their own particular values on the shape and direction of policy.[22] To the extent that they seize on the opportunity thus provided, they come to play an active political role, though not necessarily as a coherent interest group. Such chances are not confined to the "planners," as the term is normally understood; but insofar as the determination of resource allocation priorities is significantly centralized, they are likely to have a strong say in it. The fact that the central planner may be able to exercise a political role is reason enough to ask under what conditions he can do so and how he will then behave.

Broadly speaking, then, two types of situations may be distinguished. The first is one in which the regime's objectives are fairly well defined, and the role of the planner—however he may perceive it—is seen by the government itself to be fairly narrow. In these circumstances, the planner has relatively little independent room to maneuver—unless some degree of discretion resides inherently in the system—or some policy can achieve the trick of furthering both his own and official ends. Here, the critical question is whether the government itself places a high priority on solving the problems of poverty and income maldistribution. At one extreme, the government's position will be explicitly and only too clearly one of active hostility. Here it is doubtful if the planner can play any role other than a technical one, which is prescribed closely by the objectives of

---

[22]When the planner *qua* technician employs well-defined preference functions, his intention must be analytic or pedagogic. In tracing out as fully and clearly as possible the probable consequences of adopting a given policy package, or of specifying different preference functions, his aim will be to establish a more coherent and consistent set of policy objectives.

those who control the political system. At the other end of the spectrum, the government concerned will be committed strongly, and in more than words, to implementing an egalitarian strategy. In this situation, too, the planner should, in principle, have an important technical role to play, especially in keeping an eye on the macroeconomic constraints within which policy must operate. But where radical changes are afoot, the situation is bound to be confused and uncertain. The regime will be rightly obsessed with maintaining its support base and the associated pattern of alliances as it tries to keep up the momentum of structural changes. There may be little nervous energy, even concern perhaps, to weigh up some of the incidental economic consequences of actions aimed at restructuring the distribution of assets and power. In the early stages, at least, the planner is not likely to have a major say.

The second general scenario is one which corresponds much more closely to real life. Here the government is perceived neither by itself nor by others as a custodian of that difficult and ambiguous concept, the national interest. Rather it is an "operational" alliance between various interest groups which aims to grasp and preserve power, but which also needs to be continuously cemented and possibly extended. In this situation, the political leadership may be described as giving only limited guidance to the planner. Despite the agnostic position adopted here, the politicians themselves may well accept that intervention to secure improvements in the condition of the poor would lead to greater political stability, even over the time horizon which concerns them, quite apart from any intrinsic humanitarian appeal such an objective might possess. Yet even if it exists, a willingness to consider, and possibly to initiate, a poverty-focused strategy does not by itself lead to politically well-articulated objectives to which planners can respond as technicians. The regime's preoccupation with the sheer maintenance of power is often so great (and this can apply as much to a military dictatorship as to a ruling party in a parliamentary system) that the leadership's view of the future is bound to have a much shorter horizon than the decades of the historical process which their actions affect.

What role can the planner play in this sort of political context? It can be argued that this is precisely the situation where he can be most influential. Unlike the one discussed above, there is no clear, politically stated set of objectives to begin with—other than remaining in power—but the planner can work towards identifying it on the basis of such broad indications as are available, for example, other actions of political leaders, their statements on policy, manifestos, and so forth. Arriving at a set of objectives in this way is by no means easy, especially in highly pluralistic polities in which, diverse and effective interests exist and politicans are engaged in making often mutually inconsistent statements. In these circumstances, an economic strategy will have to be presented in terms of its detailed implications for particular interest groups (over politically meaningful horizons) if there is to be any sort of useful dialogue, however indirect, with the political leadership. Hopefully, the dialogue will tend towards some consensus, at least on the minimum "packages" that seem likely to satisfy the numerous and disparate requirements of competing groups. Yet this process will not provide precise or even unique answers; for in presenting his proposals, the planner must make prior decisions concerning what to omit, to play down and emphasize. To exercise such discretion is to make political choices, as we have been at pains to make clear.

In general, therefore, planners cannot expect to operate in an environment in which their role is purely technical. Depending upon the political context, and subject to the constraints imposed by the political leadership, they can contribute substantially to the formulation of an objective function out of what may be ill-defined and often inconsistent premises and policy statements. Where the leadership is coherent, this contribution may take, in part, the form of a dialogue from a politically defined starting position. Where the leadership is more amorphous and the situation is confused, the planner may be more active in the selection and presentation of alternative objectives, their relative feasibilities and their implications in terms with which politicians are primarily concerned. In either case, the interaction between the political leadership and the technical planners is an essential part of the broader process of planning and decision-making.

However, to set out the possibility of an activist role is not to recommend or sanction it. Certainly, there will be no unanimous agreement that a planner should consciously insert his own conception of what the objectives should be. As a genre, technocrats may have more progressive political inclinations than others in government. Over historically short periods in particular circumstances, they may find themselves in positions of considerable influence. But without going into the vexed question of the role of the individual in history, it remains the case that those working within the system are bound ultimately by the dictates of the groups whose interests it serves, whether they realize the fact or not. The fact that the drives and energies of individuals can thus be diverted makes it far from clear that a sustained and long run effort to alleviate poverty can spring largely from technocrats adopting the role of custodians of the interests of the poor and the unborn. This fact should give pause for thought, and a due sense of humility in assessing the value of an instrumental approach to bringing about social change.

CONCLUSIONS

There are a number of regimes for which the strategy proposed in this volume is "out of court." Some are dominated by entrenched elites who will relinquish nothing to the underprivileged except under the duress of armed force. Others have attacked successfully the causes of poverty by means far more direct and radical than those discussed here. Yet that still leaves a considerable range of societies for which the strategy is at least plausible, even though in some of them the likelihood that it will be adopted with any vigor is remote.

In such cases, the key factor is the emergence of a coalition of interests able to grasp power which sees some advantage in implementing a redistributive strategy, despite the fact that some sections of it stand to lose relatively thereby. To survive in the long run in a changing society, elites must make occasional well-timed concessions, and some of them are aware of the fact. Moreover, as the rich do not constitute a class with identical interests, potential disputes among them provide other bases for political alignments, in which the poor may have enough representation to press their cause effectively.

If a workable "reformist" coalition is formed, it will tend to be rather fragile, so the policies chosen to put the strategy into effect, which determine the distributive impact of the transfer of resources, assume critical importance. To be of any use, the impact of redistributive policies must have a measure of permanence. Thus there are two strategic options open to the regime. It can plump for rapid and drastic forms of intervention, whose effects are not easily reversible, either because they change the balance of political power or because of their intrinsic features; a radical land reform and nationalization coupled with workers' control are good examples. Such moves will probably impose severe strains on the coalition and alter its support base. Even if the government falls as a result, which is a distinct possibility, the poor may still be able to defend their gains in the aftermath. The alternative option is less tempestuous and much more likely to be adopted: to nibble away at the problem, maneuvering all the while to stay in power. With small margins of error in maintaining the viability of the coalition, success may come to depend on the quality of political leadership, particularly its ability to inspire confidence and energy. There is also the danger that exogenous events, such as a harvest failure or a balance of payments crisis not attributable to domestic policy, may administer a shock severe enough to shatter the basis of the alliance. But if the coalition makes some intitial progress, it will have to give some stimulus to the mobilization of the poor in conjunction with "visible" policy measures, to consolidate gains as they are made and to strengthen its own "reformist" foundations. The cause is not lost at the outset, but it will not readily triumph.

Chapter IV

THE SCOPE FOR POLICY INTERVENTION
Montek S. Ahluwalia

The operational limitations of any development strategy are determined by the availability of policy instruments to influence social objectives. Effective planning calls for a wide range of such instruments to give maximum maneuverability in plan implementation. The scope for reorienting development strategies along the lines proposed in Chapter II can be examined in these terms. Having defined social objectives in terms of the levels and growth of income in different socio-economic groups we need to identify instrument variables with which to influence these targets.

Areas of Intervention

In general, governments have a wide choice between alternative types of policy intervention. The level and growth of income of different groups in society are determined as part of a general equilibrium of the economy as a whole and governments can intervene at different points in this system. Six different "areas of intervention" can be distinguished in this context.[1]

(i) *Factor markets* determine factor prices, utilization levels, and factor incomes, giving us the functional distribution of income.

(ii) *Ownership and control of assets* (including both physical capital and labor skills) in the population translate the functional distribution of income into a size distribution of income. Changes in ownership patterns over time are an important element determining changes in the distribution of income.

(iii) *Taxation of personal income and wealth* operates on the size distribution of income as a fiscal corrective on market-determined income.

(iv) *Provision of public consumption goods,* or direct income transfers by the state, complement post-tax income distribution patterns and, jointly with (iii) above, determine the net fiscal impact on the size distribution of income.

(v) *Commodity markets* are closely linked to the equilibrium in the factor markets. The commodity composition of final demand obviously

This chapter draws upon an earlier paper submitted to the Bellagio working party entitled "Policy Instruments and Planning Models for Income Distribution and Employment," by Montek S. Ahluwalia and Jorge Cauas. Acknowledgements are also due to Alejandro Foxley, Ravi Gulhati, Paul Streeten, and Oktay Yenal for many valuable comments.

[1]The distinction between "areas of intervention" and the actual "instruments of intervention" is a useful one for our purposes. The precise policy instruments used to intervene in a particular area may differ in different cases. For example, taxes, subsidies, and quantitative restrictions can be used as alternative instruments to intervene in a particular direction in either commodity or factor markets. Similarly, different forms of taxation represent alternative instruments in the same general area.

affects the pattern of demand for factors and therefore factor incomes. Conversely, the income distribution directly determines commodity demand through consumption patterns.

These five components constitute a "closed loop" describing the general equilibrium determination of income in an economy. To these we may add a sixth component which is crucial although somewhat less subject to government influence.

(vi) *The state of technology* determines the level of total output and the degree of substitutability between factors.

Governments can and do intervene in many of these areas in most underdeveloped countries. The relative merits of intervening in a particular area depend upon a number of considerations. Some of these are clearly economic. The particular economic characteristics of the target groups or the economic structure of a country may make intervention in one area more effective than another. In other cases, political and institutional considerations may play a dominant role in some types of intervention being preferred to others.

The choice of areas of intervention represents in some sense a choice of strategy. A detailed prescription for this choice is only possible in the context of the particular circumstances of each case. There are, however, some general considerations that determine the success of each type of intervention and these are examined below.

Factor Prices, Employment, and Income

Intervention in factor markets aimed at promoting greater absorption of labor is a popular theme in development literature. It is well grounded in neo-classical economics, which emphasizes the relationship between marginal productivity and wages as a basis for a theory of employment and the functional distribution of income into factor shares. Proponents of factor price intervention usually point to the existence of numerous distortions of relative factor prices leading to an understatement of the price of capital and an overstatement of labor costs. From this it is argued that measures designed to reduce the price of labor relative to capital in the factor markets will encourage greater absorption of labor and will have favorable effects on growth, employment, and income distribution.

Such policies are undoubtedly important but they do not by themselves provide a solution to all distributional problems. Indeed they operate subject to important limitations which need to be examined in some detail.

The Price of Labor

Policies directed at lowering the relative price of labor fall into two categories. One set of policies attempts to lower the price actually paid to labor by removing minimum wage legislation, weakening existing collective bargaining arrangements and avoiding high wage policies for fear of "trend setting." The other set aims at reducing labor costs to employers without directly lowering the wages paid, e.g., through labor subsidies or abolition of payroll taxes. In both cases the distributional impact is limited by technological conditions of factor productivity and substitutability.

The nature of these limitations can be illustrated by considering the impact of lowering real wages in a two-factor neoclassical world with unemployed labor. We would expect lower wages would produce some increase in employment and an increase in output, since more labor is employed with the same amount of capital. The tendency of both output and employment to rise accounts for these policies being presented as "working in the right direction" as long as policy concerns are expressed in terms of output or employment. But the distributional impact of these policies is more ambiguous. If the elasticity of substitution is less than unity—as is likely to be the case—the share of wages in total income will actually fall and there is a possibility that total wages may also fall if the increase in output does not offset the decline in wage share.

In these circumstances we have three distributional changes. (i) Capitalists are better off—both relatively and absolutely—since total output is higher and the wage share lower. (ii) Workers previously employed suffer an absolute decline in income due to the loss of their protected position. (iii) Against this, there is an increase in income in the previously unemployed group which represents a distributional gain. This increase can more than offset the decline in income of the previously employed (i.e., the total wage bill can be higher) if technological conditions are right. But if these conditions are not favorable there may be a worsening of the position of employed labor with only a marginal improvement in the position of the presently unemployed.

The appropriateness of technological conditions is obviously an empirical question to be determined for particular countries and sectors, but the argument presented above suggests that, for some sectors at any rate, the distributional benefits from lowering real wages may be very small. Several empirical studies of the degree of substitution between capital and labor have come up with elasticities of substitution greater than zero but substantially less than unity at least for a wide range of industries. These estimates are subject to limitations arising from conceptual and estimation problems but there is no reason to suppose that they understate the degree of substitutability. In fact, quite the contrary, since some of the measured elasticity of substitution reflects aggregation of nonhomogeneous products with different labor requirements.

The alternative approach of reducing labor costs to employers through labor subsidies or abolition of payroll taxes appears at first sight to have marked advantages since wages are not directly reduced. But these policies involve a cost to the government budget in the form of subsidy payments or tax rebates and these costs must be compared with distributional benefits as determined by the resulting increase in employment. Since most subsidy or tax rebate schemes will have to operate on total employment instead of being limited to additional labor hired, it is the total cost of the subsidy that has to be offset by the distributional benefit from the increase in employment and output. Once again the degree of substitutability in production determines the success of this policy.

These arguments are not intended to minimize the costs of distortions in factor markets. They are simply a realistic assessment of the limitations of operating on the price of labor to promote employment and distributional objectives. In particular, they are meant to temper the excessive zeal with which economists tend to attack institutional systems traditionally designed to protect labor interests, such as collective bargaining and trade union organizations. There are many cases in which substantial gains in total wages may be achieved with only marginal reductions in output and employment, because wage bargaining occurs in sectors with low elasticities of substitution and low elasticities of output with respect to labor. These conditions characterize much of the modern sector in underdeveloped countries and particularly the foreign-owned enclave sector where collective bargaining is strongest.

Against this it is sometimes argued that "protected wages" in some sectors set targets for collective bargaining and create expectations in other sectors where substitution elasticities may be much higher and the distributional impact more adverse. In these situations it may be best to tolerate dualism in the labor market, i.e., institutional mechanisms supporting high wages should continue to exist in the modern sector (where substitutability is typically low) while leaving large parts of the market outside the scope of these mechanisms. This is in fact the case in most countries.

The above discussion of the price of labor has been concerned with the relationship between wages and labor incomes through the choice of technique in production. But there are other aspects of wage policy in underdeveloped countries which have direct relevance for distributional objectives. Two of these are particularly important for our purposes. The first relates to the impact of distorted wage structures on the demand for education. High wages in the urban formal sector create expectations of high rewards from formal education producing strong demand for high school and university education. Such expectations may actually prevent the development of a skilled labor force while at the same time produce a surplus of high school and university graduates—not an uncommon phenomenon in underdeveloped countries. The second aspect of wage policy relevant for distributional objectives relates to the direct resource costs of labor employed in the government in routine administration. In many underdeveloped countries, the government is a major employer and much of the expansion in government employment reflects strong pressures to absorb educated manpower, typically from higher income classes. Such employment is frequently justified on distributional grounds, but it should be recognized that it is really a relief measure benefitting the middle- or even high-income households which account for the bulk of surplus educated manpower.

These arguments suggest that relative wages for certain types of employment should be lowered and an incomes policy in the urban sector should be implemented to this effect. This is particularly important in determining wage policies in "nonproductive" government services.

The Price of Capital

By contrast with policies directed at lowering real wages, policies directed toward raising the cost of capital are less likely to be socially regressive. They achieve the same relative price effect but generally do not produce an increase in capitalist incomes. Indeed, in most cases, they require either the imposition of a tax on capital or the removal of explicit or implicit subsidies arising from low interest rates, exchange rate undervaluation of imported capital equipment, and various types of capital-based tax rebates and incentive schemes. In general, these policies shift income from high-income groups to the government budget. Given the fiscal constraints on the scope for implementing labor subsidies, these measures may well represent the only feasible price intervention in this area.[2]

But the key policy instruments in removing capital market distortions are not the conventional tax-subsidy-interest rate interventions discussed above. The problem in most underdeveloped countries is not one of generalized underpricing of capital, but rather of capital market fragmentation, whereby the terms on which capital is made available differ markedly between sectors. Large parts of the supply of capital are institutionally preempted for particular sectors leading to an underpricing of capital in the modern sector and a marked overpricing of capital in the market facing the traditional and unorganized sectors. Discrimination against labor use arises not simply because capital intensive modern sectors face a low price of capital, but also because labor-intensive sectors (farmers and urban small producers) face a very high price of capital. In this situation, it is the lack of availability of capital to the labor-intensive sectors which prevents labor absorption by discouraging expansion in these sectors.

While lack of availability of credit for farmers and small-scale producers can be seen as a "price distortion," this diagnosis misses the point in terms of the policy instruments needed to correct the problem. In such a situation the appropriate instruments are clearly not of the traditional tax-subsidy kinds. Instead, policy action should be devoted to ensuring equality of access for sectors currently excluded.[3] The pure relative price effect of these measures on technology choice within sectors may not be very important. They will raise the price of capital in sectors where modern technology and low elasticities of substitution prevail. They will actually lower it in the traditional sectors where the scope for substitution is greater so that the relative price effect in these sectors is not in favor of greater labor intensity. Greater labor

---

[2]For a discussion of some of the implications of tax-subsidy intervention directed at labor and capital, see Ahluwalia (1973).

[3]This is largely a matter of developing the right institutions to achieve effective financial intermediation.

absorption comes not so much from a more labor-intensive choice within sectors but from a reallocation between sectors in favor of those which are more labor intensive.[4]

OWNERSHIP AND CONTROL OF ASSETS

The determination of prices and employment levels in the factor markets gives us the functional distribution of income into factor shares. For policy purposes, however, we are interested in the distribution of personal income. For this we need to examine the distribution of income-earning factors among households.

At the root of high concentrations of income we find highly concentrated patterns of assets and human skills.[5] These patterns are the "initial conditions" for any planning strategy but there are several instruments which governments can use to alter these patterns over time. Direct operations on the pattern of asset concentrations have long been part of radical programs of social reform but they have been curiously neglected by neoclassical economists, who have focused almost exclusively upon questions of relative factor pricing and employment. In fact the ability to alter asset concentration patterns over time is an important instrument for promoting distributional objectives (see Chapter II). We can distinguish between two approaches in this context: a static redistribution of an existing stock of assets and a dynamic approach aiming at altering patterns of asset accumulation over time.

Redistribution of Existing Assets

The most immediate and also most radical approach is to undertake direct redistribution of the existing stock of assets. This redistribution may take one of two forms. First, concentrated holdings of productive assets can be directly transferred to lower-income households to raise income levels of these households. Land reform aimed at transforming tenant cultivators into smallholders is a classic example of this type of redistributive policy. An alternative form is collectivization, whereby the ownership of the asset and earnings therefrom are "socialized." Examples of such policies are land reforms aimed at collective farming or state farms and also nationalization of industrial enterprises. In the case of collectivization, the impact on income distribution depends upon the distributional rules adopted by the newly socialized sector of the economy both in terms of wage and employment policies and the use of undistributed surplus. Collectivization may be a device for state appropriation of the surplus and may not be accompanied by an immediate improvement of income distribution as usually understood.

How far are such measures likely to be effective in redistributing income, assuming that they are politically feasible? The simple answer to this question

---

[4]These sectors can also be encouraged through policies directed at the commodity market as discussed later in this chapter.

[5]If all households owned equal amounts of all factors then the distribution of income would tend to equality irrespective of prices paid for different factors.

is to compare two critical elements: (i) the direct and indirect costs to the economy of acquiring these assets, and (ii) the earning ability of the recipients of the asset. Clearly the net redistributive effect is greater the smaller the costs in terms of compensation payments and the greater the additional output produced after redistribution.

The need for compensation payments and the extent of such payments will obviously be determined by the political circumstances surrounding each case. In general, countries expropriating foreign-owned assets encounter strong pressures for compensation. Refusal to enter into compensation negotiations, sometimes dictated by political considerations, raises the danger of economic retaliation which may involve significant economic costs in terms of disruption of trade and capital flows. By contrast, the compensation issue is unlikely to generate external pressure when only nationals are involved although here the domestic political costs of such action are likely to be stronger. In both cases it may prove desirable to accept the principle of compensation for expropriated assets while negotiating minimum levels of compensation. The degree to which this approach is successful will vary from case to case, but in general there is a significant range over which negotiated compensation schemes can be devised while preserving a substantial net redistribution effect.[6]

The need to maximize the earning ability of the redistributed asset is self-evident on examination but its importance is often ignored in practice. In some cases, the productive capacity of the asset may be substantially higher after redistribution, eliminating an important source of trade-offs between growth and distribution. Thus, in the case of land reforms, it is frequently argued that land productivity may actually increase as farm size is reduced, at least over a certain range, due to more intensive application of labor inputs. This is particularly true if systematic government support can be extended to ensure application of complementary inputs and new and improved techniques on redistributed land.

In practice, redistribution of assets may be accompanied by significant reductions in productivity, due to the failure to provide the necessary institutional infrastructure and complementary inputs to maintain the earnings potential of the redistributed asset. Thus, land reform may lead to a reduction in output and prove ineffective as an instrument of income distribution if marketing channels are disrupted or other limitations in the system prevent smallholders from being as efficient producers as larger cultivators. A whole range of institutional constraints are relevant in this context—education and skill level of beneficiaries of the reform, provision of critical inputs such as marketing, credit, fertilizer, seeds, and so on. Since institutional structures providing these resources are unlikely to adapt rapidly to the changed circumstances, it may be necessary to devise package policies to deal simultaneously with these constraints, any one of which may greatly reduce pro-

---

[6]The real costs of delayed compensation payments in the form of government bonds may be significantly lower than they appear due to erosion through price inflation.

duction.[7] Failure to anticipate these difficulties has undoubtedly led to high costs—at least in the short run.

Similar problems of maintaining productivity arise with the nationalization of industry as a possible "asset collectivization" policy. Countries following such policies must ensure that efficiency can be maintained. Public sector inefficiency may be an acceptable cost in an environment where public participation is limited to traditional fields such as infrastructure, where efficiency is difficult to measure and market criteria are least applicable. It is quite inexcusable—because the costs are substantially higher—in an environment where extension of public ownership is an avowed policy.

Dynamic Redistribution: Redirecting Investment

A dynamic approach to the problem of asset concentration focuses attention not on the distribution of existing assets but on the pattern of accumulation in the economy which determines the growth of different assets over time. If lack of ownership or access to particular types of assets limits incomes in lower-income groups, the government can attempt to build up these assets by redirection of the pattern of investment in the economy. Given the existing lack of access to capital, a program of directing a target percentage of GNP toward such investment could achieve substantial results.[8] As in the static case we distinguish between social and private ownership of assets and redistribution of assets over time

Socialization over time is sometimes presented as a viable strategy for the "mixed" economies. In these economies restrictions on private sector expansion combined with a growing public investment rate are expected to produce an eventual dominance of publicly owned assets in the total wealth of the country. The main difficulty with this approach is that the transition period may be very long, and it is by no means certain that pursuit of this strategy leads to a continuous improvement in the distribution of income.

On the production side there are the familiar problems of alleged public sector inefficiency. These problems reflect, to a large extent, the failure of mixed economies to develop appropriate incentives and institutions to ensure economic efficiency of public sector enterprises. The question of public sector efficiency is invariably controversial, and in almost all cases a large number of specific explanations can be provided to explain low productivity of particular public sector enterprises. However, there can be no doubt that in many mixed economies public sector efficiency is well below the levels necessary for a generalized policy of socialization of assets to be pursued without excessive output losses. Much of this is due to the failure to develop institutions appropriate for the management of an expanded public sector. Measures to improve efficiency levels will vary in different countries but they are a necessary precondition for successful use of this instrument.

---

[7] See Chapter VI on the need for a package approach for rural target groups.

[8] See Chapter XI for an exploration of the effects of redirecting 2 percent of GNP to the poor over twenty-five years.

Apart from problems of productive efficiency, public enterprises also present problems in terms of their direct distributional impact. These enterprises are usually in the industrial sector and characterized by high wages and capital intensity, and their direct distributional impact is limited to the workers employed. These workers typically belong to middle-income groups and are usually successful in pushing wage demands substantially cutting into the socially owned surplus. Public enterprises of this type have a minimal direct impact on the distributional problem in its most serious forms: unemployment of unskilled and low-skilled labor and low productivity of the self-employed poor.

An alternative to socialization over time is a policy of direct investment support to raise incomes of the lowest-income groups. Since low incomes result from the lack of physical capital, access to infrastructure, and a wide range of complementary inputs, government policy should be directed to providing these inputs over time. Rural development programs aimed at providing a balanced addition to (and improvement of) rural infrastructure in the form of land improvement, drainage, small irrigation, feeder roads, credit and marketing institutions, and so on, provide one example of this approach. Similar programs to help the urban poor are more difficult to identify because of relatively stronger economies of scale in urban economic activity, but even here there is undoubtedly some scope for providing resources and infrastructure to support small-scale production.

The political appeal of this direct approach to poverty lies in the fact that it constitutes immediate (and politically visible) action to help target groups in the population. Its economic justification obviously rests on the economic costs in terms of productivity of capital in alternative uses appropriately evaluated in terms of distributional impact. While it is arguable that investment in the modern sector is quicker maturing and more productive than investment in the poor, if the poor are insufficiently linked to the modern sector the benefits of growth are unlikely to "trickle down" for a long time to come. In these circumstances direct programs of investment support may provide the only mechanism for raising low incomes in a reasonable period of time.

EDUCATION AND HUMAN CAPITAL

Complementary to the direct attack on patterns of asset concentration is the human capital approach, which argues that concentration patterns in human skills are as important a cause of income inequality as the concentration of physical assets.[9] On this view public policy should aim as far as possible to promote education so as to develop a more equal pattern of distribution of human capital. It is particularly popular because education is widely accepted as a sector for substantial public sector involvement and the political constraints upon implementing educational policies are on the whole less restrictive.

---

[9]The similarity should not, however, obscure the differences between physical assets and human capital. Inequality due to physical asset concentration is perpetuated by inheritance patterns while inequality due to human capital concentrations is less so.

To what extent does education contribute to the goal of increased employment and better income distribution? Proponents of the human capital approach argue that education—of the right type—increases the quality of the labor input leading to higher labor productivity, which is then reflected in higher wage earnings. Underlying this optimism about the role of education are assumptions about technology and the operation of factor markets. The technological assumption is that the marginal product of skilled labor is high and will remain relatively high even though the supply of skilled labor increases.[10] The factor market assumption is that wages paid reflect the marginal product of labor.

Against this optimistic view there is a substantial body of opinion—mainly derived from research in developed countries—that education may have little or no effect upon income concentrations. On this view formal education plays little part in imparting productive skills and upgrading the quality of labor. The role of education is perhaps better viewed as a screening device and, in the event of expansion of education, other screening criteria will be employed.

Observed associations between high wages and education obviously do not resolve this dispute. They may reflect no more than a higher propensity to spend on education in the high-income groups whose children also benefit from preferential access to high wage employment due to economic power. Choosing between these views ultimately calls for judgment rather than a detailed examination of available research results on the relationship between education and income-earning ability. This is particularly so as long as we do not have direct production function type measurements of productivity gain from education.[11]

It can be argued, however, that much of the pessimism about the role of education has only limited relevance for underdeveloped countries since the research on which it is based was conducted primarily in developed countries with very different labor market conditions and relative supplies of skilled labor. The relevance of the human capital approach to education is much greater in underdeveloped countries where there is a marked shortage of labor skills. In these countries, an adequate supply of skilled labor is a necessary condition for any sustained expansion in output and would be part of any growth-oriented strategy.[12]

The problem is not whether education is desirable but to determine what is the right kind of education and how to ensure that broadening educational programs will benefit the lower-income groups. The need for the right kind of education—curriculum reform with a shift away from the "academic" towards greater emphasis on vocational training—has long been recognized. The problem of ensuring access to education for lower-income groups is

---

[10]The main empirical basis for this assumption is the observation that relative wage rates of skilled and unskilled workers do not change with relative quantities in time series comparisons. See Bowles (1969) and Dougherty (1972).

[11]Inferring productivity from higher wages is to beg the question.

[12]See Chapter IX on the importance of skill constraints in planning models.

equally important. There is growing evidence that in many countries educational expansion, especially when it involves higher education, tends to be directed disproportionately towards higher-income groups in urban areas. Even where educational facilities are directed at the poor, the poor may not be able to benefit from them. These are formidable problems, but ones which must be dealt with if education is to be an instrument promoting both growth and equality.

TAXATION AND RESOURCE MOBILIZATION

Tax policy has been traditionally presented as an important instrument for income redistribution. Its impact on the distribution of income is twofold: (i) it provides a mechanism for intervening in the market equilibrium in both output and factor markets, and (ii) it provides a means of directly raising resources which can be transferred through various subsidy and expenditure schemes to achieve distributional objectives. This section is concerned solely with the revenue-raising role of taxation.[13]

Distributionally oriented development strategies will produce a substantial need for mobilizing resources. This is implied in any scheme for direct consumption transfers or for investment transfers of the type discussed in this volume. The net redistributive impact of these transfers obviously depends upon resources being raised through a sharply progressive tax structure.[14]

Direct taxation of both income and wealth is frequently presented as an effective means of achieving progressivity in the tax structure with minimum distortion of relative prices. But the scope for expanding the role of direct taxation is fairly narrowly circumscribed in most underdeveloped countries. Legislating progressive rates of direct taxation is, of course, entirely costless, but implementing them to cover a wide range of higher-income earners is extremely difficult. Typically, personal income taxation can be effectively implemented only in the modern corporate sector and for wage and salary earners in government. The relative importance of this group varies markedly between countries and in many countries it represents only a small part of this high income tax base. Noncorporate profit income, which should be captured by the direct tax net, typically avoids both direct personal income taxation and corporate taxation owing to difficulties of implementation. In these circumstances it is important to recognize that increased progressivity of income tax rates beyond a point simply leads to increased evasion while impinging even more severely on the narrow base in which implementation is relatively easy.

An obvious direction in which tax policy could move is in the implementation of wealth and property taxation, including in particular inheritance taxes, as a means of ensuring overall progressivity in the incidence of taxation. At present property taxes account for a small proportion of the total tax

---

[13]The impact on relative factor prices and commodity prices is examined in other sections of this chapter.

[14]Chapter XI, for example, explores the possibilities of transfer schemes transferring 2 percent of total GNP per year from the savings of the Rich to the Poor.

revenues of most countries—between 2 percent and 5 percent—and do not appear to be increasing in importance.[15] Undoubtedly there are serious problems of implementation in developing an effective system of property taxation, but a substantial improvement of existing performance is certainly possible. An important advantage in this connection is the limited range of available assets in most underdeveloped countries and the well-known high concentrations of wealth in these countries.

Taxation of urban property and taxation of land on a graduated basis are perhaps the most important avenues that need to be explored. Given the high concentration of wealth, the property tax net could be designed to cover only a small proportion of the population comprising the highest income groups, somewhat easing the administrative difficulties in effective implementation. The attempt to impose a wide-ranging property tax is a mistake. The role of property taxation should be seen as supplementing direct income taxes to achieve overall progressivity. Thus property taxation should be directed at raising the effective tax rate on the highest income levels while the personal income tax is less sharply progressive but more widely implemented.

Even with the maximum effort in direct taxation, however, indirect taxation will remain the most important source of tax income. Indirect taxes amount to over 60 percent of the tax revenue in most underdeveloped countries and there is evidence that this percentage has increased over time.[16] Progressivity in the indirect tax structure is therefore even more important than in the case of direct taxation.

Progressivity in consumer incidence requires that rates of taxation should be differentiated progressively between consumer classes. Commodities (or groups of commodities) with different income elasticities and low price elasticities provide an effective basis for discriminating between consumer classes. Higher tax rates can then be levied on commodities with higher income elasticities which represent a larger proportion of the budget in high-income classes.[17] This prescription needs to be amended if the production characteristics of different sectors are not distributionally neutral. For example, indirect taxation could attempt not only to tax high-income consumption but also to switch its composition towards labor-using commodities. In practice few countries have indirect tax systems that take account of these considerations. In most cases the structure of indirect taxation is markedly regressive primarily because it was inherited from the past and consists of a series of ad hoc impositions, largely in response to annual pressures for additional revenue. Systematic reformulation of tax structures to reflect distributional objectives could produce significant improvements in many countries.

Some of the traditional "public finance principles" on which many tax systems are based may need to be jettisoned, or at least amended. The view

---

[15]See Chelliah (1971).

[16]Ibid.

[17]Low price elasticities are important to minimize switching of consumption. If we could distinguish n commodity groups with different income elasticities and zero price elasticities we could choose appropriate tax and subsidy rates for each commodity group, so as to produce any desired net tax incidence on each income group.

that taxation of widely consumed (mass consumption) items achieves a very wide tax net is clearly irrelevant when the whole purpose is to reduce the incidence of taxation on lower-income groups. Food and other wage goods are obvious candidates for tax exemption. The view that the same rate of taxation should be applied to all commodities to avoid relative price distortions also needs to be amended to allow for distributional incidence. The aim should be to achieve the same rates across all commodities with similar income elasticity and distributional characteristics in production.

A final point of some importance in the area of tax policy is the scope for using public sector pricing policies to mobilize revenues. As a rule, public sector products and services—both economic and social—tend to be underpriced in many situations where neither the logic of relative prices nor distributional considerations calls for such underpricing. The same considerations that are applied to achieve progressivity in indirect taxation should be applied to public-sector pricing.

PUBLIC PROVISION OF CONSUMPTION GOODS

The direct provision of consumption goods financed through the fiscal system is an important instrument for any distributional strategy. It is closely related to any consumption subsidy scheme (e.g., policies directed at keeping the price of food low) except for the specific character of the transfer. Thus, public health expenditure in particular areas (designated villages, for example), school feeding and other nutrition programs, and extending rural water supply and electrification are all examples of public provision of consumer goods on an almost wholly subsidized basis. Provision of consumption goods is closely related to the production-oriented approach discussed above since many so-called consumption schemes have a direct effect on productive capacity.[18]

The importance of so-called consumption transfer schemes as an instrument of redistribution derives from two considerations. First, it operates directly to provide additional consumption. Unlike policies of intervention in the factor and commodity markets it does not rely upon other behavioral or technological responses in the system. As such it avoids many of the lags and conditional elements which limit the effectiveness of other policy instruments and may be particularly important when there is an immediate concern with alleviating extreme poverty. Second, it can operate selectively both in terms of the type of consumption good provided and in defining the beneficiaries of these schemes.

Selectivity is extremely important in identifying the most urgent of otherwise overwhelming needs which must be met through government policy. In many cases there are needs which can only be satisfied through selective supply of particular goods. Provision of rural water supply, public health, and electrification, for example, can only be undertaken by public expenditures.

---

[18]In fact, any sharp distinction between investment and consumption in this context is necessarily arbitrary. Provision of public infrastructure, health, nutrition, and education, are better viewed as parts of a package designed to raise the productive capacity of the labor force.

In other cases the scarcity of resources makes it necessary to preselect critical items of consumption and also categories of beneficiaries who must be supported. School feeding programs aimed at mitigating nutritional deficiencies in children may be identified as such a critical area. In these cases equivalent money transfers to the poverty group are unlikely to be directed wholly to these particular uses and some direct program is therefore preferable to transfer schemes relying on individual choice.[19]

The effectiveness of this particular policy instrument depends upon institutional considerations. Most underdeveloped countries do not have an organizational infrastructure through which essentially marginal amounts of consumption support can be channeled. Undoubtedly, an effective delivery system can be developed over time, but this is expensive and greatly expands the cost of otherwise marginal transfer. This suggests that consumption support schemes should be carefully chosen to minimize costs of infrastructure development. The popularity of school feeding programs, for example, is in part due to the availability of such an infrastructure.

INTERVENTION IN COMMODITY MARKETS

Intervention in commodity markets to influence both the pattern of output and relative prices is a potentially important instrument of distributive policy. The instruments used for such intervention vary widely in different circumstances. They include taxes and subsidies on domestic production and consumption, tariffs and subsidies on imports and exports, and various forms of quantitative restriction on both domestic production and foreign trade. Since much of traditional planning has been concerned exclusively with such intervention, aimed at resource allocation between sectors (although usually in pursuit of growth objectives alone), governments are quite willing to operate extensively in this area. Commodity intervention is usually recommended either on grounds of the production characteristics of particular sectors or on grounds of their consumption characteristics.

The production characteristics of some sectors tend to favor income distribution objectives due to the distributional pattern of incomes generated in that sector. The argument is usually presented in terms of the labor intensity of such sectors as construction, agriculture, various types of agro-industry, services, and so forth. Stimulating production in these sectors promotes employment and amounts to indirect factor substitution through changes in demand.[20]

---

[19]This is not irrational since low-income families are unlikley to perceive the full benefits of such consumption. In any case, part of the benefits are external, i.e., to society as a whole. It is now widely accepted that the provision of adequate nourishment at an early age has a definite impact on learning ability and thus ultimately determines the skill level of the labor force in the future.

[20]See Chenery and Raduchel (1971) on the magnitude of the indirect substitution effect. It should be noted that labor intensity is only one element in the distributional pattern of income generated in the sector. Asset concentration is the other important element and may operate in the opposite direction. This is the case with agriculture, for example, if agricultural land is highly concentrated. In such cases the distributional impact of stimulating production in the sector may not be wholly favorable.

The limitations of this approach arise from the degree of substitutability in demand between products with different factor intensities. Expanding labor-intensive sectors is a viable approach only if demand is sufficiently flexible to absorb the new output mix. Proponents of this approach argue that there is in fact substantial scope for demand manipulation. Investment demand in the economy can be altered by redirecting public investment towards such sectors as housing and urban and rural infrastructure, in which construction is a major element. Switching of consumer demand is more difficult because demand patterns may strongly favor more capital-intensive "modern" consumer goods. Even so, governments can use indirect taxation and production controls to switch demand away from these goods. Such policies are frequently implemented as part of a package to promote small-scale production of some commodities. The choice between investment and consumption demand switches should be made according to the economic costs involved which can be measured in terms of the productivity of alternative investments or in terms of consumer utility foregone. Governments concerned with expanding productive investments while facing severe resource constraints may find it difficult to switch investment towards labor-using but low-productivity projects. In such situations, it may be easier to operate on consumer demand incurring utility losses on consumers. This is especially so if the consumer classes affected belong to higher-income groups.

Where domestic demand substitution is difficult foreign trade possibilities provide an opportunity to expand labor-using sectors if export prospects for these sectors are favorable. The distributional impact of the choice between export promotion and import substitution can be examined in these terms. To the extent to which import substitution implies expanding capital-intensive sectors while export promotion favors labor-using sectors there may be some distributional advantage in pursuing export promotion more vigorously.[21]

The second approach to intervention in the commodity markets is based on the consumption characteristics of some commodities. Government policy can be directed toward maintaining the price of "wage goods" at a low level in order to achieve real income transfers to the poor. This approach is particularly important for its impact on the urban poor who receive money incomes and whose real incomes are highly sensitive to wage goods prices.[22] Theoretically, such a policy is inferior to a policy of income transfers, but most underdeveloped countries lack the institutions needed to administer direct transfers so that lowering wage goods prices may represent the only feasible mechanism for income transfer.

The problem with such policies usually arises from the absence of any viable financing mechanism to continue the transfer over time. Whether the transfer is in the form of direct subsidization of wage goods or subsidization of the inputs for producing wage goods, most underdeveloped countries are

---

[21]This is, of course, only one of the elements relevant to the choice between the two.

[22]Implicit in this argument is the view that the factor markets determine money wages and not real wages so that variations in the latter can be achieved through changes in wage goods prices.

not in a position to continue a policy of pure consumption support with a heavy drain on budgetary resources. The cost of these resources must be measured in terms of alternative investment possibilities which could provide the basis for a self-sustaining growth of incomes in the poor groups in future.

An alternative policy to keep wage goods prices relatively low is to permit imports of these goods at artificially low exchange rates. This is a viable policy for countries with a favorable balance of payments position but it has the disadvantage that the consumer gain is at the expense of domestic producers who may themselves belong to low-income groups. Attempts to operate directly on producer prices are even less satisfactory. Not only do they act as a disincentive to producers, they also reduce the total supply of wage goods making some form of rationing inevitable.

The State of Technology

The state of technology and the nature of technical progress are major influences on both the level and distribution of income in any economy. Technology and technical progress directly affect income generation in factor markets (and also relative prices in commodity markets) with immediate impact upon income distribution and growth. Unfortunately, these influences are not always benign for underdeveloped countries. Research typically responds to the needs (and resources) of developed countries so that new products and processes are not geared to the demand patterns and factor endowments of the underdeveloped countries.[23] Transplanted in underdeveloped countries they often serve only to support the expansion of the so-called modern sector and the consumption patterns of the very rich.

This has important implications for distributional strategies which call for greater use of labor intensive techniques and a shift of resources and redirection of demand away from the economy's modern sector toward its traditional sectors. The "technological backwardness" of these sectors creates a potential trade-off between growth and income distribution objectives. Statically this trade-off is reflected in the low productivity of many existing labor-using techniques. Dynamically, it may be reflected in low rates of technical progress at the labor-intensive end of the technology spectrum. A slower pace of technological progress greatly increases the trade-offs involved in making distributional choices and raises questions about the dangers of being locked into a low-level technology trap.

The scope for implementing redistributive strategies therefore depends not only on the availability of a range of labor-intensive techniques but on a steady rate of technological improvement and innovation at the labor-intensive end of the technology spectrum. Since the emphasis of research in developed countries is unlikely to change, direct action on the indigenous research capability will be necessary.

One alternative open to governments is to undertake direct support of research in "relevant" areas. The potential for such redirection is very large,

---

[23]For a discussion of some of these problems, see Marsden (1970).

covering such diverse areas as nutrition and health, low-cost housing, plant breeding programs aimed at crops grown by small farmers, dry farming techniques, and research on production and marketing problems of particular commodities suitable for labor-intensive production. Direct promotion of research does not, of course, imply closing the economy to imported technology. It is simply a realistic recognition of the fact that research efforts in developed countries are unlikely to be focused on several problems that are especially important for underdeveloped countries. In any case, even when major technical breakthroughs are internationally transferable—as in the case of high yielding varieties of food crops—substantial indigenous research may be needed to adapt these varieties to local conditions. The scope for direct promotion of research is obviously limited in many countries. The resource constraints on such programs are not merely financial; they are defined in terms of the size and sophistication of the technical and scientific base of the country. Nevertheless, there are a large number of countries in which the necessary scientific base does exist and where an active technology policy could be developed.

The scope of technology policy is not, however, limited to direct support of research. Dissemination of information on available technologies is equally important. Better knowledge of the available alternatives might prevent adoption of excessively capital-using techniques when long established designs which are much more capital-saving are available. This is particularly important when the decision on the choice of technique is actually within the control of the government, as in all public sector activity.

Closely related to the problem of technology choice is the problem of capital goods production. Techniques are typically embodied in machines and implements so that even when a technology is available (in the sense of blueprints) the machines themselves may no longer be in production. Technology policy must therefore be extended to ensure production of machines embodying the new technology. It is unlikely that the capital goods-producing sectors of developed countries will respond to demand for such goods in underdeveloped countries. Capital goods-producing industries in the more advanced of the underdeveloped countries will have to take a lead in producing the appropriate capital goods and indeed exporting them to other underdeveloped countries as needed. Only when a continuous chain is established, from research, through production, to final use and adaptive innovation, will labor-intensive techniques be fully viable.

The Choice of Policy Packages

Our review of alternative areas of intervention suggests some general conclusions which have some relevance in determining the scope for distribution strategies.

(i) There is a wide range of policy alternatives from which governments can choose in promoting distributional objectives. Some of these represent familiar areas of intervention (such as intervention in factor and product

market, resource mobilization through taxation, and so on) in which the
objectives of intervention need to be changed but the mechanisms are well
understood. Others represent new areas of intervention (such as redirection
of public investment towards the poor) which will place a heavy strain on
available resources and will need far-reaching institutional changes to be
effectively implemented.

(ii) No single type of policy intervention is likely to succeed in achieving
distributional objectives. Not only is each instrument limited but the objectives are typically multidimensional and particular types of intervention will
have an impact on only part of the distributional problem.

(iii) Some types of intervention promote both growth and distributional
objectives, raising no problems of trade-offs. This is often argued, for example, in removing distortions in the factor market, expanding education, and
promoting the search for appropriate technologies. Other types of intervention involve substantial trade-offs, at least in the near future, as for example
when resources are redirected to low-productivity long-gestation investment
projects directed at helping the poor. Given the scale of the distributional
problem, substantial improvements may not be achievable without accepting
some trade-offs.

(iv) Many types of policy intervention are strongly complementary and
require simultaneous implementation. Resource transfer policies, for example, require complementary action on resource mobilization through progressive taxation. Measures to increase labor absorption need to be accompanied
by expansion of education and training schemes to provide a skilled labor
force and other measures aimed at improving labor-intensive techniques.

These considerations suggest that the approach to formulating distributionally oriented strategies in most underdeveloped countries will have to be
eclectic rather than doctrinaire. The doctrinaire approach narrows down the
range of policy options to particular types of policy intervention which are
then elevated to something between dogma and strategy. Examples of this
approach are to be found at both ends of the political spectrum. Conservative
liberal strategies tend to focus almost entirely upon market price corrections
designed to "get the prices right" in the hope that the economic structure is
sufficiently flexible and the conviction that everyone will benefit! By contrast,
the radical solution places heavy emphasis upon breaking the concentration
of wealth and the institutional framework which both reflects and supports
this concentration.

In advocating an eclectic approach, we recognize that the conservative
liberal solutions may not be sufficient. Some action toward redressing the
extreme concentration of physical assets (in terms of ownership control and
access) is also necessary, and government can act on this front by redirecting
the flow of public investment over time. By operating at the margin, governments may be able to alter the patterns of concentrations significantly,
to an extent that may be politically impossible by operating on the stock of
existing assets alone. The ultimate justification for eclecticism is not that it
is always right but that it is most likely to be politically feasible.

Chapter V

FORMULATING A STRATEGY

C.L.G. BELL AND JOHN H. DULOY

TARGET GROUPS

A GROUP of people who are not only all poor but also relatively homogeneous with respect to the effect that a given set of policy instruments might have upon them may be defined as a *target group*. This approach requires that the definitions of target groups should, as far as possible, reflect causes rather than symptoms of poverty. With this concept it is possible to take account of the complementarity among policy instruments and hence the need for policy packages. For example, the availability of universal primary education and the elimination of illiteracy are generally accepted both as social objectives and as poverty-alleviating instruments. However, the provision of educational opportunities to illiterate sharecroppers or their children (or both) without reform in their conditions of tenancy is not likely to go far towards reducing their poverty. Conversely, a tenancy or land reform is likely to be more effective in generating higher incomes for the beneficiaries if they are literate, and therefore better able to gain access to information or to improved husbandry practices.

The concept facilitates the identification of specific forms of assets which can improve the conditions of different groups of the poor. The approach also eases the task of assessing the extent to which the benefits of policies will actually reach the target groups. The requirement of homogeneity in the definition implies that a large number of groups should be distinguished. However, this and the other components of the definition are not easy to satisfy in the absence of a well-articulated theory of how the benefits from development are distributed. We have approximated the diversity of the poor's circumstances by concentrating our analysis on four main target groups, with the definitions based largely on access to income-earning assets and to remunerative employment. The four groups are (i) small farmers, (ii) landless laborers and submarginal farmers, (iii) the urban underemployed, and (iv) the urban unemployed.

The dividing lines between these groups are somewhat arbitrary; further discussion appears both in the Appendix to Chapter V and in the relevant sections of Chapters VI and VII. In the rural groups, the basis of the dividing line is access to productive land. Small farmers are defined as those having access to sufficient land to provide at least a subsistence income to the farm family from its cultivation. (They may have other income oppor-

We are particularly indebted to Dragoslav Avramovic, Raj Krishna, Michael Lipton, and Dudley Seers for comments on various drafts of this chapter.

tunities, too, such as off-farm employment.) Landless laborers and sub-marginal farmers, by contrast, do not have access to this minimum quantity of land. Both the upper and lower limits of land-holding defining the small farmer group can only be defined quantitatively in a particular country context. The definition is usually on the basis of an absolute quantity of land of a given quality, corresponding to a given level of income which can be generated with normal cultivation practice. This level of income is likely to vary among countries, depending on their per capita GNP.

In urban areas, the concept of unemployment poses some difficulties of definition. First, *employment* and *freedom from poverty* are by no means synonymous, as shown, for example, by Fishlow's (1972) study of poverty in Brazil. Fishlow indicated that the head of over 80 percent of households in poverty was classified as "employed." Second, the poor in developing countries cannot survive entirely without work. A significant proportion of those enumerated as openly unemployed in urban areas are middle-class males waiting for positions appropriate to their training and expectations while being supported by their families.[1] This group is often politically active; but it does not necessarily form a *major* part of the poverty problem.

Tabulations of the personal or household distribution of income against these four socio-economic groups are not yet available, so that it is not possible to evaluate the extent to which they encompass all people in poverty. However, Chapter I states that the bulk of the poor is to be found in agriculture and, within agriculture, poverty is concentrated among small farmers and landless laborers. In urban areas the major poverty group comprises those referred to by the ILO Kenya mission as "the working poor" (ILO, 1972) and, to a lesser extent, the openly unemployed. We are confident therefore that, while not exhaustive, these four groups cover the bulk of those in poverty in developing countries.[2]

The proportion of the total population in poverty, the relative importance of the different target groups, and the tractability of the poverty problem in response to government intervention vary widely among countries. To reflect this variation, a typology of countries is required. Further, the numbers in poverty and the relative importance of the groups will change over time, with the time-paths for a given country type depending upon its initial conditions, its GNP growth rate, and the distributional pattern of growth. These considerations are reflected in a projection model calibrated to the country typology. We turn first to the typology.

---

[1] ILO (1971).

[2] Although these four groups can be separated for analytical purposes, there remains the problem of separability for the purposes of statistical enumeration. For example, a poor rural household typically earns part of its income from operating land and part from offering labor services to other farms. What, then, is the dividing line between a "small farmer" household and a "rural labor" household? Similarly, migratory movements between rural and urban areas, particularly short-term and seasonal movements, raise difficult definitional issues.

A TYPOLOGY OF COUNTRIES

The typology of countries developed here is designed to provide a number of country archetypes. Each archetype represents a "typical" set of initial conditions relating to the groups in poverty, and allows an evaluation of the dynamics of changes in the absolute and relative sizes of different poverty groups over time.[3] This typology also reflects the range of choice which governments of such countries have in the policy measures available to alleviate poverty. The three dimensions of the typology were chosen on a priori grounds: (i) the relative proportions of the population in urban and rural areas, reflecting also the GNP per capita of the country; (ii) the availability of land already cultivated or brought easily under the plough, whether it is abundant or scarce relative to the country's population; and (iii) the degree of concentration of land ownership, whether it is high or low.

These three binary choices lead to eight country types, defined in Table V.1. The three country archetypes which were selected for analysis are indicated by asterisks. "Latin America" (country type 1), is characterized by relatively abundant land and highly concentrated ownership, a high urban fraction, and relatively high per capita GNP among developing countries (e.g., Mexico, Colombia, Brazil, Ecuador, or Peru). "South Asia" (country type 7), is classified by land scarce in relation to population and moderately concentrated ownership, a low urban fraction, and low per capita GNP (e.g., India, Pakistan, or Indonesia). "Africa" (country type 6), is characterized by abundant land and a comparatively low concentration of ownership, a low urban fraction and low per capita GNP (e.g., countries in tropical Africa, such as Kenya, Tanzania, or Ghana). These three archetypes encompass the bulk of the population in poverty in those developing countries where the problem is amenable mainly to national policy intervention. For example, there are few countries of type 2; country type 3 is mainly confined to the Caribbean; type 4 is exemplified by countries like Taiwan and South Korea, where the poverty problem appears to be moving towards manageable proportions as a result of past and present policies;[4] countries of type 5, like South Africa and Rhodesia, are not typical; and the last, country type 8, is exemplified mainly by Bangladesh.

Country type 8 has the most difficult poverty problem in our classification scheme. Land is scarce relative to population, with little remaining scope for land redistribution in favor of target groups, and there is a low urban fraction associated with a low level of GNP per capita. Therefore, there is little prospect that even an employment-oriented industrialization

---

[3] It should be noted that this typology differs somewhat from the approaches adopted by Chenery and Taylor (1968), and by Adelman and Morris (1967), in that it is concerned specifically with poverty groups and with distributional considerations, rather than with considerations of growth strategies.

[4] This is true also for North Korea, which also fits into our type 4 category, and for other socialist developing countries like Cuba and China. Their approach to solving the problem is, of course, very different from that adopted by Taiwan and South Korea.

Table V.1: A Classification of Country Types

| Degree of Urbanization | Land Relatively Abundant | | Land Relatively Scarce | |
| | Land Ownership | | Land Ownership | |
	High Concentration	Low Concentration	High Concentration	Low Concentration
Highly Urbanized	Country Type 1*	Country Type 2	Country Type 3	Country Type 4
Less Urbanized	Country Type 5	Country Type 6*	Country Type 7*	Country Type 8

*Selected for analysis in the text.

policy will have a major impact on the proportion and numbers in poverty until many decades hence. The scope for bringing about substantial improvements in the well-being of poverty groups by means of the reorientation of national economic policy advocated in this volume seems extremely small in the context of limited resources and pervasive poverty. The margin for alleviating poverty by redistribution is extremely narrow. This fact suggests the need for a reorientation of international economic policy. Here, particular consideration should be given to reordering criteria for aid allocations to take into account fully, not only the level of development and GNP per capita, but also the long-run prospect of reducing poverty by reordering national policy priorities. Where the latter is limited, as most obviously in country type 8, then the case for special consideration in aid is very powerful.

The typology set out above could be expanded readily to take account of other considerations along the lines of the work of Adelman and Morris (1973). In particular, additional dimensions include the existence of mineral resources, size of country, the level of education of the population, the openness of the economy, the nature of government institutions, and a host of others. We have not expanded the typology at this stage, finding that it is sufficient for a discussion of the main issues with which we are concerned.

THE PROJECTION MODEL

In order to make use of these concepts, we need to determine the size of each target group and its change over time. We have therefore designed a simple projection model so as to be able to project: (i) changes over time in the total population, (ii) changes in the balance between urban and rural population, (iii) changes within agriculture in the absolute numbers and relative representation of small farmers and submarginal groups, and (iv) how these changes over time are influenced by the dynamic interactions within and between a set of initial conditions which define the country type and a set of policy variables.[5]

The dividing line between initial conditions on the one hand, and policy variables on the other, is not clear-cut. For example, we start with

---

[5]These represent the *outcome* of different policies, rather than being policy instruments.

the initial balance between urban and rural populations as a given initial condition for a given country archetype. The degree of concentration of land is also an initial condition in a particular solution of the model for a particular country type, but it can be varied among solutions for that country type in order to analyze the effect of a land reform. Similarly, the abundance of productive land relative to population can be taken as an initial condition, but it can be varied also among solutions to capture the effect of a program of land colonization and settlement where, as in the "Africa" archetype, this is a major policy option open to governments.

Other policy variables included in the model are the natural rate of increase of population, p; the rate of increase of urban jobs, u; and the rate of increase of productivity (on the initial land base) in agriculture, q, over the range of productive land-holding classes which spans the groups of submarginal and small farmers. The mechanics of the model are described in the Appendix to Chapter V. Essentially, the model utilizes three sets of relationships: (i) a set of projections of total population changes due to natural increase at a rate assumed constant over time, together with a projection of urban population at a specified rate which reflects changes in urban employment opportunities (in both the formal and informal sectors); (ii) a projection of the urban demand for rural migrants expressed as a function of the difference between the rate of increase of urban employment and the natural rate of population increase; and (iii) a set of relationships which determine the evolution over time of the sizes of target groups in the rural areas as functions of opportunities to migrate to urban areas and of shifts in the distribution of access to productive agricultural land. This last is computed taking into account the interaction between the initial distribution of land and the increase in agricultural output relative to the natural rate of population increase.

The model as described above, and in more technical terms in the Appendix, is disaggregated for the rural target groups at the expense of an aggregated treatment of the urban sector. The reason for this choice is that poverty is largely a rural phenomenon in most Third World countries, although it is becoming more an urban phenomenon in Latin America. The urban sector is discussed in more disaggregated terms in Chapter VII. For the rural sector, the model is actually more disaggregated than is implied by the description in the text; however, the results are presented only in terms of "small farmers" and "submarginals."

If our objective were to project the evolution over time of the absolute and relative sizes of the target groups for a particular country, then it would undoubtedly be necessary to use country-specific data. However, the purpose here is to convey the qualitative differences in the time-paths result from differences in the initial conditions and parameter values of "representative" country types. The basic data used are presented in Table V.2. They are of three main types. The first are averages for each of the regions for which country archetypes were selected. Included in this category are the initial share of the urban population in total population, and the growth rates respectively of the total population and the urban population.[6]

Table V.2: Initial Conditions and Standard Case Parameters

	"Latin America" Case 1	"South Asia" Case 7	"Africa" Case 6
Urban Population*	0.400	0.200	0.200
Rural Population	0.600	0.800	0.800
of which,[†] Submarginal	0.330	0.400	0.510
Small Farmer	0.170	0.150	0.140
Other rural	0.100	0.250	0.150
Total Population	1.000	1.000	1.000
Growth rate of— total population [‡]	0.030	0.025	0.030
— urban population §	0.050	0.045	0.040
— agricultural production[//]	0.030	0.030	0.035
Implicit initial GNP Growth Rate[#]	0.062	0.045	0.049

Sources: * Rounded figures for 1970 from Table 2.4 in World Bank (1973) with total population in the initial period normalized to be 1.00.

  † Sources are discussed in the text, and appear in the Appendix to Chapter V.

  ‡ Projections for 1970-90 from Table 2.1 in World Bank (1973) rounded to nearest 0.05.

  § Projections for 1970–85 from Table 2.4 in World Bank (1973) rounded to nearest 0.05.

  // Discussed in Appendix to Chapter V.

  # Discussed in Appendix to Chapter V.

The second type of data used includes a set of growth rates for agricultural production, which is used in the projection model, and a set of data which is used to compute the implicit initial growth rates of GDP presented in Table V.2. The data in this second set are *not* used in the model itself, but only for the purpose of validating the data which are used.

The third type of data— the numbers in the different target groups within agriculture— presented the greatest difficulty, reflecting the paucity of data which relate the size distribution of land holdings to farm income on a comparable basis across countries. In a country-specific context, we would have used country minimum-income classes to define cut-off points for the various groups,[7] farm survey data to translate the income cut-off points into size-holding points in various parts of the country, and a land access distribution based on land transformed into units of constant productivity to generate the estimate of the distribution of the target groups. Of course, these data are available only for a very few countries, so we resorted to an approximation procedure which rested heavily on

[6]This last is taken to be equal to the growth rate of urban employment, assuming unchanged participation rates, age composition of the population, and the proportion of the population which has some form of employment.

[7]Which, of course, would be relative across countries.

judgement and intuition in assessing such data as are available for each of the "representative" country types.

The data which were used in the projections are presented in Tables V.3 through V.5; the data underlying these tables are discussed in the Appendix to Chapter V. Briefly, the objective was to define a distribution of land of a given income-earning capacity for each of the three country archetypes.

Table V.3: Representative Land Distribution for Projection Model: "Latin America"

Target Groups	Relative Area Limits (hectares per holding)	Proportion of Rural Population	Proportion of Land	Relative Mean Size of Holding
Submarginals	≤ 2.49	0.48	0.03	0.7
Small Farmers	2.5 to 14.9	0.33	0.18	7.0
Other Farmers	15 to 29.9	0.11	0.17	21.0
Other Farmers	30 to 49.9	0.05	0.15	38.0
Other Farmers	≥ 50	0.03	0.47	205.0
Total		1.00	1.00	

The representative data for the "Latin America" archetype are presented in Table V.3. In the cases of "South Asia" and of tropical "Africa," variants of the land distribution were included in the projections to simulate the effects respectively of a land reform in a land-scarce situation, and of land settlement and colonization in a more land-abundant situation. There seemed little reason to carry out a similar exercise in the case of the Latin America data: even the relatively favorable distribution used in the projections is so skewed that an adjustment downwards of the mean size of the top 3 percent of large holdings from 205 hectares to about 130 hectares is sufficient to bring up the mean land holding of the lowest 48 percent of households (including the landless) from 0.7 hectares to 5.0 hectares. The relative importance of economic and political constraints to alleviating the worst of the rural poverty problem appears to be of a quite different order in Latin America than in Africa or Asia, and the projection exercise is directed at exploring the consequences of the persistence of economic obstacles.

The data for "South Asia" are in Table V.4. In this case, two variants are presented. Variant I corresponds to an initial distribution and Variant II to the distribution following a land reform. The land reform underlying Variant II is not radical—about 13 percent of land is redistributed, or about 22 percent of the land operated by the larger farmers—and it corresponds to a land ceiling of about ten hectares, similar to the ceiling of twenty acres—or slightly over eight hectares—analyzed by Minhas

Table V.4: Representative Land Distribution for Projection Model: "South Asia"

Target Groups	Relative Area Limits (hectares per holding)	Proportion of Rural Population		Proportion of Land	
		I Pre–Land Reform	II Post–Land Reform	I Pre–Land Reform	II Post–Land Reform
Submarginals	≤ 0.99	.50	.34	.07	.06
Small Farmers	1.0 to 1.99	.18	.31	.12	.22
Other Farmers	2.0 to 3.99	.11	.14	.12	.15
Other Farmers	3.0 to 4.99	.06	.07	.09	.10
Other Farmers	≥ 4.0	.15	.14	.60	.47
Total		1.00	1.00	1.00	1.00

(1971).[8] Following Minhas, the reform here involves distribution of land only to the smaller farmers already operating some land.[9] The "impact effect" of even this mild redistribution is to reduce the proportion of rural population defined as submarginal from 0.50 to 0.34, with a consequential increase in the proportion of small farmers from 0.18 to 0.31.

Table V.5: Representative Land Distribution for Projection Model: "Tropical Africa"

Target Groups	Relative Area Limits (hectares per holding)	Proportion of Rural Population	
		I (pre-settlement)	II (post-settlement)
Submarginals	< 1	0.60	0.30
Small Farmers	1 to 2.4	0.20	0.40
Other Farmers	2.5 to 4.9	0.10	0.20
Other Farmers	≥ 5	0.10	0.10
Total		1.00	1.00

The data for "Tropical Africa" appear in Table V.5. This set of representative land distributions is the least firmly-based of the three. The difference between alternatives I and II in the table reflect, not land reform, but the effects of a strategy of accelerated settlement and colonization in agriculture[10] leading to a reduction by one-half of the proportion of submarginals in the rural population and a doubling of the proportion of small and medium farmers, taking place over a twenty-year period. This involves bringing into effective production almost 50 percent more

---

[8]The ceilings are not strictly comparable, Minhas' ceiling applying to the projected 1970 distribution.

[9]This strategy flows simply from the consequences of the extreme scarcity of productive land relative to the size of the rural population.

[10]By "accelerated," we mean an increase in the growth rate of agricultural production over and above that implied by a given value of the parameter q, the (constant) rate of growth of agricultural production in the projection model.

land over the period, or adding about two percentage points to the overall growth rate of productivity in agriculture used in the projections.

SOME ALTERNATIVE STRATEGIES

Selected results from the projection model are presented in Table V.6. The limitations of the model itself and of the "representativeness" of the data must be borne in mind in interpreting these results, the interest of which lies mainly in their sensitivity to parametric variation.

The proportion of the total population remaining in the target groups is particularly sensitive to the growth rate of population, p. This can be seen by comparing the relative proportions remaining in the target groups for pairs of projections in Table V.6 for which only the population growth rate is varied. Such pairs are projections 1 and 2, and 4 and 5 for "Latin America," projections 1 and 6 for "South Asia," and 1 and 4, and 5 and 6 for "Africa." Of course, if the *proportion* of the population in a target group increases with a higher rate of natural increase, the *number* in that group increases a fortiori. If anything, the results from the model underestimate the impact of any given rate of natural increase of the population. This is so for two main reasons. First, the population growth rate is assumed to be the same across all groups in the population, although there is considerable evidence that the rate of natural increase is inversely related to income levels and access to education.[11] If this relationship were included in the model, then the impact on the size of the target groups of a given rate of natural increase would be increased substantially.[12] Second, the age composition of the population and participation rates in the work force are assumed similarly constant, whereas the proportion of the population accounted for by the younger age groups grows with higher population growth rates. The two main reasons for the sensitivity of the model's results to population growth are the assumptions of a fixed land base and of growth rates of urban employment and agricultural production independent of variations in the population growth rate. In labor-surplus economies, these approximations may not be far off the mark. If account is taken also of the scale effect of population growth as well as its effects on the proportions in the target groups (that is, by examining the absolute numbers of people in the target groups), then it is apparent that population policy must be at the center of a poverty-alleviation strategy.

Population policy, because of the duration of time required to bring about changes in the size of the population, must be part of a long-term development strategy. However, its importance is such that it must not be given a lower priority in any reorientation of policies in the direction of alleviating poverty.

---

[11]Cassen (1973) and Rich (1973).

[12]This relationship is included in the specification of the model which is presented in Chapter XI.

Table V.6: Results of Projections Over 20-Year Period

Country Archetype	Projection Number	Parameter Set					Results in Year 20*		
		Population Growth Rate (p)	Agricultural Production Growth Rate (q)	Growth Rate of Urban Jobs (u)	Land Reform or Settlement	Percentage Growth of Total Population	Proportion of Total Population		
							Submarginals	Small Farms	Urban
"Latin America"	0	—	—	—	Before	0	0.33	0.17	0.40
	1	0.030	0.030	0.050	Before	83	0.13	0.16	0.60
	2	0.025	0.030	0.050	Before	65	0.06	0.19	0.66
	3	0.035	0.030	0.050	Before	101	0.20	0.14	0.54
	4	0.025	0.040	0.050	Before	65	0.04	0.20	0.66
	5	0.035	0.040	0.050	Before	101	0.18	0.19	0.55
	6	0.025	0.030	0.035	Before	65	0.23	0.19	0.49
"South Asia"	0	—	—	—	Before	0	0.40	0.15	0.20
	1	0.025	0.030	0.045	Before	65	0.28	0.17	0.30
	2	0.025	0.030	0.060	Before	65	0.17	0.17	0.40
	3	0.025	0.030	0.045	After	65	0.16	0.22	0.30
	4	0.025	0.020	0.045	Before	65	0.33	0.11	0.30
	5	0.025	0.020	0.045	After	65	0.20	0.25	0.30
	6	0.015	0.030	0.045	Before	35	0.17	0.17	0.36
"Africa"	0	—	—	—	Before	0	0.51	0.14	0.20
	1	0.030	0.035	0.040	Before	83	0.43	0.23	0.24
	2	0.030	0.035	0.060	Before	83	0.31	0.23	0.37
	3	0.030	0.045	0.040	Before	83	0.37	0.33	0.24
	4	0.025	0.035	0.040	Before	65	0.37	0.32	0.27
	5	0.030	0.035	0.040	After	83	0.25	0.28	0.24
	6	0.025	0.035	0.040	After	65	0.19	0.28	0.27

*For row 0, the results apply to the initial period; for all other rows they are projected results for year 20.

It should be noted that most of the variants on the basic case which have the effect of reducing the poverty problem (i.e., those involving increases in q or u) necessarily appear at first sight to imply a higher rate of growth of GDP. To this extent, the results can therefore be regarded as optimistic. However, it must be emphasized strongly that the policy parameters — land reform, p, q, and u — are set exogenously and independently. In reality, of course, this will not be so. The key relationships among them are best illustrated by examples. First, there are those implicit in transformation possibilities: stepping up the rate of urban job creation and output (for a given distribution of earnings) will mean diverting resources away from agriculture, thereby lowering q. Second, there are complementarities: a land reform may well enhance (or reduce) the rate of increase of agricultural productivity on some farm sizes faster than others, and so change the size distribution of holdings measured on an output basis. Third, there are one-way causal connections: in a labor surplus economy, increases in the agricultural workforce may not lead to rises in agricultural production, but increases in the net output of small and marginal farm households may reduce their fertility levels. Fourth, strictly speaking, the relevant value of q is that affecting the target groups, so that, *ceteris paribus,* a rise in q could be associated with a fall in the growth of output on large farms (and perhaps of aggregate farm output too).

In this connection it should be recognized that the model was not designed to explore trade-offs between growth and distribution (unlike that reported in Chapters II and XI), and the results can be interpreted as exploring some of the distributional consequences of increments to growth occurring in different sectors. Also, the model results underline again the need for growth in dealing effectively with the poverty problem.

The model illustrates one trade-off of particular consequence in Asian and African countries. Many agricultural policies, such as encouraging productivity growth, land reform, land settlement, and colonization, may well reduce the proportion of the population in the submarginal group at the expense of increasing the proportion in the small-farmer group.[13] While such a shift undoubtedly involves an increase in the income level of some of the most disadvantaged in society, it does so by increasing the numbers of small farmers, who are themselves a target group. It may lead also to a rural structure which impedes rapid growth in the future. Clearly, the smaller the minimum viable holding size for small farmers, the larger the number of landless who can be accommodated with a given land base or with a given expenditure on opening up unsettled land. However, the smaller size is less likely to be viable in the future than a larger one, particularly as incomes increase elsewhere in the economy and because it does not seem prudent to assume that future improvements in agricultural

---

[13]For example, compare projections 1 and 3 for "Africa" in which only q is varied; or 1 and 3 for "Asia," which differ only in whether or not there was a land reform; and 1 and 5 for Africa, which differ in the pace of land settlement and colonization.

technology will be scale-neutral.[14] This raises the issue of institutional forms of land-holding alternative to small family farms, and particularly of communes, cooperatives and collectives.

The fourth general point is that, examined on the basis of different initial income levels and resource availabilities, the poverty problem is far less tractable in Asia and Africa than in Latin America.[15] This holds true even in the absence of a land reform variant in the projections for the Latin American archetype.

This rather obvious point is worth restating, because it helps to focus again on the political (as opposed to the economic) dimensions of the process of reducing poverty and also upon the priorities for the allocation of international assistance among developing countries.

For the "Latin America" archetype, the projections indicate that the proportion of the total population in urban areas is likely to increase from about 40 percent to about 60 percent over the twenty-year projection period, with accompanying declines in the relative importance of rural poverty groups. As discussed earlier in this chapter, there is a relative abundance of land in most Latin American countries and it is subject to extremely concentrated ownership. The worst of the rural poverty problem, under these circumstances, can be overcome by an effective, implemented land reform. In other words, the economic resources needed to solve the rural poverty problem exist, but an effective political commitment is required. Given this, and the increasing proportion of the total population which will be in the urban areas, the ruban poverty problem will become of increasing importance over time. Of course, a problem of urban poverty exists already in most Latin American countries. But the fact remains that this group is likely to grow at a much faster rate than groups in poverty in rural areas, in the absence of the implementation of strategies directed at alleviating urban poverty.

The persistence of poverty in the "South Asia" archetype, with demographic pressures on scarce land resources and a relatively high rural population proportion, is striking even under a wide range of alternative projections. The long-run comparative advantage of countries in this situation does not lie in agriculture, and long-run development strategy must concentrate on labor-intensive industrialization. The appropriate long-run rural strategy is then a "holding operation" for at least two or

---

[14]The extent to which improvements in agricultural technology in the past were scale-neutral is an unresolved empirical question. Three points can be made, however. Improvements in mechanization have tended not to be scale-neutral, but to have enhanced the competitiveness of large-scale operations over small. Second, improvements of a biological nature in seeds and associated inputs tend to be scale-neutral. This seems to be the case for the recent improved varieties of wheat and rice. Third, the first two points have force only for innovations actually applied on the farm; and the rate of adoption of new technologies appears to be much more rapid on large than on small farms. Some of the reasons for this are discussed in Chapter VI.

[15]Implicit in this statement is the assumption that increasing urbanization is associated with a reduction in the degree of poverty in absolute terms, although relative poverty may well increase.

three decades until the urban population proportion grows sufficiently for a given urban growth rate to have a substantial impact on absorbing people from agriculture. The main requirements of such a strategy are that it should provide relief as rapidly as possible to the most disadvantaged sections of the rural population, and that it should as far as possible not lock the economy into rural institutions which are inimical to future growth. This is not an easy strategy. While it is apparent that redistributing land to the landless on tiny plots will create massive problems for the future, it does not seem feasible to mount alternatives such as rural public works on a scale sufficient to make much impact on the problem over a twenty-year period.[16] The strategy will probably have to be mixed, minimizing redistribution of land to the "lower end." In the Asian context, the upper end of the land distribution probably requires more attention: restrictions on the upper limits of size of holding, vigorously enforced, could go a long way towards breaking a social and political structure in rural areas which reduces the access of the bulk of the farm population to production-increasing services. These issues are taken up again in Chapter VI.

For tropical "Africa," a rural-based strategy is appropriate, with maximum attention to land consolidation and settlement with appropriate ownership patterns, together with increases in the productivity of small farmers. The issues here are less those of immediate redistribution than of the availability of resources to effect a transformation of agriculture. However, to achieve these objectives, it will be necessary to solve the difficult problems of devising cheap and effective methods of delivering services and resources to large numbers of small farmers, and of preventing the evolution of privileged groups in a position to capture a disproportionate share of increases in incomes.

---

[16]This is a view contrary to the conclusions of the Bhagwati Committee on Unemployment in India. However, these conclusions have drawn severe criticism in the pages of the *Economic and Political Weekly*.

The Projection Model

The model is designed to project (i) changes in the balance between rural and urban populations and (ii), within agriculture, changes in the absolute numbers and relative representation of small farmers and submarginal groups.[17] Each projection is influenced by a set of boundary conditions—the initial urban fraction, which is given exogenously, and the initial size distribution of land holdings, which is subject to policy—and by a set of parameters which reflect the impact of government policy—the natural rate of population increase, the rate of growth of rural output, and the rate of growth of urban jobs.

The variables and parameters of the model are

Variables[18]

$N(t)$: total population (normalized at unity in year zero)

$N_1(t)$: population in landless labor households

$N_2(t)$: population in submarginal farm households

$N_3(t)$: population in small farm households

$N_4(t)$: population in other farm households

$N_5(t)$: total rural population

$N_6(t)$: total rural submarginal population

$N_7(t)$: total urban population

$M(t)$: urban demand for rural migrants (and their dependents)

$L_1(t)$: transfer rate of population from (to) the category of submarginal farm households to (from) the category of small farm households

Parameters

p: natural rate of population increase in both towns and villages

u: rate of growth of urban work force

q: rate of growth of agricultural production, taken as identical with agricultural productivity increase where the land base is constant

$\overline{x}_i(o)$: class boundaries (in land units) at year zero of different categories of farm household, $i = 1, 2, 3, 4$

$V_i(o)$: initial population in the ith farm size class as a proportion of the total initial population in landholding households, $i = 1, 2, 3, 4$

First, three accounting identities:

$$N(t) = N_5(t) + N_7(t), \qquad [1]$$

$$N_5(t) = \sum_{i=1}^{4} N_i(t), \qquad [2]$$

$$N_6(t) = N_1(t) + N_2(t). \qquad [3]$$

---

[17]We acknowledge the assistance of H. Lucas in programming this model for the computer.

[18]All the $N(o)$'s are given exogenously; $M(o)$, $L_1(o)$, and $L_2(o)$ are endogenously defined.

Next, the exogenous part of the projection, which determines the total population and the rural-urban balance. The total population grows at a constant rate p:

$$N(t) = e^{pt}. \tag{4}$$

The urban population grows at a constant rate u:

$$N_T(t) = N_T(o)e^{ut}. \tag{5}$$

The growth rates of urban population and jobs are taken to be identical, implying that rural migrants obtaining jobs bring their dependents to join them after, at most, a relatively short lag. As the natural rate of increase is the same in both sectors, this implies also that the age structures of the urban and rural populations are identical. The demand for rural migrants to fill urban jobs is the excess of new urban jobs created over the natural increase of the urban work force (population):

$$M(t) = (u-p) N_T(t) \tag{6}$$

which amounts to an assumption that participation rates among the urban workforce are not influenced by extra job chances. We assume that exactly $M(t)$ rural migrants (and their dependents) leave agriculture in year t.

The mechanistic system [4]-[6], which gives the overall rural-urban balance, covers well-trodden ground (Dovring, 1959). We turn now to the projections of the proportions of the total rural population falling into the four categories of rural households. First, it is necessary to specify which rural households supply migrants to fill urban jobs. Here, we depart from such formulations as that of Harris and Todaro (1970), which specifies an individual's decision rule for migration as a function of expected income differentials between rural and urban locations. Unless initial income levels are homogeneous, a correct procedure for aggregation to the national level requires that different income earning categories be distinguished. We have done this only on the rural side. We subscribe to a special combination of the "push-pull" debate on migration,[19] namely that the greatest "push" is on those with least land and that they will be subject also to the "pull" of an expected earnings differential as strong as (or stronger than) small or medium farmers.[20] Thus rural households are given a "priority" for migration on the basis of the income rank ordering of their land holdings. Hence net migration to the towns consists, first of landless laborers, and then of sub-marginal farmers ("slices" of the size distribution of holdings being removed sequentially from the left-hand tail).

The submarginal rural population, then, tends to rise through natural increase, to fall on account of migration to the towns, and to rise (fall) as formerly "viable" small farmers cease to be so (formerly submarginal

---

[19]See Chapter VII.

[20]This ignores the often substantial once-and-for-all costs of relocation and finding a job, which the poorest are least able to afford.

farmers become small farmers). Hence the instantaneous rate of increase of submarginals as a whole is:

$$\dot{N}_6(t) = pN_6(t) - M(t) + L_1(t). \qquad [7]$$

Likewise, the instantaneous rate of increase of small farm households is given by:

$$\dot{N}_3(t) = pN_3(t) - L_1(t) + L_2(t). \qquad [8]$$

We turn first to the $L_i(t)$ in equations [7] and [8]. Let $f(x)$ be the initial density function of the population of farm holdings (adjusted for family size),[21] *where holdings are defined in terms of their normal output levels in the base year;* as a proxy for base year household income.[22] The relationship between the transfer functions, $L_i(t)$, and the density function, $f(x)$, requires some explanation.

First, the density function reflects the base period distribution of land holdings defined in terms of their normal income-earning capacities. This *initial* distribution can be changed to reflect differences among country types; for a given country type, it can be altered to reflect the impact of a land reform or land settlement at the extensive margin or both. Second there are changes over time which must be accounted for: in the size of the population due to natural increase, and in the income-earning capacity of land due to productivity or price changes or both.[23] In their turn, these changes affect the proportions (and the absolute numbers) of people falling into the different size classes defined initially by the boundary limits $\overline{x}_i(o)$.

There are two main ways in which these dynamic effects can be incorporated into the model. The first of these is a general specification in which the class boundaries are held constant, but the density function alters over time. The second is to hold the density function constant over time but to shift the $\overline{x}_i(o)$, a procedure which is admissible because of the special migration process adopted there. The former specification is intractable mathematically if analytical solutions of the differential equations are sought. The

---

[21]Landless laborers are defined separately so that $f(o)$ is undefined, even though $\lim\limits_{\varepsilon \to 0+} f(\varepsilon) \to a_o$. Note also that

$$V_i(o) = \int_{\overline{x}_{i-1}(o)}^{\overline{x}_i(o)} f(x)dx$$

where $\overline{x}_o(o) = 0$, $i = 1, 2, 3, 4$.

[22]The existence of wage payments or receipts should not affect the rank ordering of households, and their absolute effect is allowed for in the definition of the class boundaries, $\overline{x}_i(o)$. Evidence on the close relationship between the rural income distribution and the size distribution of holdings is reviewed by Chaudhri (1974).

[23]Note that the model does not take account of changes due to transactions in land across the boundaries $\overline{x}_i(t)$. To handle this, a model of asset accumulation would be required.

latter yields equations which can be solved and which are therefore easier to apply empirically. For this reason we adopt the second approach, in which the $L_i(t)$ capture the effects of changes in the class boundaries due to population growth and productivity change, and how these interact with the density function. The $L_i(t)$ capture also the *scale* effects of net population increase.

We can now turn to a rigorous statement of the $L_i(t)$. Consider a household initially on the class boundary $\overline{x_i}(o)$. Natural increase at a constant rate p will decrease output per person at the same rate; against this, there are increases in agricultural production at rate q—in the relevant neighborhood of $\overline{x_i}(o)$—on the original holding base due to a combination of extensions of the holding area, increasing intensity of inputs (including labor) and rising productivity of inputs. Thus, at time t, the class boundary will have moved to:

$$\overline{x_i}(t) = \overline{x_i}(o)\, e^{(p-q)t} \qquad [9]$$

that is, to the left if $q > p$, and conversely if $q < p$. Now with migration by the "priority" ordering set out above, and with no net transfers of land among holding classes, the number of small farmers just losing viability at time t by the movement of $\overline{x_1}$ to the right (submarginal farmers just gaining viability by the movement of $\overline{x_1}$ to the left) will be determined by the factors: the relative frequency of holdings of size $\overline{x_1}(t)$ in the base year density function $f(x)$, and the difference between the rates of natural increase of the landholding population and the increase in productivity of the base holding over the interim period. An exactly similar statement applies to the small farmer–medium farmer boundary. In the interval δt, the number of households thus transferred will be equal to $L_i(t) \cdot \delta t$. From Figure V.1, this must equal

Figure V.1: Density Function of Farm Holdings

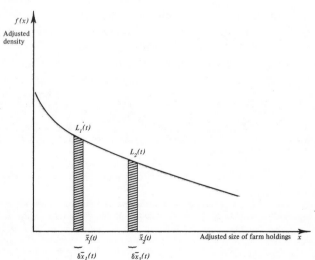

$B(t) \cdot f[\overline{x}_i(t)]\delta\overline{x}_i(t)$, where the scaling factor $B(t)$ is given by $[N_5(o) - N_1(o)]e^{pt}$, as the group transferred across class boundaries will not have been affected yet by migration loss.[24] Hence, in the limit, we have:

$$L_i(t) = B(t) f[\overline{x}_i(t)] \frac{d\overline{x}_i(t)}{dt}.$$

[10]

Using equation [9],

$$L_i(t) = [N_5(o)-N_1(o)]\cdot f[\overline{x}_i(t)]\cdot x_i(o)\cdot(p-q)e^{(2p-q)t}.$$

[11]

If $f(x)$ is specified as a polynomial, then the differential equations [7] and [8] are readily integrable.[25] For this reason, and because we found that a polynomial[26] gave a sufficiently good approximation in the region $\overline{x}_1(o)$ and $\overline{x}_2(o)$, we write:

$$f(x) = \sum_{k=0}^{n} a_k x^k.$$

[12]

Hence, from equations [5]-[8], [11], and [12] we have

$$N_3(t) = N_3(o)e^{pt} + B(o)\left(\sum_{k=0}^{n} \frac{a_k}{k+1} \{ \overline{x}_2{}^{k+1}(o)\} \right.$$

$$\left. \{e^{[(k+2)p-(k+1)q]t}-e^{pt}\} \right),$$

[13]

and

$$N_6(t) = N_6(o)e^{pt}-N_7(o)(e^{ut}-e^{pt}) +$$

$$B(o)\left\{ \sum_{k=0}^{n} \frac{a_k\overline{x}_1{}^{k+1}(o)}{k+1}e^{[(k+2)p-(k+1)q]t}-e^{pt} \right\}.$$

[14]

In view of the simple structure of this projection model, dictated largely by the need for computational simplicity, some remarks are in order. First, the model is not designed to explore trade-offs between growth and distribution endogenously. The parameters representing alternative policies—$V_i(o)$, q, and u—are set exogenously and independently of one another. In

---

[24]Note that Figure V.1 is drawn for the case where $q > p$ in the relevant neighborhood. When $q=p$ there is, of course, no transfer across boundaries, and where $q < p$ the transfer has a sign opposite to that where $q > p$.

[25]Many of the size distributions examined appeared to be exponential, a very intractable form. Note also that although $f(x)$ must be continuous in $]o, x_{max}]$, its derivatives need not be so.

[26]In the results reported here, a quartic was used and the function crudely estimated from the data, a_0 graphically and a_k $(k \neq o)$ by solving the following set of equations.

$$\sum_{k=0}^{4} \frac{a_k\overline{x}_i^{k+1}(o)}{k+1} = \sum_{j=1}^{i} V_j(o), \qquad i = 1, 2, 3, 4.$$

principle, of course, it would be possible to guess at (or estimate from other evidence) the fall in u associated with a unit rise in q (say) in the course of comparing different combinations of the policy parameters, some optimistic, others less so. The only plausible alternative would have been the introduction of a production and resource allocation structure, a much more formidable undertaking.

Second, and this is probably the weakest feature of the model, the specification of the migration process from rural areas lacks a solid behavioral foundation. Here, there is much evidence that comparatively affluent rural households dispatch many of their members to the cities, while poor ones are often deterred by the high fixed costs of relocation. Moreover, u and its associated pattern of earnings are involved, too. The upshot of this is that the above specification may err considerably on the side of optimism in predicting the time taken to shift rural submarginals into urban jobs.

Third, the model does not include a number of the adjustment mechanisms which exist in rural areas. For this reason if the model is run for too long a period, or with unrealistic sets of parameter values, or both, equations [7] and [8] will break down, the population of marginals becoming negative and that of small farmers undiminished by migration. For this reason, among others, we restricted the projections to twenty years. Over this period and for the parameter sets chosen, the boundary conditions were not violated. One example of the lack of an adjustment mechanism is that the model does not allow for the reallocation of land among the remaining pool of submarginal farmers after migration has drawn off landless laborers and commences to draw off submarginal farmers. However, this occurs in very few runs and generally to a small extent, with the exceptions of projection numbers 2 and 4 for "Latin America," both of which are based on very optimistic rates of growth of both population and urban jobs. More importantly, the proportion of land held by submarginal farmers is very small, as can be seen by examining Tables V.3 to V.5, so that the error involved is likely to be small.

Some Notes on the Data

The first data sets with which we are concerned here are a set of the rates of growth of agricultural production (which are used in the projection model) and a set of data which is used to compute the initial growth rate of GNP. It should be noted that data in this second set are *not* used in the projection model. We first define the nature of the "urban" and "rural" sectors. By the "rural" sector we mean activities *based* in rural areas, which would include both industrial and services components; "urban" activity is defined in a similar way.[27] This introduces major difficulties into attempts to arrive at base output weights for the two sectors, as most empirical work on the

---

[27]What constitutes an urban community is subject to wide differences in interpretation and definition, though a minimum population size of 5,000 to 10,000 is frequently used as the dividing line between urban and rural communities.

subject is founded on the primary/secondary/tertiary distinction. Our method was to use the cross-section relationship between GNP per capita and sectoral shares derived by Chenery (1970) with estimates of GNP per capita in 1970 for "Latin America," "[South] Asia," and "Africa" of US$500, $100, and $100, respectively (World Bank, 1972). The rural sector output weights of 0.22, 0.44, respectively, were derived from the primary sector share in GNP by making an adjustment for mining. Allowing for a much higher level of output per man in secondary and tertiary activities within urban areas, the higher urban population share of "Latin America" and the (apparently) greater importance in "South Asia" of nonfarm occupations in rural areas compared with "Africa," we selected representative rural base output weights of 0.30, 0.60, and 0.50, respectively.

The growth rates of agricultural production include a nonagricultural component of between 15 percent and 25 percent of the whole. However, such activities, being predominantly of the "informal" type, are unlikely to expand more rapidly than agricultural output proper, through increases either in employment or in average output per man or combinations of the two. Thus, we have settled for growth rates a little in excess of population increases for "Asia" and "Africa," which is in line with the experience of the past twenty years, and equal to population increase in the case of "Latin America," which is a little pessimistic.[28] Finally, to compute the initial GNP growth rates (although not necessary for the projections) it is necessary to convert the rate of growth of urban jobs into a growth rate of urban output. To do this, it has to be recognized that output grows at a faster rate than employment, due to increasing productivity of labor. The transformation was done using estimates of the elasticity of output with respect to growth in urban jobs (the Verdoorn elasticity). For formal sector industry as a whole in the period 1955-65, its value was about 2.50 in "Latin America" and about 1.75 in "Asia."[29] Taking account of the need to introduce a comparable figure for the services and informal components of the urban sector, for which this elasticity would certainly be lower (if meaningful at all), and of the inherent instability of this statistic, we settled for a figure of 1.50 across the board. Thus, multiplying the growth rates of urban employment by 1.50 to get those of urban output and weighting the sectoral output growth rates appropriately, the implicit initial GNP growth rates entered in Table V.2 may be derived.[30]

The procedures used in calculating the land size distribution included in the body of the chapter were essentially the same for all three country archetypes, although the data base was far more fragmentary for "Africa" than for

---

[28]Strictly speaking, the relevant rate of growth of this output, in the context of the model, is that affecting small and marginal farmers. The average over all farmers may well be somewhat greater and taking this into account would enhance correspondingly the growth of total GNP.

[29]Turnham (1971), p. 94.

[30]Let the rural base output be w and the Verdoorn elasticity be v, then the initial growth rate of GNP will be $g = w \cdot q + (1-w) \cdot vu$.

the other two. For this reason, we describe the procedure only for the case of "Latin America."[31]

For "Latin America," the starting point was a size distribution of farms by socio-economic levels, based on data collection in ICAD studies, and cited in Barraclough and Domike (1970). These data are reproduced in Table V.7 and provide estimates of the relative sizes of the target groups in terms of the employment opportunities on farms. However, the data exclude land-

Table V.7: Relative Number and Area of Farm Units by Size Groups in ICAD Study Countries (Percentage of country total in each size class)

Countries	Sub-family*	Family‡	Multi-family Medium#	Multi-family Large§	Total
Argentina					
Number of farm units	43.2	48.7	7.3	0.8	100.0
Area in farms	3.4	44.7	15.0	36.9	100.0
Brazil					
Number of farm units	22.5	39.1	33.7	4.7	100.0
Area in farms	0.5	6.0	34.0	59.5	100.0
Chile					
Number of farm units	36.9	40.0	16.2	6.9	100.0
Area in farms	0.2	7.1	11.4	81.3	100.0
Colombia					
Number of farm units	64.0	30.2	4:5	1.3	100.0
Area in farms	4.9	22.3	23.3	49.5	100.0
Ecuador					
Number of farm units	89.9	8.0	1.7	0.4	100.0
Area in farms	16.6	19.0	19.3	45.1	100.0
Guatemala					
Number of farm units	88.4	9.5	2.0	0.1	100.0
Area in farms	14.3	13.4	31.5	40.8	100.0
Peru					
Number of farm units	88.0	8.5	2.4	1.1	100.0
Area in farms	7.4	4.5	5.7	82.4	100.0

*Subfamily: farms large enough to provide employment for less than 2 people with the typical incomes, markets, and levels of technology and capital now prevailing in each region.
‡Family: farms large enough to provide employment for 2 to 3.9 people on the assumption that most of the farm work is being carried out by the members of the farm family.
#Multifamily Medium: farms large enough to provide employment for 4 to 12 people.
§Multifamily Large: farms large enough to provide employment for over 12 people.

Source: ICAD studies cited in Barraclough and Domike (1970).

---

[31]For "Asia," the main data base was the Seventeenth Round of the National Sample Survey as Analyzed by Minhas (1971); for "Africa" it was mainly ILO (1972), Singer and Reynolds (1973), FAO (1971), and various World Bank country reports.

less laborers, they are not in terms of a size classification of holdings, and they do not take into account changes in the size distribution due to land reform measures applied in some of the countries listed since the data were collected. Two of these problems are readily soluble: the data in Table V.7 may be used to give a size distribution of land-holdings, based also on data from ICAD studies which are available in Felstehausen (1970); data on numbers of landless laborer households are included in Barraclough and Domike (1970) for most of the countries listed. To err on the side of optimism concerning progress in land reform and in agricultural productivity since the data were collected, we made two further adjustments. The first was to redistribute land among the size classes to reduce somewhat the degree of inequality of ownership. The second, to reflect increases in productivity, was to compress the distribution proportionately to the left, in effect reducing the minimum size of holding required for subsistence.

The adjusted size distribution of holdings, and its correspondence to target groups in agriculture is given in Table V.3.

Chapter VI

RURAL TARGET GROUPS

C.L.G. BELL AND JOHN H. DULOY

IN THE previous chapter, we identified four target groups: (i) small farmers, (ii) landless laborers and submarginal farmers, (iii) the urban underemployed, and (iv) the urban unemployed. Also, we showed how the relative importance of these groups differs among three representative country types, how their relative importance changes over time, and how the time-paths of the numbers in the groups are responsive to initial resource endowments and different, broadly defined strategies to alleviate poverty.

In this chapter, we concentrate upon how some specific policy packages affect the rural target groups and upon some of the choices which have to be made in reorienting development strategy. In doing so, we attempt a synthesis applicable for different country types, rather than attempting specific recommendations for individual countries.

The main thrust of the strategy is upon increasing the productivity of the rural poor by increasing their access to complementary assets—land, skills, credit. For the landless, and particularly those precluded from operating land in countries where the land/rural population ratio is extremely unfavorable, the emphasis is more upon access to employment opportunities.

EFFECTS OF LEAKAGES

Throughout the chapter, particular emphasis is given to the problem of "leakage" in the sense of spillover of benefits from target groups to non-target groups. This problem arises in evaluating the effects of broadly applied national policies, of policies at the subnational or sectoral level, or in evaluating narrowly defined investment projects. For example, consider a feeder road system constructed in a rural area, employing landless laborers in its construction phase, and designed to benefit small farmers by reducing transportation costs for both product and inputs. In the construction phase, some of the benefits are likely to accrue to local contractors already enjoying substantial incomes, depending, of course, on the institutional arrangements involved in construction. In the utilization phase, benefits are likely to accrue also to large and medium farmers (who produce the bulk of the marketed surplus and utilize off-farm production inputs intensively), depending on the initial degree of concentration of the operation of land. Some of these benefits may, of course, lead to levels of employment of landless laborers on medium and large farms higher than would otherwise have been the case, thus offsetting the leakage to some extent. Introducing these considerations leads to a greater degree of complexity in evaluating the benefit and cost streams in project appraisal

We are grateful for the comments of Graham Donaldson, Raj Krishna, Uma Lele, and Michael Lipton.

in comparison with the more usual methods where the question of *who* benefits is of little or no concern.

The quantitative significance of leakage can be illustrated by alternative scenarios which reflect different distributional patterns of the same overall income growth in the sector. The evaluation is ex post, in the sense that the *mechanisms* of leakage are not explored.[1] The scenarios can be evaluated in terms of the different weighting schemes which are introduced in Chapter II, and which measure the utility components corresponding to each scenario. A critical element in this evaluation is the initial distribution of income, which in agriculture is approximated by the distribution of rights to productive land. These three elements—the relative growth rates of income of different groups, the initial distribution of income (or of income-producing assets), and the weighting scheme—are evaluated in a numerical example. Four groups are distinguished, of which the first two, submarginals (consisting of landless laborers and submarginal farmers) and small farmers, are target groups. The other two groups, medium farmers and large farmers, are not. The data for the example are given in Table VI.1, and discussed below.

Table VI.1: Alternative Distributional Composition of Growth by Target Groups

Group	Percentage of Population	Percentage of Income		Scenario (Relative Income Growth Rates)				
		I	II	1	2	3	4	5
Submarginals	50	10	20	2.00	0.80	0.75	1.00	0.67
Small Farmers	30	20	30	1.00	1.00	1.00	1.00	1.00
Medium Farmers	10	20	20	0.00	0.60	0.50	1.00	1.33
Other Farmers	10	50	30	0.00	0.00	0.25	1.00	1.60
	100	100	100					

Income growth rates are normalized with respect to the income growth of small farmers.

Five different scenarios of ex post relative income growth rates, presented in Table VI.1, were examined. These are all normalized relative to the income growth rate of the group of small farmers, taken here to be the main target group. Of course, the actual growth of income of small farmers varies across the scenarios, but normalizing the growth rates of income of all groups with respect to the main target group helps in highlighting the different distributional components in the descriptions of the scenarios in Table VI.1. Scenarios 1 through 5 are arranged in descending order of effectiveness in reaching exclusively the target groups. Scenario 4 represents the case where all four groups benefit equally, and Scenario 5 represents the case, which is probably uncomfortably close to past reality, where the highest income growth rates apply to the highest income groups. Scenario 3, in which the two target groups benefit a great deal

---

[1]Research on the *mechanism* of leakage, taking into account the second- and third-round effects through linkages among the various groups, is much needed.

more than the two nontarget groups, in terms of rates of income increase, is probably as favorable an outcome as is possible under the degree of land concentration and the patterns of access to the benefits of government intervention which are characteristic of many developing countries.[2] To evaluate leakage, calculations were based on a constant total increase of sectoral income (that is, a total summed over all four groups).[3]

Of the two initial income distributions in Table VI.1, the first distribution (distribution I) is similar to the observed distribution in many countries (see the data presented in Chapters I and V). The second distribution of income (distribution II) represents the effects of a redistribution of land which reduces the ratio of the mean income of the highest group to the mean income of the lowest from 25:1 to 7.5:1.

The results appear in Table VI.2, where they are normalized with respect to the most favorable growth rate case, Scenario 1. Leakage exists only in the context of a welfare function which weights increments to income differently depending upon to whom they accrue. For this reason, the use of GDP weights neither distinguishes among any of the five scenarios, nor takes account of how these were interrelated with the initial distribution of income. By contrast, the use of either "equal weights" or "poverty weights" distinguishes sharply among the different outcomes. The choice between these two weighting schemes in this example does not appear to be critical: the ordering of the various scenarios is invariant with respect to the choice and, in terms of absolute magnitudes, the difference between them is not large.[4]

Table VI.2: Normalized Welfare Variation of a Given Increase in Total Income

Welfare Weights	Initial Income/Asset Distribution	Scenario*				
		1	2	3	4	5
GDP Weights	I	100	100	100	100	100
	II	100	100	100	100	100
Equal Weights	I	100	57	45	30	21
	II	100	71	65	54	42
Poverty Weights†	I	100	52	41	24	14
	II	100	67	56	42	31

"Normalized" relative to Scenario 1.
*The scenarios are defined by the normalized growth rates in Table VI.1.
†Poverty weights are: Submarginals, 0.67; Small farmers, 0.33; Medium farmers, 0.00; Other farmers, 0.00.

---

[2] Of course, equally characteristic of the nonsocialist developed countries.

[3] If there is a trade-off between growth and distribution, there could be a lower growth rate of GNP as growth is skewed towards the target groups. This possibility is excluded from the evaluation here, but is discussed in Chapters II and XI.

[4] Of course, the choice of weighting system could make a substantial difference in evaluating other alternatives, particularly alternatives in different sectors, and alternatives where the productivity-distribution trade-off is important.

On the other hand, the initial distribution of income makes a great deal of difference. Taking Scenario 3, the "most likely" outcome of an investment program directed at reducing poverty, the leakage as measured by either of the non-GDP weights is strongly influenced by the initial distribution, as shown by the difference between distributions I and II in Table VI.2. The arithmetic of these results is not the end of the story. With a more equitable initial distribution of income and assets, it is less difficult to achieve patterns of relative increases in income favorable to the poor. This observation takes account of considerations of access to publicly supplied goods and services and of the power structures in society, as discussed in Chapter III.

The Rural Poor

The bulk of the poor in developing countries is located in rural areas. This phenomenon can be seen, for example, from the data in Table I.3 and from the data presented in Chapter V. From a static viewpoint, this statement on the location of the poor is unexceptional; taking a more dynamic view, it requires some qualification. A major conclusion from the projection model in Chapter V is that poverty in many Latin American and other middle-income countries will become relatively more of an urban phenomenon over the next few decades, paralleling the shift in the locus of poverty during the early and middle stages of industrialization of many European countries. By contrast, of the total population of people in poverty, the *proportion* of them in rural areas is likely to remain high in most countries of tropical Africa and South Asia for many decades. This is not to deny the importance, in terms of absolute numbers, of the urban poverty problem in such cities as Calcutta and Bombay. But the number of people in poverty in such urban areas is small *relative* to the number in poverty in rural areas, and is likely to remain so for a long time.

This is not the only contrast among these three broad groups of countries. Problems of rural poverty are far more tractable, in economic and resource availability terms at least, in Latin America than in most other parts of the developing world. A redistributive land reform can go a long way towards a solution in a relatively short period.[5] Without such a reform, however, it is difficult to see much prospect of major advances in reducing poverty in rural areas, apart from the process of attrition associated with increasing urbanization or expanded programs of settlement of new land or both. The immediate issues are therefore more political than economic. There are, of course, also economic issues. In particular, a land reform needs to be associated with a rural development strategy to have a really major impact on rural poverty.

---

[5]It is worth recalling that many Latin American countries, unlike most of those in Africa and Asia, were colonized by metropolitan powers which were feudal rather than capitalist. Many of these are still handicapped by the persistence in rural areas of an imposed feudal structure.

The major difference between archetypal "Asia" and "Africa," broadly defined, turns on the availability of land relative to population (see Chapter V). For the former, long-term comparative advantage appears to lie in labor-intensive manufacturing, with a "holding operation" being mounted in rural areas designed to alleviate some of the worst of the problems of poverty. For the latter, a long-term strategy of rural development seems appropriate to the relative resource endowments. This difference aside, rural development must have high priority in the development strategy of both African and Asian countries over the foreseeable future.

We do not propose to review the large and growing literature on rural development. Instead, we focus on a limited number of the critical decisions[6] which face governments concerned with improving the well-being of the rural poor. We turn first to some issues which affect the poor generally in rural areas, and then to some issues affecting more particularly the two sets of target groups, the small farmers and the submarginals.

Population Policy

The first of these issues is the importance of measures which reduce the rate of natural increase of population, as a component of a strategy designed to reduce the proportion and, a fortiori, the numbers in poverty. The importance of population policy is underlined both by the results of the projection model given in Chapter V, and by the results obtained from an entirely different type of model in Chapter XI.

A population policy with the explicit goal of fertility reduction will normally include a family planning program, intended to make the number of children that parents have conform to the number they want. Such a policy may also include a variety of measures, ranging from simple propaganda to elaborate systems of positive and negative incentives, designed to influence the desired number. The extent to which the provision of family planning services unaccompanied by other measures can be demographically effective is controversial. Universally, fertility in developing countries remains significantly higher than in the industrialized countries, whether or not these have had family planning programs, and in some instances a fall in fertility apparently resulting from a program has appeared to have leveled off well above replacement levels. Induced abortion and traditional methods of contraception are widely practiced in virtually all societies. Some acceptance of contraceptive measures through family planning programs must involve a substitution of modern methods for traditional ones, which would imply a net gain in individual welfare rather than a demographic effect. Well-organized family planning programs appear to have played little part in the decline of fertility in developed countries.

On the other hand, the very prevalence of abortion is a sign of high potential for family planning services. Clearly large numbers of conceptions

---

[6]We are indebted to Raj Krishna for suggesting this approach.

are unwanted and it is impossible to believe that all such end in abortion. There is also evidence that family planning acceptance is related to the degree of effort made in the program. For example, those states in India that provide better program coverage do get better results. Berelson (1974) has pointed out that the degree of national commitment appears to be a critical ingredient determining the relative success of national programs.

Other evidence that many unwanted children are both conceived and born is provided by a great many surveys which ask about desired family size and compare it with what actually occurs. These surveys frequently find that average family size is well above the number which respondents think ideal for families in their circumstances. These surveys usually show, however, that desired family size is very much larger than the number that would eventually stabilize the population. For this reason, most governments have attempted to influence the norms which couples hold with respect to family size. Usually this influence is confined to simple propaganda. Monetary incentives for accepting family planning may supplement simple propaganda; such is the case of cash payments for sterilization in India. More complicated incentive systems have been tried only on an experimental basis—these entail deferred rewards for non-pregnancy. Where governments provide extensive services to individual families it may be possible to control the allocation of these to favor those with socially desirable demographic performance, though only Singapore and China appear to have explicit policies in this respect.

Such schemes are generally too recent to provide much indication of their potential. The record of their predecessors—pro-natalist policies in developed countries trying to buck the trend of falling fertility—is not very encouraging. Unless, like China, governments are prepared to attempt very substantial intervention, exerting very heavy social and economic pressures on such individual decisions as when to marry and when to have children, there appears to be a severe constraint on the ability of governments to control the socio-economic forces which determine fertility. Most would find such intervention both politically impossible and morally objectionable.

These forces are still not clearly understood but they are evidently very powerful. In less developed countries, cultural factors, and probably economic ones as well, keep the demand for surviving children high. On the economic side, even young children often contribute economically to their families; later they supply some form of insurance against disability or old age. In addition, high levels of infant and child mortality mean that individual families must have more conceptions than they desire survivors both as a replacement for those already lost and as an insurance against future child deaths. Universally, modernization has meant that ultimately fertility has fallen to levels which imply population growth rates of less than one percent a year. This has been true whether or not modern contraception has been available, and whether or not religious forces permitted the use of contraceptive measures. It has come about through a combination of a rising age at marriage and lower marital fertility, but the relative strength of these factors has varied greatly. Usually lower marital fertility has been dominant, but in Ireland, where contraceptive practice appears to have been effectively discouraged by religious and legal forces, an increase in the age of marriage and a reduction in its incidence has been the major cause. In most instances, but not universally, the fall in fertility has been preceded by a fall in infant and child mortality.

Other than the fall in mortality, important causal factors include employment and educational opportunities for women. In many cross-country surveys, the level of a woman's education is the factor most highly correlated (negatively) with her fertility. This correlation is probably a reflection of the woman's employment opportunities outside the home. Whether or not this factor can be harnessed by deliberate policy measures in countries with high levels of underemployment is uncertain. In general, the modernization which has brought about the fall in fertility is indistinguishable from the process of development itself. Nevertheless it has been suggested, with particular reference to contrasts between Taiwan and Korea and many Latin American countries, that the more equal the distribution of income, the more the critical elements of modernization affect the poor and the faster fertility will fall (Rich, 1973; Kocher, 1973). Though this can hardly be said to have been rigorously established, it is both plausible and encouraging that measures to reduce population growth and policies which attack poverty are mutually supportive.

Land Ownership

The second issue concerns patterns of ownership of land and how it is operated. In the case of many Latin American countries, we have already stated our position. We consider an effective land reform to be a necessary condition for the type of strategy propounded in this volume, and that the immediate problems are primarily political rather than economic. We should enter a qualification at this point. The *objective* of a land reform in the Latin American context is not only to increase the area of land available to small farmers and tenants, but also to break the semifeudal structure of labor bondage which still persists in the rural areas of many Latin American countries. There are alternative means open to achieve the same basic objectives. These are increasing the rate of creation of urban jobs and increasing the pace of settlement of new land. Both of these can achieve the objective by the geographical shift of people from the *latifundia* system; whereas a land reform can achieve the objective with less spatial movement of people. There are three dimensions in which the two alternative courses of action may be compared. These are the political "cost," the economic cost, and the timeliness of the process.

Land reform clearly involves difficult political decisions and confrontations, if it is to be effective. On the other hand, combined with a rural development strategy, land reform could offer a reasonably rapid relief of rural poverty problems, and at a low economic cost apart from the short-term dislocations to production which are likely to be associated with it. Increasing the rate of urban job creation may be difficult politically because of the issues it poses in urban centers. However, in the short run, the creation of urban employment probably does not involve a direct confrontation with rural interests.[7] The economic costs are likely to be higher than those associated with a land reform, measured relative to a given objective for rural target groups. As well, it is likely to be a relatively slow process, being a process essentially of attrition rather than of direct intervention. Expanded settlement and colonization, in the short run in particular, is likely to be a politically acceptable course of action, particularly as it is often justified on nationalistic grounds. However, the economic costs are likely to be very high — and the availability of resources to finance the volume of new investment in infrastructure which is required is likely to place constraints on how rapidly the process can proceed. Therefore, trade-offs are involved. However, the political issue is not so clear-cut as a static viewpoint would suggest. This is so because, as either settlement or urban job creation begins to have a perceptible effect on the work force available on the *latifundia,* powerful rural interests are likely to begin to oppose these strategies. In other words, while some form of confrontation can be delayed and made easier by the delaying, it generally cannot be avoided.[8]

Political issues were in the forefront of our discussion of land reform in the South American continent and, of course, land reform is clearly always an intensely political issue. However, there are also difficult economic issues in the cases of most African and Asian countries.

In Africa, decisions have to be taken on the allocation of scarce development resources among the following three broad approaches. First is the settlement and colonization of new areas, that is, expansion at the extensive margin. Next would be providing highly intensive services to increase the productivity of existing small farmers; these would include land registration and stabilization of holdings, packages of improved seeds, inputs, extension advice, credit, and market access. Last is the provision of more thinly spread services to reach a larger number of small farmers. In principle, the appropriate mix of these three approaches could be taken on the basis of evaluating benefits relative to costs, using the type of weighting scheme for both costs and benefits which is described in Chapter II. In practice, however, the type of data required for such exercises is generally unavailable.[9] Further, the need to ensure equity in the allocation of public resources across different tribal groups living in

---

[7]Except insofar as the allocation of public investment is concerned. But this is an issue clearly less divisive than issues of static asset redistribution.

[8]These issues were taken up in Chapter III.

[9]The information base for decision-making and for generalizing from experience gained in various forms of rural development projects and programs is improving rapidly, through such studies as the World Bank's "Africa Rural Development Study" (Lele, 1974) and the African Rural Employment Study being conducted at Michigan State University.

different areas imposes constraints on how these resources are allocated. Settlement schemes based on individual holdings are extremely costly relative to the number of people who benefit. This argues for greater emphasis being placed on improvements at the intensive margin, designed to reach large numbers. It also argues for experimentation with different forms of land ownership, perhaps along the lines of the *ujàmaa* villages in Tanzania, which, in principle, allow both for a large element of "self-help" and for reaching large numbers of people relatively cheaply through the purposive grouping of households and farms.

While the advantages and disadvantages of different institutional forms in rural areas are by no means yet clear, it is evident that a strategy based on rural development requires, in many African countries, a reallocation of resource flows in favor of agriculture. This implies more than government budgetary items and pricing policy; it requires also the redeployment of scarce administrative and technical skills into rural areas. Implementing such a policy is not likely to be easy, running counter to the perception of many members of the administrative structure that their best chances of advancement lie in city postings, close to the central government. Such problems can be overcome, however. In particular it may require salary differentials to be paid either for service in rural areas, or to make the completion of a tour of duty in rural areas mandatory in the relevant branches of government, or for both. This approach can be complementary to the development of urban growth poles in rural areas discussed in Chapter VII.

Similar issues and considerations apply also to many countries in Asia. However, the situation in these countries is made much more difficult by the scarcity of land relative to population. Some of these difficulties are brought out by a study by Minhas (1970) of a possible form of land reform in India. He analyzed the impact on India's landless of a "radical" land reform with three provisions: (i) no household ownership holding is to be larger than 20 acres of a defined productivity equivalent; (ii) non-land-owning, noncultivating households are not to receive any land; and (iii) extra land is to be distributed amongst households operating less than 0.5 acres of land per capita in such a way as to equalize per capita ownership among this group of small farmers.

Such a reform would involve the transfer of some 43 million acres from the largest land-holding group. At Minhas' estimate, this type of reform would reduce the number of rural people below the poverty line by some 20–25 million. This may seem impressive. However, executing the plan would merely reduce the proportion of the rural population living in poverty from about two-fifths to about one-third! This remaining one-third, comprising about 80–100 million people, would remain landless labor households.[10]

---

[10]While many such schemes have been discussed in the Indian context, and land reform legislation has been enacted in all states, little progress has actually been made in the implementation of such reform.

Bluntly, as seen from the Minhas study discussed above, there simply is not enough land available to provide holdings of a viable size for all the rural population. The options are to accommodate a great many families on smaller holdings or a smaller number on less small.[11] We recommend essentially the latter, in order to avoid the problems created for the future by the establishment of a very large number of holdings of a marginal size. However, in any land reform, consideration should be given to making available to landless laborers house-plots which are large enough to support some horticultural and animal husbandry operations. Such a step could go a considerable way toward reducing the dependency status associated with having housing provided by, and under the control of, big farmers, who are the principal employers.

Associated with a land reform, there would be shifts in the demand for hired labor. Yet even the direction of such shifts is uncertain. While the greater labor-intensity of production on small farms relative to large is well established, this is due primarily to the relatively high family labor/land ratio on small farms. Thus, a land reform along the lines discussed by Minhas is likely to increase the total utilization of labor. But such a reform could well involve the increased utilization of underemployed family labor on small farms which obtained additional land, at the expense of landless laborers formerly hired by large farmers who lost land in the reform. The issue is at best uncertain, particularly since smaller farms, to the extent that they utilize hired labor, frequently do so only at harvest.

Public Investment

A program of public investment, and particularly of labor-intensive rural public works, is an essential component of a strategy to alleviate poverty. However, in countries where the distribution of the ownership of land is highly skewed, a land reform makes it much easier to devise opportunities for productive investments in which benefits accrue mainly to the poor — in other words, in which the leakages are relatively small. Without a land reform, leakages are likely to be large for such forms of investment as large- and small-scale irrigation works; other forms of land improvement such as consolidation of holdings, bunding, terracing, and leveling; and investment in infrastructure, feeder roads, improved marketing facilities, clinics, clean water supplies to the villages, and the like. Taking consolidation of holdings — the regrouping of scattered parcels of land into a contiguous block[12] — and land improvements as an example, this is

[11]There is, of course, a third option, that adopted in China: communal ownership of land and diversified production activities to absorb labor *in situ* in rural areas. This option is not available in the context of the political framework set out in Chapter III.

[12]Minhas (1970) presents some interesting data from the 1966 NSS on the extent of parcelization of holdings in Indian agriculture. For example, for all size classes of holdings, the estimated average area operated is 6.5 acres, split into about 5.7 parcels of less than 1.2 acres each. Small holdings are not unaffected by excessive parcelization: taking the size class of operational holding of 1.00 to 2.49 acres as an example, the average total size is about 1.7 acres, divided into almost 4.5 parcels averaging less than 0.4 acres each.

clearly an appropriate area for government programs in the interests of smallholders. Market forces alone are unlikely to achieve consolidation (particularly in the face of demographic pressures and traditional inheritance laws) and there are marked externalities in land improvements, particularly those associated with the efficient use of irrigation water. Reinforcing this observation is the fact that land consolidation is unlikely to prove successful alone and that it is more likely to prove acceptable to farmers if accompanied by investments which directly enhance the productivity of the land involved.

Equally clearly, such programs and investments can only be efficiently applied to spatially defined agroecological areas, and not to particular size classes of farms within the boundaries of such areas. In the absence of land redistribution, and in countries or districts where the distribution of land ownership is highly skewed, even the direct benefits from such programs of government investment will extend beyond the target groups. Many other forms of investment, such as feeder roads, marketing facilities, and the like are similarly subject to leakages.

The combination of a far-reaching land reform with rural public works directed at increasing agricultural productivity is a relatively untried program, but one which seems to us to hold out more chances of success than uncoordinated programs either of land redistribution alone, or of rural public works alone. All the same, one's hopes must be tempered by the thought that, except under the conditions of an extremely far-reaching reform which distributes land to the landless, those who labor to construct such capital will capture most of the benefits, in the form of wages, only during the construction phase and subsequent annual maintenance. These will not be the sole or even major beneficiaries of the extra output stream yielded by investments during the utilization phase because they will not own the land which such investments complement. The landless *will* gain much more during the utilization phase, to the extent that permanent employment opportunities are created. For this reason, irrigation, which at least doubles the demand for labor per unit of land, should have high priority in the public works program.

A portion of public investment expenditures should be reserved for those investments in social infrastructure, such as clean water supplies in villages and education, the benefits of which are essential for improvements in living standards in rural areas but which are difficult or impossible to quantify. A considerable body of literature has attempted to quantify the benefits from education in economic terms. There are also admittedly unquantifiable benefits: education enhances the ability of the rural poor to perceive their own interests and to pursue them more effectively. In this connection, it is worth noting that some of the successful land reform cases—in Taiwan, Japan, and Korea—were associated with a peasantry possessed of a relatively high level of education. For these political as well as economic reasons, education programs in rural areas should have high priority.

In the past, public investment in infrastructure has been heavily concentrated in the major urban centers. This is the phenomenon which Lipton (1968) terms "urban bias." As part of a strategy to alleviate poverty, we strongly recommend a reallocation of public investment away from urban and towards rural areas.

Pricing Policy

The third major issue which affects the rural sector as a whole, rather than mainly particular groups within it, is government pricing policy and, in particular, the barter terms of trade between agriculture and the rest of the economy. The terms of trade are affected by a wide range of government policy interventions, both directly, e.g., through agricultural product price legislation, and indirectly, e.g., through trade policy and a host of other measures which bear differentially on the relative prices of agricultural and manufactured products. In many developing countries, the net effect of these various policies is to bias the terms of trade against agriculture, measured relative to international prices.[13]

Where such distortions exist on a broad scale, they should be removed on both growth and equity grounds, given the generally lower levels of incomes prevailing in rural as opposed to urban areas. This last consideration has particular relevance in the light of the fact that the impact of changes in the barter terms of trade differs greatly between rural and urban target groups. Clearly, increased relative prices of agricultural products (which constitute a large share of the consumption bundle of low-income wage earners) reduce the real wage. This phenomenon, of course, works to the benefit of the producers of marketed agricultural products and the suppliers of labor services to them. These considerations argue at least for neutrality in pricing policy; they also raise the issue of price support in agriculture.

Within agriculture, the effects of increasing product prices upon the rural target groups vary according to the distribution of production among different size groups (reflecting the size distribution of land ownership), and this in turn varies substantially among different products.[14] Clearly, the leakage away from poverty groups to nontarget groups associated with government price support for any particular crop depends upon the proportion of that crop marketed by farms of different sizes and upon how the elasticity of marketed supply varies over size classes. The proportion of different crops produced by different farm size classes varies widely among countries and among crops, so that no generalizations are possible. All that can be said is that the effectiveness of product price support, with the objective of alleviating poverty, can be increased greatly by a careful selection among products. In such a selection, the indirect effects upon the level and conditions of employment of rural laborers through an ex-

---

[13]Of course, the effects of intervention on the barter terms of trade have differed widely over time within a given country. (See Krishna, 1967.)

[14]See, for example, FAO (1970).

pansion of output should be taken into account, as well as the direct effects upon groups of producers.

SMALL FARMERS

The lower limit of farm size of a given productivity which divides "small farmers" from "marginal farmers" is a holding size sufficient to provide at least subsistence income for the farm household. This limit clearly varies among countries, but can be established by combining data from farm management surveys with a definition of what is considered to be a minimum acceptable subsistence income in the particular country. The upper bound is more difficult to specify, although in practice such a bound is used in many countries.[15] However, a precise specification of the bound is not crucial, particularly if the benefits from various policies and projects are evaluated using a weighting scheme for benefits which puts higher weights on income increases for the poor than for the less poor. The important point is that the small farmer is defined to have sufficient land to yield at least a subsistence income for himself and his family. This income can be increased by measures which increase the productivity of small farmers. Different measures are required for those farmers with insufficient land.

The small farmer is characterized by low levels of household income and limited access to land. While certain features of his situation vary greatly from country to country, some general common characteristics may be noted. Of particular importance is the mix of factors employed in production, which tends to vary with the size of farm operations. There are three main reasons for this variation.[16] The first has to do with differential pricing of factors by farm size, the second with risk, and the third with different relative initial factor endowments.

On the first, it is well known that large and small farms have differential access to credit. If the average prospensity to save is an increasing function of farm income, then small farmers are more dependent on credit for purchased inputs than are large ones. For this reason, at a given mix of factor inputs, small farmers are likely to require proportionately more credit for purchased inputs than their large counterparts. Given the inherent riskiness of agriculture, small farmers—even if equally efficient—are therefore likely to be less creditworthy than large ones for a given mix of factors, and therefore can be expected to have to pay a higher price for capital. Second, even without monopolistic or oligopolistic elements in the capital market, the transaction cost of lending per unit of capital is higher

---

[15]For example, the upper limit of holding size for eligibility under the Indian Small Farmer Development Agency is five acres.

[16]In this discussion we assume that the available technology set is the same for large and small farms; and in particular that the production function is homogeneous of degree one. Although increasing returns may exist associated, for example, with the fixed costs of mechanization, it is likely that the new technology of seeds and fertilizer is scale-neutral.

to small than to large farmers.[17] This point reinforces the first, leading to the expectation of higher interest charges for small than for large farmers. Third, there are, of course, oligopolistic elements in the capital market. This particularly is the case in the common situation in which small farm operators borrow from the landlord, who is frequently in the strongest position to enforce recovery of the loan.[18]

These factors taken together lead to the conclusion that, for a given mix of factors and efficiency of use, small farmers would require proportionately more credit than large farmers and they have to pay a higher price for it. The effect, of course, is to increase the *effective* price payable by small farmers for such purchased inputs as improved seeds, fertilizers, and other chemicals. Their response is to use less of these inputs than would otherwise have been the case, and to use proportionately less than large farmers who enjoy access to cheaper sources of credit.

Although the evidence is far from conclusive, it does not appear that small farmers face differential prices *directly* in markets for material inputs; that is, it seems likely that these markets are competitive.[19] This is not surprising given the large number of traders in developing countries and the ease of entry into trading activities.

The second main reason which can be advanced for different factor mixes by farm size classes is the differential response to risk of large and small farmers. For example, Bell (1972) has shown that small farmers will tend to use less purchased inputs per unit of land than large farmers, basically because their subsistence requirements per unit of land are higher. In order to assure that their subsistence requirements are met, they will use purchased inputs only up to the point where the total expenditure upon them will leave a sufficient margin for subsistence even in bad crop years.

Lastly, farms of different sizes typically have relatively different initial factor endowments. In particular, in cross-section observations, the size of the farm family household tends to increase less than proportionately with the size of the area operated. If members of the household are prepared to work on the land operated by the household at a marginal return less than the wage for hired labor (i.e., if the "reservation price" of family labor is less than the wage rate) and if the availability of family labor is not binding for significant portions of the agricultural year (i.e., if there is

---

[17]This statement requires qualification to the extent that the transaction cost includes the risk of default. Lele (1972) has surveyed evidence which suggests that the risk of default may be larger for large farmers than for small. An important reason advanced by her for the good repayment records of small farmers is "their lesser ability to get away with overdues compared to large farmers who wield considerable political power."

[18]The analysis here is purely in economic terms and is reinforced if we introduce considerations of differential power and influence of large farmers, which typically lead to their having far readier access to subsidized sources of credit provided by governments in the rural areas.

[19]See, for example, Minhas (1973), and the evidence surveyed by Lele (1972).

seasonal unemployment of family labor), then small farms operate with a higher ratio of labor to land than larger farms.[20]

It is likely that these conditions hold in most areas of most developing countries, and it is probably this difference in labor intensity of production which goes a long way towards explaining the frequently observed higher output per land unit on small than on large farms.

The differential impact of technical change upon farmers in different size groups should be considered in light of the foregoing considerations. The most important recent advances in technology in agriculture involve mainly land-augmenting technologies, coupled with "packages" of improved seeds, fertilizers, pesticides, and irrigation. These advances apply mainly to the two staple cereal crops, rice and wheat. Evidence from various studies points strongly to the conclusion that, while the new technology is scale-neutral, it has benefited large farmers relatively more than small ones. The main reasons for this are three. (i) Large farmers tend to adopt the new technology earlier than small for a variety of reasons. Of particular importance is the fact that, to be fully exploited, the new technologies demand a four- to five-fold increase in working capital per unit of land and small farmers, as discussed above, typically pay a higher price for credit than do large farmers. Other considerations include the greater willingness (and ability) of large farmers to bear risk, their greater access to information, their higher levels of education, and the greater attention they receive from extension workers. (ii) With other factors of production, including labor, available in highly elastic supply, most of the gains from the new technologies accrue as increased quasi-rents to land (of which large farmers have a relative abundance) and the supply conditions of labor have permitted an expansion of employment without increases in real wages, even though the new technology is labor-demanding. (iii) The benefits of the new technologies have been concentrated in regions of irrigated agriculture—regions which, in general, permit higher farm incomes than dry-land regions.

In the absence of government intervention in their favor, these factors point to a relative worsening of the income position of small farmers, pessimistic conclusions which are supported by some direct empirical evidence in rural India.[21] However, government intervention can redress the balance, or tilt it in favor of small farmers. Some of the policies or policy packages available for this purpose are evaluated below. The effectiveness of these policies is greatly enhanced if they are preceded, or accompanied, by the implementation of policies of land reform and of the creation of in-

---

[20]The availability of family labor frequently is binding at harvests in many countries and, during these seasonal peaks of labor demand, labor is hired even on small farms. However, this does not affect the argument advanced in the text, because the labor intensity of harvesting operations generally has slight effects upon yields. Further, the use of hired labor for harvesting operations on small farms is consistent with the capital rationing argument set out above—hired harvest labor is frequently paid in kind from the proceeds of the harvest and therefore credit is not required for wage payments.

[21]Dandekar and Rath (1971).

frastructure in rural areas through public investment. This is not to suggest that implementation be delayed; rather, it is to draw attention again to the importance of complementarities among policy measures.

Factor Prices

The first issue which we take up is that of pricing policies for factors of production, product pricing having been discussed earlier in the chapter. For small farmers, the most important component of pricing policy has to do with the price and availability of capital—particularly, of working capital—one of the areas where they are particularly disadvantaged compared with larger farmers. It is unrealistic in this connection to call for policies directed to making cheap capital available to small farmers. In many developing countries, public institutional credit mainly goes to large farmers who are charged subsidized and low money interest rates. Frequently these rates are so low that, taking inflation into account, the implicit real rates are near zero or, in some cases, negative. Attempts to expand the supply of credit at such low interest rates in order to reach small farmers, or even to direct it towards them by various rationing devices, are likely to be futile and are almost certain to lead to leakages towards larger and more influential farmers. A more realistic approach, and one which we support strongly, requires an overall reform of credit pricing, with higher real interest rates in the institutional credit market (both public and private). This will reduce somewhat the incentive for large farmers to take a disporportionate share of public institutional credit. But this is not sufficient. The gap in interest rates between the institutional market and the private moneylender market is likely to remain large, even after an interest rate reform as advocated above. What is required is to change the conditions of access to institutional credit. In this connection, it should be noted that institutional credit typically accounts for a relatively small proportion of total credit used in agriculture.[22] Clearly, an expansion of the supply of credit to agriculture is required. Further, in situations where the same institution supplies credit to both small and large farmers, the latter obtain a disproportionate share of credit and the former have to resort to the private money market. We recommend that the whole of public institutional credit should be reserved for small farmers, with special institutions—be they cooperatives, or a nationalized bank, or a government agency—set up to identify small farmers and supply their credit needs.[23]

A Package Approach

Small farmers are disadvantaged in a number of ways: in their access to credit and extension advice, in the impact upon them of risk and uncer-

---

[22] The remainder coming from private moneylenders.

[23] This implies that larger farmers would perforce have to resort to other institutions for credit. Given their creditworthiness on conventional banking criteria, this could lead to an expansion of commercial banking activities in agriculture.

tainty, and in the mix of factors they employ, reflecting an inability to take early advantage of the opportunities to increase incomes associated with the new technologies. To overcome these disadvantages, a coordinated rather than a piecemeal approach is required. Here we set out the outlines of a package approach to improving the incomes of small farmers, under the assumption that the technology to do so is available, but that its application requires a substantial increase in the use of purchased inputs, and that small farmers are reluctant to incur these additional costs on account of their assessment of the uncertainty involved in so doing. This is a situation which corresponds to that in many developing countries, where small farmers are conspicuously lagging behind the large in the adoption of the new technologies.

The first objective of the proposal is to assist small farmers in taking the step from a traditional variety or cropping pattern to the use of a new and income-enhancing technology in situations where they perceive that the outcome is uncertain. It is *not* designed to reduce the normal risk in agricultural production associated with climatic variation. The second objective of the proposal is to minimize the supervision and extension costs associated with helping small farmers make the change.

To explain the proposal, we assume that, for a given crop, the yield required just to break even using the improved variety and heavily increased use of purchased inputs is, say, double the yield obtained using the traditional variety. That is, a doubled yield with the new variety will yield the same net income, after deducting the increased expenditure on purchased factors of production, as the yield using the traditional variety. The expected yield from the use of the new variety combined with the associated increased variable capital and good husbandry is likely to be substantially greater than doubled. This must be the case if the use of the new technology is income-increasing for the farmer. For expositional purposes, let this expected yield be *greater than* tripled. The package we suggest requires an Agency for Small Farmers (ASF) which conducts a combined credit, extension, crop insurance, and input supply operation. The ASF would enter into a contract with registered small farmers with the following provisions. (i) the Agency is to supply the farmer with the appropriate combination of improved seed, fertilizer, pesticides, credit, and the like, together with extension advice on their best use.[24] (ii) If the farmer obtains an actual yield with the new variety less than doubled (that is, below the break-even point for the new technology compared with the old), he is allowed a remission of his debt to the ASF equal to the shortfall in yield. (iii) If the farmer obtains a yield greater than doubled, the ASF charges him a substantial premium (say, 20 percent) on the incremental yield up to a yield of equivalent to a tripling. (However, no premium is

---

[24]Variants of this provision are, of course, possible, For example, it is not material to the essential concept of the proposal if the ASF itself supplies the inputs or if these are supplied through contractual arrangements with private traders, or if the credit is supplied by a bank upon presentation of a chit from the ASF.

levied on any incremental yield in excess of the expected yield). (iv) The farmer can opt, for any new crop year, to accept all the components of the ASF package apart from those relating to insurance, extension assistance, and premiums.

The main properties of this proposal are three. (i) The proposal *guarantees* the small farmer who decides to adopt the new technology at least the subsistence return which he would have obtained from the use of traditional techniques—he cannot lose from the four- or five-fold increase in the use of variable capital associated with the new technology. (ii) Initially, the proposal is extremely intensive in supervision requirements, in extension advice on the use of the new inputs, and particularly in the measurement of yields. However, the proposal has built into it a device for reducing over time the supervision required. As the farmer learns from experience that he can regularly obtain yields *at least* doubled (the break-even point), he has an incentive to withdraw from the insurance component of the contract in order to avoid the premium on the yield increase between doubling and tripling. This eliminates the major component of the supervision needed, which is the verification of yields. (iii) The proposal allows for simple and effective measures of the performance of the ASF. These are, in addition to the number of small farmers entering the scheme, the proportion of those who obtain better than doubled yields (and who are therefore able to repay in full the cost of the additional inputs), and the number who, over time, withdraw from the insurance component but continue using the new technology and take advantage of the credit component. Note also that the ASF has an incentive to provide extension advice and inputs at the right time—if it does not do so, it stands to sustain operating losses on the remissions of debts for shortfalls in yields below the break-even point.

This proposal is only one of many which could be, and have been, devised to assist the small farmer, However, it has no chance of success unless the ASF is provided with full power and control over the various components—extension, yield measurement, credit, insurance, and input supplies.[25] The need for supervision and extension advice to the small farmer is among the heaviest demands on resources which it makes. But we see no possibility of success in improving the conditions of small farmers if governments are unwilling or unable to make such resources available. The scheme is open to corruption, particularly through collusion between farmer and ASF agent in the measurement of yield. But this is characteristic of all proposals which involve the nonmarket allocation of valuable goods and services.[26]

---

[25]Note that the lack of such power has been suggested by Jodha (1973), as the major reason for the limited success of the Small Farmers Development Agency in India. This Agency can only coordinate and request the services of other agencies which actually control the various required components.

[26]The possibilities for collusion can be reduced somewhat if yield verifications are done by an independent agency.

In conclusion, the ASF proposal should be seen as an example of the type of institution required to assist the small farmer. While the scheme is intensive in administrative and supervision costs, it is likely to produce substantial increases in the productivity of small farmers, and its educational component—that of learning by doing with protection against the risks associated with innovation—may well be more productive than additional years of traditional formal education.

Tenure Reform

In many countries, large numbers of small farmers are able to operate a good deal more land than they own by renting land from others (who usually have big holdings which they choose not to manage entirely themselves). Thus the nature and conditions of the rental contract affect large numbers of poor farmers.

Tenure reform is really a comparatively weak substitute for land reform. If the degree of local monopoly is high and the mobility of tenants is low except in the very long run, then intervention to lower rents can aim simply at reducing them to what would be their competitive levels. Should intervention seek to lower them further, cast-iron security of tenure in legally binding form must be granted to tenants simultaneously. In practice, of course, clauses relating to security of tenure are left to the slow due process of law. Landlords then are able to evict tenants in the interim. Despite these caveats, tenure reform is often advocated precisely because the element of expropriation is likely to be smaller than would be the case in an outright redistributist land reform and may therefore be more palatable to powerful rural interests which stand to lose in the event of either.

Second, the nature of the tenancy system itself has a bearing both on the allocation of resources and on equity between tenant and landlord. Traditionally, the main target of attack, both in the literature (Marshall, 1890) and the statute book, has been sharecropping. Sharecropping is especially widespread in Asia and has deep historical roots. As traditional theory would have it, the practice of a fixed division of the *gross* product between landlord and tenant introduces a strong tendency for variable inputs to be used less intensively than is optimal when the owner is also the operator. More recently, the traditional view of resource misallocation has come under a strong attack (Cheung, 1968; Newbery, 1973), causing others to spring to its defense (Bardhan and Srinivasan, 1971; Mazumdar, 1973). We do not propose to enter into a detailed discussion of this debate. Suffice it to say that two points appear to us to be important. First, insecurity of tenure (whatever the system) is a powerful deterrent to long-term investment by the tenant in the land to raise its productivity. This conclusion applies *a fortiori* if the landlord automatically receives half of the resulting extra stream of gross output. Second, the essence of the Marshallian position seems to stand if, in addition to labor (the traditional input), nonlabor purchased inputs (fertilizers, pesticides, and so forth), and the entrepreneurial skill that must accompany their use, become important.

One form of lease which does ensure allocative efficiency under certainty with any number of inputs is the so-called cost-share lease in which the landlord contributes to the cost of variable inputs in the same proportion as he shares in output. Moreover, unlike fixed cash or kind rents (which are allocatively efficient), cost-share leases divide the burden of risk between landlord and tenant fairly evenly (as does sharecropping). A general move towards this form of tenure will encourage tenants to use purchased inputs more intensively, thereby raising their gross outputs. A desire for still more equity requires that the landlord's legal share be reduced. On implementation, to the extent that registered tenants can be brought into organized credit markets, the provisions can be enforced by debiting landlords concerned with an appropriate share of the liabilities thus contracted by their tenants. Whether or not a radical redistributist land reform is carried out, tenancy reform is important and, in our view, the cost-share lease merits close attention.

Most importantly, the share of proceeds, or the levels of rentals, or both, are set by economic forces and the relative bargaining power of landlord and tenant. Legislative or administrative action is ineffective to the extent that its provisions run contrary to these realities. Changing the relative bargaining position is therefore important. This can be done, for example, by making tenants or sharecroppers eligible for credit, insurance, and extension advice from an agency such as the Agency for Small Farmers discussed above, instead of leaving them dependent on the private moneylender who, in practice, is often also the landlord.

Research and Development

The direction as well as the volume of research and development is another of the difficult issues which have to be faced. There is an obvious need for an expansion of R and D in the developing countries themselves. What is perhaps less obvious is that different objectives of R and D can have marked distributional implications, and can have quite different impacts upon the alleviation on poverty. Two polar extremes illustrate this point. Research and development can be directed at, say, developing improved varieties suitable mainly for use in irrigated areas where farmers are already well-off, and at the improved utilization of large-scale mechanization. Or, on the other hand, R and D can be directed at seeking improved varieties for use by small farmers on unirrigated land and at developing improved simple implements which increase the efficiency and competitiveness of labor-intensive methods.

Most R and D effort falls somewhere in between these extremes. It is difficult to evaluate ex ante, not only the likely costs and benefits of R and D expenditures, but a fortiori the distribution effects. It seems likely, however, that R and D of the kind in the first example set out above may

appeal more to scientists as having more chance of success and of bringing more prestige. Whatever the facts, we would suggest that at least a portion of the total R and D budget should be reserved for research, the objectives of which are clearly associated with reducing poverty among
specified poverty groups.

Submarginal Farmers and Landless Laborers

We have defined the lower limit of the groups of small farmers as having access to a holding size sufficient to provide at least subsistence income for the farm household. Marginal farmers and landless laborers are
then defined as having access to land below this minimum size. Of course,
all the households in this latter category are not necessarily "poverty"
families: many receive incomes in fact which are larger than those received by small farmers. However, many of the most desperately poor are
in this category.

The definition as it stands is static; it also requires a dynamic dimension.
Where it is possible to increase land productivity faster than the rate of
population growth, or to increase the availability of land to this group by a
land redistribution or expansion of land at the extensive margin or both,
then some households previously in this group will be transferred to the
group of small farmers. This is the process which is quantified by the
dynamic projection model in Chapter V.

The situation of the rural landless or those who operate very little
land,[27] who depend for their livelihood mainly on hiring out their labor
services, constitutes one of the most intractable problems facing developing countries. It is a problem, also, which does not lend itself either to generalized analysis or to generalized approaches to policy. The dimensions of
the problem also vary greatly across countries and over time (see Chapter
V). The problem is most acute in the high population and relatively dense-
ly settled countries of Asia (India, Bangladesh, and Indonesia), less acute
in most Latin American countries (with some notable exceptions such as
northeastern Brazil), and the problem takes quite different forms in most
African countries (although even in many of these there are areas of acute
population pressure upon the land). In these last countries, the problem is

---

[27]The dividing lines between landless laborers, marginal farmers, and small farmers are
somewhat arbitrary and change over time. Families operating small farms typically hire out
their labor for some periods of the year on other farms even though, over the year as a
whole, they are probably not net hirers of labor. Similarly, households classified as "rural
labor households" frequently operate some land themselves. But to draw the distinction on
the basis of net transactions in nonfamily labor is to make an a priori judgment of the nature
of the problem. Taking the principal source of income and its size provides a better guide.
However, while we draw a distinction between small farmers on the one hand, and submarginal farmers and landless laborers on the other (the "submarginals"), we do not attempt
a further distinction within the latter category. Any attempt to do so would be entirely arbitrary and would add little to the analysis.

less one of land scarcity or land reform, than of settlement, consolidation, and colonization.

The major policy measures which can substantially increase the demand for rural labor are increases in the prices of labor-competing farm machinery which will bring these up at least to the level of international prices, and the implementation of rural public works programs. Both of these policies, which we firmly support, were discussed earlier in this chapter. However, a few additional points should be added on rural public works, as they affect the submarginals. First, there are a number of types of public works which can *directly* add to permanent employment, as well as employment during the construction phase. These include in particular the establishment of forestry and fishing activities, and of labor-intensive animal husbandry activities. Second, if schools and hospitals and other social infrastructure are included in rural public works, and if the submarginal group is guaranteed access to free services from these institutions, they add a continuing stream of benefits in kind to the employment benefits associated with the construction phase. Third, investment in irrigation, constructed as part of a rural public works program, can substantially increase the intensity of cropping on otherwise dry land, and can therefore substantially increase the continuing demand for labor.

Measures to increase demand for labor can be expected to lead both to an increased volume of employment for the remaining members of this group and to increased wage levels. However, the magnitude of the problem is so large that it will require many decades to bring about marked changes in numbers and conditions of employment. Some direct intervention to increase wages is required. We are *not* suggesting only minimum wage legislation; this has been attempted in a number of countries and has proved ineffective where the underlying conditions of supply, demand, and relative bargaining power between employer and employee lead to a "natural" wage below the legislated minimum.

In addition to minimum wage legislation, two proposals to increase the bargaining power of rural laborers are worthy of consideration. The first is to include provision for household plots (of a size sufficient to support some intensive productive activities) as an integral part of a land reform.[28] This provision will to a major extent reduce the dependency of the employee upon his employer. The second proposal is, at first sight, more radical. This is to provide central government funds to organize rural laborers (including those engaged in public works projects) along the lines suggested by Krishna (1973), in order to stop leakages out of their wages to overseers and contractors, and to increase their bargaining power with respect to private employers. In this context it is interesting to note the marked differences in wage trends which were observed by Bardhan (1973*d*) between the Punjab and the state of Kerala. This was over a period when production was increasing far more rapidly in the former than in

---

[28]Similar to "sites and services" projects in urban areas.

the latter, but when labor was organized in the latter and not in the former. Unfortunately, data are not also available on the relative trends in total employment over the same period.

It must be recognized that the implementation of the various measures suggested here, while improving their condition, will still leave many in poverty in rural areas for some decades in many countries in Africa and Asia. The alternatives are a policy of inaction or forms of labor utilization which have been adopted with apparent success, but at largely unknown cost, in China. Neither of these alternatives seems to be acceptable in the light of the political framework discussed in Chapter III.

CONCLUSIONS

The strategies for improving the incomes of the rural target groups discussed in this chapter vary substantially across the three country archetypes. In "Latin America" we see the need for structural changes in the rural sector, which can be achieved by land reform, by land settlement at the extensive margin, or by some combination of the two. In "South Asia," the option of expansion at the extensive margin is not available in most countries, and a redistributive land reform, even a radical one, cannot provide sufficient land for all the landless and submarginal farmers to produce a minimum subsistence household income. A land reform which breaks the power of large farmers and the rural elite will, however, provide a framework within which public goods and services can be directed to the target groups with minimum leakage. In "Africa," the structure of rural institutions and of land holdings is less rigid than in the other two archetypes, and governments' freedom to maneuver is correspondingly greater. Here, the emphasis has been upon settlement at the extensive margin and registration of land ownership on existing small farms. However, we would stress that the lack of rigidity in much of tropical Africa makes possible interventionist policies designed to create new forms of rural institutions, such as the *ujàmaa* villages in Tanzania, which can provide for the more efficient use of public infrastructure, agricultural capital, and such government-supplied services as extension, health care, and education.

In addition to these structural changes it is necessary to create special institutions and programs, such as the ASF and rural public works, designed to increase the productivity and incomes of rural target groups. The evaluation of such programs should take account of productivity in the sense of increased GDP, efficiency in reaching the target groups in the sense of minimizing leakages and, in particular, the indirect effects upon the target groups due to linkages among various groups in the rural economy. This last point is most important in the case of the submarginals, who are difficult to reach by direct action.

Chapter VII
URBAN TARGET GROUPS
D. C. Rao

THE PRODUCTIVE ROLE of the urban poor is as much at issue now as was that of their rural counterparts ten years ago. The landless and the small farmers were widely regarded as bound to traditional modes of production, and steeped in ignorance. They were seen as being unwilling to change in response to economic incentives and in response to opportunities opened up by new technologies. They were not regarded as being potentially productive, and their problems were consequently largely ignored — in practice if not in rhetoric. These views of the rural poor have now, of course, been radically revised and a similar reexamination of the economic role of the urban poor has recently begun.

Studies of urban poverty previously focused on those who were unemployed but now explicitly consider the problems and the potential of the "working poor." Examination of the problem of urban poverty suggests that government policy towards the urban poor is often characterized by benign neglect and sometimes by active discrimination. Perhaps struck by the survival power of squatters and migrants in the face of such odds, some observers have concluded that the informal sector of the urban economy has "the potential for dynamic, evolutionary growth" and could be "the source of a new development strategy" (ILO, 1972, p. 505).

However, no development strategies have been focused directly on the urban poor. The complexity of the problem of urban poverty and its neglect by governments and researchers are two reasons for the paucity of data about the poor. To define corrective strategies, it is necessary to correlate the characteristics of poverty, defined on the basis of income, with other economic and social characteristics. Existing surveys are more helpful in providing information on the indexes of poverty (income, consumption patterns, and so on) than on the causes of poverty, i.e., the human and physical wealth of the poor. Surveys of household income and expenditure typically do not present much data on corresponding occupation or at best present them in very broad categories. On the basis of conventional industrial or occupational classifications, the urban poor are inextricably interwoven with the not-so-poor in the same sectors or activities.

There is a considerable amount of data on employment collected in surveys of the labor force.[1] But surveys relating employment status to income levels are extremely rare. Such evidence as is available suggests that there is only a weak relationship between unemployment and poverty. A study of eight cities in Colombia estimates that more than half of the unemployed are those who

---

I have had the benefit of discussions with Raj Krishna and many other colleagues at the World Bank, who have been generous with their time and their unpublished work on this subject.

[1]Surveys of employment data are available in Turnham and Jaeger (1974) for LDCs, Frank (1971) for Africa, and Hofmeister (1971) for Latin America.

aspire to high-income jobs, or have been unemployed for less than five weeks, or live with their families (being first-time job-seekers); the group of unemployed poor is smaller than the group of employed poor (Berry, 1972b). An analysis of the socio-economic sample survey of households in West Malaysia in 1967/68 shows that the age-specific unemployment rate is highest among secondary school leavers and that new job-seekers accounted for 60 percent of the male and 72 percent of the female unemployed (Mazumdar, unpublished). These data support a general impression that poverty and unemployment are not closely related: it is not much of an exaggeration to state that the poor cannot afford to be unemployed. Conversely, one who is employed (especially one who is self-employed) can still be poor because he cannot find remunerative employment for as long as he would like or because even "full-time" work does not pay well enough.[2]

While we may agree that the poor generally tend to be occupied in some way, the sectoral labels now in use are strikingly inadequate in helping us locate the urban poor. The labels *small-scale* or *traditional sectors* are both too broad and too narrow: the former includes capital-intensive engineering firms but excludes construction activities; the latter includes rich shopkeepers but excludes bicycle tire repairers. The ILO report on Kenya (ILO, 1972) introduced the label *informal sector* and gave it a fairly broad definition.[3] Some components of the definition (e.g., ease of entry) are important features of occupations accessible to the poor. But the informal sector cannot only be identified with the urban poor.

Available information does not permit the presentation of a well-researched profile of the urban poor. Any generalizations that one can hazard at this stage are subject to two major limitations.

First, the definitions of *poverty* and the occupations of the poor vary considerably between countries at different levels of income, urbanization, and industrialization. Fragmentary evidence on how poor households (defined as those falling in the lowest quartile of the urban household distribution) differ from other households leads to significantly different profiles of the poor in various countries. Data on Nigeria, India, and the Philippines suggest that a higher proportion of heads of poor households are self-employed than for urban households as a whole. The reverse is true in Mexico. There is no significant difference between poor and other households in this respect in eight Latin American cities.[4] In comparison with other urban households, a higher proportion of poor households derive their main income from farming and fishing-related activities in the Philippines, from unskilled

---

[2]These characteristics have been used to define "underemployment." For an excellent exposition of the conceptual relationship between underemployment and poverty, see Krishna (1973).

[3]The ILO report illustrates the nature of informal activities as characterized by: (a) ease of entry, (b) reliance on indigenous resources, (c) family ownership of enterprises, (d) small scale of operation, (e) labor-intensive and adapted technology, (f) skills acquired outside the formal school system, and (g) unregulated and competitive markets (ILO, 1972, p. 7).

[4]Reported in Figueroa and Weisskoff (1974).

service occupations in India, and from blue-collar occupations in the eight Latin American cities.

Second, and perhaps even more fundamental, it is extraordinarily difficult to allow for the fact that poverty is a household phenomenon and not an individual one. While almost all available data identify the occupations of individuals, it is essential, for a profile of urban poverty, to know how many secondary workers and dependents there are in each household. The social structure in less developed countries makes it absurd to base inferences on an assumption of nuclear family relationships. The size of the household is not independent of its economic status for reasons other than differential fertility rates. Households can annex aged, wealthy uncles, as well as young nephews looking for their first job. Secondary workers may work in the informal sector to increase family income. It is impossible to go beyond vague, subjective impressions in this area until we have surveys that relate per capita household incomes with employment status and household characteristics (size, age structure, education levels, and migration status). Furthermore, some urban workers may maintain close links with rural areas.[5] Urban workers who remit a considerable part of their earnings to rural dependents may be poor despite a high per capita urban household income.

Subject to these major limitations, one may hazard the following generalizations. The urban poor usually include: (i) self-employed persons in the services sector (the oft-cited hawker, shoeshine boy, repair and maintenance workers, barbers); (ii) unskilled workers who are employed in the manufacturing, construction, or services sectors—some of them in the modern sector, perhaps irregularly; (iii) recent migrants who have taken on casual work while looking for better jobs; (iv) skilled workers, usually self-employed, some of whom have relatively obsolete skills (pottery, hand-spinning) and do not enjoy much demand for their product; others, such as tailors and carpenters, who operate on a very small scale; and (v) aged and disabled persons who are not in the labor force—in developing countries they are usually dependents rather than independent households. Conversely, the urban poor usually exclude skilled operatives in modern industry, government employees, working proprietors even of small firms with employees, educated unemployed, and those in technical and professional occupations. In general, unionized employees are not among the poor. This is by no means an exhaustive list and does not allow sufficiently for regional differences. It is sufficient, however, to illustrate the diverse occupation and skill backgrounds of the urban poor, which is why it has been so difficult to encapsule them into a single label. For expository convenience, however, we shall continue to use the term *informal sector* to refer to the economic activities of the bulk of the poor.

---

[5]For an interesting study of this subject see Bhattacharya and Chatterjee (1973). A survey of jute industry workers in Greater Calcutta revealed that while 56 percent reported no agricultural work experience, 79 percent owned houses in their native villages and 58 percent made regular financial remittances.

STRATEGY OPTIONS

It is now clear that continued reliance on a capital-intensive expansion of the modern sector to solve the urban poverty problem would be a disastrous mistake. Skepticism about the employment absorption capacity of the modern sector is based on the rapid growth of urban population, the small share of the modern sector in urban employment and the low employment elasticity of modern sector growth. Even assuming a slowdown in the rate of urban growth, the United Nations projects the rate of growth of urban population in developing countries with market economies at 4.1 percent over the 1960-2000 period, which is higher than historical rates for any developed economy except North America between 1850 and 1920 (Bairoch, 1973). The rapid growth of urban population is the result of both migration from rural areas and a high natural rate of increase of population.

Estimates of the structure of urban employment highlight the limited role of modern industrial employment. Data for urban areas in twelve countries reported by Turnham and Jaeger (1974) show that the services sector generally has a much higher proportion of employed persons than either industry or commerce. Industrial employment varies around one-third of urban employment, and the proportion employed in modern industry is even smaller. The latter proportion is estimated at only 7.7 percent in Latin America in 1969 (Turnham and Jaeger, 1974). Establishments with more than five workers employ only 30 percent of manufacturing workers in the Philippines and account for only 3 percent of total employment (ILO, 1973). Self-employed and unpaid family workers constituted 50 percent to 60 percent of manufacturing employment and over 80 percent of employment in commerce in urban areas in Pakistan (Hofmeister, unpublished). Even though manufacturing accounts for more than 15 percent of GDP in Pakistan, total employment in registered factories (those employing more than ten persons) is less than the annual increase in the labor force.

It is easy to infer that even under optimistic assumptions about the rate of expansion and employment elasticities, growth of the modern manufacturing sector cannot absorb the major part of the increase in the urban labor force. It is necessary therefore to consider strategies that would have a more direct impact on the incomes and welfare of the urban poor.

A striking feature of the strategy discussion of the rural target groups in the previous chapter was the crucial role of asset transfers. In contrast, the desirable urban stratgey is more diversified for a number of reasons. First, urban conditions are rather more diverse across countries and cities of different sizes and perhaps also cities of different ages. As discussed in Chapter V, countries differ considerably in their levels of urbanization, with consequent differences in the economic characteristics of the urban poor and in the applicability of various strategies. Even within a single city, the poor consist of groups of various employment status and occupational skills. A corresponding mix of strategies is necessary to reach them.

Second, the greater potential for exploiting economic linkages in the urban sector opens an additional strategy option that is not effective in the rural sector. Within the rural sector, the bulk of production units in developing countries meet most of their own consumption needs and market their surplus outside the rural sector. It is, therefore, common to see development of small segments of the rural sector (large landowners, irrigated areas) without the benefits being shared to any large extent by their neighbors. In the urban sector, on the other hand, the relationships between producing units can run both wide and deep. This is reflected in higher ratios of intermediate inputs to value-added in production processes and in the mobility of factors among the wide range of urban activities. Consequently, the condition of the urban poor can be improved without necessarily focusing action so directly on the poor.

A third consideration is the great difficulty in identifying the poor in terms of occupational characteristics, a problem we have previously discussed. The difficulty in identifying the recipients puts an obvious restraint on a strategy to transfer assets. Thus in the urban sector there is no direct analogue to the redistribution of land to small farmers. But neither is redistribution of existing assets so important when new assets are constantly being produced. The pattern of asset ownership in the urban sector can be changed by measures that promote very small-scale production units and change the pattern of allocation of public "human capital" expenditures so as to benefit the poor directly. In this context, it is important to expand the scope of action beyond manufacturing industry to a host of other economic activities, such as transport, construction, commerce, and other services.

Some countries at relatively high income levels can afford to finance programs for consumption transfers directly to the poor. These can take the form of school feeding programs, unemployment benefits or massive support for low-income housing. They can also extend more public utility services to the poor without affecting the standards of service to the middle- and upper-income groups. However, most less developed countries do not have the resources to implement a major consumption transfer strategy, and we shall not discuss the specifics of such a strategy. The strategies explored below are designed for the consideration of countries which face severe resource constraints.[6]

The basic strategy that we propose is a mixture of the asset redistribution approach of the previous chapter with a more conventional approach of increased labor absorption in the producing sectors. One class of strategies, discussed in the following section, has the objective of improving the income earning opportunities of the poor, whether they are employed or seeking employment in the modern or informal sectors producing goods or services. In the modern sector this primarily involves the removal of existing factor price distortions so as to increase the direct and indirect employment absorption capacity of the industrial and construction sectors. In addition, a variety

---

[6]The provision of public services at prices below cost does amount to a transfer. The role of such public expenditure policies is considered later in this chapter.

of measures is needed to encourage the labor-intensive small producers, partly by developing greater links between the modern sector and small suppliers either on the basis of subcontracting or market relationships, and partly by providing special benefits to small producers in carefully selected sectors. The provision of special benefits immediately raises the question of the trade-off between redistribution and efficiency in production. We shall argue that it may be necessary to compensate small producers for the various handicaps under which they operate, which themselves interfere with efficient allocation and all of which it may be impossible to eliminate.

It is frequently stated that the employment generated in the modern sector depends not only on the techniques of production but also on the composition of output. Defining products on the basis of the needs they satisfy rather than on their physical attributes, different qualities of the same product may well require very different factor intensities in their production.[7] Consequently, changes in the composition of output may be a potent means of influencing the labor absorption capacity of the modern sector. The potential and the limitations of this approach are fully discussed in Chapters IV and IX and will not be considered here. Suffice it to say that while the evidence is not conclusive on the relation between income distribution and the product mix, there is a critical shortage of instruments by which to influence the composition of demand directly.[8]

A second class of strategies consists of measures which will more directly increase the real income of the poor. They consist of redirecting public policy and expenditures, especially on education, health, and housing so as to benefit the poorer sections of the urban population directly. In addition to the direct impact on the real living standards of the poor, this could improve their productivity and increase the efficiency of labor-intensive techniques relative to capital-intensive ones.

There is some overlap between these two classes of strategies (the production sector strategies and the transfer strategies) because they are highly complementary. The themes underlying this mix of strategies are that the poor deserve as much access to public infrastructure as the rich and that the small producer is frequently as efficient as the large one and should be given equivalent access to scarce inputs. Throughout this chapter we shall draw attention to the many ways in which governments have tended to discriminate against the small and the poor while according significant economic privileges to the rich and the not-so-poor, usually in the name of efficiency.

While these strategies may be expected to improve the consumption standards of the urban poor, they might not help in eradicating the problem of urban poverty. This paradox is explained by the likelihood that rural-urban migration will increase when the conditions of the urban poor are improved.

---

[7]See Stewart (1972) for a careful discussion of these propositions.

[8]The two instruments available are indirect taxation, which is already widely used, and government demand, which is subject to obvious budget constraints.

There are a number of models attempting to explain rural-urban migration which hypothesize that migrants respond to their expected earnings in the city.[9] These models have not been fully tested so far but their hypotheses are plausible.[10] The conclusions of one of the models of this genre is that any improvement in the employment or earnings opportunities in urban areas will increase the number of those underemployed in the informal urban labor market.[11]

Of course, migration does have some positive aspects. It improves labor mobility and liberates the migrants (and their families) from a rigid, rural ascriptive base that might restrict achievement. However, a rapid rate of growth of urban population imposes an additional resource cost on the economy in providing infrastructure to cope with more congested living conditions.

These considerations highlight the dominant importance of rural development in coping satisfactorily with the problem of urban poverty. Not only is rural development necessary to restrain the flow of migrants to urban areas, it is also necessary to increase the supply of wage goods and demand for the products of the smaller urban manufacturers (either of which may otherwise prove a binding constraint on employment growth in urban areas).

The close relationship between rural and urban strategies is also evident in policies concerning the degree of concentration of urban growth. In most countries, metropolitan areas attract government investment in infrastructure and private investment in industry. An alternative strategy, however, is for the government to encourage the growth of a larger number of small towns dispersed across the country. The evidence on the relative costs of different sizes of cities is not conclusive. However, there are some evident advantages to more decentralized urban growth. Widely dispersed small towns can serve as market towns for the rural hinterland. The resulting improved supply of agricultural inputs and the ready market for perishable crops such as vegetables (the production of which is labor-intensive) will accelerate rural development and, indirectly, assist in tackling the problem of urban poverty.

Small towns may also improve employment prospects by attracting manufacturing industry and providing off-season employment to agricultural workers. By bringing some of the attractions of modern urban life (e.g., cinema) close to the rural areas, small towns might discourage rural migration to more congested metropolitan cities. By reducing the costs of migration, decentralized urban growth will tend to raise the proportion of migrants coming from poor rural households, even though it might encourage rural-urban migration in the aggregate.

---

[9]One of the earliest formal models is Todaro (1959); see also Harris and Todaro (1970) and Stiglitz (1973). Mazumdar (1973) defines expected earnings in the city as a weighted average of their earnings in the modern and informal sector, the weights being given by the expected probabilities of finding employment in each of these sectors.

[10]Empirical tests are underway in some countries. See Rampel and Harris (forthcoming) on Kenya; studies are now in progress in Tanzania by Richard Sabot (at the Oxford Institute of Statistics) and in Indonesia by John Harris (at Massachusetts Institute of Technology).

[11]Mazumdar (1973).

The interaction of rural and urban strategies can thus be seen to be extremely complex. Both strategies must be jointly conceived and executed. In the following sections we shall discuss production sector strategies and transfer strategies in the urban context. It should be understood, however, that closely analogous policies also exist in the rural sector (as discussed in Chapters V and VI), and that the relative balance between the two sectors is a matter of strategic importance.

Production Sector Strategies

Correct Factor Prices

A large and significant volume of literature suggests that encouraging the use of more labor-intensive techniques of production in a labor-abundant economy is principally a matter of removing existing distortions in factor prices. The scope of government-induced distortions in factor markets and the neoclassical assumptions on which policy prescriptions are generally based have been explored in Chapter IV. The belief that the removal of factor price distortions will significantly influence the level of employment in the modern sector relies on the strength of a presumed relationship between factor prices and factor intensities. The evidence for such a relationship is suggestive but not conclusive. Numerous econometric attempts to estimate the elasticity of substitution between capital and labor using aggregative production functions have been inconclusive (Morawetz, 1974). Microstudies appear to be a more useful approach although economists have yet to learn how to cope successfully with the complexity of real world production processes and each microstudy can analyze only one or a few of the myriad products of modern society. Nevertheless, Acharya (1974) concludes tentatively "that microstudies are on the whole encouraging about the scope for capital labor substitution given the existing available technology."

Some additional support for the importance of correcting factor prices to increase employment is provided by isolated studies on individual countries and economic sectors. The findings of such studies do not have universal applicability, but their relevance ought to be considered in specific country contexts. Studies relating to the level of capacity utilization have pointed to the importance of night wage rates in determining multiple shift operation of machines; the widely remarked importance of adaptive technological innovation underscores the relevance of the factor prices to which innovators adapt; there is scope for labor substitution in peripheral activities in the manufacturing sector (materials handling, packaging, storage) even if the core process is insensitive to factor prices; and there is substantial engineering and economic evidence of fairly large scope for the greater use of labor-intensive techniques in construction activities.[12]

The possible benefit from the elimination of factor market distortions depends on how widely these distortions affect the economy. In countries

---

[12]See Harral et al. (1974) for a thorough investigation of the spectrum of alternative efficient techniques in civil construction.

where the modern manufacturing sector is large, the effect could be considerable. See, for example, a study of Venezuela by Tokman (1972). However, in most countries the modern manufacturing and construction sectors are relatively small. Furthermore, the consequences of the removal of price distortions on the distribution of income and the pattern of growth will depend crucially on the initial distribution of income and assets.[13]

The use of labor-intensive techniques may also be inhibited by institutional and legal measures that do not operate directly on factor prices, such as restraints on firing workers, requirements for severance pay, and the granting of import licenses for raw materials on the basis of installed machine capacity. Unless the institutional climate is more conducive to employing more labor, the removal of price distortions may not have much impact on relative factor intensities. Thus, while correcting factor prices has an important role to play in employment generation, it is far from a sufficient strategy.

Promoting Small Producers

Removing discrimination against small producers and, in selected areas, a more deliberate policy of promoting small producers can increase employment and improve the earnings of the self-employed poor. There is strong evidence that, taking manufacturing industry as a whole, capital-output ratios and capital-labor ratios are higher among large firms than small firms.[14] The evidence is less striking in studies of individual branches of manufacturing, but still broadly supports the hypothesis that smaller firms tend to use more labor-intensive techniques of production.[15]

Although we cannot support a completely general statement that small-scale units would be more effective than large-scale units in either output or employment generation with given capital stock, there are undoubtedly industries where small units are no less efficient than large units. For examples, see ILO (1973) on the Philippines. Prominently mentioned industry groups where small-scale units can be expected to be efficient in specific branches are wood and leather products, truck and bus assembly, agricultural tools, construction goods, and miscellaneous household goods. Nonetheless, it is not uncommon to see government subsidies extended to large, capital-intensive units in these industries. ILO (1973) cites a strong positive correlation between incentive benefits and the size of firm and capital intensity in the Philippines.

The promotion of small units will also lead to a more systematic exploitation of backward and forward linkages within the urban sector. A deliberate

---

[13]It is likely that the success achieved by Taiwan and Korea in using this strategy is partly explained by the relatively low concentration of asset holdings, especially in agriculture.

[14]Data relating to Japan, India, Pakistan, and Mexico are cited in Berry (1972a), Chile in Marsden (1969), Philippines in ILO (1973), and Malaysia in Suh (1974).

[15]For evidence on four industry groups covering 80 percent of industrial capacity in Karachi in 1957, see Ranis (1961); findings relating to engineering industry in Bombay, seventeen of twenty industrial branches in the United Arab Republic, and twenty-two major industrial branches in the United States are reported in Marsden (1969).

effort to increase the strength of these linkages could be the basis for an increase in the incomes of the urban poor both by increasing employment and by improving the income opportunities for the self-employed.

Production linkages between firms of different sizes were a striking feature of the economic structure in countries that industrialized in the last century. Large enterprises subcontracted work heavily and efficiently to small ones in the early stages of industrialization. The same pattern has been followed by Japan, Korea, and Taiwan. In most other recent industrializers, however, there has been a tendency towards vertical integration rather than a reliance on either subcontracting or market relationships with suppliers.

The reasons for this trend are probably the same as those that have led to vertical integration in developed economies—the desire to assure supplies and simplify management. These influences have been reinforced in developing countries by the greater regional concentration of industrial development, the greater uncertainty of obtaining supplies of intermediate inputs in import-constrained economies, the levy of cascading indirect taxes, and the sheer advantage of being large in terms of privileged access to credit, import licenses, and influential policy-makers in government. Vertical integration restricts the income-earning opportunities of the poor in two ways. First, it eliminates small entrepreneurs who, as discussed earlier, tend to use labor-intensive production techniques. Second, because of the diseconomies of scale in managing labor, vertical integration also means a heightened preference for capital-intensive means of production.

To alter this tendency, a conscious effort should be made to increase linkages between large and small production units in the urban sector. Although industrial estates for small-scale industries have not been conspicuously successful so far, they could offer a means of strengthening market relationships between large and small firms, as for instance in Hong Kong and Singapore. This should be a major criterion in planning the composition of firms in industrial estates and the location of the estates. At a broader level, what is needed is the deliberate promotion of small firms so that they can compete efficiently in supplying intermediate inputs to large firms.

Measures that are widely suggested to encourage small production units include the elimination of special incentives (such as subsidized credit, cheap foreign exchange, and licensing procedures) that favor large firms; establishment of agencies that can advise small firms on technical and managerial matters; reform of the interest-rate structure and credit allocation mechanisms; and improvement of access to scarce materials, skilled labor, and markets.

Improvement in the functioning of the capital market deserves special emphasis. Credit flows are determined by "modern" financing institutions such as commercial banks, nonbanking cooperative institutions, commercial relationships between traders, and also by the activities of moneylenders. Of these, it is probably trade credit that provides the bulk of the needs of the very small producers. This is because commercial banks have stringent collateral requirements which the poor are unable to satisfy; and membership of cooperative institutions does involve the contribution of one's own savings to a common pool that all members can draw on.[16] While credit from suppliers is thus the major means by which poor producers can supplement their own net worth to meet their capital requirements, it is obvious that the supply of trade credit is related to market conditions. When commodities are in short supply, which is frequently the case in developing countries, trade credit will also be less forthcoming. Consequently, unless collateral requirements on bank credit are relaxed, production activities will tend to be restricted to those who have sufficient wealth to meet their capital needs.

Many countries have established special institutions with the sole purpose of encouraging small-scale production units in manufacturing and have adopted at least some of the measures listed above. However, there are ample grounds for caution in designing policy packages. The observed lower capital and import intensity of the small units may be the result of the fact that they tend to face factor prices that reflect social costs. We have already remarked that small units have restricted access to and pay higher prices for capital and imports. Studies also show that they tend to pay lower wages. There is the danger (and some evidence suggests it is a real one) that if small firms are given the same access to subsidized credit and foreign exchange now enjoyed by larger firms, they will increase the capital intensity of their production. In general, therefore, the emphasis should be on the elimination of subsidies to large firms rather than the extension of the benefits to small ones.

When there is reliable evidence that small units are as efficient as large ones in their use of inputs (valued at social costs), policy should go beyond the measures listed above. Special steps could be taken to reserve scarce inputs (e.g., imported intermediate inputs and capital) for the special use of small industries. In designing these reservation mechanisms, it is necessary to ensure an adequate supply of scarce inputs and safeguard against their diversion to well-established larger users. An additional step could be the use of industrial licensing procedures to reserve appropriate branches of industrial production exclusively for small units.[17]

Although these measures have usually been debated in the context of manufacturing, they are applicable also to transport, commerce, and other service sectors. They are particularly suited to the promotion of extremely small producers and the self-employed. Tailors and carpenters need credit to buy tools and machines; hawkers need working capital for inventories; all of them need a place to do business. But they generally do not have access to credit institutions and property rentals are extremely high in central urban locations. Governments can assist them by providing special incentives to (or requiring) financing institutions to give credit to very small producers and self-employed workers; by reserving land for them in the vicinity of

---

[16]See the discussion of "chit funds" and "nidhis" in Government of India Banking Commission (1971).

[17]The identification of economic activities where small producers are at least as efficient as large ones is an important empirical task which is unfinished. For a discussion of the consequences of attempting to protect an inefficient technology, see the chapter on labor-intensive technology in Dandekar and Rath (1971).

industrial developments and in central urban locations; by assisting in the provision of cooperative marketing facilities; and by removing onerous licensing and registration requirements that have no purpose other than to restrict entry to specified occupations.

More detailed planning to increase linkages between different categories of producers requires more detailed information. Information on production relations is available in the conventional Leontief transactions matrix which, however, is not disaggregated by size of firm. Similarly, final demand for products is generally not disaggregated by type of household—whether rich or poor. Information in this disaggregated form would assist analysis of policies with respect to urban target groups, but it is not yet available. Table VII.1 presents a simple scheme which illustrates a useful basis for collecting the required data.

Table VII.1: A Schematic Transactions Tableau

Purchasing Sector	Goods			Services			Households		Government
Supplying Sector	Large scale	Small scale	Infor- mal	Large scale	Small scale	Infor- mal	Rich	Poor	
Goods:									
Large scale	X_{11}	—	—	—	—	X_{16}	H_1^1	H_1^2	G_1
Small scale	X_{21}					:	H_2^1	H_2^2	G_2
Informal	X_{31}					:	H_3^1	H_3^2	G_3
Services:									
Large scale	X_{41}					:	H_4^1	H_4^2	G_4
Small scale	X_{51}					:	H_5^1	H_5^2	G_5
Informal	X_{61}	—	—	—	—	X_{66}	H_6^1	H_6^2	G_6

This matrix serves a dual purpose. It can be used to identify the bottlenecks in increasing the supply of goods and services consumed by poor households. More importantly, the matrix would help in assessing the extent to which production units in the informal sector are linked to other producing and consuming sectors in the economy. For instance, one could measure the extent to which government purchases involve production by the informal sector and identify sectors in which remedial measures are most likely to be effective.

TRANSFER STRATEGIES

There are a number of uncertainties about how effective an employment generation strategy will be in alleviating poverty. One thing that is certain, however, is that it will take a long time to show results even under very favorable circumstances. Even assuming that the entrepreneurs react immediately and predictably to the new set of prices, changes in factor intensity of production techniques can be reflected primarily in new investment and only to a small extent with existing capital equipment. Indirect employment generation through changes in the pattern of demand and development of linkages between various production sectors will also be rather slow. It is necessary, therefore, to consider measures that will operate more directly to improve the living standards of the urban poor.

An important determinant of the real living standards of the poor is the quality of public services provided to them. Although the scope for improvement in urban public services in less developed countries is only too evident, its feasibility is severely constrained by the overall scarcity of resources and the existing imbalance between urban and rural areas in infrastructure investments. For instance, per capita expenditure on primary education in the Federal District, Mexico, is twice as high as the countryside average, and the figure for secondary education is four times as high. Hence, we do not recommend a large program to provide more urban infrastructure. However, it is necessary to restructure both public policies and public expenditures so that the poor benefit more fully in the areas of public utility services, housing, health, and education.

The poor are doubly deprived by their reduced access to the services of government-owned public utilities. Because of the fiscal constraint, local administrations provide some services (such as water, telephone, and electricity) only to those who can pay for them. Even roads are sometimes financed by valorization of properties surrounding a road construction scheme and hence are not built in poor localities. The paucity of roads in turn worsens the supply of public transport, fire and police protection, and refuse collection. The poor who have to settle outside the city limits have even less access to public services. The cost of water is twenty times as high for those in squatter settlements outside Karachi as for those who are served by piped water connections. The clear correlation between low income and poor-service areas, apparent even to the casual observer, has been documented in recent World Bank studies of cities in Peru, Zaire, and Mexico. If the costs of the provision of public services were fully recovered from the users, the distributional consequences of the imbalance in the provision of services would not be a serious matter. But for a variety of reasons, many public services are provided free or at prices below costs. Because of the nature of public expenditures, the implied subsidy probably tends to benefit the rich- and middle-income groups rather than the poor.

Health, housing, and education are major aspects of the standard of living. This is sufficient reason to argue that the poor should get a better share of public expenditures in these areas and should not be discriminated against in the formulation of policy. In addition, however, it is also likely that if the poor receive more of these services, their productivity will increase. But evidence is fragmentary, not of uniform quality, and inconclusive in some respects.

Some studies have shown that improved health will increase the ability of the poor to supply labor (through reduced absenteeism and mortality) and increase the productivity of labor (through reduced debility, increased work effort and a less fatalistic attitude toward their environment).[18] Parasitic diseases lead to an unnecessary increase in the demand for food.[19] The social rate of return to primary education has been estimated to be quite high.[20] While there is no direct evidence that better housing will improve the productivity of employed labor, the urban poor make intensive use of residential accommodation for economic purposes (e.g., tailoring, craft activities).[21] A controlled nutrition therapy program in Indonesia resulted in a 19 percent increase in labor productivity of anemics for negligible cost.[22] There is also considerable evidence that better health, education, and housing reinforce each other. Improved health enables better absorption of education. Improved housing reduces the incidence of diseases (such as tuberculosis) which spread in overcrowded and unsanitary living conditions. Improved education can result in better personal hygiene and dietary habits. Better nutrition at infancy significantly increases preschool intelligence and probably has a cumulative effect through schooling which is reflected in later income earning ability (Selowsky and Taylor, 1973).

The enormous significance of the benefits of improved housing, health, and education, which operate both in the short term and in the long term (and through generations), makes it vital that the urban poor have adequate access to public expenditures in these areas. An improvement in the distributional consequences of these expenditures requires a reassessment of priorities in each of the areas and some very hard political choices. They are discussed further in the following sections.

Health

The type of health care financed by government expenditures in developing countries is, in large part, unsuited to the needs of the poor and the manner in which it is provided usually restricts their access to its benefits and reduces their participation in the health industry.

The most striking feature of health expenditures in less developed countries is the great emphasis on curative medical care despite the prevalence of diseases whose incidence could be greatly reduced by preventive measures. The proportion of public health expenditures on preventive health care is rarely above 20 percent although there is considerable variation among countries (Table VII.2).

Most of the remainder (nearly 70 percent to 80 percent of the budget) is spent on curative care, with the primary emphasis on in-patient hospital care. While there is little hard evidence to support this assertion, it is likely that relatively few of the poor get such care. (This is definitely true when

---

[18]Feldstein, Piot, and Sunderasan (1973) and Malenbaum (1970, 1973).

[19]HEW (1972).

[20]The median of the social rates of return for fifteen LDCs estimated by Pscharopoulos (1972) is 20 percent.

[21]Twenty percent of all houses in Bogota, Colombia, are estimated to have some home-based economic activities such as retail food outlets, carpentry, tailoring, etc.; the proportion for the poor houses is estimated at 50 percent by Nelson (1973).

[22]Basta and Churchill (1974).

Table VII.2: Composition of Public Health Expenditures
(Percentage)

Country	Year	Preventive Care	Curative Care	Training & Research
India	1965/66	37.0	55.5	7.5
Sri Lanka	1957/58	23.3	74.4	2.3
Colombia	1970	18.7	79.3	2.0
Chile	1959	18.3	77.7	4.0
Venezuela	1962	18.0	76.5	5.5
Israel	1959/60	14.3	81.1	4.7
Kenya	1971	5.2	83.8	11.0
Tanzania	1970/71	4.9	80.3	4.4

Sources: Brian Abel-Smith, *Paying for Health Services, WHO Public Health Paper 17.*
Brian Abel-Smith, *An International Study of Health Expenditures, WHO Public Health Papers 32.*
India: Government of India, *Health Statistics of India,* 1965.
Iran: John Z. Bowers and Lord Rosenheim, *Migration of Medical Manpower,* p. 92.
Colombia: *Economic Growth of Colombia,* Vol. IX, (IBRD), p. 11.
Kenya: Ministry of Health, *Recurrent and Development Budget, 1971-72.*
Panama: A.I.D. *Syncrisis: The Dynamics of Health,* Vol. I, U.S. Dept. of H.E.W.
Tanzania: Malcolm Segal, "The Politics of Health in Tanzania", *Development and Change,* IV, No. 1 (1972-1973), pp. 37-50.

hospitals are run by social security organizations exclusively for their members; where special hospitals are established for the poor, the quality of care is relatively low.) Furthermore, hospitals and clinics tend to be used only by those in the immediate vicinity. The relatively low emphasis on the dispersal of clinics with out-patient facilities (or mobile clinics) suggests that the poor have less access to publicly provided health facilities, particularly those who live on the outer fringes of the cities (or in rural areas).

There is a long list of diseases to which the poor are particularly prone and which can be prevented by the better provision of environmental sanitation projects, piped water, and insecticides.[23] There are also a number of diseases susceptible to control by mass immunization campaigns.[24] The diversion of public resources to hospitals that provide high quality care for relatively few people rather than environmental sanitation and mass immunization is a costly social waste at the expense of the poor. One consequence is shown by a study in Morocco which estimates that the costs of saving a life average $2,500 in general hospitals but only $40 with mass vaccination programs (Barlow, in press).

This antipoor bias in health care also shows itself in the way medical personnel are trained. The shortages of paramedical and auxiliary personnel, who could be used to spread health care more equitably, is frequently more

---

[23]Malaria, typhoid, bilharzia, typhus, hookworm, cholera, plague, dysentery, onchocerciasis, dengue, schistosomiasis, and filaria.

[24]Smallpox, diphtheria, polio, tetanus, measles, cholera, and onchocerciasis.

severe than the shortage of doctors in developing countries. There is also a reluctance to introduce modern medical practice to other schools of medicine (e.g., homeopaths, ayurvedics, and other traditional systems) which vary in effectiveness but are nonetheless trusted, frequently preferred, and more accessible to the poor.

In summary, health policy in developing countries should reverse existing priorities—placing greatest emphasis on environmental sanitation, followed by mass immunization, out-patient care in clinics, and quantity oriented hospital care. There should also be a big expansion in the number of paramedics and auxiliary personnel trained to augment health services for the poor and a reduction of subsidized programs to produce highly qualified doctors.

Housing

The horrifying conditions in which vast numbers of the urban poor live are so widely known that they do not require elaboration.[25] Poor housing conditions, like poor diet and poor clothing, are only a manifestation of the poverty of the poor. It is worth remarking, however, that the poor who live in city slums are perhaps better off (in terms of infrastructure and public services) than the bulk of the poor who live on the outskirts of the cities. Indeed, many of those who live on city streets in Asia own shacks on the periphery of the city but cannot afford the cost of daily transportation to their work in the city. There are one million people who live on a dry salt lake bed on the outskirts of Mexico City, and who face frequent flooding, typhoid in the wet season, and bronchial pneumonia in the dusty dry season (Fox, 1972).

The acute lack of physical access to work sites at reasonable transport cost is a problem of the urban poor that can be solved at relatively low cost in real resources, although it does involve politically difficult policies. Segregated zoning policies tend to keep poor residential areas away from commercial areas and rich residential areas where the poor may find work. Most poor walk to work; some cycle or take public transport if available. A study in Kinshasa showed that some of the poor have to commute to work about two hours each way. This implies a considerable loss of energy and foregone earnings, both of which are especially serious when they afflict the poor: the former because the poor are unable to afford an adequately nutritive diet,[26] the latter because the poor are peculiarly dependent on casual labor, hourly paid work, and moonlighting (either for work or for education). The additional commuting time, therefore, tends to represent a substitution from alternative occupations rather than from leisure.

Government attempts to improve the housing conditions of the poor have not been generally effective for two main reasons. First, public housing projects rarely reach the poor. Second, there can be no serious housing policy

---

[25]A World Bank survey of principal cities in forty developing countries showed that more than half of their population lived in slums and uncontrolled settlements in seventeen of the cities; only twelve cities had less than a third of the population living in these conditions.

[26]When first priority is given to the food needs of the income earner, the result is malnutrition of infants which has long-term consequences on their income-earning ability.

for the poor without a bold land policy, and such a land policy faces grave political obstacles.

Experience with public housing projects has shown that they rarely reach even the poorest 40 percent (and very rarely the poorest 20 percent) of the population. This has partly been due to the reluctance to design cheap houses. Factors that have tended to perpetuate this situation are housing standards that are well beyond the reach of the poor, plus pressures from builders and local groups in government to meet demands of middle-income groups, and housing finance institutions that lend only on credit-worthiness criteria that exclude the poor. Even site and service projects have tended not to reach the poor because of the high price of the sites. An alternative approach effectively tried in some countries has been to improve water, sewerage, road, medical, and social services to existing squatter settlements. While this approach avoids the problems of housing design and land cost, and deals with the very real problem of inadequate public services, it does not solve the problem of physical access to work sites.[27]

A comprehensive attempt to solve the housing problem of the poor is not possible without a forceful policy of acquiring land for public use. The scarcity of centrally located urban land is the single most critical factor restricting the ability of the poor to acquire adequate shelter with reasonable access to employment. The cost of land is frequently up to 50 percent of housing costs in developing countries.[28]

Private rights of land ownership are deeply embedded in the legal systems of developing countries and are not completely eliminated even in centrally planned economies. There is, of course, an established tradition of public ownership of land in the British and French tradition which has been passed on in the colonization process; there is also a tradition of communal ownership of land in Africa. However, governments in developing countries now tend to own only small parts of urban land[29] and find it extraordinarily difficult to acquire more.

There are many legal obstacles to public acquisition of land: a requirement to pay "fair compensation" to the owner, based on the land's current market value but which is beyond the fiscal capacities of governments to pay; legal restrictions on the uses for which land might be acquired, which do not always include the construction of housing; long delays while legal battles are fought over tiny parcels of land without which the project cannot proceed.

The outright large-scale nationalization of land has sometimes been suggested as a necessary part of the solution. There is much to recommend this view considering that urban landowners are reaping a scarcity rent arising out of public investment and growing urban concentration to which they

---

[27]Unfortunately, this approach has been shunned by international aid agencies until very recently.

[28]This proportion varies a great deal with the location of the land, the type of housing, the cost of building materials, and the wage level of construction workers.

[29]A notable exception is Hong Kong, which owns all the land and leases the right of use at periodic public auctions.

contribute little. But there has not so far been any city where this solution has been successfully applied.

The political and economic obstacles to the nationalization of urban land necessitate the adoption of a variety of measures to improve land use policies for the benefit of the urban poor. Growing cities, especially new ones, can legislate a governmental monopoly on the acquisition of land on the urban fringes.[30] Without abridging private property rights, it is possible to prohibit the payment of compensation for land value appreciation resulting from publicly financed developments. Governments may also acquire preemptive rights of purchase at appraised prices which are linked to the values declared for tax assessments.

While all these measures will undoubtedly assist the public acquisition of land, they are unlikely to provide adequate centrally located land to make a significant difference in the housing and commercial facilities for the urban poor. The prognosis for a satisfactory land policy within the existing legal framework in most cities has to be gloomy. The fact remains, however, that without such a land policy, there is no possibility of a comprehensive solution to the housing problem of the urban poor. Nevertheless, a variety of second-best solutions should be pursued with vigor. These include the provision of public services to existing squatter settlements, cheap transportation for the poor to places of work, and land-use policies that will place poor residential areas close to opportunities for employment in growing cities.

Education

The potential role of education in reducing the unequal distribution of income has already been discussed in Chapter IV. While there are considerable doubts about the general validity of the "human capital" model in analyzing the benefits of education, there is ample evidence that the poor also tend to be less well educated. Without necessarily accepting a causal connection between education and income levels, it is worth examining whether education policy in less developed countries can be modified so as to make public expenditures on education (estimated at nearly 4 percent of GNP on average) more directly beneficial to the poor.

A striking feature of education policy in less developed countries is the very great emphasis on secondary and higher education compared with developed countries. These countries' governments allocate a higher proportion of their expenditures to university education, where they have a smaller proportion of students than developed countries. The annual per student expenditures on secondary and higher education, expressed as ratios to the expenditures per student at the primary level, are much higher in developing than developed countries. (See Table VII.3.)

But students from a poor background account for a much higher proportion of primary students than of university students. There is little empirical evidence on this subject but the available data for Tunisia (see Table

---

[30]Land so acquired could then be auctioned to finance the required compensation payments for the acquisition of centrally located land.

VII.4) and for Colombia (reported in Jallade, 1974) are likely to be quite typical of many less developed countries.

The pattern of allocation of education expenditures is thus strongly discriminatory against the poor. The relatively high public subsidy of university education directly benefits the middle- and upper-income groups. The smallness of the share of total education expenditures that is directed to primary education directly affects the poor. The insufficient spread of schools in rural areas is responsible for the poor educational level of migrants who probably form a large proportion of the urban poor (especially in Africa). The lack of financial resources also affects the quality of primary education, rendering it less effective in preparing the student for a productive economic role. Bhagwati (1973) argues that the costs of education are also greater for the poor even at the primary level if one allows for the opportunity cost of labor and the higher cost of capital. These factors are reflected in the high dropout rates of students at even the primary levels in less developed countries.

Table VII.3: Index of Recurrent Expenditures per Pupil
(Primary level expenditure = 1.0)

	2nd level		3rd level	
	Median	Range	Median	Range
More advanced countries	1.7	(1.03- 3.1)	5.7	(2.1- 9.8)
Less developed countries	3.5	(1.04-12.2)	18.6	(7.2-155.6)

Source: Joan Maruhnic (1973).

Table VII.4: Socio-Economic Status of Students' Fathers in Tunisia (1970)
(percentage of students with fathers in each category)

Socio-economic Status	Primary (1)	Secondary (2)	Higher (3)	Ratio (3)/(1)
High 1	1.2	5.9	10.5	8.8
2	26.5	40.0	26.2	1.0
3	12.7	20.8	17.6	1.4
Low 4	43.5	17.3	11.9	0.3
Other	16.1	16.0	33.0	2.0
Total	100.0	100.0	100.0	
Students (thousands)	113.9	7.8	0.6	

Status: High 1: Highest white collar, professions, heads of firms and employees
        Category A.
      2: Employees Categories B and C, businessmen and skilled workers.
      3: Foremen, semiskilled, or unskilled industrial workers.
    Low 4: Agricultural laborer and nonindustrial unskilled workers.
    Other : Retired, without occupation, and father dead.

Source: Compiled by John Simmons using data from Ministère de l'Education Nationale, Bureau de Planification, Tunis.

The reduced access of the poor to educational opportunities has exceptionally serious consequences when educational qualifications are required as credentials for employment even when they have no relevance to the execution of the job. Arbitrary barriers, which are simply a reflection of the distribution of power in society, are used by the middle- and upper-income groups to reserve scarce jobs in a labor abundant economy. It is noteworthy that governments are themselves major employers in less developed countries and are at least as prone to these practices as private employers.[31] The elimination of these arbitrary barriers would reduce socially wasteful investments in irrelevant formal education and improve the access of the poor to jobs.

A second major step that is needed is to make education more relevant to the needs of the poor by expanding the opportunities for training in skills. Experience in providing training in formal vocational schools has not been generally satisfactory.[32] There are many reasons for this, the most important reason being the inability to predict the needs of the labor market and to respond flexibly to changing demands for skills.

One way to remedy the lack of relationship between trainers and employers that handicap formal vocational schools is to have employers provide training. Self-interest would ensure that the training developed skills that the employer needed and the trainees would either already have or be guaranteed a job. It is necessary, however, not to make the training so narrow that the worker loses mobility or is unable to cope with changing job requirements. Extension of these in-plant training opportunities can be encouraged by tax incentives (which have been successfully tried in Latin America) and by providing teachers and teaching facilities.

By upgrading labor skills, these measures could increase the profitability of labor-intensive techniques and lead to the substitution of skills for capital, especially in the manufacturing sector. The impact on the urban poor could be significant in countries at a relatively advanced stage of industrialization.

In countries where the poor tend to work in very small enterprises rather than in the modern sector, special organizational innovations would be necessary to expand nonformal training schemes. The establishment of training cooperatives and government subsidization of programs operated by trade associations should be considered.

In the final analysis, it should be recognized that education, like health and housing, is an important determinant of the quality of life and should not be regarded only as a means of increasing economic productivity. Putting more resources into primary and nonformal education and making higher education more accessible to the poor through the introduction of generous loan schemes are two ways in which the poor can get more education. Eliminating irrelevant entry requirements in the labor market will help

---

[31]For example, see Blaug, Layard, and Woodhall (1969) on minimum requirements for government hiring in India.
[32]See Zymelmann (1973) for a discussion of the issues.

ensure that the poor have equal access to the job market, even if they have not had equal access to education.

CONCLUSIONS

The complexity of the problem of urban poverty, the great diversity in the levels of urbanization in different countries and the almost total lack of precise information about the economic characteristics of the urban poor are good reasons to view the generalizations in this chapter more as hypotheses than settled conclusions. Perhaps the main conclusion is that we need to do a great deal more to subject the numerous hypotheses in this area to vigorous empirical testing. We need to learn more about why people flock to cities, how the unskilled poor behave in imperfect urban labor markets, what constrains the growth of informal production units, which industrial branches can be efficiently reserved for the small-scale sector, to what extent the poor benefit from public services, and many other questions. A primary require-ment to shed more light on these subjects is the execution of systematic surveys aimed directly at the informal household production activities in the urban sector.

Although we have been unable to provide more than some tentative gen-eralizations about who constitute the urban poor, it is clear that the group is rapidly growing because of the high natural rate of population increase in less developed countries and a rapid process of urbanization. It is also clear that government policies are partly responsible for the condition of the poor by restricting their access to the benefits of public services and by biasing the economic environment in favor of large-scale producers. The chap-ter has focused on possible corrective measures in these policy areas. The principal recommendations concern: (i) correcting factor-price distortions and adopting other measures to increase wage employment and encourage small entrepreneurs; (ii) the provision of better facilities to the poor both for housing and productive enterprise based on a bolder policy for land acqui-sition and a new approach to the provision of public services to squatters; and (iii) the reorientation of priorities in health and education to ensure a more equitable distribution of benefits from public expenditures.

Implementation of these recommendations will no doubt be stoutly resisted by large industrialists who will resent the loss of subsidies and privileges; by urban real estate investors who will resent encroachment on the private right to own land; and by the middle-income groups who are probably the principal beneficiaries today of public utility, transport, health, and education facilities. An attempt to provide more services to the poor without reducing services to the not-so-poor will only accentuate the existing urban/rural imbalance in the provision of these services and is probably beyond the fiscal capacity of most governments.

Even if all these recommendations are successfully implemented, the urban poverty problem will be far from fully solved in most countries. We have noted that the increased employment resulting from these measures can be of significant magnitude only in those countries that have a major portion of the labor force employed in the modern manufacturing or construction sector. Second, fiscal and political constraints will restrict the extent to which the poor can be provided with better housing or other facilities. Finally, success in ameliorating the condition of the urban poor may well result in a growth in their numbers resulting from in-migration.

We have also noted the dominant importance of rural development in restraining migration, increasing the supply of wage goods and the demand for urban manufactures. Finally, it is worth reemphasizing that rural and urban development strategies must be jointly conceived and executed. This applies to the allocation of infrastructure investment; the design of health and education policies; and the development of small towns which could serve as market towns for the rural hinterland, as growth poles for manufacturing industry offering off-season employment and wider access to urban facilities.

Chapter VIII
INTERNATIONAL DIMENSIONS
RICHARD JOLLY

MOST OF this volume is about inequality *within* countries and the need for policies combining redistribution with growth to deal with it. Such policies within countries cannot be separated in theory or in practice either from international inequality between countries or from national and international policies designed to tackle such inequality.

These international policies must not be thought of as simply adding positive elements to an otherwise unaffected situation. To many observers the starting point is almost exactly the inverse—a situation in which the economic wealth, power, and interests of the rich countries interact with key groups and interests within the Third World to become a major obstacle to the adoption of redistributive policies.

As this is being written, in early 1974, difficulties in the international arena are compounded by major changes in the world trading system introduced by sharp and unprecedented increases in world oil prices. It is too early to assess the full repercussions of these events, though almost certainly their net effect will be to inhibit growth within the oil-importing countries and to make more difficult the adoption of redistributive policies by them.

Nevertheless, there are still some small grounds for optimism, primarily because there are many areas in which both rich and poor countries could gain from a mutual adoption of certain policies and, ironically perhaps, because the major changes in the world economy wrought by the oil-producing countries have revealed how much redistribution between countries is possible if potential bargaining power is pressed much more strongly than in the past. The scope for the exploitation of such bargaining power in other areas at the moment appears to be strictly limited—but in the longer run could grow and lead to significant concessions, if only because an orderly measure of redistribution is likely to be preferred to disruption.[1] What is required in the years ahead is the extension of this process by international agreements and through developmental institutions. Constraints that hinder countries from adopting and pursuing redistributive policies domestically may in these ways be reduced.

This chapter attempts to explore such policies, starting with a summary of the present dimensions of inequality among countries. The analysis of international factors is then considered for policy in three crucial areas: international trade, technology and private investment, and international agencies and development assistance. Primary emphasis is on what the

I am grateful for helpful comments from Robert Cassen, Michael Lipton, Hans Singer and Dudley Seers.

[1]During the 1960s, independence brought some redistribution of political power to many countries, just as nationalization of key industries brought a measure of formal, if often not effective, control.

rich countries and international agencies could do. As far as possible, highlights fall on issues and policies which could seriously be put on the agenda for international discussion within the short and medium run. But changes which at present seem likely to be acceptable only in the long run are also mentioned at several points. The extent of world inequality and poverty is too serious and persistent a problem for adequate remedies to be found only within the range of currently realistic debate.

THE DIMENSIONS OF INTERNATIONAL INEQUALITY

The poorest 10 percent of the world's population in 1962/63 accounted for less than 2 percent of world consumption, whereas the top 10 percent enjoyed 35 percent. The bottom 30 percent of the world's population consumed only about 10 percent of world consumption.[2]

As elsewhere in this volume, we must begin with a warning that the statistical data on which such quantifications of inequality rest are extremely inadequate. Nevertheless, what data there are on economic inequality between countries prompt three suggestions. (i) Both absolute and relative differences in per capita income between rich and poor countries have been steadily growing over recent decades, especially between the very poorest (and largest) and most other groups of countries.[3] Judged against the sweep of history, present world inequalities in income (and wealth) are recent and unprecedented.[4] (ii) The international size distribution of income and real consumption per capita between countries at present is more unequal than that within the majority of countries, developed or developing. Measured by Gini coefficients, the international size distribution of income is comparable to the size distribution of income within countries of *high* inequality.[5] (iii) These differences in incomes and real consumption, though more loosely linked to differences in human welfare and the incidence of poverty, are closely correlated with differences in the use of world resources and with differences in the economic and political power of different countries.

The enormous gap between the rich and poor countries of the world should not disguise widening gaps between different parts of the Third World. Latin America is both richer and, since 1950, has (with East Asia) been pulling ahead faster in aggregate terms than Africa and South Asia. Within all these areas major differences exist between countries.

---

[2]Beckerman and Bacon (1970), p. 62.

[3]Kuznets (1972).

[4]Patel (1964).

[5]The estimated Gini coefficient for world distribution of consumption was about 0.57, virtually identical in 1954/55 and 1962/63, and broadly comparable to the Gini coefficients of the 16 low- or middle-income countries of high inequality. See Table I.1 and Beckerman and Bacon (1970). Andic and Peacock (1961) produced broadly comparable estimates for the period 1949 to 1957. Note that these estimates are all calculated on the assumption that within each Third World country incomes are equally distributed. The estimates must accordingly be treated as orders of magnitude, with the bias that they *overstate* the share of the poorest group in the world economy.

More significant are the differences between the group of countries which appear to have institutionalized rapid growth and those which have not. The former includes countries from the poorest to those of middle-income levels and encompasses a reasonable proportion of the population of the middle-income and poor country groups shown in Table VIII.1. This group would include, for example, Kenya, Korea, Israel, Mexico, and Turkey, with the recent addition of those oil-producing countries likely to benefit greatly from rises in oil prices. Poverty and income inequality remain serious in many of these countries, but the challenge is to adopt redistributive measures and to make changes in the structure of growth without losing the momentum achieved in many sectors.

Table VIII.1: Population and Output: Levels and Growth Rates 1960-70
(Averages of countries grouped by level of average income)

| Country Group | Gross National Product (constant 1970 prices) | | | | Population | |
| | 1970 | | 1960-70 Growth Rate | | 1970 | 1960-70 |
	Per Capita ($)	Total ($ bil.)	Per Capita (% p.a.)	Total	Total (mil.)	Growth Rate (% p.a.)
Rich	2,790	2,570	4.4	5.5	920	1.1
Middle-Income	870	270	4.5	6.5	310	2.0
Poor	300	155	3.2	6.0	520	2.8
Very Poor	120	230	1.8	4.0	1,930	2.2
Total	880	3,225	4.1	6.1	3,680	2.0

Source: Calculated from *World Bank Atlas, 1972,* pp. 227-36.

More difficult are the problems of those countries, also at a variety of income levels, in which poverty and inequality are serious but in which the adoption of measures of adjustment and structural change is made more difficult by their failure over the last decade or two to achieve more than slow or negligible growth. Within this group, and perhaps most difficult of all, are those very poor countries of the world's population in which poverty for many of their population is extreme and for which little momentum of growth has been achieved. Many of the countries classified by the United Nations as *least developed* would be included as well as others, like Bangladesh, in which land scarcity and a moderately egalitarian pattern of land distribution provide much less freedom of maneuver. In total, this group would include nearly half of the population of very poor countries and nearly one-third of the population of the Third World. The very poor countries had per capita incomes under $130 in 1970 and as a group experienced over the 1960s growth rates of less than 2 percent per capita, under half the world average. These comparisons are all in terms of income-weighted growth rates. As Table II.1 showed, the income growth rates among the poorest 40 percent within each country have frequently been lower.

One implication for policy is that strategies of redistribution with growth in most of the really poor countries must give as much attention to accelerating growth as they give to measures of redistribution. This is a particularly important conclusion for eradicating world poverty, since the poorest countries contain over half of the world's total population and over two-thirds that of developing countries.

In terms of international policy, several important conclusions can be drawn from the existence of this extreme inequality between countries in income and consumption. First, as will be elaborated later, this extensive inequality *between* countries appears in several respects as a major *cause* of inequality *within* countries and a major constraint on the domestic adoption of policies of redistribution with growth. The repercussions of world inequality are transmitted particularly in the areas of technology; economic, political, and military power; and trading, investment, and monetary relationships.

Second, strategies of redistribution with growth within individual countries will by themselves do little to diminish world inequality. Virtually every projection of the next decade or two, if not longer, suggests that the absolute gap between incomes in most of the poorest countries[6] and most of those in all other groups of countries is likely to continue to increase.[7] If, therefore, the constraints imposed by inequality between countries on the adoption of redistribution with growth strategies *within* Third World countries are to be diminished, deliberate policies will be required, some beyond those at present seriously contemplated anywhere.

Finally, over the long run, international inequality on the present scale will itself almost certainly become a target for reform. At present, such talk still appears idealistic or nonsensical, though environmental concerns and competitive pressures for resources have already begun to make it respectable, at least as a topic for popular discussion. But long before the gaps have reached the levels projected for the year 2000, we can expect serious work—if not serious remedial action—on what should be done about it.

BACKGROUND TO INTERNATIONAL POLICY

The immediate need is to identify measures to deal with those aspects of world inequality, particularly rich country actions and policy, which set constraints on the adoption of redistributive policies within Third World countries. These measures must touch on the main economic interactions

---

[6]Except those with substantial oil exports such as Nigeria and Indonesia. The need to make major changes to accelerate growth in the oil-consuming poor countries is all the greater, given the pessimistic prospects indicated by projections made even before the increases in oil prices had their full effect. World Bank projections in November 1973 estimated that average growth of GDP in non-oil-producing countries would be nearly 6 percent or more for developing countries of medium or high per capita income. In contrast, for the countries of per capita income below $200 in 1973 projected growth during the period 1973-78 is only just over 4 percent, or about 1.5 percent per annum per capita. See World Bank (1973b).

[7]Strategies of redistribution with growth within countries could easily widen some of the intercountry gaps further, to the extent that growth rates increase relatively more in the richer than in the poorer countries.

in the areas of trade, technology, private investment, capital aid, and technical assistance. Moreover, there are interactions in the areas of diplomatic and military activities. There is the more tenuous but important range of economic, social, and cultural influences, for instance, on consumption patterns, emanating from the rich countries and spreading throughout the world.

Whenever possible, international measures should focus in support of the four thrusts of domestic policy, which, as shown in Chapter II, are all usually involved in a strategy combining redistribution with growth: (i) accelerating GNP growth, (ii) transfer of existing assets, (iii) creation of new assets and redirection of investment in favor of the poor, (iv) transfer of income in the form of direct support of consumption of the poorest groups.

Some further changes are mentioned here under the headings of trade, technology transfer and private overseas investment, and development assistance and international policy. Before turning to these, three general points should be mentioned.

First, the impact on world poverty of any international measure of policy or new development depends on *which* countries are affected, as well as on which *groups* within each country. In both respects, a conscious concern for the distributional impact of the development process and of changes in policy under consideration is required. It is still common in discussion of international economic policy to concentrate on the costs and benefits to different countries with little concern for the differential impact on countries of different levels of income. What is now needed is both concern for which countries are affected and concern for the differential impact on different income groups within countries. In terms of policy, a major decision will be whether to choose policies which benefit more the poorer countries or countries the overall strategy of which is more clearly directed at improving the welfare of the poorest.

Second, the types of policies thought necessary will be heavily influenced by the viewpoint — or paradigm[8] — within which interactions are analyzed. In the world of international economic analysis three major paradigms exist at present: the neoclassical, the structuralist, and the dominance/dependence.[9] In essence, *neoclassicists* stress the gains from trade (usually within a static framework) to both parties and hence the payoffs to removing barriers to trade, though they concede that the resulting intercountry and intracountry distributive consequences are not always desirable. *Structuralists,* who are essentially eclectic, emphasize structural rigidities in the economic systems which set limits on the scope and speed of adjustment through changes in prices. Recently, struc-

---

[8]For more on paradigms, see Kuhn (1962).

[9]Every man has his own examples of archetypes, perhaps archangels or archdevils. Mine in the area of international economics would include: neoclassicals Harry G. Johnson and Jagdish Bhagwati; structuralists Hollis Chenery, Gunnar Myrdal, and Dudley Seers; dominance/dependence analysts Paul Baran and Gunder Frank.

turalists have put greater emphasis on differences in bargaining power which stem from differences in wealth, income, and technological capacity; their policy prescriptions tend to be strongly "interventionist" but ad hoc. *Dependence* theorists see the world system as providing for the systematic exploitation of poor countries by rich ones, so that development can proceed only under a regime of almost total autarky—economic, political, and military, but especially in relation to private investment and assistance.

Such frameworks of belief exert widespread and serious influences on policy-making and action. Policy choices touching on income distribution and poverty are particularly sensitive to them. In these areas of policy, values and ideologies are close to the surface. Additionally, most issues of international policy have so many ramifications that it is impossible to trace every consequence of each policy alternative under review given present knowledge and data. Even if it were possible, time would scarcely permit it. Thus most policy-makers, consciously or unconsciously, make use of these or other paradigms to simplify and order the facts and issues if not, as too often, to prejudge them.

Finally, one needs to distinguish "zero-sum game" situations—where each party can gain only to the extent that another party loses—from those in which a change can bring gains to both parties. The first raise real conflicts of interest; shifts in bargaining strength may be a precondition for action. The second offer scope for cooperative activity, though redistributive measures must be combined with them to make them acceptable (see Chapter III). For example, it has long been argued that more liberalization in international trade would bring benefits to all countries involved. Part of the reason why such policies are opposed is that the repercussions on distribution within countries would be prejudicial to some groups who are well organized. If these policies are combined with distributional measures, such opposition can sometimes be reduced.

INTERNATIONAL TRADE

The volume and terms on which international trade is conducted between countries exert at any point in time incomparably the largest influence on the flows of income *between* countries. In 1972, total export earnings of the developing countries were about $74 billion, roughly eight times the flow of net development assistance or net private long-term capital. Moreover, in the last few years, export earnings have been rising rapidly over a period in which aid inflows have in real terms been falling and inflows of direct foreign investment have been more than offset in the aggregate by outflows of income on accumulated past investments.[10]

The importance of the terms of trade for redistributing incomes among trading partners has been dramatically made clear by the recent and

---

[10]See section on private overseas investment below.

unprecedented increases in oil prices—which by the beginning of 1974 reached levels 4.5 times those of twelve months earlier and 6.5 times those of 1970.[11] In a situation still so fluid, it is impossible to assess future trends in prices or even the full implications on the balance of payments of present levels. But as an order of magnitude, the changes in oil prices by January 1974 were estimated to transfer over the following twelve months an additional $65 billion to the oil-producing countries. Roughly $55 billion of this sum would come from oil-importing industrialized countries and some $10 billion from Third World countries. Whatever the final result of this adjustment process, this shows the crucial importance of the terms of trade for changing income distribution among countries, a point of general significance to which we return later.

Moreover, changes of this magnitude in world economic relationships will have major effects on the ability of countries to pursue policies combining growth with redistribution. One can indicate the main problems very briefly even if quantitative estimates must remain speculative.[12]

The immediate effects on the oil-producing countries are the easiest to assess. Clearly they will benefit dramatically, and to such a degree that in most of them there will be ample resources for their domestic poverty-focused programs, whatever other claims may be pressed.[13] Hopefully, the potential for improving the position of the poorest, citizen and non-citizen, in these countries will be taken. Nevertheless, however desirable these changes may be in themselves, in terms of relieving world poverty, the direct impact will be limited to countries totaling some 70 million of population in the Middle East and some 200 million more in Nigeria, Indonesia, and Venezuela. Many of the oil-producing countries already have a range of welfare state services built on their very high per capita incomes, and those which have not may already be receiving oil revenues near the limits of what can be absorbed by poverty-focused activities, given the present supply of skilled manpower and the present administrative structure.

As regards the impact on the oil-importing countries, by far the majority of the Third World, a crucial question concerns the impact of higher oil prices (and reductions in supply) on the level of economic activity in

[11]World Bank estimates, January 14, 1974.

[12]To the extent that we use numbers, they are crude estimates based on oil prices of January 1974, designed to provide orders of magnitude of what might be involved, but not to imply that we have any reason to think present levels of prices will remain unchanged.

[13]Two decades ago, the risk of other claims preempting oil revenues at the direct expense of the poor was greater. "If these sums, plus what can properly be borrowed against future income, are spent on scientific agricultural development, industrialization, communications, and education, health and other social services, it may be possible to bring the living standard of the Arabs up to a level approaching that of Western countries within a generation. On the other hand, if the oil royalties are used principally for the importation of private motor cars and other luxuries by a few wealthy merchants, government officials and landowners, and if the wages of the oil company employees are spent on commodities from abroad which ought to be produced locally, the newly discovered wealth will contribute little to the economic well-being of the vast bulk of the people of the Middle East." Mikesell and Chenery (1949), p. 84.

the industrialized countries. With effective international action to provide means for financing the additional costs of oil imports and for avoiding internal deflation and a round of beggar-my-neighbor policies, the level of world economic activity may only be moderately reduced for a limited period. Without such action, a major world deflation could follow. Given the phenomenal size of the additional oil bill, the range of possibilities is very large. It is difficult to believe that some reduction in world economic growth can altogether be avoided.

Export prospects and foreign exchange receipts (from trade, private investment, and aid) in most Third World countries will be heavily influenced by this outcome, particularly Third World exports which are sensitive to the level of investment activity in the industrialized countries. But they will also be heavily influenced by the second-round effects: the extent to which higher prices of petroleum-based synthetics switch back demand to Third World exports of natural products. For some Third World countries, the net effect on both the volume and price of their major exports could be highly favorable. But for the majority it seems likely that on balance export prospects will suffer, and there will be a general tightening of the foreign exchange constraint in many of them, at least in the next few years.

How any particular Third World country is affected will thus depend on (a) how these direct and second-round effects in the world economy affect its export prospects, in price and volume; (b) the extent of its oil imports and dependence on oil products; and (c) its capacity to bear additional foreign exchange costs from other foreign exchange receipts or reserves. This amalgam of effects seems likely to be very unevenly distributed among Third World countries, though several of the poorest—India, Bangladesh, and Sri Lanka in particular—seem likely to be hit the hardest. Even if short-term remedies can be found, the long-run impact could be disastrous, precisely because they are among the poorest group of countries in which growth as well as distribution is so necessary and which will be most severely constrained by a continuing shortage of foreign exchange. Although it seems unlikely that many other countries will be hit as hard as these, most seem likely to lose in one way or another, either by the indirect effects on the level of world activity or in other ways.

The other crucial factor is the magnitude and direction of capital flows. However rapidly expenditures build up within the oil-producing countries, for several years there will almost certainly be considerable surpluses, channeled to other countries as financial investments, loans, or grants. Traditionally the major part of these has flowed as investments to the industrialized countries and it seems likely that much of this will continue. Nevertheless, there could be advantages if an increasing share was directed into Third World investments. The Third World countries could gain by this augmentation of capital inflow from new sources, particularly if some of it were on concessional terms. The oil-producing countries could benefit, not merely by a diversification of their assets but by a judicious choice of the countries and industries in which they invest.

Two obvious areas of joint investment suggest themselves in which substantial gains could be reaped both by oil-producing countries and by Third World countries. First, oil-producing countries could supply capital and feedstock for the development of petrochemical industries in, and geared to, large Third World markets (e.g., fertilizer). Second, joint ventures could be started to develop capital goods production in the Third World. At present, developed countries enjoy a virtual monopoly in the supply of capital goods, and the development of Third World capacity in this area is long overdue. The oil-rich countries would benefit since their demand for capital goods is likely to expand, given additional investment resources. More generally, production of capital goods in the Third World is essential for the development of the right kind of technology.

The advanced countries would not lose from this redirection of investable funds. The underlying asymmetry in world trading relationships is such that the rich countries would also benefit in demand for their exports, even if a sizeable fraction of the original surplus was directed to the Third World. In effect, the rich countries would be gaining in export trade much of what they would lose in import cost and direct inflows of capital and, over the longer run, possibly much more.

If the oil producers channeled even a quarter of their total additional oil revenues to other Third World countries this would not merely compensate entirely for the additional cost of oil imports but, in addition, would transfer financial assistance equivalent to half the existing annual net flow of official aid.

These are enormous magnitudes. Their significance is not simply that they show the very large transfers which could take place if only those with the resources were willing. After all, this has always been true with aid from the industrialized countries, had they been willing to transfer more than a fraction of a percentage of their national income.

The real significance of these very large sums is that they show how much additional revenue might be transferred from the rich countries to the Third World as a group, if only (a) potential monopolistic power is used more fully, and (b) mechanisms are developed, bilateral or multilateral, on a regional or continental basis, enabling a substantial part of the additional resources to flow to the Third World (whether in trade, aid, or investment) and not simply to flow directly to the rich countries in a form which benefits the Third World little if at all.[14]

The two crucial conditions for success are some degree of Third World solidarity and acquiescence, willing or reluctant, from the rich countries. Complete Third World solidarity is not required, and it may sometimes be possible to buy it where it does not exist. At present oil prices, as shown

---

[14]Moreover, some of the richer oil-producing countries have already been allocating substantial sums in assistance to poorer countries. A recent estimate for Kuwait, for example, suggests that grants and loans to Third World countries have recently exceeded 10 percent of GNP.

above, $10 billion is sufficient to compensate all Third World importers for assisting the oil-producing countries to gain an additional $65 billion. Economically, it is a bargain — though whether it is politically or administratively possible even for groups of countries remains to be seen.

Will the rich countries acquiesce? This also is difficult to assess. There are obvious risks of retaliatory price increases and embargoes, to say nothing of heavy political influence, manipulation, and military intervention. In the medium run, there are also possibilities of producing known technological substitutes, as well as searching for and developing others yet unknown.

Whatever happens, the world of economic relationships will never be quite the same again. The potential for bargaining in other areas has been dramatically revealed, no doubt to an extent and at a speed which is unlikely to be matched again. But bargaining to much greater degrees is possible in other areas, if only bargaining strength is developed and exploited. Such possibilities include: (i) monopolistic price increases for other primary commodities, (ii) strict embargoes on export of strategic materials, and (iii) restriction of overflying rights or use of military bases.

Such proposals and others similar have been suggested before. But the experience of oil price increases suggests new potential in them, if ways can be found to win more widespread Third World support.

In the longer run, the world as a whole, rich countries and poor, could tire of the instability stimulated by such actions and support moves towards a more rational world system, involving orderly financial transfers within, for example, some form of world income tax. More fundamentally, the whole structure of world production could be rationalized within the world economy, accelerating industrial development within the poorer countries and enabling them to obtain, by agreement or takeover, a larger share of the benefits.[15]

Immediate and obvious difficulties at present arise with all such developments which make them appear visionary and unrealistic. At the same time, interdependence within the world economy increases steadily, in ways which make the need for coordinated action more necessary and cooperative action mutually beneficial. Recent oil developments are merely one example. Arms and pollution control, supplies of basic commodities, world monetary management, and control of multinational corporations are others for achieving gains by the poorer countries through the exploitation of mutual advantages, no doubt requiring tougher bargaining, but for mutual gains, not just at the other parties' expense. A wide range of agencies and institutions have parts to play in these

---

[15]Lest this seem a purely visionary suggestion, it is worth noting that the Japanese Federation of Economic Organizations has already published a proposal for the "Reform of Japan's Industrial Structure," which envisages a shift of the basic primary stages of Japan's industrial production to nearby Third World countries. Processing to be shifted would include production of pig-iron, steel, refined petroleum products, fertilizers, and all car production. Although the motivation seems in large part to shift pollution-intensive production out of Japan, the proposal is of much wider significance.

developments, which must be followed through in bilateral as well as multilateral negotiations. The international agencies have a particular role in developing a rational framework less obviously dominated by rich-country interests, but at the same time not condemned simply to fruitless debate.

Although at present this may seem somewhat idealistic, there is much for both parties to gain from orderly moves towards redistributive policies and the use of international resources in support of them. Recent experience has already made clear the enormous risks and high price of un-controlled interdependence. The costs of conceding a fairer world system may increasingly appear less than the costs of meeting haphazard and disruptive exploitations of bargaining power by those Third World countries whose possession of natural resources gives them a bargaining weapon. Without some planned and negotiated measures to ensure a fairer distribution of world income, it seems impossible to avoid the haphazard distribution of benefits and additional costs which follows from a rise in the price of a commodity like oil which is exported by a few countries, imported by many. And from the viewpoint of the Third World there is real advantage in retaining some bargaining power with the developed countries and avoiding extreme confrontations which may lead to a rapid withdrawal into technological substitutes.

A crucial question will be how to ensure changes which benefit not just Third World countries as a group, but particularly the poorer countries among them and the poorer groups within individual countries. We have already considered the position of the poorer countries. What of the effects of changes in foreign exchange earnings on different income groups and social classes within countries?

Four main characteristics determine the direct effects of an expansion of foreign exchange earnings from exports on employment creation and income distribution: (i) the form of organization and ownership of export production; (ii) technology, particularly the extent to which production is capital-intensive or labor-intensive and whether it is resource-based or technology-based; (iii) the role of government in the trade sector; and (iv) the general stance of a government's policies towards those with low incomes, both rural and urban.[16] The total impact of exports on income distribution and growth in any economy is more likely to be influenced by the overall set of a country's policies than by the particular production characteristics or first round effects of the export under analysis. This leads to the important conclusion that the effects of changes in international trade on poverty and income distribution within Third World countries depends more on *which* Third World countries will gain or lose from the changes in question, rather than on the direct production characteristics of the particular commodities involved.

In terms of policy there are various reasons for doubting the desirability of trade policies which would discriminate by individual countries. One

[16]See, for example, Singer, et al. (1973).

might, however, consciously adopt policies which would ensure that the benefits of trade expansion would accrue more widely within the Third World and thus that each country would get at least some benefit. The poorer developing countries could, for example, be given "free quota floors,"[17] under which they would obtain free access for exports up to a specified maximum without tariffs or quota limitations (or on an equal footing with countries enjoying "most favored nation" treatment). Such measures could provide a guaranteed degree of trade benefit for each Third World country individually, but without introducing the risks of individual discrimination.

An additional approach would be to discriminate in favor of those particular products or sets of products which generate income for the poorest groups. Here the problem is that there is a great risk of the argument being used unscrupulously by groups pleading a self-interested case (e.g., to keep out manufactures). Moreover, the multiplier, linkage, and secondary effects often outweigh the immediate direct impact on employment and income distribution. Hence one cannot be certain, for example, that an expansion in exports of labor-intensive agriculture and processed primary products produced by small-scale firms or manufacturers in one country will necessarily do more to improve the incomes of the poor than an equivalent expansion of exports of some more capital-intensive product in another country.

Even so, with respect to Third World countries as a whole, one can be reasonably confident that concessions in favor of agricultural exports (raw and processed), handicrafts, and other labor-intensive manufactures would tend to do more to benefit poor people and poor countries than concessions in relation to capital-intensive manufactured products.[18] This would be so for several reasons. Rural and small-scale producers are generally poorer than urban manufacturing workers. Second, local multiplier and linkage effects are likely to be higher than with modern manufacturing. Next, the least developed countries have less manufacturing and more primary exports than better-off developing countries. Last, agriculture and handicrafts and other labor-intensive manufactures tend to generate at least some income for the poorer groups, while capital-intensive manufacturing production in developing countries by definition provides incomes for relatively few local persons and tends to have links with foreign investors and greater risk of expatriation of profits.

It is thus in the area of agricultural exports, raw and processed, and handicrafts and other labor-intensive manufactures that particular efforts are required internationally to ensure that international trade contributes not only to growth by increasing foreign exchange earnings but does so in

---

[17]Proposed by Angus Hone in Singer et al. (1973). Many other measures of this sort have frequently been proposed, and endlessly debated, for instance in UNCTAD. As in many other areas the real question is: what chance for implementation?

[18]For handicrafts, see Ho and Huddle (1972).

ways which will also contribute to the welfare of the poorer farmers and to an improvement in income distribution.

TECHNOLOGY AND INVESTMENT

The dominance of the industrialized countries in the generation and control of technology has long been recognized—though its full extent and influence exceed what many people even today perceive. Not merely is the share of the Third World in technological expenditure minute, even much of that which takes place is influenced by the preoccupations and techniques of rich-country institutions.

A few statistics may help to document the extent of this technological dominance. Ninety-eight percent of all expenditure on research and development in the nonsocialist countries takes place in rich nations, and 70 percent occurs in the United States alone. Expenditure in the under-developed countries accounts for only 2 percent of the world total. Moreover, over half of rich-country research is in the fields of defense, space, atomic energy, and supersonic aircraft, at most of marginal value to the Third World and often against their interests.[19]

More serious than the location of this research are the unfortunate effects of its focus. Although the general advance in technology undoubt-edly has led to major increases in productivity in the *world* economy, its preoccupations have concentrated many of the benefits on the rich coun-tries.[20] At the same time, the successive advances of technology and in-novation in the rich countries have had negative backwash effects on Third World development. Over a wide range of products and factor in-puts used in the rich countries, the development of substitutes has diminished export possibilities of Third World primary or intermediate products and, at the same time, increased import demand in the Third World for the rich-country products.[21] Modern products often are or are thought to be superior in quality in ways which shift consumers' demand away from Third World manufactures. Moreover, the use of imported rich-country technology often brings with it a commitment, technological or commercial, to use inputs from the rich countries. Outflows in patent payments are high.[22]

This makes clear that the problem is not only the dominance arising because the origin of most technological development is the rich coun-tries but the biases which enter into the selection of technologies within

---

[19]United Nations (1970). See also OECD (1970).

[20]Griffin (1974) suggests that major increases in total factor productivity have occurred in rich rather than poor countries. Increases in output in poor countries seems to have been more related to increases in factor inputs than to factor productivity—suggesting that even in respect of its positive contribution to economic growth, technology has done more for the rich than for the poor countries.

[21]This trend may currently be slowed or possibly be reversed by the rise in oil prices and of synthetic products derived from petroleum.

[22]Vaitsos (1973).

the Third World. Often of course there are close links — commercial, technological, or cultural — between those developing the technologies and those choosing which to import. Even when no limits exist, choice may be biased, if only because information on what the choice entails — or should entail — is totally inadequate.

Effects on Growth and Distribution

The net effect on Third World *growth* of these technological influences is extremely difficult to assess in general terms. Neoclassicists would emphasize the mutual benefits of technology. Dominance/dependence theorists tend to emphasize the negative effects. The structuralists tend to recognize both positive and negative effects, with the net influence uncertain. In few countries are there adequate data to make any rigorous, even if partial, evaluation. Nevertheless, it would probably be fair to conclude that the trend of recent studies in different countries has tended to shift professional opinion towards a more pessimistic and certainly more cautious assessment of the net benefits. Few persons would now argue, with respect to economic growth, that technological advances in rich countries have had a purely beneficial effect on poor countries. Many would conclude that Third World growth has been partially constrained, at least compared to what might have been possible had technological advances been less biased by the rich-country context in which they were developed.

It is with respect to *distribution,* however, that the most serious effects of rich-country technological dominance appear to have been felt. The effect of this dominance on employment has long been emphasized: the simple result of adopting techniques developed in a capital-intensive context in situations where capital is scarce and labor is surplus. More recently, the biases which follow from the adoption of rich-country technology within poor rural economies have received greater emphasis. One may identify four main areas of influence. First is the direct effect on income distribution of the adoption of capital-intensive techniques in capital-scarce situations, both in raising the share of capital[23] and in concentrating the share of labor on a limited number of usually skilled and almost always higher-paid workers (higher-paid, that is, in terms of average local wage levels). Next is the effect on consumption patterns, the result of the pattern of demand generated by a highly skewed income distribution and by a style of large-scale manufacture based on imported technology for which products are intensively promoted and advertised. The third is the effect on the location and organization of production, usually urban-biased, with a style of labor relations and an approach to payment systems heavily influenced by international norms. This often leads to the remuneration of the higher executives and professional manpower at international rates with

---

[23]Strictly the share of capital depends on the elasticity of substitution. If this is less than unity, the wage share would tend to rise if capital is priced "too cheaply."

operatives and manual labor paid much less (though often still above local, domestic, small-scale, rates). Fourth is the effect on local education and aspirations, by reinforcing the attractiveness of careers in large-scale urban industries using international technology, which rapidly attract more persons to higher education and to the urban areas than can be productively absorbed in the local economy and, for some of the more talented, leads on to an international brain drain.

These are ways in which the adoption of rich-country technology creates and sustains a local enclave of rich-country incomes, consumption and production patterns, far removed from what is possible throughout the economy at large. Usually the enclave is urban based and often its existence widens the gap with the local rural economy and contributes to excessive rural/urban migration. All of these tend to exacerbate income inequality within the country and set constraints on the adoption of redistributive policies.

Internationally also, the adoption of rich-country technology often serves to reinforce existing imbalances in international relations and thus to second-round effects constraining Third World growth and increasing the maldistribution of income in the world economy.

To counteract these effects, action is needed over a wide range of areas — to change the locus of research and technological development, to alter its preoccupations, and to control its unwanted repercussions. In the first place, the focus of this work must be changed — in favor of rural as opposed to urban development. The development of IRRI rice, Mexican wheat, and other rich-country supported research shows what is possible. Much more is needed in a whole range of areas. Second, within each type of research, new technologies must be developed to offset the imbalances identified above. It must be stressed that this process is not one of detached academic or technological endeavor but of working out technologies that are appropriate to practice.

Perhaps the major need, in terms of redistribution with growth strategies, is for research relevant to providing employment and raising the productivity and living standards of the four target groups identified in Chapter V: the small-scale peasant, the landless laborer, the urban unemployed, and workers in the informal sector. These technologies will not be universally applicable but must be adapted to the different environmental contexts.

Two examples may make clear the wide range of changes required and how far there is to go. Consider, first, technological developments relevant for the small-scale farmers, who in most countries form the most numerous of the four target groups. The UN World Plan for Science and Technology has identified long lists of priority fields for agricultural research covering new seeds (especially for millet and sorghum), fertilizers and techniques both for basic foodstuffs and for nutritionally improved foodstuffs, seeds suitable for arid and semiarid regions and regions of unpredictable rainfall, simple implements for crop production, and food preparation, together with other technological advances linked to improvements in the living standards of the family and village community. In spite of this recognition of need, most agricultural research strategy is still far from pursuing such goals, being instead focused on technological improvements primarily adopted by, if not exclusively relevant to, the large farmer. Too often the universities and agricultural training institutions reveal the same biases:[24] concentrating on large farm problems in spite of the fact that the largest number of peasant farmers—and the poorest—farm at most a few acres, have low incomes, and are highly susceptible to risk and uncertainty.

As a second example, one may take health and welfare. Simple rural health systems, preventive campaigns, clean water, and basic sanitation are the priority needs for the majority of the rural poor. Although much that is needed is already known, much is not. Research and experimentation are required for inexpensive, simply organized, low skilled but effective delivery systems to provide such services on a mass scale throughout the country. In spite of these needs the lion's share of medical expenditure on research and training goes to urban, hospital-oriented, curative activities, beyond the resources and incomes of those who need them most.[25] But as with agriculture and so much other technological development, the problem is not only that so little gets spent directly on relevant technological research but also that work on rich-country problems achieves such intellectual and material eminence that it actively diverts attention from the more pressing problems of those in far greater need.

Private Overseas Investment

These failures or distortions of technology in areas directly related to the welfare of the poorest groups are serious. Less obvious may be the repercussions of technological dominance elsewhere in the economy. The import of technology often begins with a hard bargain and leads on to a continuing relationship with the parent company of a multinational corporation in which later purchases of capital equipment or intermediate goods are at monopolistic prices, though often concealed by transfer pricing arrangements, patent payments, management expenses, and so on. The net result is that the growth of multinational corporations in the developing countries—supported by, if not solely caused by, technological power—appears to have been accompanied by a sizeable increase in the outflow of income from past investment. This has been true of both oil-producing and non-oil-producing countries. At the same time, the current inflows of foreign direct investment have increased little, if at all.

[24]A textbook on farm management which is probably the most widely used in agricultural departments of Third World universities begins by stating in its preface that it is primarily concerned with US farming systems and not relevant to peasant agriculture.

[25]Navarro (1973) estimates that annual operating expenditure in the three open heart surgery units in Bogota equaled the cost of supplying a half-liter of milk a day to a quarter of the city's children, adding that among the city's two million population the main health problems are gastroenteritis, infectious diseases, and malnutrition.

Thus, the net balance of *outflows* over inflows has risen, in total, according to UN estimates for forty developing countries, from $1.8 billion in 1965 to $3.7 billion in 1970.[26]

One cannot be sure of the effect of this on growth, since the *total* impact on foreign exchange earnings and the balance of payments may still be positive, providing the direct contribution of the investment to net exports more than outweighs the net outflows of capital, interest, and profits. If the total effect is increased foreign exchange availability, economic growth can be enhanced. But the effects on income distribution seem less equivocal, particularly those operating via the structure of production and income generation. The large integrated firm brings in a style of employment and wage structures which often introduces or reinforces very large differentials in the local wage structure.

What can be done in terms of policy? Clearly, anything which improves the terms on which the investment is made or continued and thus reduces the net outflows from the developing country can be a gain — though the overall, long-run effect can only be judged by taking account of wider effects on the *total* inflows and outflows of investment and the net impact in total on growth and distribution in the country. In relation to the policy instruments identified in Chapter IV, the terms on which investment is accepted can be influenced by changes relating to prices, technology, taxation, rights to transfer profits abroad, and so on. Particularly important are policies or conditions in agreements concerning asset redistribution, especially nationalization of foreign-owned assets. Crucial issues for policy are the extent to which compensation is paid and to which control and the objectives of management are shifted. Potentially the impact of international transfer of assets can be large — but often the actual effects of income distribution on the welfare of the poor are far less than their potential because complementary policies have not been adopted.

THE ROLE OF INTERNATIONAL AGENCIES AND AID

The dominant factors in relationships between the rich countries and the Third World are technology, trade, private investment, and political and military influence. As in political matters so in economic, the international agencies can play only a modest role, particularly on issues where direct interests of the larger and richer countries may be threatened. Nevertheless, this modest role is not unimportant and, over the longer run, can be highly significant, particularly: (i) to alter the framework within which economic transactions take place and thus the terms on which they take place and (ii) to provide supplementary sources of finance, technical assistance, information, and so forth, in ways which assist strategies of redistribution with growth within countries and within the world economy at large.

---

[26]United Nations (1973), Table 42.

The need to alter the framework of international economic relationships is of course only part of wider changes needed. We emphasize here some starting points if attempts to alter the international framework are to be successful.

The initial step is for the international agencies to provide active support or at least adopt a tolerant stance toward the various measures which redistribution with growth within countries will require. Some important moves toward this have recently been taken, both by the international agencies and by some of the bilateral donors. But so far, the declarations have been mainly with respect to aid policy, and very little in relation to the other changes in rich-country policy needed to permit, if not to encourage, the adoption of redistributive policies within the Third World.

Indeed, it would be naive not to recognize the sensitivity — many would say bias — with which international agencies have responded in the past to domestic changes of policy in some countries which have been — or sometimes just been seen as — prejudicial to the interests of the major industrial powers.[27] Indeed, donor countries have frequently used their own power to undermine regimes having what they regard as unfavorable ideologies and have used their influence in international agencies to achieve support for their policy, or at least acquiescence. In recent years there have been some signs of more moderate use of such policies (Chile, perhaps, being the outstanding exception). But it should be obvious that much greater restraint by the rich countries will be required if the range of international forces which constrain Third World countries is to be altered.

Even within the international agencies this will not be easy. Three-quarters of the financial resources of the World Bank and IDA, for example, comes directly or indirectly from the capital markets, the central banks, and the governments of its six principal rich member-countries. Almost all the rest comes from the other rich countries. Hopefully this position will now alter with the channeling of oil revenues to the Third World as earlier discussed.

One benefit of diversification of sources of funds is that it might help to diversify the range of interests represented and the views on how funds should be used. Certainly, the terms on which financial support is sought and given and the assumptions of subscriber-control over the way it is used by the international agencies must change considerably if the resources are to be available for the active pursuit of redistributive policies within the poorer countries.[28]

As a first step towards this shift of attitude, firm endorsement by each of the international agencies of the importance of redistributive policies

---

[27]Nationalization, changes in taxes, tariffs, foreign exchange regulations, or exchange rates are areas where obvious conflicts arise. No less important is international understanding and support in the form of capital aid and technical assistance to meet the strains on the balance of payments or elsewhere arising from domestic reactions to redistributive policies.

[28]Reid (1973).

would be useful. Such endorsements should include frank recognition of the repercussions which serious pursuit of redistributive policies within countries may have internationally—and, where possible, proposals and machinery for providing support for these policies and for continuing aid (or compensation) to minimize any negative reactions from particular sections of the world community. These measures are important, for it is hardly possible to expect extensive redistribution of income and assets within a country without any repercussion on foreign interests; they involve controls or increased taxation on foreign-owned assets and income and a variety of commercial and trading repercussions following major changes in the local structure of incomes and demand.

As a second step, the development of criteria to assess the extent and effectiveness of a country's redistribution and growth policies would be useful. Such criteria would be necessary if international agencies are to move more explicitly in support of such strategies. More objective criteria might also help to take some of the ideological heat out of the debates and evaluations involved in decision-making. As noted in Chapter V, criteria for assessing a country's redistribution and growth policies would need to consider the need and potential for such policies as well as performance. Poor countries with high population/land ratios which have already achieved fairly equal distribution of land may have much less scope for further redistributive measures than countries which are much richer or have extremely unequal land distribution. Indeed, land reform is so crucial a measure for improving peasant welfare that it should be given central importance in any criterion of growth and redistribution policies.

The adoption of such criteria would also help to legitimize the concern of international agencies—and possible donor governments—with redistributive policies, sometimes argued to be matters solely of domestic concern. To the extent that such criteria are used to set the terms on which international support is given, no more interference with internal policies is involved than has long been accepted for aid provided to meet other agreed objectives. All countries retain their sovereign rights not to apply for or to refuse what is offered. Nevertheless, it is worth making clear that the adoption of criteria involving explicit concern with redistribution is likely to involve some questioning of the extent to which donor countries are themselves pursuing such policies internally. Such questions could be helpful, not only in bringing change within the rich countries but in breaking down the tendency to consider the development policies of the rich countries as totally separate issues.

Just as internal public revenue and expenditure policy provide a vehicle for implementing redistribution with growth, so international redistribution with growth can be implemented through aid strategy. Five years ago, the Pearson Commission recommended that 0.7 percent of GNP in each rich country should be transferred in the form of aid to the Third World. At present, net transfers of official development assistance are about half this percentage and have been falling. International redistribution with growth would imply not only achieving the 0.7 percent target, but increasing it.

At the moment, any talk of increasing aid among the larger donors looks unrealistic, even more so after the recent oil increases. It is only objective to point out the contradiction between this position and the protestations by some rich-country representatives of the need for the oil producers to provide substantial sums of aid. Most of the rich countries have for years been far richer than the majority of the oil countries. The moral is that more transfers are needed from both groups.

Nevertheless, if the increase is combined with continuing growth within the rich countries the burden would still be modest even with a rapid expansion toward the 0.7 percent target. This is the rationale for arguing that international redistribution is possible without either severe conflicts with domestic interests or without sacrificing poverty-focused programs within the rich countries themselves. If only 2 percent of the increment of growth in the rich countries were channeled to the Third World, official development assistance would within five years achieve the 0.7 percent global target.[29] Yet 98 percent of new resources would still be available for domestic use within the rich countries, including their domestic redistribution programs.

Just as important is the need for a more rapid shift in the whole focus of aid toward more explicit concern with alleviating poverty and providing support for countries and programs in pursuit of redistribution with growth. As a first priority, this would suggest that much greater priority should be provided to countries whose development policies showed an open and effective commitment to poverty-focused strategies. (The development of objective criteria mentioned earlier could help in assessing this.) For the same reasons that export earnings will do more to benefit the poor in countries whose general set of policies are poverty-focused than in countries whose policies are regressive, so also would increased aid. If a country's policies are clearly set in this direction and it has the capacity to implement them, then effective, genuine, untied program aid support is the most effective assistance that can be given. A shift in priority of this sort would be greatly assisted if a general endorsement of strategies for growth with redistribution were reinforced by revised criteria for aid allocations, national and international. Criteria are needed which take into account more systematically a country's policies of redistribution (and the extent to which they are being *implemented),* as well as its level of per capita income and efficiency.

Clearly, aid criteria must continue to give considerable weight to the level of development and the need for growth: as already stressed, the majority of the world's poor are in very poor countries and growth as well

---

[29] Assuming total growth of GNP of 5 percent and initial percentage of net official development assistance is 0.34 of GNP (as in 1972). If 2 percent of GNP increments were allocated, official transfer would reach 0.7 percent of GNP in just over five years.

as redistribution is a necessary part of the solution. For countries at this level, aid criteria should clearly give weight to both growth and redistribution.

But what of Third World countries of medium or high levels of per capita income? Here there is a strong case for revising the aid criteria to stress primarily the extent to which the programs lead to unambiguous additional benefits for the poorer sections of the country.

Even this approach is debatable, for it can be argued that a country with medium levels of per capita income already has sufficient resources to pursue redistributive and poverty-focused policies, without the need for outside support. (Indeed additional resources from outside could even be used to substitute for local resources which might otherwise be used for poverty-focused programs.) Nevertheless, given the size of the international gaps in income between the rich countries and even the richer of the Third World, there is a reasonable case for concessional transfers providing they are clearly linked to programs and policies which help to relieve and preferably abolish the conditions of poverty.

So far we have talked of countries in which there is an unambiguous set of policies toward redistribution with growth and some areas of effective implementation. What of the other countries where the general set of policies is more ambiguous or less effective? Even in these, official assistance could usefully be directed in support of poverty-focused programs and projects, and aid allocation criteria should provide for this. But in these situations the case for general support is weak and much more attention must be given to particular programs or projects, to ensure that as far as possible they will lead to net additions to the incomes and welfare of those in poverty, particularly persons in the four target groups. Often these groups appear to be bypassed by official aid, in spite of increasing support for agricultural and rural projects and growing emphasis on projects benefiting chiefly low-income groups. To reach the small farmer and other members, rural and urban, of the four target groups is not easy and will require devising ways to channel loans through a variety of local and national institutions which can allocate them in amounts which do not smother—or corrupt—local initiative.

All this provides further urgent reasons for national donors to move seriously towards untying of aid. Tying, as has so often been shown, effectively raises the cost of the capital goods purchased with aid finance, by limiting the range of choice. But more important, from the viewpoint of poverty-focused planning, tied aid concentrates a donor's support on products that can be purchased from its own exporting firms. This often leads to a concentration on capital-intensive large-scale projects when the small-scale, labor-intensive is required. In general, more flexibility in procedures, especially in permitting local-cost financing, will be necessary if serious support is to be given to poverty-focused programs.

Project evaluation criteria also must be changed to give much greater weight to concern with poverty and income distribution. Some preliminary ideas on this appear in Chapter XI. But this is a matter not only of changing formal criteria but of carrying concern with poverty and income distribution into the day-to-day thinking and procedures of donor agencies, both national and international. The vested interests in aid-giving may be often exaggerated in comparison with the slowness with which thinking and bureaucratic procedures are changed. Active steps need to be taken, therefore, to ensure that broad endorsements by international and national agencies in support of redistributive policies are followed up with specific changes in procedures at all levels. Brave words should become brave actions.

CONCLUSIONS

The first point to stress in summary is that action on the international front must be part and parcel of action domestically if there is to be any effective shift which gives greater emphasis to poverty-focused policies. Such action is needed as much to remove external impediments which hinder the adoption or implementation of such policies within Third World countries as to provide supplementary resources or support to carry them out. The impediments to implementation arise in each of the main areas of international interaction: trade, technology, private investment, monetary arrangements, military activities, and aid, as well as in the way in which the whole international framework of negotiation and agreement operates.

The second point is that international action, to be commensurate with the scale of the problem, must involve broad and deep changes economically, politically, even culturally and socially. As such, the perspectives of what is required must be set by desirable long-run changes in the structure of world production, income distribution and consumption, and the implied pattern of world economic relationships underlying them. At the same time the long-run scenarios of what is desired must be related to the short-run realities of the present world economy with its extremely unequal relationships among economic structure, international power, and influence.

The third point is the need to distinguish options where both countries can gain from options (zero-sum) where one country can gain only to the extent that some others lose. Action in both areas is required. There are important opportunities of the first type open in the areas of trade and technological development—but they are frequently left unexplored or declared unacceptable through the opposition of interested parties within countries who might lose without regard to the others who would gain. The coordinated design of internal policy measures may help to release such opposition and set in motion changes in these areas of policy. Frank and dispassionate analysis of policy options is needed to make clear what is possible.

The second area of policy change is that in which poorer countries can gain only to the extent that richer countries lose; this area of change thus

depends on a shift in the balance of bargaining power. The recent rises in
oil prices provide a dramatic example of the magnitude of the changes
which are possible in favorable circumstances, even though the set of factors and interests which have made those changes possible — or will make
it possible to continue them in the future and with other products — is not
entirely clear. Here again, we only begin to understand what might be
possible, let alone work out the institutional arrangements, domestic,
regional, and international, which will make possible effective implementation in ways which spread the costs and benefits of such changes more
fairly.

If increases in the price of oil can in one year virtually double the
money value of all Third World exports and exceed by eight or ten times
the net flows of private investment or official development assistance, it
seems difficult to argue either that present arrangements are optimal or
that nothing can be changed. Instead, recent changes of this magnitude
pose the challenge as to what other changes are desirable and feasible — to
move the world system of trade, technology, and transfers to new forms in
which rich and poor countries alike will be freer to adopt policies which
will eliminate poverty from within their border.

Part Two: Quantification and Modeling

Chapter IX

AVAILABLE PLANNING MODELS
HOLLIS CHENERY AND JOHN H. DULOY

THE DEVELOPMENT of long-run planning models over the past twenty years has focused on factors identified as the main limitations to growth: capital stocks and foreign exchange. Starting from simple aggregated models of the Harrod-Domar type, the structure of production has been increasingly disaggregated and related to the structure of demand and trade. The empirical foundation for this type of planning model is the input-output accounting system, which has now been applied in most developing countries in which industry has reached a significant proportion of total output.

Since the main objective of planning has been conceived to be the increase of output, principal attention has been given to modeling the productive structure of the economy and to identifying the factors limiting its expansion. As the importance of distributional objectives has been increasingly recognized, however, the multisectoral models of production have been extended to include factors affecting the income levels of different groups, such as employment, education, and the regional location of economic activity.

Although considerable use can be made of existing planning models for the analysis of income distribution and employment,[1] they have several inherent limitations that should be recognized at the outset. Existing models are largely concerned with the organized sectors of the economy, which are the main users of scarce capital and foreign exchange. Since small-scale production is not distinguished, these models are not sensitive to policies aimed at strengthening it. While existing models determine the growth of value added and employment by sector of production, they do not link these aggregates to income generation by size or by socio-economic group. The structure and ownership of assets, which are crucial to the analysis of changes in income distribution, have not yet been incorporated in planning models.

Despite these limitations, some valuable distributional implications can be derived from existing planning models or simple extensions thereof. These implications are taken up in the present chapter, which discusses the supply and demand for labor and the effects of changes in income distribution on the productive structure. This evaluation of the relevant features of existing economy-wide models leads us to propose alternative types of model in Chapters X and XI, designed to treat the factors that have a direct bearing on the incomes of poverty groups more explicitly. A realistic application of these ideas would require a combination of the types of models discussed in these three chapters.

---

[1] An extensive survey of theoretical and empirical aspects of multisectoral planning models is given in Blitzer, Clark, and Taylor (forthcoming).

ALTERNATIVE FRAMEWORKS FOR ANALYSIS

The policy conclusions that can be derived from economic models are determined as much by their basic structure as by the statistical estimates of the parameters involved. The art of modeling, therefore, to a large extent consists of making simplifying assumptions that will facilitate the empirical application of the model without biasing the results that it produces for specified purposes. Too often, however, this logic is ignored in applying a given model to purposes other than those for which it was initially designed.

The implementation of production-oriented models in the past has had a substantial impact on the types of data which have been collected and which are available for future economy-wide models. National income and product accounts now exist in some form for almost all developing countries and input-output accounts have been compiled for perhaps fifty, including almost all of the larger countries. Employment data, however, typically cover only the modern sectors of the economy; employment in the informal and rural sectors is only inferred from infrequent censuses and samples. Data on income distribution and the structure of asset ownership are typically extremely weak, if they exist at all.[2]

The existing data sources and sector classifications make some form of input-output framework the logical starting point for any effort to introduce distributional considerations into planning models. From the existing materials, it is possible to make alternative classifications of economic activities, to reallocate analytical effort away from exclusive concern with production toward income generation and consumption, and to consider alternative types of aggregation when economy-wide models are used. We will comment briefly on the differences between a production orientation and a distribution orientation in model design before taking up the applications that can be made with relatively little modification of existing models.

In a plan designed to maximize output over time, economic activities should be classified in such a way as to reveal the direct and indirect uses of the scarce factors of capital, skilled labor, and foreign exchange. This criterion leads to a rather detailed disaggregation of manufacturing and imported agricultural products, since essential commodities not produced must be imported. However, there is little reason to disaggregate the remaining large traditional rural or urban services sectors, since the unskilled manpower to man them is in plentiful supply.

When we shift our interest to the sources of income for the poor, the first requirement is to classify productive activities quite differently. Since labor is less mobile than capital, more information is needed on the regional location of economic activity, which is typically ignored in economy-wide models. The productive sectors need to be broken down

---

[2]Priorities for future data collection and analysis are discussed in Chapter XII.

by size of establishment, since (as shown in Chapter VII) the small establishments use more labor and less capital per unit of output and hence have a different impact on distribution. Perhaps most important, we need an explicit analysis of the urban informal sector and of nonagricultural activities in rural areas, both of which provide some income to workers who cannot find other forms of paid employment.

Along with these differences in classification of economic activities, a shift in the objectives of planning models requires us to consider different forms of interdependence. Models designed to maximize output tend to take the composition of demand as given and to trace the links from demand to commodity production and the uses of scarce factors. The policy alternatives considered in such models are primarily the choice among ways of satisfying the balance of payments and investment constraints. Employment can be determined as a by-product of the determination of production levels, but is rarely a limiting factor.

When we shift our interest to the effects of alternative production strategies on the structure of incomes, we need to add several other types of linkage to those incorporated in the traditional planning models. Since at least half the income of poverty groups comes from wages, this is the first element to be added. Wages vary considerably both among regions and among skills. A certain amount of detail on wage structure is therefore needed to model this link between the poverty groups and the organized sectors. For the informal sectors, which produce both commodities and services, it is important to determine to what extent their products are substitutable for those of organized producers and to include these demand linkages. For these sectors also, the linkage between the firm and the household, particularly expressed in production for subsistence, is important. Finally, we need to recognize the possibility of a transfer of income or consumption to the poverty groups and determine its effects on demands from other sectors.

The shift from production to distribution as a social objective implies that we should try to include the determinants of employment and income and their repercussions on demand within the model structure. Under the heading of "closing the model," this has been a familiar topic of input-output research for some time although it has not taken the particular form needed to analyze poverty groups in developing countries.

Several extensions of this kind are illustrated in the remainder of this chapter, in which the links from production to employment and consumption are added to the type of input-output system that is normally used in planning. The simple linear relations that are assumed should be regarded as first approximations adopted in the absence of sufficient data to make econometric estimates. As data become available to analyze these relations in more detail, these assumptions can be replaced with more complex functional forms estimated from time series. In this regard, the modeling of the determinants of income distribution is at a stage comparable to that of Keynesian models or input-output systems some years ago, when the data only supported the simplest formulations.

The numerical solution of the more complex models needed to combine production and distributional relations is probably the least serious of the problems raised by the proposed reorientation of planning methods. In the absence of well-specified welfare functions, simulations of the evolution of production and incomes over time are likely to be the most practical form of application, as they have been in the planning applications of existing models of production and trade. Numerical solution to the models discussed in this and the following chapters is not likely to be a major problem with the computing equipment now available to most of the countries that can implement this type of approach to planning.

Planning models usually start from an aggregate estimate of income growth and then work from the composition of demand to the required levels of production and imports and thence to the demand for labor and capital. We will follow this sequence in considering the modifications that can be introduced to make the standard techniques more responsive to the needs of poverty-focused planning. The single-period analysis typical of five-year plans involves the following sequence:

(1) Statement of demand by sector
(2) Determination of production levels
(3) Demand for labor (from organized sectors)
(4) Determination of labor supply
    (a) Education and skills
    (b) Supply to informal sectors
(5) Income determination by groups (Chapter XI)
(6) Taxation and income transfers (Chapter XI)
(7) Modification of domestic demand

This sequence covers the principal aspects in which a recognition of distributional objectives can be readily incorporated into standard planning methodology. We will try to bring out the nature of the modifications without going into great detail.

The modeling of other aspects of income generation and employment requires larger departures from the existing planning methodology, some of which are taken up in the following two chapters. Although the several types of models do not in their present form comprise an integrated whole, they can be made compatible and used together through the method of informal linkages explained in Chapter X. In particular, the more aggregated dynamic model of income determination and growth of Chapter XI is designed to be used with a disaggregated single-period model of the type discussed here.

PRODUCTION AND THE DEMAND FOR LABOR

The nature of the economies with which we are concerned has been described in Chapters V–VII above. In most countries there is an abundant supply of unskilled and semiskilled labor to the organized sectors of the economy.[3] Workers who cannot be absorbed in those sectors find some form of lower-paid employment in the urban informal sector or remain in rural occupations. Given the substantial differences in productivity and wages between the organized sectors and most of the alternative sources of employment, the rate of absorption of labor into the organized sectors is one of the major determinants of income distribution.

Conventional interindustry planning models are concerned mainly with production in the organized sectors and its effect on the supply and demand of scarce capital and foreign exchange. In this context agriculture is important mainly as it affects the balance of payments.[4] Furthermore, since agricultural output is limited by land and productivity growth, it is often analyzed separately and taken as given in economy-wide models.[5]

Given the design and orientation of existing interindustry models, they are of much greater use in analyzing the urban sectors of the economy. For example, they can determine the rate of growth of urban jobs (by sector and skill), which is one of the basic elements used in Chapter V to determine the distribution of population among the various target groups. The steps in this analysis can be outlined as follows, using the conventional terminology of input-output analysis.[6]

Assuming no shortage of labor, we can first project production levels from assumptions about domestic demand and trade and then derive employment by skill category in a second stage. The first step in this approach is typically carried out by using an open input-output system with exports estimated separately and domestic demand related to the level of GNP. In this formulation, the supply-demand relations for each sector of the economy are written:

$$X_i + M_i = \Sigma_j \; a_{ij} \, X_j + D_i + E_i \quad (i = 1 \ldots N) \qquad [1]$$
$$(j = 1 \ldots N)$$

where X_i is gross output of sector i, M_i is imports of commodity i, D_i is domestic final demand and E_i is exports. The solution to this set of N equations gives production levels as a function of domestic final demand (D_j) and net trade $(E_j - M_j)$ in each sector:

$$X_i = \Sigma_j \; r_{ij} \; (D_j + E_j - M_j) \qquad [2]$$

---

[3] We follow the terminology of Chapter VII in treating the organized sector for statistical purposes as comprising establishments employing five or more employees. The coincidence with the "modern" sector of dual economy theory is not exact, particularly in the service sectors.

[4] A disaggregated form of agricultural analysis more focused on distributional problems is taken up in Chapter X.

[5] See, for example, Tims's (1968) description of the model used as a basis for the Pakistan Third Five-Year Plan.

[6] More detailed discussions of input-output planning models and of alternative formulations of the basic relations are given in Chenery and Clark (1959) and Blitzer, Clark, and Taylor (forthcoming).

where r_{ij} are the elements in the inverse of the Leontief matrix $(I-A)^{-1}$.

In the second stage we assume labor to be classified by S skill categories. The total demand for labor of each type is determined as the sum of the labor required by each sector. As in the rest of the input-output model, the increase in the demand for labor by a sector is assumed to be proportionate to the growth of its output. This assumption implies that the total demand for labor in the sth skill category, L_s, is:

$$L_s = \Sigma_j \ e_{sj} \ \overline{X}_j + \Sigma_j \ e'_{sj} \Delta X_j \ (s = 1 \dots S) \qquad [3]$$

where e_{sj} is the average labor of type s needed per unit of output in the base year and $\overline{X}_j$ is the initial level of production. In this formulation the incremental labor coefficients e'_{sj} represent the increase in labor demand for each type of labor resulting from an increase in output in each sector ΔX_j over the plan period.[7]

This formulation permits the elasticity of employment with respect to output to be greater or less than unity, according to whether the marginal labor coefficient is greater or less than the average. In addition, employment elasticities can differ by type of labor as estimated from available time series.

Although it is realistic to assume an elastic supply of unskilled labor at fairly constant real wages in many developing countries, this is unlikely to be true for many higher skill categories. It is thus necessary in an overall planning model to predict the skill composition of the labor force from assumptions explained below. This gives an estimate of labor supply by category, L_{st}, for each year. The total supply of labor of type s in each period t must be greater than or equal to the demand determined by equation [3]. The imposition of constraints of this sort is readily handled in a linear programming framework. In practice, however, planners usually make trial adjustments in the vector of final demands to achieve a feasible solution or investigate the possibilities of substituting less skilled labor in some of the sectors using the scarce category.[8]

The imbalance between the skill composition of the labor force and the skill composition required by existing levels of production has been stressed as one important aspect of the unemployment problem.[9] In many

---

[7]Manpower projections based on equation [3] assume that whatever changes have taken place in labor requirements in the past as a result of substitution among skill categories and productivity increases will continue in the future. Since the available data rarely permit a separation to be made between substitution and technological change, employment elasticities less than 1 are commonly attributed to the latter factor, and future substitution possibilities are ignored. While this assumption may be valid when relative prices of different types of labor are fairly constant, it is likely to overstate the requirements for types of labor for which relative wages will rise more in the future than in the past.

[8]Good discussions of the evidence on opportunities for substitution among skill categories are given by Blaug (1967), Bowles (1969), and Dougherty (1972). Unfortunately, their conclusions as to high substitution are based on cross-section data of relative wage structures and provide little evidence on substitution possibilities over a relevant plan period of five years or so.

[9]See ILO reports on Sri Lanka (1971a) and Kenya (1973).

countries the existence of an excess of qualified workers requires them either to accept employment normally requiring lower qualifications or to remain unemployed until more satisfactory opportunities arise. This queuing phenomenon explains the growing unemployment of young educated workers, particularly in urban areas.

LABOR SUPPLY AND EDUCATION STRUCTURE

In order to model a system in which underemployment or other imbalances in the labor market can persist, the supply of labor must be studied independently of labor demand. We therefore summarize the ways in which labor supply has been modeled before turning to labor use.

Projections of Total Population

Demographic techniques for projecting total population are well developed and range from the simplest exponential projection to more sophisticated simulations of the actual process of population growth under specified assumptions of age-specific marriage and fertility rates. In the latter models, the crucial marriage and fertility rates may be assumed to change over time.[10]

Two general conclusions emerge from a review of the methodology of population projections. First, the basic processes of population growth are fairly well understood, readily modeled and widely incorporated in planning procedures. However, the accuracy of demographic projections to date is still far from satisfactory. Experience with projections in countries having a wide range of apparently reliable data reveals a large margin of error over the past two decades. This margin of error must be allowed for in projections of labor supply in the long run, but it does not affect medium-term plans.

Projections of Education Structure

Techniques are also well developed for modeling the flows of population through the formal educational system and the effects over time on the educational structure of the total population.[11] The flows of students through the system over time reflect the rates of continuation, repetition, and dropout at each grade and level within the system. These rates in turn depend on the interaction between the supply of places at each grade and level and the demand from students, which reflects their ability and willingness to take up the places available. Studies on the determinants of repetition and dropout rates make clear that of the many factors involved,

---

[10]The classic work in modern development literature in this field is Coale and Hoover (1958). For standard treatments of projection methodology see particularly the publications of the United Nations Population Division's Department of Social Affairs.

[11]See Tinbergen et al. (1969) and references in Blaug (1970).

the levels of current family income and the economic advantage to be gained from further education are dominant.

The interconnection between the flows of education within the school system and the stocks of educated manpower available to the economy can be modeled with various degrees of sophistication. Providing migration is not significant, the age-specific structure of educational attainment in the population at large will closely reflect school enrollment ratios at different periods in the past. On such assumptions, the future educational structure of the population can be projected.

Underlying this preoccupation with formal education is the assumption that it is a crucial characteristic (as opposed to, for instance, nonformal education) because of its effects on labor force participation, migration, access to high level occupations, and lifetime earnings. However, this is only part of the story; formal education in many situations seems to be increasingly less important than nonformal and informal education. The apparent importance of formal education is explained partly because it is more widely documented and partly because of its closer links with job opportunities in the formal sectors. While there is probably a good case for continuing to model formal education, one must not overlook the many other forms of education.

Given projections of the age, sex, and educational characteristics of the total population, we are in a position to make more specific projections of several categories of labor supply. These require estimates of age and sex-specific participation rates, which are quite widely available. There is evidence that these rates vary considerably by levels of formal education. It may therefore be useful to estimate age, sex, and education-specific participation rates and project the labor force accordingly.

. It is only in the organized sectors of the economy that a useful separation can be made between the demand and the supply of labor. Given the higher wages in the organized sectors, we assume that their demands for different types of labor, as determined by equation [3] above, will be satisfied first. The remaining work force must be allocated among the several rural and urban groups of marginal, largely self-employed workers.[12]

This procedure more fully indicates the basis for the projections of the size of the several poverty groups that were outlined in Chapter V. Since the labor force is growing rapidly in developing countries as a result of the drop in the death rate in the 1950s, the organized sectors for which a labor "demand" can be calculated typically do not take up more than half of the

---

[12]Estimates of labor force participation in the unorganized sectors have little meaning. In Kenya, for example, the official estimate is that the rate of female labor force participation is 45 per cent. In fact, there is good evidence that almost all women in rural and a high proportion in the urban areas are engaged in economic activities for many hours a day — in routine agriculture and house-building activities. It is clear that in this case formal participation rates are not only factually in error but are misleading in attempting to draw a sharp line between economic and noneconomic activities, both of which can be equally important for alleviating poverty.

increment of the labor force unless total output is growing in excess of 6 percent per year. Policies of education, "correct" pricing of capital and labor, and increased export of labor-intensive commodities can all increase the labor absorption coefficients (as discussed in Chapter VII) although these factors are offset by increased productivity.

In some cases, the comparison of labor demands from the organized sectors with the supply of particular skills will reveal areas of shortages. In a long-term projection, these can be filled by changes in the output of the educational system. In medium-term planning, however, adjustments in the demand for labor and substitution among skill groups also need to be explored. While this can be done formally by means of linear programming, less formal methods will usually suffice.

Most of this section has been concerned with models of labor force supply and demand, with labor measured in physical units. In terms of income distribution, it would be desirable to carry forward the projections of labor force supply and demand into projections of wage structure. One would then have the basis for estimating the major components of income from work in a form which could be linked to the size distribution of income. This, together with income from assets and with estimates of demand functions, would close the production-income-demand-production loop. Such models are still at the experimental stage. We turn now to the demand-production relationship under the assumption of an exogenously given change in the distribution of income.

CONSUMPTION AND INCOME DISTRIBUTION

There are two main links between the structure of production and the distribution of incomes among economic groups. The primary linkage is via the ownership of productive assets and the distribution of labor income, which is taken up in a dynamic framework in Chapter XI. Of equal importance to distribution policies in the short run, however, are the effects of changes in income distribution on consumer demands and the ability of the productive system to supply these demands.

The issue of major concern is whether a shift toward more equitable income distribution would reduce the demands for scarce resources—particularly capital and foreign exchange—and hence make possible a more rapid increase in total income within given constraints. The input-output model is well suited to analyze this problem and has been applied for this purpose in several countries. We will first outline the methodology involved and then summarize the results of a recent extensive study by the Indian Planning Commission (1973).

Effects of Redistributing Consumption

One of the principal types of distributional strategy discussed in Chapter II is the redistribution of consumption and income by a combination of fiscal measures and direct subsidies of essential consumer goods. To make this approach operational, it is necessary to base it on a meaningful disaggregation of income recipients and to recognize the limits to the policy instruments available for redistributing income among them. Specifically, a judgment will have to be made as to the feasibility of limiting consumption of upper income groups and transferring purchasing power (or public goods) to poverty groups.

A methodology for studying the effects of the redistribution of income among specified categories of recipients has been developed in several recent studies;[13] its basic features are five. (i) A pattern of income redistribution is assumed, based on either targets for the lowest group, other social objectives or taxation possibilities. (ii) The impact of the redistribution on savings and total investment is calculated from aggregate consumption functions for each group, plus assumptions as to external capital flow. (iii) The total consumption of each income group is broken down into component parts using Engel curves or other forms of demand function. (iv) The new levels of total consumption for each commodity are used in an input-output system to determine changes in production, imports and employment, which are then compared to an initial projection without income redistribution. (v) Where capital coefficients by sector are available, the changes in capital requirements can be determined in the same way as the labor estimates.

One important use of this methodology is to estimate the effects of a hypothetical income redistribution on the factors limiting growth: domestic savings, investment requirements, foreign exchange, and external capital flows. Once these are determined, the effect on total output can also be estimated. The welfare effects of income redistribution can then be summarized as: (i) a growth effect (positive or negative); (ii) a redistribution effect (positive); and (iii) an employment effect (hopefully positive).

The studies made so far are inconclusive as to the general nature of the effect of income redistribution on growth and employment. In the cases studied, the effects measured have been relatively small. For example, moving from a Brazilian to a British income distribution in Brazil would, in Cline's estimate, have little effect on total employment. In most studies, the savings rate is reduced somewhat, but this is offset by a fall in the aggregate capital-output ratio. As a result, the growth rate might be slightly increased if negative responses from domestic and foreign investors (and other factors omitted from the model) did not work too strongly in the other direction.

---

[13]Recent examples of input-output studies of the effects of income redistribution include Cline (1972) for several Latin American countries, Weisskoff (1973) for Puerto Rico, Lopes (1972) for Brazil, and Bardhan (1973c) for India. A discussion of the methodology of demand estimation is given in Taylor (forthcoming).

The Indian Planning Commission Model

In preparing the Fifth Five-Year Plan (1974-78), the Indian Planning Commission has made use of a variant of this methodology that provides a useful example of its value as well as its limitations.[14] The Indian approach is designed to test the feasibility of bringing the lowest 30 percent of the income recipients up to a specified minimum consumption standard (20 rupees a month in 1960 prices) by 1978. This would involve a 60 percent rise in the average per capita consumption of this group over the five-year period. It is further assumed that income redistribution would not affect the overall rate of growth of GDP (taken to be 5.5 percent), and that a reduction in the average per capita consumption of the top 30 percent of income recipients of 3 percent (instead of an increase of 16 percent with no redistribution) would therefore be required. Since these assumptions are widely regarded as politically unrealistic, they probably indicate the upper limit to the potential effects of a redistribution policy in the Indian context. (The impact of recent increases in oil prices has made the assumptions even more unrealistic.)

The analytical procedure used by the Planning Commission follows the five steps outlined above. The consumption functions of different groups of income recipients were estimated from family budget studies, while exports and public consumption were kept unchanged. The new final demands were then translated into production and import levels by means of a sixty-six-sector input-output model.

One of the most interesting results of these simulation experiments concerns the effect that redistribution of consumption would have on the production levels of most industrial sectors. In twenty-two of the sixty-six sectors, consumption redistribution causes a change in the annual growth rate by more than one percentage point. Requirements for foodgrains and textiles are appreciably increased, while consumer durables are significantly lower. Although the calculation shows a reduction in import requirements due to income redistribution, this result assumes that the increase in consumer demand for foodstuffs can be met from domestic production. On recent performance, this seems very optimistic.

The feasibility of this type of redistribution policy depends on the possibilities for limiting upper income consumption through taxation, which in the Indian context would have to be mainly in the form of indirect taxes on luxury consumer goods. In principle, as Bardhan shows, it would be possible to compute the level of excise taxes needed on the basis of the price elasticities for each commodity, although this calculation is not given.

While the Indian model does not analyze the process of income generation and the instruments for intervening in it, it represents one of the

---

[14] The methodology and results are given in Indian Planning Commission (1973). The present summary is based on Bardhan (1973c) in which the use of indirect taxes as the principal instrument for redistribution is also explored.

most interesting official attempts to explore the implications of distributional policies for planning.

CONCLUSIONS

We have shown that planning models can be extended from their traditional concern with the structure of production and international trade to the analysis of employment and the effects of changes in demand resulting from shifts in income distribution. The limits to this methodology derive more from the way in which production and employment data have been collected than from the logical structure of the models. In fact, most of the experimental models of income distribution outlined in Chapter XIII make use of an input-output model as part of a more comprehensive system.

Within the interindustry system itself, the model structure would be much more useful for the analysis of employment if large-scale units were separated from the small-scale and handicraft techniques that are now aggregated in each sector of production. Experimental applications of this type of disaggregation are being made by Pyatt and Thorbecke (1973). A similar differentiation on the demand side would permit a better analysis of substitution and clearer definition of the role of the informal sectors, which constitute a large part of the poverty problem. Other extensions of existing models are taken up in Chapters X, XI, and XIII.

Chapter X

SECTORAL, REGIONAL, AND PROJECT ANALYSIS
John H. Duloy

·The poor tend to be particularly concentrated in agriculture; to a lesser extent, in depressed geographical regions. Modeling policy alternatives for a particular sector or region requires models with properties different from those of economy-wide models. These properties include detailed specification of technological alternatives, the behavior of product and factor markets, the spatial dimension of economic activity, and the asset structure of the sector or region.[1] Models or extensions thereof are available which capture most of these details. However, these models cannot at the same time adequately reflect the constraints imposed on programs to alleviate poverty by the availability of scarce economy-wide resources. One means of obtaining an adequate picture is by a process of planning at different levels, and by linking models. Some issues of multilevel planning are taken up first; a discussion of sectoral, then regional, models follows. This chapter concludes with a brief account of some problems of project evaluation.

Multilevel Planning

The literature on multilevel planning and on the decomposition of planning models has two main strands.[2] The first, initiated by Dantzig and Wolfe (1960 and 1969) is concerned primarily with solving large-scale linear programming models by decomposing a larger system into smaller components. This approach is based upon the mathematical structure of large-scale models, which commonly can be broken down into a number of equations having some nonzero elements in all or most of the blocks of activities and a second part of the model which is block-diagonal. The first set of equations often represents the central decision-making unit in the decomposed model. The block-diagonal components are likewise interpreted as a number of "peripheral" decision-making units. From this simple breakdown, a number of solution procedures can be derived, involving a transmittal of vectors between the periphery and center containing the former's response to the center's signals.

While the various decomposition algorithms have not, in practice, proved useful in the solution of large-scale models, they have given rise to a second strand of the literature, concerned with the simulation of decentralized planning procedures subject to central resource constraints and centrally defined objectives. Much of the work in this area was initi-

---

[1] Methods are available to include some of these properties in economy-wide models. See Duloy and Hazell (forthcoming).

[2] A recent review is contained in Geoffrion (1970).

ated by Kornai (1969a) and Tinbergen (1958). Kornai was primarily concerned with developing a descriptive theoretical model of the planning process. Tinbergen proposed "planning in stages" as a procedure for practical planning, which overcomes the difficulties associated with encompassing both the micro- and the macro-levels in one large system.[3]

In this chapter we are concerned primarily with the second approach. In this connection we will refer frequently to "linkages" between models or between different levels in the hierarchy of planning organizations. By linkages we understand the transmittal of information on an organized basis from one model to another or from one level of planning to another.

In practical planning, and in designing models for application to planning situations, the need for linkages between models arises for a number of reasons. The first is the need for detailed and disaggregated studies at the micro-level in order to come to grips with problems of poverty and unemployment. Some examples include investment projects defined at a local level and at a substantial degree of technological detail, changes in land tenure systems in particular districts, the choice of education strategies for different strata of the population, and charges for irrigation water which vary from district to district, by crop or by farm type. Second, at the micro-level, it is necessary to incorporate into the analysis information which can only be obtained from models or analysis at the economy-wide level. This information includes the prices (or the quantitative allocations to the micro-level) of such national resources as capital, skilled labor, and foreign exchange and, in particular, allocations for the government budget. In turn, the micro-level can supply information flows which can be incorporated into the higher-level analysis. This information consists essentially of the transmittal of technology sets and substitution possibilities.

The form of the information flows (or linkages) between models at different levels in the planning hierarchy can be either formal or informal. The former apply to models which are decomposable and soluble by precisely defined algorithms. Our main concern here, however, is with informal linkages, which allow information flows between otherwise incompatible models or sets of analyses. These flows can consist of only a few key numbers, for example, the prices of a few major resources from the center to the periphery, or some particular coefficients computed from a sector model and incorporated in an economy-wide model. The analyst must use his judgment concerning the information and relationships which can be disregarded. Further, in an informal linkage, unlike the formal, it is not necessary to iterate amongst models until the system converges upon a solution.

---

[3]The distinction among these strands is by no means clear-cut. For example, the work of Kornai and his colleagues has incorporated both strands, from the use of decomposition methods for the solution of large models, to major contributions to the theory of multistage planning as a description of the planning process and to the construction of a set of models (some linked) as part of the planning process in Hungary.

An example may help to explain these points. In an informal linkage between an economy-wide model and an agricultural sector model, the information provided by the economy-wide model may consist of the growth rate of GDP, the prices of capital, labor, and foreign exchange, and the government budget allocation to agriculture. The agricultural sector model could provide a set of vectors to be incorporated in the economy-wide model, each of which would consist of a different feasible technology. In an informal linkage it is not necessary to have many iterations, nor to continue iterations until convergence; a substantial amount of information can be obtained from only a few, or even from one iteration.

The major requirement of the informal linkage approach is that there is a common set of definitions for the variables which constitutes the information flows between models. For example, if three skill classes of labor are distinguished in an economy-wide model, and fifteen skill classes are distinguished in an education-sector model, then it is essential that the various definitions of skill classes be such that the fifteen can be aggregated into the three by prior-defined rules.

The main model components for such planning would be at least two. First, an economy-wide model constructed so that it is *compatible* with models at the sectoral and regional levels, and which can incorporate information flows from these lower-level models. The usefulness of the economy-wide model can be greatly increased if it can distinguish between public and private investment and if it explicitly incorporates a treatment of the government budget. Second, models at the micro-level, which may include models of particular sectors (and especially agriculture and the informal sector) or regions, and information from special studies. All of these may have different structures and different coverage, but they can be linked into the economy-wide models if uniformity of definitions is adhered to in respect of the main economy-wide resources.

SECTORAL MODELS

While multisectoral economy-wide models attempt to cover all sectors and draw upon macroeconomic theory, sectoral models are partial in coverage and draw primarily upon sectoral policy issues and instruments. In attempting to define a sectoral model, it is necessary to distinguish a model of a sector such as agriculture, power, construction, or mechanical engineering, from a model of a sector component, such as an agricultural district, a "typical" farm, or a particular power plant. The former attempts to encompass all sources of product supply and relate total supply to aggregate demand. The latter covers less than the total supply and demand, and the problem is often one of minimizing the cost of producing an increment to supply. While many models have analyzed the components of a sector, few attempt to model a sector as such.[4] For this reason, this sec-

---

[4]The major exceptions to this generalization are the steel and energy-producing sectors in which, unlike mechanical engineering, for example, the product is relatively homogeneous. There are few "sectoral" models as defined here cited in a recent review of sectoral modeling in agriculture by Thorbecke (1973).

tion draws upon an example: that of a linear programming model of the agricultural sector of Mexico, CHAC (Duloy and Norton, 1973a).[5]

The narrower focus of sectoral models enables a greater degree of disaggregation. The model may be disaggregated in one or more dimensions:[6] *spatially,* across regions or districts within regions; *temporally,* with time more finely divided than typical in economy-wide models;[7] *by product definition,* including both differentiation across clearly different products (wheat and tomatoes, for example) or different qualities of the same product; *by technology for producing a given product,* allowing the possibility of substitution among both primary and intermediate inputs; *by source and quality of primary factors,* land or labor, for example; and *by size of producing unit,* distinguishing between large and small farms, for example.

CHAC, the model of the agricultural sector of Mexico, provides an example of these possibilities for disaggregation. Spatially it is disaggregated into four regions further subdivided into a total of twenty districts. Time is disaggregated into months, in order to reflect the agricultural calendar. The model distinguishes thirty-three different crops, and different end products or uses associated with many of these. There are 2,300 different technology vectors. Although the coefficients are fixed in each vector, the inclusion in the model of a wide range of technologies overcomes many of the problems of lack of substitutability in planning models. That is, planning models of this type can, by incorporating a set of alternative technologies based on observed variation in production processes across firms or farms, utilize a formulation of factor substitution possibilities intermediate between the two extreme assumptions of continuous substitutability in neoclassical theory and zero substitutability in the Leontief technology set. For example, corn can be produced with a highly capital-intensive technology on irrigated farms with mechanization and substantial investments in land improvements and the use of intermediate inputs such as improved seeds, fertilizer, and pesticides. Or, at the other extreme, it can be produced with a highly labor-intensive technology, on dry land, using men and mules rather than machinery, and using a minimum of intermediate inputs. These extremes and a large number of intermediate technologies are included in the model. The most important disaggregation of a primary factor is the differentiation of land among different quality types both within and between the distinction between dry and irrigated land. Farm size distinctions are made in one district submodel of CHAC but, in order to keep to a manageable size, not throughout the model.

Another property of the model should be noted: while built in a linear programming framework, the objective function and many of the con-

---

[5]CHAC takes its name from the rain god of the Maya.

[6]This listing of dimensions, of course, is not exhaustive. Further, disaggregation in some of these dimensions is possible in economy-wide models.

[7]This case is relevant where intrayear seasonality is important as, for example, in agriculture or in the demand for electricity.

straints have been replaced by approximations to nonlinear functional relationships. By using the sum of producers' and consumers' surpluses as the objective function (rather than value added at constant prices), product prices become endogenous in the model. This enables the model to be used to evaluate price support and subsidization policies. It also enables an analysis of price-responsive substitution among factors and products. For example, an exogenously determined increase in the user price of capital upon employment in such a model has the combined effect of: (i) a reduction in employment associated with the lower level of sectoral output due to an increase in the price of one of the factors of production; (ii) an increase in employment due to substitution in production of labor for capital; and (iii) an increase in employment through substitution in demand and trade, due to a relative price increase in products requiring capital-intensive technologies and a relative increase in the consumption of products which are labor intensive (and, of course, an overall increase in the prices of the sector's products, with adverse effects on consumers).

The net effect upon employment is by no means certain, particularly if the increase in the user price of capital applies to capital goods complementary with labor, such as, in an agricultural context, investments in irrigation or land improvements.

The model does not include a labor constraint as such. Instead, it includes a labor supply function, which is approximated by a step function. The first step is the supply of family labor at a nonzero reservation wage less than the wage for day labor. The second step is the supply of region-specific landless labor at an exogenously given institutional wage. The third step is given by the migration of landless labor into a region from other regions at a cost. The fourth step is given by the movement of farm family labor from nonirrigated land into the regional pool of landless laborers at an endogenous cost no less than the institutional wage, plus migration cost.

Policy instruments, such as the premium on foreign exchange, the users' price of capital, the institutionally fixed wage rate, the price for irrigation water in particular regions or districts, and so forth, are explicitly incorporated in the model. These can be varied parametrically, either varying one instrument alone while keeping others constant, or by evaluating the effects of a number of instruments applied simultaneously.

Some CHAC results are illustrative. By means of a Bruno (1967) type calculation the comparative advantage of Mexican agriculture in international trade was evaluated. The results indicated that, for Mexico, the comparative advantage lay with the agricultural sector rather than in manufacturing. Further, within agriculture, the ranking of crops by their efficiency in earning foreign exchange adhered closely to their ranking by labor intensity. From this result it is evident that substantial additional employment in agriculture could be generated by a revision of the government priorities and policies for agricultural exports expressed in crop-specific targets and import restrictions.

The model showed that out of the total labor time available for the production of short-cycle crops, about half was not used. This degree of total and seasonal unemployment is consistent with the level revealed in a recent survey by the Centro de Investigaciones Agrarias (1970). The seasonality of employment throughout the agricultural year was very marked and seasonal unemployment is not easily reduced. There is a trade-off between total employment generated in agriculture and the seasonality of employment. For example, if the user price of capital (including farm machinery) is increased, then there is an expansion in the use of labor. This, however, is accompanied by an increase in the index of seasonal employment, due mainly to the fact that the expansion in the use of labor occurs primarily in the harvesting season for corn, coinciding with the peak demand for labor in Mexico.

Not only is there this trade-off between total employment and its seasonality, but the model shows limited responsiveness of employment to conventional policy instruments, such as changes in the user price of capital or changes in the institutional wage rate. This result applies over a wide range of values of different instruments in spite of the fact that the model, as described above, has built into it many possibilities for factor substitution both in the technology set and in demand. To evaluate other possibilities of increasing productive employment in agriculture, one district in CHAC was modeled in greater detail than other districts; it distinguished four farm types defined by the two dimensional classification of large and small farms by dry land and irrigated land. In the results, the technology chosen on small farms was far more labor-intensive than that chosen on large farms, although both farm size groups in the model had access to an identical technology set. The main reason for the different choice of technology between the two types of farm lies in their different relative factor endowments.

The conclusion which can be drawn from these results is that while the conventional policy instruments showed little scope for increasing productive employment, substantial increases in employment in the agricultural sector could be obtained by policies which led to changes in the size distribution of farms, and which had the effect of reducing the number of large farms and of increasing the number of small.

There are trade-offs also between different policy objectives. This is most readily seen in Table X.1, which shows the qualitative impact of a number of policy instruments upon selected policy objectives.

For example, an increase in the user price of capital leads to a moderate increase in employment mainly through substitution. The increase is at the expense of a lower level of production and of exports, and of higher prices paid by consumers for agricultural products, reflected in Table X.1 by a reduction in consumer surplus. Given the low price elasticity of demand for agricultural products, the lower level of production and the higher product prices lead to an increase in the income of farmers. To add to the difficulties of the policy-maker faced with trade-offs of this type, the impact of different policy instruments is not additive, so that it is not possible to obtain a linear combination of the different policy instruments which will be optimal in some sense in terms of the different target variables. To investigate different combinations of policy instruments, it is necessary to investigate each combination separately.

Table X.1: Qualitative Impact of Selected Policy Instruments

Target \ Instrument	Foreign exchange premium	Interest rate change	Wage change	Chemical subsidy	Water tax	Supply controls
Producers' income	++	++	++	+	−	++
Consumers' surplus	−	=	=	++	−	=
Employment	+	+	=	=	−	−
Exports	++	−	−	+	−	++
Budget	−	n.a.	n.a.	−	+	n.a.
Production	++	=	=	++	=	−

Key: ++   strongly positive
        +   positive
        =   strongly negative
        −   negative
      n.a. not applicable

Cases chosen: Foreign exchange premium = 15%; interest rate raised to 18%; wage rate raised by 22%; supply controls imposed to increase farmers' incomes by 30%.

CHAC is an example of a model constructed to evaluate, among other things, the impact upon employment of various forms of government intervention. This model was not designed to study changes in the distribution of income, although such changes are implicit in its solutions. The model could readily be adapted to provide distributional measures, based on two main characteristics of its structure. The first characteristic is the spatial disaggregation of the model, and the distinctions made between dry land and irrigated land and between farmers and landless laborers, which coincide with some major determinants of the agricultural income distribution in Mexico. Next is the distinction, in the one district which was modeled in detail, between farms of different size. To measure the differential effects upon the incomes of these various groups requires adding a set of accounting identities to the model, or using ex post an appropriate report generator.

REGIONAL MODELS

Development planners have concentrated primarily on planning in terms of economy-wide aggregates, particularly the consumption-savings choice, imports and exports, and investment allocation among sectors. Models for planning have naturally tended to reflect these concerns. By and large, planners, particularly in formal planning, have neglected the spatial dimension. This neglect is shown in the paucity of applied planning models with a spatial dimension.[8]

Here we take a narrow focus. We are not concerned with the efficiency aspects of the location of particular industries nor with the large and recently growing body of literature concerning the spatial aspects of economics.[9] Instead, we concentrate on one main issue: planning in the context of a depressed region in a national economy.

In both developed and developing countries, the phenomenon of depressed regions is well known. Examples include the Mezzogiorno in Italy, Appalachia in the United States, the northeast of Brazil, and the southern, tropical areas of Mexico. Depressed regions have some common characteristics. Levels of poverty and unemployment are high, frequently both in absolute terms and relative to the remainder of the country. Sectoral composition of output differs from the national economy and is associated, as both cause and effect, with the lower levels of per capita income. The growth rate of incomes is lower than the rest of the economy. Production tends to specialize on sectors facing a low rate of growth in demand. There is a resistance to institutional change. Neoclassical theory, with its assumptions of factor and product mobility and substitutability, does not encompass the problems of unevenness of development among regions which arise from the immobility of factors. In this situation, the mobility of labor manifested in migration out of depressed regions may actually accentuate regional disparities due to the fact it is often the "wrong" people (i.e., the young and the skilled) who move.

Planning models, of course, do not provide an appropriate tool for the analysis of institutional rigidities, although application of their results may require changes in the institutions. However, they can throw light on the constraints to regional development on both the supply side and the demand side.

The four approaches to regional modeling surveyed here all focus on the use of asset transfers from the rest of the economy to the depressed region as the main policy instrument for reducing a regional disparity in income levels. This is one application of formal models to the analysis of the strategy of asset transfers from growth discussed in Chapter II although the poverty group in this case is a region in an aggregate sense rather than particular groups delineated by their socio-economic characteristics. The approaches, however, differ in other important respects. The first (Chenery) demonstrates the need for a structural shift in the sectoral

---

[8]This generalization is intended to apply to models used in the planning process in developing countries. Regional input-output models have been used extensively for planning in socialist countries [see, e.g., Kaser (1968) and Ellman (1968)] and there have been many regional input-output studies in other countries [see, e.g., Bourque and Cox (1970)]. There are, of course, exceptions to the generalization concerning developing countries. An example is the study of regional planning in Korea, Korean Development Association (1967).

[9]Some recent contributions in this area include Bos (1965), Serck-Hanssen (1970), Mennes, Tinbergen and Waandenberg (1969), and Takayama and Judge (1971). A guide to the earlier literature is contained in Friedman and Alonso (1964).

composition of output, but does not include a mechanism to bring about such a shift. The second and third (MacEwan and Norton) similarly are concerned with sectoral shifts but, being optimizing models, contain a mechanism for production adjustments. The fourth (Enos) represents a different line of approach which emphasizes the modeling of nonlinear behavioral functions at the expense of sectoral disaggregation.

An early study by Chenery (1962b) of regional development patterns in Italy, concentrating particularly on the Mezzogiorno, illustrates how even a very simple model can be used to evaluate both the reasons for different income growth rates among regions and the broad outlines of alternative development programs. The model itself is extremely simple. It covers twelve sectors in three regions — north, center, and south — and allocates a given growth in gross national product among regions and sectors according to the values of a number of parameters (national growth rates of exports by sector, income elasticities of demand for national and regional sectors and regional resource transfers). The model is parsimonious in data requirements. The two essential features of the model are, first, the treatment of a number of "policy variables" (which are either policy instruments in the sense of Tinbergen, or variables which reflect the effect of government policies) and, second, the distinction between changes in regional output by sector proportional to changes in total demand and changes due to structural shifts in sectoral output patterns.

Applying the model to past data, it was apparent that the lagging growth rate of the south was due primarily to a concentration of regional production in sectors facing low income elasticities of demand. The transfer of resources to the region over the period was not sufficient to offset the effects of the sectoral pattern of production. The model was also applied to an analysis of three possible development strategies to obtain a target growth of per capita income involving respectively a continuation of past policies, a set of policies focusing mainly on agricultural developments, and a set of policies directed at inducing structural changes in sectoral production patterns. The income target is obtainable under the first strategy only in association with extremely high rates of emigration from the region. The second and third strategies both indicate the need for increasing emphasis on industrialization, with emigration rates substantially lower in the third than in the second. The results from the model show that previous policies of resource transfers directed mainly at improving infrastructure facilities constitute only one aspect of development policy for this depressed region; structural shifts in production patterns are required also, and those incorporated in the third strategy are broadly consistent with the results of previous studies of national industrial patterns.

A substantial extension of Chenery's approach has been implemented by MacEwan (1971), in the case of Pakistan. The model is a static, multisectoral, two-region linear-programming model, based on input-output matrices for each of the two regions. Of particular interest is the treatment of agriculture, which is frequently treated as one sector in planning models, but which is disaggregated by six commodities or commodity groups in this study. Furthermore, in a departure from the usual Leontief technology specification, the model incorporates production response functions for the main food grains with fertilizer and other nontraditional inputs as arguments. The objective function in the basic solution is aggregate consumption and the model has three main overall resource constraints: the supply of funds and each region's ability to earn foreign change. With this formulation, and maximizing aggregate consumption (i.e., "valuing" increases in consumption equally for both the richer and the poorer region), the solution of the basic model must lead to greater relative consumption increases in the region where incremental consumption is cheapest in terms of the constraining resources. In the particular solution, this region was East Pakistan [now Bangladesh] with a larger share of agricultural goods in its marginal consumption bundle. These were evidently relatively cheap to produce at low levels of growth. At higher levels of resource availability, and, therefore, at higher levels of growth, the model switches to favoring the West. This result depends also on the assumed degree of success in the adoption of new techniques in agriculture: consumption increases in East Pakistan depend critically on its being able to supply its own rice, through the adoption of new techniques. The realism of the assumptions incorporated in the model is open to question, but this is not our concern here.

As MacEwan points out forcibly, the question of relative income increases in the two regions is not only (or even mainly) a matter of the relative cost of incremental consumption: it is a political question. The model is used to trace out the interregional resource allocations which correspond to different (policy-determined) weights applied to consumption increases in each region. The marginal rate of substitution of per capita consumption in the East for per capita consumption in the West was close to unity, over a wide range. "Consequently, in terms of national per capita consumption, no great loss would result from placing strong emphasis on the development of one of the regions."[10]

A similar conclusion was reached by Norton (1971a), based on results from a four-region multisectoral planning model for Korea. The structural characteristics of this model are basically similar to MacEwan's model. However, the model for Korea incorporates transportation activities for most products, allows some variation in the commodity composition of demand as a function of the sectoral composition of output, and the results on regional per capita incomes take account of interregional migration computed ex post from a simple migration model.

In Norton's model, unlike MacEwan's, the device used for exploring the transformation frontier defined by the feasible set of regional income levels is the specification of minimum (target) levels of income-generation in the lagging regions. This approach leads to more extreme solutions;

---

[10]MacEwan (1971), p. 150.

that is, solutions which incorporate more radical structural shifts in regional production patterns than those coming out of the solutions to MacEwan's model.

These three studies arrive at broadly similar conclusions: that structural shifts in sectoral production patterns are required to reduce regional income disparities, that such shifts are not costly in terms of *national* consumption foregone, and that government intervention is required to bring about these changes. It is perhaps not surprising that the results of these studies are similar; they allow broadly similar shifts among regions in the sectoral composition of production and in resource transfers. While they address directly interregional per capita income, they do not analyze the intraregional income distribution nor do they consider the level of productive employment.

A regional planning model which does focus upon employment is that constructed for the northeast of Thailand by Enos (1970). This model differs greatly from the three models previously discussed, being a simulation model, in the sense of a nonoptimizing model based on a linked system of nonlinear equations, rather than a model based upon Leontief technology matrices. As such, it incorporates a great deal of richness of specification in terms of nonlinearities and substitution in demand and in production. This is at the expense, however, of a paucity of specification of sectoral disaggregation and of resource allocation. The model focuses on the northeast per se, and not upon the region as part of the national economy, and it is used to evaluate the effects upon regional employment of a number of policy interventions.

The lack of applied regional planning models for developing countries reported in a literature which is rich in abstract formulations points up the difficulties of empirical studies in this area of planning. The importance of policies focused upon raising the incomes in a depressed region as part of a national income redistribution strategy and the useful insights which even simple models can provide indicate a need for a reordering of priorities on the part of practitioners of planning. These studies are of particular interest in the context of poverty alleviation because, in this dimension of the problem, there does exist an operational theory, that of economic growth. This can be applied to explore the trade-offs between the growth rate of the aggregate economy and reductions in the inequality of the interregional distribution of income.

PROJECT ANALYSIS

The purpose of project appraisal is to assist decision-making between alternative investment opportunities or to provide an acceptance or rejection criterion for a particular investment opportunity. The importance of project selection criteria derives from the fact that poverty-focused strategies may have to rely to a large extent upon fairly specific investment projects designed to raise incomes of particular target groups. Experience with such schemes suggests that they often prove to be insufficiently productive or are of a make-work type which is perhaps less effective than direct subsidy. The importance of finding productive opportunities for direct investment packages aimed at raising incomes of low income groups has been emphasized in Chapters II and VI. Project analysis provides a possible way of ensuring the productivity.

The methods traditionally used are based implicitly on the maximization over time of GNP or net output. Each method provides ways of measuring costs and benefits through the use of appropriate prices, and ways of aggregating them over time (by the use of an appropriate discount rate) to yield a measure of the net output effect of an investment project. The bulk of the research conducted in this field has been directed at deriving rules for estimating prices for the heterogeneous set of physical goods, services and factors of production in the context of various forms of market imperfection. This is the shadow price problem.[11] It applies, for example, in the common situation of a fixed rate of exchange of domestic currencies in terms of foreign currencies associated with tariffs or quantitative restrictions on imports, or both.

A second main line of research has been to explore how to shift away from GNP as a measure of social utility by superimposing on the traditional project appraisal schema a method of breaking down income (or net output) generated by the project into income streams accruing to individuals at different income levels. By weighting these income streams differently according to whether they accrue to individuals at higher or lower income levels, the multiple income streams can reflect the different social premia on its components. The weight to be attached to each component would be derived from some general welfare function, to be used also as a basis for obtaining weighted growth rates of GNP as discussed in Chapter II. The application of these weighting schemes to decision-making is still very much at the experimental stage.

This is a very brief summary of the main lines of the methodology of project appraisal. It does less than justice to the subtleties involved; and it entirely ignores the conceptual and practical differences amongst different methods, although outside observers may find these differences rather less than their proponents maintain.

Taking the framework of analysis of project appraisal as given, there still remain some less than satisfactorily resolved issues. These include questions on the transitoriness or permanence of the market distortions which give rise to the use of shadow prices, the use of shadow prices as a problem of the second-best, the different criteria of the public and the private sectors, the budgetary and fiscal implications of adjusting distorted market prices to shadow prices, shifts in shadow prices over time, the interrelationships amongst the shadow prices of different goods and factors of production, and the definition of a social welfare function. These problems are formidable, and the application of the newer methods of project

---

[11]See UNIDO (1972) and OECD (1969).

evaluation is still largely on a pilot basis. Some of these problems could, in principle, be overcome by obtaining shadow prices from the dual solution of dynamic multisectoral linear programming planning models. In practice, however, neither the formulation of these models nor the results from them are such as to lead to much confidence in using their dual variables for project appraisal.[12] This is understandable: the usefulness of these models does not lie in the results of a single solution; their appropriate use is to explore sets of alternative strategies, the consequences of alternative policies, and the trade-offs among different objectives. Used in this way, no particular primal solution is taken as "optimal" for the economy; there is, therefore, no particular set of optimal dual variables.

In addition to the problems of defining appropriate weighting systems for different income groups and appropriate discount rates, there are two other major difficulties which arise in the context of a poverty-alleviation program. First, we need to be able to translate the costs and benefits of poverty-alleviation projects into measurable quantities. This is relatively easy on the cost side. But, given the nature of the outputs in many cases (health, education, nutrition, and access to public services such as clean drinking water), it is difficult to quantify the benefits even in GNP terms. Second, there is also a problem in identifying precisely the beneficiaries of the project-generated net income streams accruing at different income levels. These are both essentially information problems.[13]

The first of these problems, relating to the benefit side of some poverty-alleviation projects, is intractable for rigorous evaluation. It appears to us that recourse must be had to essentially rule of thumb procedures. In this context, the procedure of some planning offices of making separate allocations of investment funds to the "productive" sectors on the one hand and to the "social" sectors on the other, is probably as useful a practical approach as any. Within the constraint set by the total allocation to the social sectors, the priorities can be set in relation to the most pressing needs as identified by the "poverty surveys" which we advocate in Chapter XII. For expenditures of this type, while the benefits cannot be quantified, the costs certainly can be. The requirement then is for the setting of objectives and standards and for the monitoring of expenditures.

The second of these problems is more tractable, particularly for direct or first-round effects. For large investments which are at the core of a poverty program — those which are designed to increase the access to income earning assets of the poor — we suggest that the appropriate procedure should include, first, the setting of aggregate target levels of investment funds to be allocated for this purpose, and second, the evaluation of projects utilizing a weighting system for benefits according to the income levels of the recipients. One modification is suggested. In the usual project

---

[12]This point is discussed in Taylor (1973).

[13]There is also the more substantive problem of the leakage of benefits from the intended recipients. This is similar to the problem of restricting the benefits of public services so that they flow only to the target income groups, discussed in Chapter IV.

appraisal, benefits and costs are generally measured both in shadow prices for an "economic" appraisal and in market prices for a "financial appraisal." Analogous calculations to those involved in the latter must be done with respect to the net benefits which accrue to individuals, who receive incomes and pay costs in market, not shadow, prices.

Particular problems of a practical nature arise in those poverty-alleviation programs which involve a very large number of projects and decentralized decision-making. These problems are exemplified by the public works program in Indonesia, which in 1972 accounted for about 2800 projects at the village and urban district level and which is directed at both "social" and productive investments. In this program, the objectives are set centrally, together with a requirement to use labor-intensive methods of construction and a proscription on projects of certain types (monuments and public offices are cases in point); the particular projects are selected locally; and the expenditures are monitored by state governments. Even if formal project appraisal techniques were applicable to all the projects of this type, the sheer number of sometimes very small projects in scattered villages would preclude their application. Probably the best which can be suggested in such cases as these is that expenditures be monitored rigorously in an accounting sense, and that a sample of projects be more carefully appraised on a regular basis.

In this connection, it is worth noting that in selecting projects which form part of a poverty-alleviation program, as in project decision-making generally, the formal appraisal is not the essence of the process. The importance of appraisal criteria is that they provide guidance concerning the types of projects to be sought and concerning the design of projects. In most situations where investment decisions are taken, it is rare for a project to be rejected on the basis of its appraisal; projects unlikely to meet the criteria tend to be weeded out much earlier by project planning staff who have acquired good judgment in selecting projects which are likely to meet the criteria. However, to achieve this, the rules of the game need to be set out in precisely defined evaluation procedures.

CHAPTER XI

A MODEL OF DISTRIBUTION AND GROWTH
Montek S. Ahluwalia and Hollis Chenery

THE GENERAL THEME of this volume is that distributional objectives should be treated as an integral part of development strategy. They should be expressed in terms of the growth of income and consumption of different socioeconomic groups, with special weight being given to growth in low-income "target groups." The survey of planning models in Chapter IX shows that existing multisectoral models are largely inadequate for formulating development strategies in these terms. They can be extended to analyze some aspects of the distribution of production, but a much more basic reformulation is required. We need a model that provides a unified treatment of the determinants of both the growth and distribution of income in different groups.

In this chapter we present a simple model focusing on some of the main features affecting distributional patterns in underdeveloped countries that are omitted from conventional planning models. Principal among these are the following:

(i) The dualistic nature of production in developing economies, in which capitalistic modes of production characterized by the use of hired labor coexist with traditional modes characterized by self-employment and family labor.

(ii) Concentration in ownership of capital, which is generally more extreme than the concentration of incomes.

(iii) Differential access of socio-economic groups to employment possibilities and therefore to wage incomes generated in the capitalist sector. These differences may reflect geographical and social barriers to mobility or differences in educational and skill characteristics.

(iv) Differences in savings behavior of different socio-economic groups, which reinforce concentration patterns in assets over time.

(v) Differences in natural rates of population growth between different socio-economic groups.

These features have often been examined in isolation in the context of both growth and income distribution, but they have not been combined in formal models so as to examine interactions among them. Since they represent crucial constraints on both growth and income distribution their exclusion necessarily exaggerates the degree of flexibility in the economic structure and leads to a distorted picture of the feasibility of alternative policies.

The chapter is organized as follows: we first describe the structure of the model and use it to examine the interactions among the several structural factors affecting growth and distribution patterns over time. We then compare three principal approaches to improving the welfare of the poorest groups indicated in Chapter II: a "consumption transfer approach," an

Acknowledgments are due to Shankar Acharya, Irma Adelman, Kenneth Arrow, Bela Balassa, Robert Cassen, Richard Eckaus, and Raj Krishna for many valuable comments, and to Shail Jain and John Chang for computational assistance.

"investment reallocation approach," and a version of the "maximum growth approach." The model provides a framework in which these strategies can be evaluated dynamically in terms of growth rates of income of the poor, relative income shares, and trade-offs against GNP growth.

A Growth Model for a Segmented Economy

The structural characteristics of technological and institutional dualism, limited access to complementary assets, and differences in socio-economic behavior can be examined using the concept of a segmented economy. The members of society are divided into socio-economic groups which differ in terms of their ownership or access to productive assets, physical and human. These groups are explicitly linked through the employment of labor by the capital-owning groups, which leads to payments of wages from one group to another.[1]

In a realistic application there might be a large number of such groups to allow for regional differences as well as finer subdivisions by asset ownership and socio-economic characteristics. The regional dimension is particularly important because many policy instruments are regionally focused or because the characteristics of income groups differ by regions.[2] For present purposes, however, we limit ourselves to three groups, which suffice to illustrate the main features of a dynamic distribution model and the implications of different distributional strategies. We assume that the households in the economy are divided into three socio-economic groups based on their ownership of physical and human capital (and access to publicly owned assets). For simplicity, the groups will be identified as *Rich, Middle,* and *Poor.* These socio-economic groups correspond initially to the top 20 percent, the middle 40 percent, and the lowest 40 percent of the population ranked by income levels.[3]

Segmentation does not, however, imply partitioning. While the ownership of assets is highly concentrated in the Rich, output produced by physical capital owned by one income group flows in part to other income groups in the form of wages. Such income linkages are crucial for the analysis of policy and have an important role in the model. They bring out the relationship between the internal dynamics of growth in each segment of the economy and the growth of income in other segments. It is this interdependence between growth in one group and growth in another that is the core of an integrated theory of growth and distribution.

The growth theory built into the model is based on the familiar Harrod-Domar assumptions applied to a segmented economy. The growth of per capita income in each group therefore depends on (i) its own saving, which determines the accumulation of owned capital; (ii) the productivity of its

[1] The groups are also implicitly linked by commodity trade, since changes in the commodity composition of demand will have an important impact on the factor markets, but these linkages are not explored here.

[2] See Chapters VI and VII for analyses of the differences in policy packages for rural and urban target groups.

[3] This classification by income level permits us to compare the results to the data on intercountry variations in Chapter I.

capital; (iii) the nature of the wage linkages; and (iv) rates of population growth.

The distributional theory emerging from this analysis departs from the traditional exclusive emphasis on the division between profits and wages. Instead, there are two sources of income inequality in the model.

The first is the distribution of output into profits and wages, in which the wage bill itself is disproportionately divided among income classes. This differentiation between different kinds of labor is entirely realistic and reflects the fact that a large part of the employed labor force falls in higher-income groups in underdeveloped countries. The second source of income inequality is the concentration of physical assets in the Rich and the perpetuation of this concentration through higher rates of savings. This aspect is particularly important given the fact that almost half the income of the poorest groups in society derives from self-employment either in peasant farming or the urban "informal sector."[4] For these groups the constraint on income growth is determined as much by access to land and other forms of capital as by considerations of wage and employment levels.

The integration of growth and distribution theory comes from the dual roles of the stocks of capital. The growth rates of the various stocks of capital determine both the rate of growth of the economy as a whole and the pattern of distribution between income groups.

The detailed structure of the model is given below. The following notation will be used for the variables in the model (all variables should be read with a time subscript).

$$Y_1, Y_2, Y_3, Y = \text{Incomes of the Rich (Group 1), Middle (Group 2),}$$
Poor (Group 3), and total income.

$$C_1, C_2, C_3, C = \text{Consumption of the Rich, Middle, Poor, and Total}$$
Consumption.

$$W_1, W_2, W_3 = \text{Wage income accruing to the three groups.}$$

$$P_1, P_2, P_3 = \text{Nonwage income accruing to the Rich, Middle, and}$$
Poor groups.

$$K_1^l = \text{Capital owned by the Rich, using hired labor.}$$

$$K_1^n = \text{Capital owned by the Rich, not using hired labor.}$$

$$K_2^l = \text{Capital owned by the Middle group, using}$$
hired labor.

$$K_3^n = \text{Capital owned by the Poor, used for self-employ-}$$
ment with no hired labor.

$$K_3^t = \text{Capital transferred to the Poor through the fiscal}$$
mechanism.

$$Q_j^i = \text{Output from capital stocks with corresponding su-}$$
perscript and subscript.

$$N_1, N_2, N_3, N = \text{Population of Rich, Middle, Poor, and Total Popu-}$$
lation.

$$T = \text{Annual amount of transfer from the savings of the}$$
Rich to the Poor.

---

[4]See Chapter I.

Production Relations

In a realistic application of this approach it would be useful to distinguish at least five types of capital stocks: (i) capital used in commodity production with employed labor; (ii) capital used by the self-employed; (iii) land which is a nonreproducible form of capital and cannot be increased over time; (iv) human capital embodied in the labor force; (v) overhead facilities (transport, education, power, water supply, and the like). In this chapter we will deal explicitly only with (i) and (ii). The stock of land may be thought of as part of the stock of capital owned by each group but the model does not reflect the special problems arising from its nonreproducible character. The stocks of human capital will be reflected in differences in the wage shares for each group but are not measured explicitly. Access to the initial stock of overhead facilities will not be treated explicitly although the distributional potential of redirecting the increases in public capital will be considered explicitly in terms of redirecting investment to the poor.

With these simplifications, we can focus attention on the output of the two types of capital used to produce goods and services, K^l and K^n, where the superscripts indicate whether the capital is "linked" or "nonlinked" in terms of wage flows to other income groups. K^l is owned (in different amounts) by both the Rich and the Middle groups and uses hired labor, thus generating income linkages. K_1^n is the capital owned by the Rich which is not linked to incomes of lower income groups. We may think of this as capital which uses only highly skilled labor which is itself part of the Rich group, or capital invested abroad; in either case it does not directly contribute to employment or wage income flows. K_3^n is the capital owned by the Poor and used for self-employment. It is nonlinked because any labor employed belongs to the same income group.[5]

An extended treatment of production would require that a production function be defined for each type of capital, specifying the required inputs of different types of labor (i.e., skills possessed by the high-, middle-, and low-income groups) and the output produced. For simplicity we assume a fixed proportions technology of the Leontief or Harrod-Domar type (as in Chapter IX) although allowance can be made for substitution without greatly complicating the analysis.

These assumptions yield the following production equations for the four types of capital in the economy:

$$Q_1^l = a_1 K_1^l \qquad \text{[1a]}$$
$$Q_1^n = b_1 K_1^n \qquad \text{[1b]}$$
$$Q_2^l = a_2 K_2^l \qquad \text{[1c]}$$
$$Q_3^n = b_3 K_3^n \qquad \text{[1d]}$$

---

[5]Note that the structure of income linkages in the model is a downward flow. Capital owned by a group does not hire labor from a higher-income group. The absence of a demand structure rules out linkages flowing from incomes of lower-income groups to incomes of higher-income groups owning assets used to produce mass consumption goods—an important omission.

where a_1 and a_2 are the output capital ratios of "linked" capital owned by the Rich and the Middle, and b_1 and b_3 are the output capital ratios of nonlinked capital owned by the Rich and the Poor and used in self-employment. For purposes of simulation, any predictable changes in the productivity of capital over time can be incorporated in terms of changes in these coefficients.[6] Since in aggregate terms the productivity of capital does not show much change over time, we will assume each coefficient to remain constant except where specified.[7]

The Distribution of Income

The output of each capital stock is distributed between wages and non-wages (which may be either profits or total net output in the case of nonlinked capital). In any given year, the total wage income to each group (W_i) is specified as follows:

$$W_1 = w_{11} Q_1^l \qquad\qquad\qquad [2a]$$
$$W_2 = w_{21} Q_1^l + w_{22} Q_2^l \qquad\qquad [2b]$$
$$W_3 = w_{31} Q_1^l + w_{32} Q_2^l \qquad\qquad [2c]$$

where w_{ij} is the wage share of output Q_j^l received by group i.

These wage parameters are summary reflections of the complex processes determining the functional distribution of income, that is, the amount of labor employed in the production of Q_j^l and the real wage paid. In principle our formulation is completely general only if we solve explicitly for the wage parameters in each year according to some process of wage and employment determination. For simplicity we assume the w_{ij} are constants given at the beginning of the period. This is obviously an extreme assumption limiting the generality of functional distribution theory built into the model.[8]

The distribution of nonwage incomes can be written as a residual after payment of wages:

$$P_1 = p_1 Q_1^l + Q_1^n \qquad\qquad [3a]$$
$$P_2 = p_2 Q_2^l \qquad\qquad\qquad [3b]$$
$$P_3 = Q_3^n \qquad\qquad\qquad\quad [3c]$$

where $p_1 = 1 - (w_{11} + w_{21} + w_{31})$ and $p_2 = 1 - (w_{22} + w_{32})$.

Total income of each group is the sum of wage income and nonwage income and can be written as follows:

---

[6]When this is done in the simulations reported below, the change affects new investment only, i.e., we assume a putty-clay world.

[7]The relative constancy of capital-output ratios that is observed reflects offsetting effects of substitution of capital for labor and technological progress, which have not been satisfactorily separated in econometric estimates of production functions.

[8]In a neoclassical world we would expect the wage share to vary except when the elasticity of substitution is unity. In the case of unit elasticity factor price and employment changes leave the wage share unchanged but the output capital ratio changes, so that the total wage bill may change. These relationships are ignored in this chapter.

$$Y_1 = W_1 + P_1 = w_{11} Q_1^l + p_1 Q_1^l \qquad\qquad + \qquad Q_1^n \qquad [4a]$$
$$Y_2 = W_2 + P_2 = w_{21} Q_1^l + w_{22} Q_2^l + P_2 Q_2^l \qquad\qquad\qquad [4b]$$
$$Y_3 = W_3 + P_3 = w_{31} Q_2^l + w_{32} Q_2^l \qquad\qquad + \qquad Q_3^n \qquad [4c]$$

Substituting for the Q_j^l from equations [1a]–[1d], these equations can be written in terms of the various capital stocks in the economy. In other words the distribution of income among the Rich, Middle, and Poor groups is determined by the distribution of the capital stocks and the wage and productivity parameters.

The nature of the income linkages in this system is brought out in Table XI.1 which shows the initial distribution of capital stocks and a set of parameter values which generate income shares of 56.5 percent for the Rich, 30.9 percent for the Middle, and 12.6 percent for the Poor.[9] The shares are comparable with shares reported in Chapter I for underdeveloped countries with moderate to high inequality. Total wages constitute 42 percent of income, but the bulk of this goes to the upper and middle income groups. The Poor receive income in comparable proportions from employment by each of the other groups and from self-employment. This division is important in evaluating the effects of policies that operate indirectly by increasing employment and wage income from capital owned by higher-income groups compared to those that operate directly on the capital constraints on the Poor group, which limit output and income for this group.

Savings and Capital Accumulation

The dynamic character of the model derives from the growth of each of the capital stocks. Capital accumulation by each group is assumed to be equal to the savings of that group. This assumption is modified to allow for transfers between groups (which will be introduced below) but, in the absence of transfers, the growth of each type of capital can be written as follows:

$$\Delta K_1^l = \qquad q s_1 Y_1 \qquad\qquad\qquad [5a]$$
$$\Delta K_1^n = (1-q) s_1 Y_1 \qquad\qquad\qquad [5b]$$
$$\Delta K_2^l = \qquad s_2 Y_2 \qquad\qquad\qquad [5c]$$
$$\Delta K_3^n = \qquad s_3 Y_3 \qquad\qquad\qquad [5d]$$

where Δ indicates the increase in the specified capital stock between time t and time $t + 1$.

The model assumes in effect a fragmented capital market in which savings by each group lead to investment by that group. Since the Rich own two kinds of capital, the savings of the Rich are divided between K_1^l and K_1^n. For simplicity we assume they are divided in fixed proportions given by q and $(1-q)$ as indicated in equations [5a] and [5b].[10]

---

[9]It should be emphasized that the same overall distribution patterns could be generated by a different parameter set.

[10]This arbitrary assumption is necessary because of the absence of any capital market allocation mechanism which would allocate savings between capital stocks to equalize returns. The value of q used in our simulations maintains the base-year proportions between K^l_1 and K^n_1.

Table XI.1: Income Structure of the Economy in the "Basic Solution"

Initial Year Values

	Linked Capital (Using Hired Labor)				Nonlinked Capital		Total
	Profits	Wages	Profits	Wages	Self-Employment Income	Self-Employment Income	
1. Value of Capital Stocks	$K_1^l = 200$		$K_2^l = 50$		$K_1^n = 60$	$K_3^n = 15$	325
2. Output from each Capital Stock	$Q_1^l = 0.33K_1^l = 66$		$Q_2^l = 0.30K_2^l = 15$		$Q_1^n = 0.35K_1^n = 21$	$Q_3^n = 0.35K_3^n = 5.25$	107.25
3. Incomes by Group							
Y_1	$0.40Q_1^l = 26.4$	$0.20Q_1^l = 13.2$			$Q_1^n = 21.0$		60.60
Y_2		$0.32Q_1^l = 21.12$	$0.60Q_2^l = 9.0$	$0.20Q_2^l = 3.0$			33.12
Y_3		$0.08Q_1^l = 5.28$		$0.20Q_2^l = 3.0$		$Q_3^n = 5.25$	13.53
Total Y	26.4	39.6	9.0	6.0	21.0	5.25	107.25

Total wages: 45.6
Total profits: 35.4
Self-employment: 26.25
107.25

Parameter values:

$a_1 = .33$	$w_{11} = .20$	
$b_1 = .35$	$w_{21} = .32$	$w_{22} = .20$
$a_2 = .30$	$w_{31} = .08$	$w_{32} = .20$
$b_3 = .35$	$p_1 = .40$	$p_2 = .60$

Following the discussion in Chapter I, we assume that savings rates differ among income groups with the poorer groups saving a significantly smaller proportion of their income. The savings rates of the Poor, Middle, and Rich are therefore set at 5.54 percent, 7.55 percent, and 21.45 percent initially. These savings rates, if maintained over time, would yield a "balanced" growth in all capital stocks and incomes of each group at the rate of 5.0 percent per annum. However, the assumption of constant savings rates over time as income in each group rises is not consistent with the available evidence. Accordingly we assume that initial differences reflect differences in income levels and that the savings rates of the Poor and Middle will rise with per capita income, reaching a maximum of 21.45 percent when per capita income of each group equals that of the Rich in the base year (see Figure XI.1).[11]

The consumption equations of the model follow directly from the savings behavior described above and can be written

$$C_1 = (1\text{-}s_1)\ Y_1 \qquad\qquad\qquad [6a]$$
$$C_2 = (1\text{-}s_2)\ Y_2 \qquad\qquad\qquad [6b]$$
$$C_3 = (1\text{-}s_3)\ Y_3. \qquad\qquad\qquad [6c]$$

Population Growth

The growth of population is obviously a crucial variable for the analysis of income distribution and poverty.[12] The population equations of the model are specified so as to permit each socio-economic group to grow in size according to an exogenously specified rate of growth of population.

$$N_{1t} = N_{10}\ (1+n_1)^t \qquad\qquad\qquad [7a]$$
$$N_{2t} = N_{20}\ (1+n_2)^t \qquad\qquad\qquad [7b]$$
$$N_{3t} = N_{30}\ (1+n_3)^t \qquad\qquad\qquad [7c]$$

There is considerable evidence that fertility rates decline with the level of urbanization, health care, education, and other characteristics associated with higher income, although the nature and timing of the underlying mechanisms are not yet well understood. In most of our simulations, we will assume that in the typical case the net effect of these factors will be to produce rates of growth of population of 2 percent, 2.5 percent, and 3.0 percent in the Rich, Middle, and Poor groups, respectively. For simplicity we assume these rates remain constant over time.[13]

---

[11]The assumption of savings rates rising with per capita income over time is a familiar one in most theoretical work. It is also consistent with the available evidence on aggregate savings in crosscountry and intertemporal analysis. For a recent review, see Mikesell and Zinser (1973). In our model we assume that the savings function (with the savings rate as dependent variable) is approximated by linear segments connecting observed savings rates at the per capita incomes of the three groups in the base year.

[12]See Chapter V, where it is shown that the growth of population worsens the concentration patterns in land with distributional consequences for the rural population.

[13]These population assumptions imply that the rate of growth of total population accelerates slightly over time from 2.6 percent initially to 2.66 percent in the fortieth year. Note that over time the three socio-economic groups do not correspond with the initial percentile grouping of the top 20 percent, the middle 40 percent, and the lowest

Figure XI.1: The Savings Function*

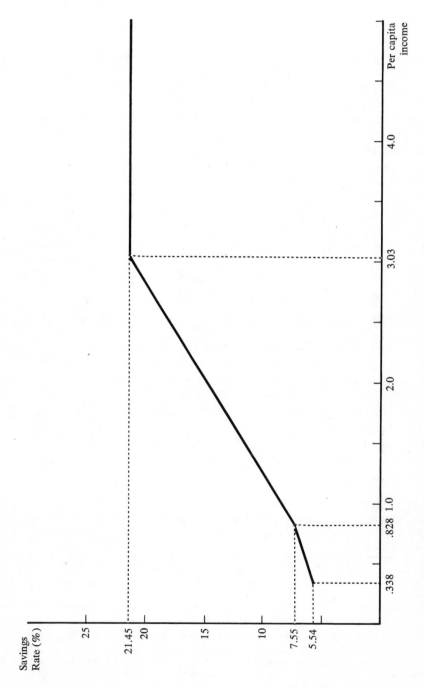

*The savings function is a linear interpolation between the savings rates observed for the three socio-economic groups in the base year given the per capita incomes of these groups in that year.

The growth of population affects both the rate of growth and the distribution pattern through its impact on the rate of saving. A higher rate of population growth leads to a lower rate of growth of per capita income and this in turn slows down the rise in savings of the Poor and Middle groups.[14]

The model described above provides a simple but integrated explanation of the processes determining growth and distributive patterns in an economy. In effect, it gives us three Harrod-Domar economies—with different capital stocks, savings rates and population growth—which are linked by the downward flow of wage incomes between them. The linkages ensure that the growth of income in one group is not simply a function of capital accumulation in that group but also the growth of production and income in other groups. In a dynamic context therefore the determinants of the distribution of income cannot be separated from the determinants of growth in the economy.

An important weakness of the model is the absence of explicit modeling of the structure of demand and its implications for production and distribution. Since demand patterns are not neutral to the pattern of functional income determination, a more complete analysis of distribution and growth requires that the segmented framework described above be combined with a disaggregated treatment of output and demand patterns.[15]

SIMULATING GROWTH AND DISTRIBUTION PATTERNS

The dynamic properties of the model outlined in the previous section are best examined by simulation rather than by analytical techniques.[16] In this section we present two versions of what we call Basic Solutions of the model, which illustrate the interactions between the different parameters in determining growth and distribution. Next we illustrate the sensitivity of the model to changes in such key parameters as the rates of growth of population of the different socio-economic groups. Taken together these simulations give us some idea of the factors determining growth and distribution patterns in the system.

Basic Solution A

The calibration of the model in the Basic Solutions is not designed to reflect the structure of any particular country. There are as yet no country studies

---

40 percent. By the fortieth year, the Poor have grown to 46 percent of total population. A more realistic assumption would be to allow the population growth rate of the Poor to decline as their per capita income increases thus allowing for a demographic transition.

[14]The savings rate of the Rich is already at the maximum 21.45 percent and is not affected by reductions in the growth rate of per capita income.

[15]The treatment of alternative patterns of demand in conventional models is discussed in Chapter IX.

[16]The model can be written as a set of simultaneous difference equations where the coefficients are determined by the parameters of the model. Since we allow some of the parameters to change over time, it is difficult to discuss the model in terms of any analytical solution.

that provide estimates of all the parameters required by the model. But while our particular estimates cannot be formally verified, we have attempted to reflect one of the three general country types described in Chapter V, namely, the Latin American case. This is done by ensuring consistency of our Basic Solution with various aspects of economic structure reflected in a number of comparative studies that have been made of Latin American countries.[17]

Table XI.2: Parameters for the Basic Solution

Output Capital Ratios	Wage Parameters	Savings Parameters*	Population Growth Rates
$a_1 = 0.33$	$w_{11} = 0.20$	$s_1 = 0.2145$	$n_1 = 0.020$
$a_2 = 0.30$	$w_{21} = 0.32$	$s_2 = 0.0755$	$n_2 = 0.025$
$b_1 = 0.35$	$w_{31} = 0.08$	$s_3 = 0.0554$	$n_3 = 0.030$
$b_3 = 0.35$	$w_{32} = 0.20$	$q = 0.7692$	
	$w_{22} = 0.20$		

*Note that the savings parameters for the Middle and Poor are not constants. They are determined by the savings function (Fig. XI.1) and rise over time as per capita income of these groups rises. The values given for s_2 and s_3 are base-year values corresponding to per capita incomes of the Middle and Poor in the base year.

The parameters for Basic Solution A were chosen so that initially the economy would show moderately high inequality and would grow at 5 percent with population growing at 2.6 percent, as was typical of the decade of the 1950s. The relative growth of each group thereafter and the changes in the distribution of income between the groups are determined by two sets of factors working in opposite directions. First, the savings behavior of the different groups is such that as the per capita income of the Poor and Middle rises their savings rates increase, while the Rich are already saving at the maximum rate. This process accelerates capital accumulation by the Middle and Poor reducing the initial concentration in capital stock ownership and permitting their incomes to catch up over time.[18] Against this we have the pressure of population growth, which directly reduces the rate of growth of per capita income and also slows down the equalizing process generated by the savings behavior described above.

The resulting pattern of growth and distribution is summarized in Table XI.3. The rate of growth of income of both the Middle and Poor increases over time as their savings rates rise. The distributional implications of these

---

[17]See, for example, Chenery and Eckstein (1970); Landau (1971); Rich (1973), Annex D: "Fertility Levels and Social Indicators for Developing Countries of the Western Hemisphere, 1970."

[18]The equalizing impact over time of a concave savings function has been explored by Stiglitz (1969). This relationship between savings and the distribution of income is very different from that envisaged by Kaldor (1956) and Pasinetti (1962) in which the distribution of income adjusts to equilibrate total savings with exogenously determined investment. Note that the equalizing impact of savings behavior is reduced if the Poor and Middle groups lack opportunities for holding their savings in a form which maintains real values and earns an appropriate rate of return.

Table XI.3: Basic Solutions A and B

Basic Solution A

Year	Total Income				Growth Rates of Income*				Per Capita Income				Per Capita Consumption				Relative Income Shares		
	Rich	Middle	Poor	All	Rich	Middle	Poor	All	Rich	Middle	Poor	All	Rich	Middle	Poor	All	Top 20 Percent	Middle 40 Percent	Lowest 40 Percent
0	60.6	33.1	13.5	107.2	5.00				3.03	0.83	0.34	1.07	2.38	0.77	0.32	0.91	56.5	30.9	12.6
5	77.3	42.4	17.3	137.1	5.00	5.06	5.06	5.03	3.50	0.94	0.37	1.21	2.75	0.86	0.35	1.02	56.9	30.7	12.4
10	98.7	54.7	22.3	175.7	5.00	5.22	5.21	5.09	4.05	1.07	0.42	1.36	3.18	0.97	0.39	1.15	57.1	30.7	12.2
15	126.0	71.1	29.0	226.1	5.00	5.39	5.38	5.17	4.68	1.23	0.47	1.54	3.68	1.11	0.44	1.29	57.1	30.8	12.1
20	160.8	93.3	38.1	292.1	5.00	5.58	5.58	5.26	5.41	1.42	0.53	1.74	4.25	1.27	0.49	1.46	56.9	31.0	12.1
25	205.2	123.8	50.5	379.5	5.00	5.81	5.81	5.37	6.25	1.67	0.60	1.99	4.91	1.46	0.56	1.66	56.4	31.5	12.1
30	261.9	166.4	67.9	496.2	5.00	6.10	6.11	5.51	7.23	1.98	0.70	2.28	5.68	1.70	0.65	1.89	55.7	32.1	12.3
35	334.3	227.7	93.0	655.0	5.00	6.47	6.49	5.71	8.36	2.40	0.83	2.65	6.56	1.99	0.77	2.17	54.5	33.0	12.5
40	426.6	319.1	130.8	876.5	5.00	6.99	7.05	6.00	9.66	2.97	1.00	3.11	7.59	2.37	0.92	2.52	52.8	34.3	12.9

Basic Solution B

Year	Total Income				Growth Rates of Income*				Per Capita Income				Per Capita Consumption				Relative Income Shares		
	Rich	Middle	Poor	All	Rich	Middle	Poor	All	Rich	Middle	Poor	All	Rich	Middle	Poor	All	Top 20 Percent	Middle 40 Percent	Lowest 40 Percent
0	60.6	33.1	13.5	107.2	5.01				3.03	0.83	0.34	1.07	2.38	0.77	0.32	0.91	56.5	30.9	12.6
5	77.4	42.4	17.3	137.2	5.01	5.08	5.07	5.04	3.50	0.94	0.37	1.21	2.75	0.86	0.35	1.02	56.9	30.7	12.4
10	99.0	54.9	22.4	176.3	5.05	5.30	5.26	5.15	4.06	1.07	0.42	1.36	3.19	0.98	0.39	1.15	57.1	30.7	12.2
15	126.9	72.0	29.2	228.1	5.09	5.55	5.49	5.29	4.72	1.24	0.47	1.55	3.70	1.12	0.44	1.31	57.0	30.9	12.1
20	163.1	95.7	38.7	297.5	5.15	5.85	5.77	5.45	5.49	1.46	0.54	1.78	4.31	1.30	0.50	1.49	56.7	31.2	12.1
25	210.4	129.5	52.1	392.0	5.22	6.24	6.13	5.67	6.41	1.75	0.62	2.06	5.04	1.52	0.58	1.71	56.0	31.8	12.1
30	272.4	179.6	71.8	523.8	5.31	6.76	6.62	5.97	7.52	2.14	0.74	2.41	5.91	1.81	0.69	1.99	55.0	32.7	12.3
35	355.1	255.8	101.7	710.5	5.33	7.33	7.20	6.29	8.83	2.69	0.90	2.87	6.93	2.20	0.83	2.34	53.3	34.1	12.6
40	457.7	375.6	149.7	983.0	5.33	7.99	8.03	6.71	10.36	3.50	1.15	3.49	8.14	2.75	1.04	2.80	50.9	35.9	13.2

*Average annual rate for preceding five years.

patterns of growth in each group can be examined in terms of shares of total income accruing to the top 20 percent, the middle 40 percent, and the lowest 40 percent. Because of different rates of growth of population the three socio-economic groups no longer correspond to the top 20 percent, middle 40 percent, and lowest 40 percent over time. We have computed these shares for the top 20 percent, middle 40 percent, and lowest 40 percent by appropriate adjustments for population growth.[19]

Table XI.3 shows that the share of the lowest 40 percent first declines and then rises. The initial deterioration in relative income share reflects the faster growth of population in the Poor and also the slower rise in savings rates at low income levels (Figure XI.1). The share of the middle 40 percent also declines slightly in the earlier years but begins to rise much earlier, reaching 34 percent in the fortieth year compared to 31 percent in the base year.

Effects of Productivity Growth: Basic Solution B

Changes in productivity over time are an important source of growth in theoretical models and can easily be incorporated in our model by changing the output capital ratio for particular types of capital.[20] As we would expect, both the growth and distributional results of the model are affected by assumptions about the nature of technical progress. In general higher productivity of any type of capital stock in the system raises the growth rate of the economy and its impact on different socio-economic groups depends upon which group owns the capital stock affected and how the other socio-economic groups are linked to it through wage flows.

Perhaps the most important type of increase in productivity is that associated with a general improvement in living conditions for the labor force, leading to an increase in labor quality. The precise mechanism by which this occurs and the way in which its benefits are distributed between capital and labor are not well understood. For the moment we assume that the package of better nutrition, health, and access to education opportunities that goes with a gen-

---

[19]Since the Poor become larger than the lowest 40 percent, we classify the excess as belonging to the middle 40 percent. Similarly individuals belonging to the Middle group are reclassified with the Rich to form the top 20 percent. The individuals so reclassified have the per capita incomes (and asset ownership) of the socio-economic group to which they originally belong but in an ordinal ranking of the population they are now included in a higher percentile group.

Define $X_1 = N_2 + N_3 - 0.8N$ i.e., the population spillover of the Middle and Poor groups above 80 percent of total population.

$X_2 = N_3 - 0.4N$ i.e., the population spillover of the Poor group above 40 percent of total population.

Total Income of Top 20 percent $= N_1 \cdot \left(\dfrac{Y_1}{N_1} \right) + X_1 \cdot \left(\dfrac{Y_2}{N_2} \right)$

Total Income of Middle 40 percent $= (N_2 - X_1) \cdot \left(\dfrac{Y_2}{N_2} \right) + X_2 \cdot \left(\dfrac{Y_3}{N_3} \right)$

Total Income of Lowest 40 percent $= (N_3 - X_2) \cdot \left(\dfrac{Y_3}{N_3} \right)$

[20]In all such simulations we assume a putty-clay world in which productivity changes affect only the new investment in the model. Since we are dealing with net investment rather than gross investment, this understates the productivity impact.

eral betterment of economic conditions of the labor force will lead to an increase in the output capital ratio in sectors using hired labor. This process is simulated in the model by assuming that the output capital ratios for K_1^l and K_2^l rise as per capita consumption of the Poor rises.[21] The wage share parameters are unchanged, implying that all groups benefit proportionally.

The effect of incorporating this assumption is identified as Basic Solution B (Table XI.3). Comparing Basic Solution B with Basic Solution A shows that per capita income and consumption is higher for all three groups as a result of the assumption of increased productivity. The relative income share of the middle 40 percent is slightly higher because this group benefits from ownership of K_2^l and linkage with K_1^l.

In the rest of this chapter we will use Basic Solution B as a basis for comparison with all other simulations.

The Effects of Population Growth

The effects of population growth on the levels of living and the pattern of distribution can be illustrated by comparing the Basic Solution B with two other solutions reflecting alternative population assumptions. Case II reflects a more optimistic population assumption in which population in all groups grows at 2 percent, and Case III a more pessimistic assumption in which all groups grow at 3 percent. Table XI.4 summarizes the results both in terms of per capita incomes of the different socio-economic groups and income shares of percentile groups.

The direct effects of alternative population assumptions on per capita incomes of the different groups are quite predictable. In Case III the per capita incomes of the Rich and the Middle are lower than in Basic Solution B because of higher population growth. Over time, however, the per capita income of the Poor is also lower than in the Basic Solution even though their population grows at the same rate in both solutions. This is because of the indirect effect operating through income linkages with the Middle group. The higher population growth rate in the Middle group reduces the growth of per capita income in this group and slows down the rise in their savings rates with adverse effects on capital accumulation in K_2^l and the wage flow from Q_2^l.[22] Conversely, in Case II the per capita income of the Poor is higher than in the Basic Solution because (i) their lower rate of population growth produces a higher per capita income; (ii) the acceleration in their own savings rate increases accumulation in K_3^n and raises self-employment income Q_3^n; and (iii) there is a beneficial effect from income linkage with the Middle group due to a more rapid rate of accumulation in K_2^l.

The importance of indirect effects of population growth can be seen by comparing Case II, in which all groups grow at 2 percent, with Case III, in

---

[21]They rise linearly with per capita consumption of the Poor from $a_1 = 0.33$ to $a_1 = 0.363$ and from $a_2 = 0.30$ to $a_2 = 0.33$. In each case the output capital ratio reaches the higher level when per capita consumption of the Poor doubles and remains at that level thereafter.

[22]Since the Rich are at the maximum savings rate to begin with, there are no indirect effects from their slower growth of per capita income.

Table XI.4: Effects of Population Growth

| | Per Capita Income | | | | Percentage Income Shares | | |
| | | | | | Top 20 Percent | Middle 40 Percent | Lowest 40 Percent |
Year	Rich	Middle	Poor	All			
I: Basic Solution B							
$n_1 = 0.02$; $n_2 = 0.025$; $n_3 = 0.03$							
0	3.03	0.83	0.34	1.07	56.5	30.9	12.6
10	3.94	1.04	0.41	1.33	57.1	30.7	12.2
20	5.49	1.50	0.54	1.78	56.7	31.2	12.1
30	7.52	2.14	0.74	2.41	55.0	32.7	12.3
40	10.36	3.50	1.15	3.49	50.9	35.9	13.2
II: Low Population Growth							
$n_1 = 0.02$; $n_2 = 0.02$; $n_3 = 0.02$							
0	3.03	0.83	0.34	1.07	56.5	30.9	12.6
10	4.07	1.13	0.46	1.45	56.1	31.2	12.7
20	5.54	1.66	0.67	2.04	54.3	32.5	13.2
30	7.63	2.69	1.09	3.04	50.2	35.4	14.4
40	10.52	4.77	2.10	4.85	43.4	39.3	17.3
III: High Population Growth							
$n_1 = 0.03$; $n_2 = 0.03$; $n_3 = 0.03$							
0	3.03	0.83	0.34	1.07	56.5	30.9	12.6
10	3.68	1.02	0.42	1.31	56.2	31.1	12.7
20	4.52	1.30	0.53	1.64	55.1	31.9	13.0
30	5.60	1.77	0.72	2.11	53.1	33.4	13.5
40	7.01	2.58	1.05	2.85	49.2	36.1	14.7

which all groups grow at 3 percent. Per capita incomes of all groups are higher in Case II than in Case III but the Poor benefit proportionally more than the other groups. In the fortieth year the per capita income of the Poor is twice as high in Case II as in Case III whereas that of the Rich is 50 percent higher and that of the Middle 80 percent higher. This is because the Poor benefit not only from the acceleration in their own savings rate but also from the accelerated savings of the Middle due to the wage flow from K_2^l. A uniform reduction in the rates of growth of population not only raises per capita incomes in all groups, but also improves relative income shares. The share of income of the lowest 40 percent in the fortieth year is 14.7 percent in Case III compared to 17.3 percent in Case II.

REDISTRIBUTION THROUGH GROWTH: SOME POLICY ALTERNATIVES

The treatment of growth and distribution in the previous section has been conducted in a laissez-faire world, taking no account of the potential effect of government intervention. The way in which different economic groups benefit from growth was made to depend on initial conditions such as the stock of capital owned by these groups, structural parameters such as capital productivity, relative wage shares and rates of population growth, and rates of saving generated by per capita incomes.

In this section we will examine the scope for policy-induced changes in the pattern of growth and distribution aimed at accelerating the growth of income of the Poor. In principle the model described above can be used to simulate any type of policy intervention which can be summarized in terms of its impact on the parameters and initial conditions of the model. We will focus on three major alternative strategies that have been outlined in Chapter II. The strategies and the constraints under which they operate can be summarized as follows:

(i) *Consumption Redistribution* involves transferring a specified fraction of total income to the Poor in the form of additional consumption. This policy operates subject to a fiscal constraint, that is, transfers amount to 2 percent of GNP in each year for twenty-five years.

(ii) *Investment Redistribution* involves directing public resources to build up capital stock available to the Poor so as to raise their incomes. We assume that this policy involves productivity trade-offs in the use of capital and that it operates subject to the same fiscal constraint as (i) above, involving a transfer of 2 percent of total income for twenty-five years. For purposes of comparison a variant involving a 3 percent transfer is also explored.

(iii) *Wage Restraint* involves holding down real wages in the modern sector in order to increase the share of profits, thus redistributing income towards the Rich in the hope of higher growth and higher incomes for the Poor in future. We assume that this policy can operate so as to increase profits out of Q_1^i by 15 percent at the expense of wages paid to the Middle and Poor.

These strategies have an element in common which is of special interest for our analysis. Each involves trade-offs between the growth of income of the Poor and the growth of income of the other groups. Our emphasis on strategies with trade-offs does not of course imply that distributional goals always involve trade-offs with growth. We recognize that there are situations in which governments can increase incomes of all groups in society through measures promoting economic efficiency. These measures are desirable in themselves but in general they are not likely to be sufficient. Hence the need for formulating distributional strategies which accept trade-offs where necessary.

Modifications to Simulate Transfer Policies

Simulating the effects of transfer policies requires modification of the model to allow for fiscal intervention. Rather than specify a complete set of equations for the public sector as a fourth group, we add a simplified mechanism by which a target level of resources can be raised from the Rich and transferred to the Poor. The target transfer for consumption (uY) and investment (vY) are each defined as a proportion of total income.

$$T = (u + v)\, Y \tag{8a}$$

The costs of such a strategy depend crucially upon the incidence of the transfer. If the transfer is achieved by a reduction in consumption of the Rich the cost is simply in terms of consumption foregone. But when the transfer involves a reduction in saving, the cost of the transfer is in terms of future income foregone, part of which would have accrued to the Poor through linkages. In this section we assume that the transfer comes entirely from the savings of the Rich and leads to reduced investment in both types of capital stock owned by the Rich. This requires modifications in equations [5a] and [5b]

$$\triangle K_1^l = \quad q \ [s_1 \ Y_1 - T] \qquad\qquad [5a']$$
$$\triangle K_1^n = (1\text{-}q) \ [s_1 \ Y_1 - T] \qquad\qquad [5b']$$

The assumption that transfers come entirely from the savings of the Rich calls for some explanation. An alternative would be to assume that increased taxation reduces the disposable income of the Rich and that the savings propensity of the Rich applied to lower disposable income determines savings. On this view the incidence of T is largely on the consumption of the Rich and only partly on savings. Such a specification substantially reduces trade-offs in terms of income growth over time. In order to illustrate the distributional benefit of transfer strategies under relatively pessimistic assumptions regarding trade-offs, we assume that total savings cannot be raised, so that any transfer has to come out of the savings of the Rich and is reflected in a lower rate of accumulation in K_1^l and K_1^n.[23]

The operation of transfers requires us to add equations [5e] and [1e] to the model and modify equation [3c].

$$\triangle K_3^l = vY \qquad\qquad [5e]$$
$$Q_3^l = b_4 K_3^l \qquad\qquad [1e]$$
$$P_3 = Q_3^n + Q_3^l \qquad\qquad [3c']$$

To allow for the impact of consumption transfers, the consumption equation of the Poor needs to be rewritten:

$$C_3 = (1 - s_3) \ Y_3 + uY. \qquad\qquad [6c']$$

The net effect of including resource transfers is to add another linkage to the segmented system which can be directly manipulated by policy. The nature of this linkage determines the trade-offs between consumption and investment policies as described below.

A final modification for the evaluation of alternative policy simulations is the incorporation of an explicit measure of welfare for each simulation. For our purposes the per capita consumption of each group provides an adequate measure of welfare in that group.[24] The results of each simulation are pre-

---

[23]Since we do not show the government sector separately, we can think of such a transfer being effected by a redirection in the use of public investment funds which would otherwise benefit the Rich. Alternatively, it corresponds to transfers financed by taxation in a situation where government propensity to save is equal to the propensity to save of the Rich and government consumption benefits only the Rich.

[24]The use of per capita consumption rather than income permits comparison between the consumption and investment strategies.

sented in these terms in Table XI.5 and Figure XI.2. Since our strategy alternatives involve trade-offs between per capita income and consumption levels
of different groups, we also need a summary measure that will evaluate these
trade-offs. This is best done by using a social utility function where social
utility can be written as a function of per capita consumption of different
groups.

Using the social utility formulations described in the Appendix to Chapter
II, we define U_e as per capita social utility from the "equal weights" form of
the social utility function and U_p as per capita social utility from the more
egalitarian "poverty weights" form. This gives us two alternative measures
of utility:

$$U_e = \left[N_1 \bullet \log\left(\frac{C_1}{N_1}\right) + N_2 \bullet \log\left(\frac{C_2}{N_2}\right) + N_3 \bullet \log\left(\frac{C_3}{N_3}\right) \right] \bullet \frac{1}{N} \qquad [9a]$$

$$U_p = \left[N_1 \bullet \log\left(\frac{C_1}{N_1}\right) + 2\,N_2 \bullet \log\left(\frac{C_2}{N_2}\right) + 6\,N_3 \bullet \log\left(\frac{C_3}{N_3}\right) \right] \bullet \frac{1}{N} \qquad [9b]$$

Each policy simulation of the model yields per capita consumption of each
group which can be aggregated into a single utility stream which can be used
to compare per capita utility from each strategy.[25] These streams are plotted
in Figures XI.3 and XI.4 for a forty-year period for each strategy.

Strategy I: Consumption Transfers

A strategy of consumption transfers in which 2 percent of total income is
redirected to the Poor succeeds in raising their consumption levels substantially above the Basic Solution for the first twenty-five years (Figure XI.2).
Since productivity of K_1^l and K_2^l is assumed to be a function of per capita
consumption of the Poor it also accelerates the increase in productivity. But
the transfer is achieved at the cost of reducing accumulation by the Rich. This
means not only that the growth of income of the Rich is lower but, because
of income linkages, the growth of income of the Middle and Poor, and capital
stock accumulation by these groups, is also reduced.

The welfare impact of this strategy can be examined in terms of per capita
consumption levels of the different groups. The Rich and Middle are worse
off throughout the period because of lower income growth rates. The Poor
are better off for the first twenty-five years because the transfer offsets the
slower growth of income, but when the transfer stops, the per capita consumption of the Poor drops to the level sustainable by their per capita income.
Since all per capita incomes are now much lower than in the Basic Solution,
everyone is worse off from the twenty-fifth year onwards.

The trade-offs implied by this strategy can be evaluated by reference to the
alternative utility indexes plotted on Figures XI.3 and XI.4. Social utility
from this strategy falls below the social utility generated by the Basic Solution
after the twelfth year using the equal weights formulation (or the twentieth
year with poverty weights). It is typically a strategy with a short-run payoff.

---

[25]Since population growth rates are exogenous, per capita utility is an acceptable index
for comparing different strategies at the same point in time.

The above statement of this strategy deals only with the very broad characteristics of this approach and as such may exaggerate some of its shortcomings. Our assumption that the Poor do not increase their saving as a result of consumption transfers may be too severe. Also, the simulation probably understates the importance of consumption transfers in specific cases. The productivity benefits of a consumption strategy may be much larger than we have assumed. Several specific types of consumption support schemes, for example those focused on nutrition and school feeding programs for undernourished children, are particularly important in this context. Such schemes are directed at target groups which can only be reached through consumption transfers, and in these cases transfers may have a marked effect on future productivity as discussed in Chapter IV.

Strategy II: Investment Redistribution

A strategy of investment redistribution provides a more efficient alternative to the consumption approach discussed above. It calls for the use of the resources mobilized not for consumption but for investment in various forms of capital assets so as to raise production and incomes of the Poor directly.

The need for such direct support and the various forms that it might take have been discussed elsewhere in this volume. For present purposes we assume that provision of credit and physical inputs, access to physical infrastructure, investment in human capital, and public investment to improve productivity of owned capital of the Poor (that is, access roads, irrigation, drainage, and so forth) are all alternative forms in which public investment can be directed to raise incomes of the Poor.[26] These diverse types of investment are all encompassed by a single capital stock in the model, namely K_3^t, which is built up by fiscal transfers and which generates output Q_3^t that accrues to the Poor.

In practice, capital so used may have a lower productivity than in alternative uses in the modern sector. To be conservative, we reflect this productivity loss in two assumptions. First, this investment has a five-year lag compared to a one-year lag for other investment in the model. Second, the output capital ratio on investment for the first five years of the transfer is only $b_4 = 0.22$. This rises to $b_4 = 0.30$ for investment undertaken after the fifth year but is still below $a_1 = 0.33$ and $b_1 = 0.35$, the output capital ratios for the two kinds of capital owned by the Rich (K_1^t and K_1^n respectively).

The investment strategy differs from the consumption strategy in that the resulting increases in per capita consumption, although initially smaller, are self-sustaining over a longer period. The transfer of 2 percent of GNP over twenty-five years reduces the income growth of the Rich and the Middle groups but it accelerates the rate of growth of income of the Poor substantially.[27] When the transfer stops the Poor have acquired a stock of

---

[26]See Chapters IV, VI, and VII for a discussion of various aspects of this approach.

[27]Income of the Poor which grew at about 5.5 percent per annum over the first twenty-five years in the Basic Solution grows at about 7.5 percent per annum under the Investment Strategy.

Table XI.5: Comparison of Alternative Strategies

O: BASIC SOLUTION B

Year	Per Capita Consumption Levels				Shares of Disposable Income		
	Rich	Middle	Poor	All	Top 20%	Middle 40%	Lowest 40%
0	2.38	.77	.32	.91	56.5	30.9	12.6
10	3.19	.98	.39	1.15	57.1	30.7	12.2
20	4.31	1.80	.50	1.49	56.7	31.2	12.1
30	5.91	1.81	.69	1.99	55.0	32.7	12.3
40	8.14	2.75	1.04	2.80	50.9	35.9	13.2

I: CONSUMPTION TRANSFER

Year	Per Capita Consumption Levels				Shares of Disposable Income*		
	Rich	Middle	Poor	All	Top 20%	Middle 40%	Lowest 40%
0	2.38	.77	.37	.93	54.5	30.9	14.6
10	3.00	.93	.44	1.11	54.4	31.2	14.4
20	3.69	1.16	.53	1.34	53.7	31.9	14.4
30	4.87	1.54	.59	1.67	54.6	32.7	12.7
40	6.71	2.20	.84	2.27	52.3	34.7	13.0

II: INVESTMENT TRANSFER

Year	Per Capita Consumption Levels				Shares of Disposable Income		
	Rich	Middle	Poor	All	Top 20%	Middle 40%	Lowest 40%
0	2.38	.77	.32	.91	54.5	30.9	14.6
10	2.95	.93	.44	1.11	53.2	30.6	16.2
20	3.68	1.16	.67	1.40	50.2	30.5	19.3
30	4.88	1.56	.98	1.85	49.7	30.9	19.4
40	6.73	2.22	1.28	2.49	47.9	33.2	18.9

III: WAGE RESTRAINT

Year	Per Capita Consumption Levels				Shares of Disposable Income		
	Rich	Middle	Poor	All	Top 20%	Middle 40%	Lowest 40%
0	2.54	.70	.29	.90	60.2	28.4	11.4
10	3.49	.90	.34	1.16	61.6	27.8	10.6
20	4.85	1.19	.43	1.51	62.1	27.8	10.1
30	6.80	1.65	.58	2.03	61.3	28.7	10.0
40	9.69	2.47	.86	2.85	58.2	31.3	10.5

*We use the concept of disposable income to allow for the impact of the fiscal mechanism in transferring between groups. Disposable income for the Rich excludes *T* while for the Poor, it includes consumption transfers but not investment transfers. When there are no transfers as in the Basic Solution and the Wage Restraint strategy (or after the twenty-fifth year in the other two cases) disposable income is identical to total income.

Figure XI.2: Per Capita Consumption in Alternative Simulations

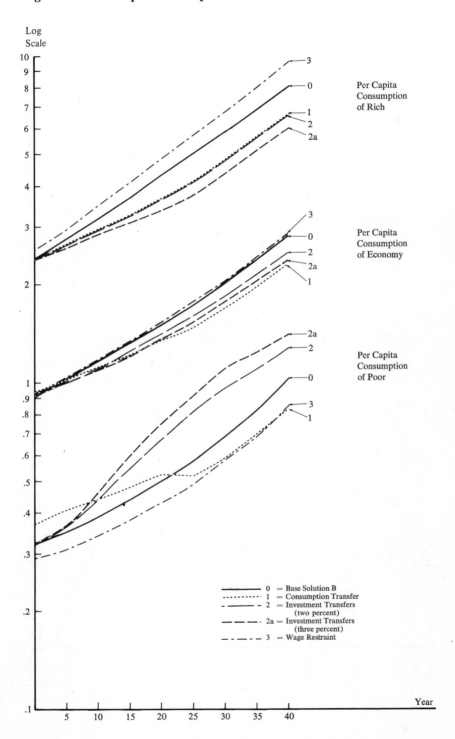

Figure XI.3: Welfare Evaluation with Equal Weights

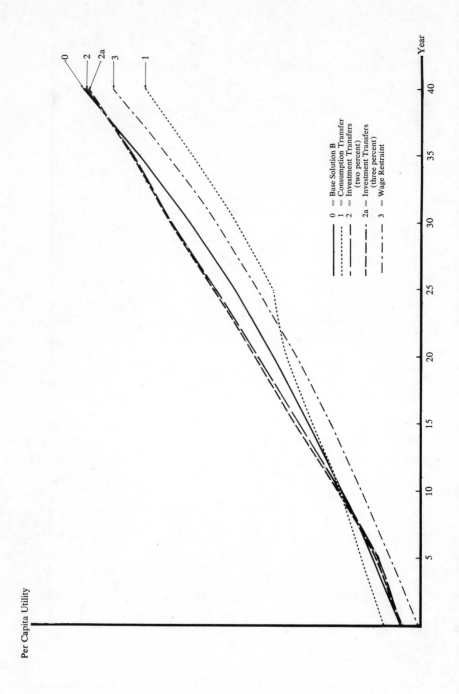

Figure XI.4: Welfare Evaluation with Poverty Weights

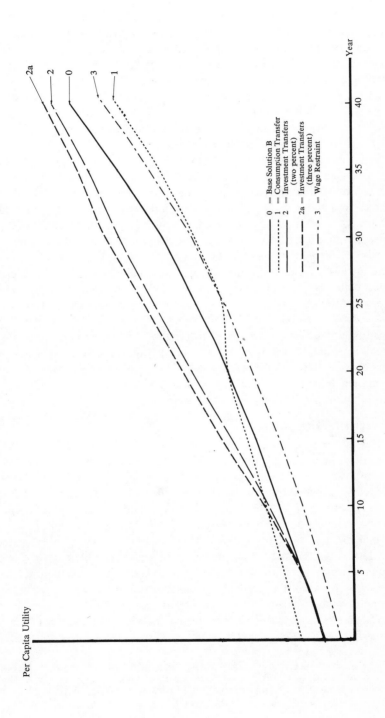

assets $K_3^n + K_3^l$ amounting to 166, compared to 56 for the same year in the Basic Solution (Table XI.6). While the cessation of transfer leads to a deceleration in their income growth rate, the additional capital stock represents a permanent addition to their productive capacity. As in the consumption transfer case, consumption of the Rich and Middle is lower than in Basic Solution B, but in this case consumption of the Poor remains above the Basic Solution even after the transfer stops (Figure XI.2).[28]

The summary evaluation provided by the utility stream shows that this strategy yields higher social utility than the Basic Solution after the eighth year, but more importantly it is also higher than the consumption strategy after the tenth year (Figures XI.3 and XI.4).

These results suggest that a significant impact on incomes of the Poor can be achieved by operating on the availability of productive assets to this group through allocation of appropriate amounts of public investment. In the example given above the investment redirection was maintained at 2 percent of total income over twenty-five years. A much larger impact on per capita consumption of the Poor can be achieved by implementing a transfer of 3 percent of income over twenty-five years. Figure XI.2 shows the results of such a transfer. The cost to the Rich is noticeably greater but the Poor are much better off. In the twenty-fifth year, when the transfer stops, the per capita consumption of the Poor is 80 percent higher than in the Basic Solution compared to only 55 percent higher with the 2-percent transfer. The quantitative impact of investment transfers on this scale is reflected in the size of the capital stock owned by and made available to the Poor ($K_3^n + K_3^l$). This exceeds the capital stock owned by the Middle in the twentieth year. Even though the transfer stops in the twenty-fifth year, it is not until after the thirtieth year that this situation is reversed.

Strategy III: Wage Restraint

The two strategies discussed above can be contrasted with an extreme form of growth strategy that is clearly in contrast to the redistribution of growth toward poverty groups advocated here. This strategy would actually promote concentration of income in the hands of high savers (the Rich) through policies of wage restraint.[29] We simulated this strategy by reducing the share of wages paid to the Middle and Poor from Q_1^l (w_{21} falls from 0.32 to 0.28 and w_{31} from 0.08 to 0.06). This raises profits from Q_1^l by 15 percent and lowers per capita incomes in the Middle and Poor. The decline in per capita consumption of the Poor also leads to slight reductions in productivity in K_1^l and K_2^l according to the linear relationship described above between output-capital ratios and per capita consumption of the Poor.

The results suggest that the benefits of "trickle down" strategies may be somewhat exaggerated. There is an acceleration in income and consumption

---

[28] The distributional impact of this strategy in terms of income shares of percentile groups can be seen from Table XI.5. The share of the lowest 40 percent rises to 19 percent in the fortieth year compared to about 13 percent in Basic Solution B.

[29] It could also be encouraged by lower taxes on profits or other fiscal measures.

Table XI.6: Capital Stock Ownership

(Figures in parentheses are percentages of total capital stock)

Year	Basic Solution B				Investment Transfer 2%				Investment Transfer 3%			
	Rich $K_1^l + K_1^n$	Middle K_2^l	Poor $K_3^n + K_3^t$	Total	Rich $K_1^l + K_1^n$	Middle K_2^l	Poor $K_3^n + K_3^t$	Total	Rich $K_1^l + K_1^n$	Middle K_2^l	Poor $K_3^n + K_3^t$	Total
0	260(80.0)	50(15.0)	15(5.0)	325	260(80.0)	50(15.0)	17(5.0)	327	260(80.0)	50(15.0)	18(5.0)	328
10	423(79.0)	85(16.0)	25(5.0)	533	390(74.0)	83(16.0)	53(10.0)	526	374(71.0)	82(16.0)	67(13.0)	523
20	692(77.0)	157(18.0)	42(5.0)	891	587(69.0)	145(17.0)	119(14.0)	851	538(64.0)	140(17.0)	156(19.0)	834
25	886(76.0)	223(19.0)	56(5.0)	1165	726(67.0)	197(18.0)	166(15.0)	1089	651(61.0)	185(18.0)	217(21.0)	1053
30	1137(74.0)	329(21.0)	77(5.0)	1543	933(66.0)	276(20.0)	202(14.0)	1411	816(61.0)	251(19.0)	263(20.0)	1330
40	1883(65.0)	819(29.0)	159(6.0)	2861	1550(62.0)	610(24.0)	341(14.0)	2501	1388(59.0)	520(22.0)	435(19.0)	2343

of the Rich but consumption levels for the Middle and Poor are initially reduced and also grow more slowly. The higher accumulation resulting from the shift in income to the Rich does not trickle down to the Middle and Poor. Their per capita consumption remains below the level of the Basic Solution for the entire forty-year period. The summary evaluation of this strategy given by the utility streams reflects the adverse distributional impact. Although total consumption is higher (Figure XI.2), both utility streams are lower over the entire period than for the Basic Solution or for the investment transfer strategy.

CONCLUSIONS: THE CHOICE OF STRATEGY

The policy simulations discussed in the previous section are necessarily limited by the highly simplified structure of the model and the hypothetical calibration. They should be viewed as illustrating some of the methodological issues in formulating a distributional strategy and also highlighting the major characteristics of some alternate strategies. Our general conclusions along both lines can be summarized as follows.

The most important methodological issue is the need to provide an integrated explanation of growth and distribution in planning models. This follows from the complex nature of the interactions involved in evaluating the impact of a particular policy. Policies originally designed to benefit one target group may have adverse effects on the other groups and because of income linkages may even hurt the target group itself. Since these effects take time to work themselves out, we need a dynamic model in which alternative strategies can be compared over time. The importance of the time period over which choices are made is illustrated by the welfare evaluations in Figures XI.3 and XI.4. Although the consumption strategy has a high pay-off in the short run, it is not optimal when evaluated over a longer time horizon.

Since many policy alternatives imply trade-offs between income accruing to different groups, we need an explicit statement of relative weights to evaluate these trade-offs. Economists tend to simplify this problem by assuming —as we have done—that the complex considerations that determine these weights can be summarized in the form of a welfare function. This approach has important advantages. Once defined, the welfare function can be used both for economy-wide and micro-level planning. In the former it can be used to evaluate alternative strategies involving different rates of income growth for different groups. In micro planning it can be used to determine weights for project appraisal consistent with the economy-wide plan (see Chapter X). In practice, of course, such weights cannot be determined with any precision and planners may have to work in terms of broad ranges for these weights. Our results suggest that the choice between the different strategies is not much affected whether the weights used correspond to the equal weights form of the utility function or to the more strongly egalitarian poverty weights form.

Our major conclusion as to the choice of strategy is that there is considerable potential for raising income in low-income groups through a policy of "investment transfers." Such a strategy, although operating at the margin, can achieve substantial improvements in patterns of asset concentration over time. If income in the poorer groups is constrained by lack of physical and human capital and access to infrastructure, then reallocation of public resources can provide a powerful mechanism for removing these constraints. The extent of resource transfer involved—2 percent of GNP per year for twenty-five years—is not small, but it should be feasible in many countries. Most countries have substantially increased the percentage of GNP mobilized through taxation, although much of the increase is absorbed by higher government consumption. Some combination of increased resource mobilization and redirection of investment should make it possible to finance the transfer. Since such a strategy is aimed at raising production in low-income groups, the precise form of the investment is of great importance. In our simulations we have assumed that opportunities for productive investment exist, although at some cost in terms of lower productivity in GNP terms. In practice, identifying such projects may prove to be as much of a constraint on this approach as the availability of resources.

The distributional strategies discussed above are alternatives only in their approach to the problem. They need not be mutually exclusive as components of an overall strategy. Different strategies are likely to have different pay-offs in terms of the time scale of benefits or the needs of particular target groups. In practice, therefore, an optimal choice is unlikely to lead to the adoption of any one of the alternatives in its pure form. It will consist of a mix of different approaches depending upon the character of the target groups and the scope for each type of intervention. The importance of mixed strategies is greatly reinforced when we consider that governments have additional possibilities for achieving distributional objectives without trade-offs. These should obviously be part of any overall strategy.

The present analysis constitutes only a first step toward the needed reformulation of planning models to incorporate distributional objectives and constraints. Despite its limitations, the results seem sufficiently promising to warrant further work along these lines.

Chapter XII

STATISTICAL PRIORITIES

C.L.G. BELL AND JOHN H. DULOY

THE PRIORITIES in the work programs of most statistical offices have been and generally continue to be determined by the data requirements of a growth-oriented development strategy. Work has concentrated on the measurement of output growth and on the constraints to growth. With these priorities, serious attempts are made to collect accurate information on the production activities of firms in the growing modern manufacturing and services sectors and on the growth of marketed output from agriculture. Little attempt is made to collect accurate information on the informal sector in urban areas or on production for own consumption in rural. As a consequence of this orientation, the data base for planning, designing, and monitoring policies which are directed at alleviating poverty, and for conducting research on the poor, is fragmented and unreliable.

These deficiencies can, of course, be overcome. To do so will involve reordering priorities for data collection and processing and redesigning the work programs of statistical offices. There are two major classes of requirements for new data. First, there are data needs for monitoring purposes: initially, to trace the extent of poverty and inequality and, in later stages, to assess progress in dealing with them. Essentially, these involve the concepts and measures required to map the "poverty contours" outlined in Chapter I. Second, there are data needed as inputs into other parts of policy analysis both for formal models treated in Chapters IX, X, and XI and for particular pieces of micro-analysis (such as the distributional consequences of a rural works project). In all of these cases, it is desirable to begin by assessing whether or not simple retabulations of existing data series will serve at least some of the demands arising from a reorientation of planning. At the same time, this review of statistical needs may well identify other current statistical activities—the full implementation of the System of National Accounts (UN, 1968) is one—the priority of which must be seriously questioned.

This chapter begins with a discussion of the first priority for new data collection: we set out a method for drawing the "poverty contours" and discuss the possibilities and merits of attempting to implement a standard frame for less developed countries. We then examine some of the major priorities for building on the existing framework, particularly of the input-output table, to meet the requirements for the analysis of poverty issues at the economy-wide level. These suggestions apply to the regular work program of statistical offices. The last section contains some proposals for special-purpose studies, with data collections on an irregular basis, and relating mainly to micro issues.

This chapter draws on the Bellagio conference working group report on poverty-focused planning and on Seers (1973); it benefited also from the comments of Ralph Hoffmeister.

The Poverty Profile

The first priority is the poverty map because a clear identification of poverty groups and their economic and social characteristics is an indispensable component of policy diagnosis and design. For this purpose, the basic requirement is for a statistical framework within which a range of survey results can be set.

The statistical frame will no doubt usually be compiled by the main government statistical office, and much of the data subsequently used to elaborate details within it will also come from government sources (though many not from the statistical office itself). But in addition, nongovernment groups will need to be able to contribute data in a form which can be set within the general frame, as a means to assessing their possible wider significance.

The essential units of the statistical framework should be households, with information on the socioeconomic characteristics of each member, income, assets, and consumption. Although the extent to which data can be collected will vary widely among countries, the following is a basic list which should be within the capacity of most statistical offices.

(i) The composition of the household. At a minimum, one wants the following types of information about *all* family members (with appropriate definitions of "family" to reflect prevailing customs): age, sex, relevant ethnographic data, migrant status, region, educational levels, rural/urban residence, and role within the family unit.

(ii) Family income and consumption. These data will provide basic information on the family's ability to subsist and can be related to nutritional norms. Knowledge of income flows within the extended family will be useful when framing policy interventions which affect specific family members—for example, workers in urban areas who remit payments to rural relatives. It is important to record the source of income, distinguishing among income from wages, profits, rent, transfers and remittances, and self-employment, and also distinguishing between monetary and nonmonetary income sources. Direct taxes and subsidies should be included too. In collecting consumption data, it is very useful to define consumption categories in such a way that it is possible easily to map to and from consumption categories in the household surveys and production categories as defined in the national accounts, input-output matrices, and surveys of firms and farms. Price data should be collected as well as quantity data on consumption.

(iii) Ownership of, and access to, assets and the institutional characteristics of income recipients. Here we have in mind both physical and human capital (education and skills) as assets. Both play a role in determining the intergenerational transmission of inequality. Land ownership patterns are a vital determinant of income levels in very poor countries, and are often easily ascertained (as opposed to holding patterns of financial assets). Institutional data should cover land tenure status, housing conditions, and rudimentary data on access to publicly provided goods and services such as health, education, pure water, extention advice, and the like.

(iv) Workplace data. These should also be gathered, with questions designed to elicit information about the role of each family member in the labor market. At a minimum, information is required on the sector of the economy, basic occupational class of family workers, how much and at what wage rates they work per week, in what season, at what skill level, and how near to home they work. A particular need is to ensure that data on individuals can be linked to similar data on the other members of their families.

Although the volume of data listed above is great, we judge that it can be collected using a well-designed household questionnaire of moderate length. Naturally, an appropriately large and stratified sample should be drawn.[1] This sort of sampling is not beyond the capacity of the statistical offices of many developing countries although, with the possible exception of household budgets, it may lie outside their usual work patterns. Unless these offices can be persuaded to modify their methods, it will be difficult to collect data suitable for the development of programs focused directly on the poor and the causes of poverty.

These socio-economic data can be used to quantify the poverty mapping and to suggest possible intervention programs. Data collected on a uniform, consistent and comprehensive basis will allow the results of particular studies, for example, in the fields of public health and nutrition, to be related to national poverty standards, something which in the past has proven very difficult.

While the "poverty profile" will yield much valuable information about the general characteristics of poor households, it will not reveal a great deal about them as producer-consumer units linked, if only partially, with the rest of the economy. As shown in Chapter I, about half of the poor are self-employed in household enterprises or on small family farms. Correct diagnosis and policy design demand an understanding of their behavior as both producers and consumers. Crop-cutting experiments coupled with aggregate acreage counts will implicitly include small farmers' production in estimates of overall output for the purposes of compiling national accounts, but they will shed no light on the intensity of family labor use, access to public goods and services, the fraction of output marketed, and related issues. Only rarely are the activities of small urban household enterprises employing fewer than five to ten workers covered by official surveys. The pattern of their transactions with other firms and the income levels of the consumer of their products are usually matters of pure surmise. For these reasons, we advocate that statistical offices give serious

---

[1]Countries with good statistical offices should also consider instituting continuous panel surveys of poor families.

consideration to undertaking a consolidated production and consumption survey of household enterprises and small farms regularly.[2]

Weighing its undoubted complexity against its indisputable importance, we judge five-yearly frequency to be right. The main categories of data to be sought are set out below. They overlap, in part, with those in the "poverty profile," thus allowing more detailed inferences to be made from the latter than its own contents would permit. It will be noted also that the implicit degree of disaggregation in various transactions accords closely with the System of National Accounts (SNA). The critical difference is that we are pressing for the emphasis to be on measuring the activities of small farms and households and small-scale enterprises rather than on completing reliable transactions matrices for the economy as a whole (which would entail concentrating on the organized sector).

A. Small Farms
   family composition and size;
   land area and quality, tenure status, region;
   output level and structure, marketing and market access;
   input structure, with special attention to the distinction between
      inputs supplied by the family, by other households, and by the
      nonfarm sector;
   nonfarm activities (householding, services, and so on);
   rents, interests, and taxes;
   transfer payments and receipts;
   access to, and use of, public goods and services for production and
      consumption;
   consumption patterns, with particular attention to consumption out
      of own production and the extent to which nonfood items are
      produced by the small-scale cottage sector.

B. Urban Small-Scale Household Enterprises
   The coverage would be similar to the above (with appropriate
   changes in terms and definitions, of course). On the production
   side, the main emphasis should be on obtaining a clear picture of
   the technology employed and the kinds of firms and households
   from which inputs are purchased and to which outputs are sold.

One important question which arises immediately is whether or not great efforts should be put into the development of a standard statistical frame (à la SNA) for the Third World in general or for particular regions or countries of different levels of national income. This might provide a core set of concepts, definitions, and data applicable generally among countries and not incompatible with the SNA itself. If it proved to be feasible, the

---

[2]In India, the National Sample Survey attempted such a consolidated survey, though the results have yet to be published.

advantages of a standard frame would be very great. It would permit cross-country comparative analysis of programs and performance, allow the partial transfer amongst countries of the experience gained from particular programs and policies, and provide a basis for that inductive generalization from experience which is the basis for advances in operational theorizing.

The primary disadvantage of attempting a standard frame is obvious and has strong parallels with the debate in the 1950s over whether or not a standard system of national accounts could be developed.[3] It is this: can the elements and processes we wish to measure, coming as they do from quite different socio-cultural and institutional environments, be crammed into particular conceptual boxes without doing them mortal violence? Plainly, the answer to this question is an empirical one. What is needed is a pilot study, covering perhaps half a dozen countries, which would subject concepts and methods to a severe test and, if the results were encouraging, provide the basis for a standard frame.[4] But lest anyone be pessimistic about the possibilities, it is worth recalling the debates in the 1950s about whether a standard system of national accounts could be developed. The real question is not whether it is possible but whether the gains from compatibility and international pressure to compile the data would outweigh the possible losses from over-standardization of concepts and priorities.

PRIORITIES FOR AGGREGATE ANALYSIS

Turning now to the more aggregate aspects of policy analysis, and recalling the doubts expressed above concerning comparability, it is only natural to begin by questioning the desirability of having statistical offices in less developed countries concentrate their efforts on implementing SNA *in full*. It has comparatively little direct bearing either on the problem of measuring poverty or on diagnosing its causes and the impact of policy. The more recent proposals to extend the system by linking it with demographic, manpower, and social statistics represent a step in the right direction.[5] However, it is not clear that the implementation of the full system can be justified in terms of the benefits to poverty-focused planning in relation to the statistical effort involved. This carries the implication that, with limited statistical resources, various components of SNA should be drawn on in a selective way. The ones that we would emphasize are those connected with the demands made by the sorts of models discussed in Chapters IX, X, and XI.

Of the issues which can be tackled by the available macro models which are based on an input-output framework, the most straightforward are:

---

[3]National Bureau of Economic Research (1957).
[4]The World Bank might well be an appropriate sponsoring agency.
[5]UN (1970).

first, the relationship between changes in the level and composition of gross output and changes in employment by skill category; and second, the relationship between a change in the distribution of income (as it affects the composition of final demand) and the associated shift in the level and composition of gross output. Unfortunately, inadequacies of existing data affect the reliability even of these straight-forward calculations.

In the former case, the labor input coefficients for the agricultural, service, and informal sectors, which together account for an overwhelming fraction of total employment in less developed countries, are often highly notional. Greater disaggregation and data from the surveys outlined above would do much to ground them more firmly in reality. Even then, the uncertainties surrounding the degree of substitutability between skills (and their tenuous relationship with formal educational attainments) will make it difficult to project demands for different categories of labor with great accuracy.

Plainly, the incorporation of the effects of changes in the distribution of private consumption on the level and composition of gross output (and thence on employment) requires, in addition to an input-output table and a set of rules for mapping its sectoral definitions into consumption categories, a set of demand functions. Thus, the existence of a household expenditure survey is indispensable if this line of inquiry is to be pursued.

Thus far, we have assumed implicitly that the proposed extensions are simply tacked onto an existing input-output table. But our preoccupations with poverty, inequality, and unemployment have major implications for the basis on which such tables are constructed, implications which deserve serious attention prior to the building of new tables. The crucial issue here, as always, is the set of criteria for disaggregation. The extensive literature on this subject does not deal with the requirements of poverty-focused planning. These are sketched below in barest outline. Clearly, this area demands sustained work by specialists at a detailed technical level.

As far as possible, disaggregation should be sought on the basis of distributional attributes. This is easily said, but it raises one particularly important issue: that the type of disaggregation which we recommend here involves the need to measure certain quantities which, by their very nature, are extremely difficult to measure precisely. On this point, we have embraced the principle that it is better to measure the right variable crudely than to measure the wrong more precisely. For example, if the distinction between "large-scale" and "small-scale" agriculture is of the essence, then agriculture should be disaggregated along these lines, in spite of the fact that it is far easier to measure output and intermediate inputs for agriculture in the aggregate than it is in the context of a disaggregation on the basis of farm size categories. The latter is likely to require, initially at least, the use of informal estimates resting on the judgment of such agricultural specialists as agronomists, livestock experts, and so on. We are aware that the explicit use of such subjective estimates is a marked departure from the usual practice of well-organized statistical offices. However, if these agencies are to be responsive to the data demands of a reorientation of policy and planning toward poverty, some changes in established practice will be necessary.

The first priority for disaggregation is by product category. For example, it is too often the case that "agriculture, forestry, and fisheries" are lumped together as a single sector in the input-output tables and national accounts. A finer disaggregation is required for any meaningful analysis focused on poverty. The second priority is a disaggregation within sectors by mode of production, whether it be "traditional" and "modern," or "organized" and "informal." Clearly, such a disaggregation is not required in all sectors — steel, for example, is not (except in China) produced other than in large-scale plants. Then again, the appropriate definition for this disaggregation will be difficult, and it will vary among sectors, for any particular country, and among countries for a given sector. To give an example, agriculture in Mexico might well be meaningfully disaggregated by irrigated and nonirrigated categories and in Indonesia by small-holder and estate.

At this stage, we hesitate to advocate further stages of disaggregation. If a single important sector is subdivided into n sectors and further disaggregated by the two categories above, then we have already suggested adding $x \leqslant 2n - 1$ rows and columns to the interindustry transaction matrix of the input-output table. However, for some sectors or subsectors, the size of the producing unit may be important regarding employment or poverty alleviation policies. In such cases, a further disaggregation should be attempted. Once again, this does not necessarily mean that all components need to be so treated. In agriculture, for example, some crops or groups of crops are not typically produced by all farm size categories.

On the consumption side, similar considerations apply where rich and poor consume different categories of goods, yet which are not distinguished as such. "Textiles" is an example, covering as it does highly finished fabrics for the former and coarse cotton cloth for the latter. The prior disaggregation in the production sectors may capture much of this sort of detail, but that is far from certain. To continue the textiles example, large enterprises in India produce both grey cloth saris and high fashion variants at ten times the price. The difficulties created by such complications are obvious, especially when what are essentially different products are made in the same plant. Once again, a resort to informal estimates, based on expert opinion and "engineering" data, rather than reliance on orthodox industrial censuses may be necessary.

The above basis for disaggregation will also increase the size of the matrix (and hence the work involved in constructing it). Thus, if the risk of this activity swamping all others is to be averted, the number of goods must be cut down. To give a strictly hypothetical example, this may mean collapsing four categories of steel products into one — to the detriment of the matrix's performance on other respects. Of course, this is just the crux of the matter. It is our view — and we concede its presently intuitive foundation—that the *net* payoff to a distributionally based scheme of disaggregation will be positive.

Special Surveys

Special-purpose surveys are required on an ad hoc basis to provide information which is not obtained in the regular survey program. Such surveys, wherever possible, should be carried out in conjunction with the regular survey program. For example, if information in depth is required on labor force participation rates and the socio-economic characteristics of the labor force, it should be obtained by adding an expanded section on labor to the questionnaire of the regular household surveys discussed above. The expanded questionnaire can be applied to the whole sample or to a subsample. This approach is more efficient than a separate survey because it permits the special information on the labor force to be crosstabulated with the larger set of data from the household surveys.

As discussed in Chapter VII, very few data are available on urban establishments and firms with fewer employees than the minimum number required (usually five to ten) for inclusion in the census. For this reason, there is very little information on the urban poor, many of whom are self-employed, underemployed, and in the informal sector. Special-purpose surveys are urgently required to repair this deficiency. Some valuable information on the informal sector would be forthcoming from the household surveys discussed above, and these could provide the framework within which are set the more detailed special-purpose surveys. These latter should be directed particularly at investigating the conditions under which small-scale firms and firms in the informal sector could be made more productive. They should therefore cover in detail such areas as the asset structure, the skill composition of the workforce, the sources of demand for products or services, the prices paid for factors of production and, in particular, the impact upon these firms of discriminatory pricing, and regulatory and licensing powers.

Throughout this brief account, we have attempted to stress that a reorientation of policy and planning towards poverty requires a reorientation of the priorities and, in certain respects, the practices of statistical offices. In particular, we have stressed the need to collect new series of integrated socio-economic data, to disaggregate input-output matrices in meaningful ways (disaggregation which may be offset by some aggregation over existing sectoral definitions), to give increased attention to agricultural statistics, and to give much more attention to the informal sector. These new data can be used for formal quantitative analysis, more rule-of-thumb approaches leading to the formulation of poverty-focused programs, and the monitoring of the effects over time and space of different policy measures. The range and detail of the data required mean that they will be drawn from many sources, both within government and outside, in a variety of operational and research institutes. This is the main reason why the statistical office must give top priority to the compilation of a statistical frame containing basic but highly selective information on household characteristics, incomes, and assets, to which special-purpose statistical surveys and operational programs can be related.

Chapter XIII

RESEARCH DIRECTIONS
Hollis Chenery and John H. Duloy

In this report we have described the existing distribution of income in developing countries and proposed a reorientation of policies designed to improve it. Throughout the analysis we have commented on the limitations of existing theories and empirical methods as a basis for policy-making. In this concluding chapter, we will survey some of the research that is under way to remedy these deficiencies and indicate some of the promising lines of policy analysis.

The present weaknesses in our analytical tools stem from several sources:

(i) the concentration of research effort in response to the concern of policy-makers with increasing total output rather than with the distribution of income;

(ii) the consequent focus on the modern sectors of developing economies and on the obstacles to their more rapid development;

(iii) the fact that both the statistical systems and the theoretical apparatus borrowed from advanced countries are more suited to the analysis of the organized sectors than to the poverty groups in the economy.

Although a variety of reasons can be advanced for the relative neglect of the traditional sectors in earlier work on development, perhaps the most basic is the unstated premise that they constitute transitional problems whose importance will diminish rapidly as the modern sectors expand. However, the rapid growth of population has dissipated this excessive optimism in most countries and forced the recognition that the transitional period is likely to persist for fifty or a hundred years. Furthermore, the ability of a country to accelerate the transition is intimately connected with its ability to provide an adequate share of the benefits of growth to all groups in the society.

Although relatively neglected in the earlier phase of research on developing economies, a substantial volume of work is now under way on both theoretical and empirical aspects of distribution.[1] Our comments will focus on the critical problems that have been identified in the preceding discussion and the analytical techniques that are needed to provide a better basis for policy.

Toward a Theory of Income Distribution in Developing Countries

The formulation of a general distribution theory for developing countries is not likely in the near future, nor is it necessary for better policy-making. However, it is both feasible and desirable to broaden the range of socio-economic factors that are recognized as having an important influence on income distribution and should be incorporated in policy analysis. As demonstrated earlier these include the determinants of population growth and

---

[1] A useful survey of recent and ongoing research is given by Cline (1973).

migration, the availability of land and natural resources, the possibilities of labor absorption and productivity growth in different economic sectors, and the factors affecting asset accumulation and control.

The main contribution of the present report to this discussion is to cast doubt on the usefulness of separating the analysis of income distribution from the study of growth. We have argued that not only do governments of developing countries do very little to redistribute income in favor of the poor but large income transfers would probably not play a continuing role in an effective strategy for more equitable growth. We therefore stress the need to formulate and test the missing links in present models of development, starting with a more meaningful grouping of income recipients than the simple functional division between recipients of wages and profits. Preliminary tests of segmented models in this study suggest that further research should concentrate on the definition of relevant socio-economic groups and the linkages among them for different types of country, the analysis of the productive functions of the unorganized (or informal) sectors of the economy, and the processes of asset accumulation. This research agenda can be usefully pursued at both the economy-wide and sectoral levels, since each complements the other.

Economy-wide Analysis

Two broad conclusions can be derived from our survey of economy-wide planning models. First, there are no established models which have been constructed directly for the purpose of analyzing the distributional aspects of development. However, useful results are obtainable by the imaginative adaptation and extension of existing models.

Modeling the income distribution in particular countries is an area of growing research interest, and a number of studies have been completed or are in progress. Among these are Cline (1972), Weiskoff (1973), Lopes (1972), Pyatt (1972), Adelman and Robinson (1973), Adelman and Tyson (1973), Indian Planning Commission (1973), Foxley and Muñoz (1973), and Pyatt and Thorbecke (1973). The work of these authors is along broadly similar lines. The approach is that of general equilibrium, modeling the flow from changes in the distribution of income through changes in the level and composition of demand to changes in the sectoral composition of output and back to the distribution of incomes. The studies also differ in important respects, including the treatment of disequilibrium in major markets, the determination of factor incomes, and the rules for translating factor incomes into the personal or household income distribution.

These studies are designed primarily to explain the way in which employment and income distribution have been generated in particular countries. Once their explanatory power has been tested, they can also be used to determine the effects of other policies that might have been followed. For example, the series of experiments reported in Chapter IX on the effect of income distribution on the pattern of consumption and production in a number of countries (India, Brazil, Mexico, Puerto Rico, and so forth) casts doubt on the possibilities of easing the investment and trade limitations to growth in this way.

A second line of empirical analysis which is likely to prove useful is to build on the dual economy framework of Lewis (1954), disaggregating it into a segmented model which distinguishes a number of socio-economic groups. A start on this approach was reported in Chapter XI. However, the next steps should be to define socio-economic groups on the basis of access to different forms of assets, incorporating an explicit production structure with input-output matrices estimated for the production activities of different groups. The model can be extended to cover labor markets and migration and to include the government sector and foreign trade. In this way, the constraints on growth set by savings and foreign exchange, which are the focus of conventional models, can be analyzed together with distribution.

The disaggregation into a number of socio-economic groups allows for the analysis of a wide range of policy instruments. If the interrelationships among the groups are carefully specified, the indirect effects of policy intervention can be evaluated.

Such improved planning models for policy analysis are best constructed in the developing countries themselves. However, the experience gained from models of this type is likely to be very useful in developing a more general theory of distribution. Because of the diversity of countries, a typological approach is more likely to provide an empirical basis for theory than an attempt to encompass all developing countries in a single formulation. Preliminary explorations of the factors relevant to such a typology have been made by Adelman and Morris (1973) and in Chapter V.

PARTIAL ANALYSIS

Economy-wide models must be supplemented by more detailed studies of those aspects of the system that are particularly important to the design of policy. In Chapters VI and VII we have identified a number of areas in which the empirical knowledge of target groups as productive sectors or the effects of policy instruments is so inadequate as to limit even the general design of distributional strategies. These areas suggest several priorities for empirical research. Among the types of study needed for the design of policy, we would give particular emphasis to the study of poverty target groups (rural and urban), the evaluation of specific instruments, and the analysis of depressed regions.

Perhaps the highest sector priorities, although not necessarily requiring the use of formal model building, are the study of the problems of the informal sector in urban areas and those associated with rural development. These issues have been largely neglected by researchers because they are not readily accessible to conventional economic analysis. The major policy objective here is to develop programs which, at low cost, can reach large numbers of very poor people who are frequently little affected by market forces. A number of programs are being implemented by national governments, such as public works programs in both urban and rural areas and minimum package programs for rural development. These programs raise a wide range of theoretical and institutional questions, such as the choice of technology, the size and composition of a minimum policy package, the form of delivery systems, and the assessment of benefits which do not directly increase production, such as the effects of improved village water supplies.

Our analysis of the requirements of distributional policy has led us to focus on a set of instruments by which governments can hope to reach particular target groups. While there have been studies of the effectiveness of some of these, such as land reform or rural public works, in other cases an evaluation of the available experience is badly needed. For example, the design and use of simpler and less capital-intensive forms of infrastructure is an important aspect of our proposed strategy for urban development, but there has been little systematic assessment of the experience in this field.

In many of the larger countries—such as Brazil, Thailand, Iran, and Mexico—the problems of inequality stem, in large part, from the excessive concentration of economic activity in the advanced regions of the country to the neglect of other areas. As shown in Chapter X, analytical tools and prototype examples are available for empirical studies of the sources of this problem and for testing alternative solutions. Here the need is for realistic applications to develop a regional strategy that has a stronger empirical foundation and is directed at poverty groups within lagging regions.

CONCLUSIONS

Acceptance of the main theme of this volume, that distributional objectives should be treated as an integral part of development and growth strategy, implies a significant reorientation of development research. We stress three major interrelated areas of research which are likely to be most promising for policy analysis.

First, research should concentrate on the definition of relevant socio-economic groups in different types of countries, on their production, savings, and consumption activities, and on the interrelationships among the groups. Studies which identify the linkages among socio-economic groups provide the basis for an integrated analysis of growth and distribution.

Second, as is stressed in Chapter VI, the effectiveness of policy measures and government investment programs in alleviating poverty is greatly affected by the leakage of benefits to people other than the intended recipients. The mechanism of leakage and the relationships between reducing leakage and efficiency in GNP terms need to be explored.

Closely related to these two areas is the question of access to both privately and publicly supplied assets and services. The former opens up questions on the functioning of markets and the ownership of resources. The latter involves studying nonmarket allocation through the budget with the objective of improving the access of poverty groups to public goods. Some promising lines of research in this area have been commenced by Schaffer (1969) and his coworkers.

Reorientation of research alone does not go much of the distance towards alleviating poverty. A sustained political commitment is the primary condition. However, by evaluating the dimensions of the problem and by demonstrating the effectiveness of different strategies and policies, research can contribute to a climate of opinion strongly favorable to that commitment.

PART THREE: ANNEX AND BIBLIOGRAPHY

ANNEX

REDISTRIBUTION WITH GROWTH:
SOME COUNTRY EXPERIENCE

AN OVERVIEW–RICHARD JOLLY

IN THIS ANNEX, we turn from policies proposed, if not always carried through into action, to the experience of policies implemented. We begin with a brief assessment of antipoverty policies in India, where half the population live below a modestly estimated poverty line. This is one of the highest proportions of any country. Since India's population of 550 million represents almost a sixth of the world total, India's situation is of direct significance, apart from its indirect importance as an example of the general problems of implementing antipoverty policies.

It would have been desirable, had data permitted, to include a comparable commentary on economic growth and redistribution in China, the policies of which contrast in crucial respects with those of India. Unfortunately, this was not possible. Even had it been, there is value in considering a wider range of experience. We have therefore included five brief case studies, summarizing developments with respect to redistribution and growth over the last decade or two in Cuba, Tanzania, Sri Lanka, South Korea, and Taiwan. The experience of these countries covers a range of policies from the explicitly socialist to the explicitly capitalist. In size these countries are more typical of the Third World and all appear to have moved significantly toward greater equality during at least some of the period examined.

Annex Table 1 provides some comparative statistics to set the case studies in perspective. Many of the figures must be treated as orders of magnitude rather than firm estimates.

Annex Table 1: Population, Income, Growth, and Inequality in Six Countries

	India	Cuba	Tanzania	Sri Lanka	Korea	Taiwan
1. Population (1970) mill.	537	8	13	13	32	14
2. Per capita GNP ($1970)	110	530	100	110	250	300
3. Growth of GNP (constant prices, 1960-70) %	3.5	1.5	6.1	3.9	9.4	10.0
4. Inequality: year	1961-4		1967	1969/70	1970	1964
Gini coefficient	.46	n.a.	.48	.37	.36	.32
5. Percentage of Income: top 20%	54	n.a.	57	46	45	40
6. middle 40%	32	n.a.	29	37	37	40
7. bottom 40%	14	n.a.	14	17	18	20
8. Total	100		100	100	100	100

Sources: Lines 1-3: *World Bank Atlas;* inequality data: Table I.1, which see for cautionary comments.

These are brief and personal commentaries rather than full case studies. Each has been written by an economist well acquainted with the country, who was asked to summarize country experience with respect to growth and distribution over the last decade or two, and to identify the main factors responsible, including how they were consciously linked to government objectives and policy. A few general points may help to set the country studies in perspective.

First, the experience in these six countries, although diverse, has been exceptionally favorable with respect to distribution—and for some of them, also, fairly exceptional with respect to growth. A broader review would need to take account of experience in the large majority of developing countries in which distribution has not improved and often worsened. There are many more cases of this sort than of the favorable ones examined, whether, as in India, redistributive poverty-focused policies had been formally adopted by government or not, as in many other countries.

Second, the decade or two under review is a brief period by which to judge long-run tendencies with respect either to growth or redistribution. This qualification is all the more serious, given the weak basis on which assessments of long-run prospects for both growth and distribution must necessarily rest. Moreover, analysis in this area is heavily influenced by the paradigms and ideological frameworks within which the analysis is conducted. In particular, most socialist paradigms stress the long-run tendencies for a capitalist mode of production to lead to even greater concentration of income and wealth. Because income and wealth are closely correlated with power, these paradigms usually lead to the conclusion that it is difficult if not impossible to introduce and maintain redistributive measures that would ensure a more equitable distribution of consumption, without involving a substantial prior redistribution of assets and consequent changes in the structure of production. On the other hand, many analysts working within essentially capitalist paradigms tend to stress the impossibility of combining high growth rates with strongly egalitarian policies because of the difficulty of maintaining adequate incentives for economic activities. Empirical investigation can help to take the heat out of some of these disputes and substitute light. But the absence of adequate, long-run data inevitably will leave many issues only dimly illuminated at present.

Conclusions drawn from these latter five case studies, therefore, must be tentative. But the studies can nonetheless raise questions. The most important conclusions are seven.

(i) Favorable trends in income distribution have taken place in régimes of considerable difference in political ideology and approach from Cuba to Taiwan. In Cuba, Tanzania, and Sri Lanka the income redistribution has been in large part the direct result of conscious government policy; in Korea and Taiwan, it seems that improvements in income distribution, while welcomed after the event, have been largely the by-product of policies aimed primarily at economic growth.

(ii) In all cases, successful redistribution seems to have been preceded or accompanied by changes in the structure of asset ownership, particularly by land reform. In Taiwan and Korea, much of the stimulus for land reform came from outside; in Cuba and Tanzania it has come from within, the direct consequence of socialist policies. In Sri Lanka, land reform has been long delayed. The unequal ownership of land is a major cause of the failure to carry through the welfare state policies.

(iii) In all five cases, the most marked changes in income distribution are traced to changes in the structure of economic production, except possibly in Cuba. Subsequent changes in the pattern of post-tax incomes and consumption have been effected but only to a limited extent.

(iv) Deliberate manipulation of relative prices has seemed to have had an important influence in Cuba and Sri Lanka, though to have played little part elsewhere.

(v) Free health and education policies (human capital formation by asset creation, in the terminology of the volume) have been adopted in all five cases though their long-run effects on income distribution are difficult to judge. In Sri Lanka and Korea, expansion of secondary and higher education has led to widespread unemployment of the educated. In four of the sample countries (Cuba excepted), education has been clearly associated with wide inequalities in the wage structure.

(vi) Nevertheless, the provision of various types of government services and infrastructure appears to have helped the poorer groups in Cuba, Tanzania, and Sri Lanka. In Korea and Taiwan, the impact of such services on income distribution appears to have been small while, in India, the rich farmers and traders appear to have appropriated the bulk of the benefits.

(vii) From these five cases, it is difficult to identify clear evidence of a trade-off between growth, however defined or measured, and distribution. Except for Cuba, redistribution has been accompanied by significant growth and in two cases by very rapid growth. Even in the case of Cuba, it is not at all clear that the widespread measures of redistribution themselves have been in any way a significant cause of the very slow rate of growth. And in the other cases, redistribution has been successfully combined with growth, in some cases growth at very high rates in comparison with what most other countries have achieved.

INDIA–PRANAB K. BARDHAN

Removal of social and economic injustices and assurance of minimum levels of living have been among the most important Directive Principles laid down in the Indian Constitution. Right from the inception of planning these have been among the most prominent explicitly stated objectives of government economic policy. In the last two decades or more, a whole host of policy measures (at least ostensibly resembling many of the suggestions made in different parts of this volume) had been taken towards achieving these objectives. Yet, by most accounts, about half of the total population continue to live in abject poverty and the distribution of income, wealth, and economic power continues to be extremely unequal.[1] The Indian experience, therefore, is highly instructive in understanding the nature of various types of constraints on the effective implementation of good-intentioned redistributive policies in the framework of a so-called mixed economy.

Asset Redistribution Policies

Let us first take the set of policies aimed at direct redistribution of existing assets. The most important asset in India is land. On paper, the volume of land reform legislation in India is very impressive. Laws setting ceilings (often fixed at reasonably low levels) on the private ownership of land with provision for the redistribution of surplus land adorn the statute books of all states in India. Yet by the end of 1970, for the country as a whole, the "declared surplus" has been only 2.4 million acres and the "area distributed" just half of that, or 0.3 percent of the total cultivated land. (Even then this distributed land includes, to a large extent, very poor quality land, wasteland, and the like.) Laws were frequently enacted with deliberate loopholes and telltale exemptions designed to induce fictitious transfers of land to close and distant relatives and to keep the size of permissible retentions high. These laws were executed by a local bureaucracy largely indifferent, occasionally corrupt, and biased in favor of the rural oligarchy; they were enforced by an enormously costly and excruciatingly slow judicial process. For roughly similar reasons, equally miserable has been the fate, except in a couple of states, of tenancy legislation designed to bestow occupancy rights or security of tenure on the tenant cultivators. Implementation has been particularly hampered by a lack of systematic land records (with most of the tenancy existing on the basis of informal and oral lease) and weak revenue administration in many states. Quite frequently, protective tenancy legislation (actual or anticipated) may have worsened the condition of tenants; it has led to resumption of land by the landlords and eviction of tenants under the guise of "voluntary surrender" of land.

As for nonland assets, the major attempts at redistribution have been indirect through the substantial extension of public ownership over the last two decades. The public sector now owns more than 25 percent of the total reproducible tangible wealth in the country, which is a large increase over its share twenty-five years ago. But it is doubtful if this has had any significant impact on personal income inequalities. Much of the "nationalization" has been on payment of heavy compensation and the poor utilization of capacity and low rate of profits in many public enterprises (several exceptions notwithstanding) have led to a lower surplus available for either growth or distribution. The general tendency of many public enterprises to underprice their products and to yield relatively easily to union pressures on wage

---

[1]For a survey of estimates of income inequality and poverty in India see Bardhan (1973b).

and salary settlements and provision of relatively liberal housing and other amenities to workers does not necessarily mean that the benefits of the public sector flow to the really poor people, most of whom do not belong to the organized sector and do not in general consume products which are highly intensive—directly or indirectly—in what the public sector produces.

Public Investment

From the point of view of poverty, a more important class of policies is related to public investment in the provision of various types of facilities and to infrastructure aimed at helping to raise productivity and asset formation on the part of the poor themselves. In the 1950s, major attempts in this direction were made through state-sponsored or state-patronized institutions like village cooperatives (to provide subsidized credit) and Community Development Programmes (to provide extension services and to create various infrastructural facilities). But by the end of the 1950s it was admitted on all hands (including reports of the Programme Evaluation Organization of the Planning Commission) that most of these benefits in the rural areas were being appropriated by rich farmers by virtue of their social and economic dominance in the countryside and their political and administrative control over these new institutions. The cooperatives became essentially sources of subsidized credit for the big farmers and village moneylenders; the Community Development Programmes provided some of the infrastructure (like roads, land improvement, and so on) to be utilized mostly by the big farmers and traders. Similar has been the case with the large amount of public investment in major irrigation programs, partly because the powerful and "well-connected" people in the villages have direct influence on the distribution of canal water and partly because the small farmers do not have the finances to invest in tubewells, pumps, and other mechanical devices for supplementary water supplies. In the industrial sector also, the overwhelming share of benefits of public investment in the creation and operation of public financial institutions for long-term lending has gone to the rich.

Credit and Services for the Rural Poor

In very recent years some special agencies like the Small Farmers Development Agency (SFDA) and Agency for Marginal Farmers and Agricultural Labour (MFAL) have been created to aid improvements in the productive capacity of the rural poor. It is as yet too early to attempt an evaluation of the performance of these agencies. But one may point to some inherent problems in their effectiveness. The task of the special agencies is to identify and promote viable activities for the poor and to activate and subsidize existing institutions (like cooperatives, commercial banks, extension agencies, and the like) to provide inputs, services, and credit to the small and marginal farmers. But there are problems of identifying economically viable activities for the individual small farmer because of deficiencies of *farm level* infrastructure (for example, the frequent recommendation of dairy farming as a way of making the small man viable often ignores the limitations imposed by a small or no-land base); on the other hand, attempts to compensate for these deficiencies are made by strengthening the *area-level* infrastructure (like development of general facilities of marketing, processing, storage, transport, and so forth), but these additional facilities, being in their very nature area-specific rather than individual farm-specific, largely flow to those who are better off and more well equipped to utilize them. Second, as the mode of operation of the special agencies essentially involves subsidizing and underwriting the loans of existing institutions like cooperatives, the implicit assumption is that these institutions have not been effective in helping the poor so far, primarily due to lack of adequate resources and, particularly, of risk funds (some studies have, however, shown that the extent of default on repayment of cooperative credit has *not* been larger in the case of smaller farmers). If big farmers, moneylenders, and traders continue to control the operation of cooperatives and other existing institutions, it may not be difficult for them to influence the priorities and flow of benefits from the special agencies. There are already several reports that big farmers—who, in view of the land ceilings legislation, have fictitiously parceled their land among several relatives—are now taking advantage of the subsidies of the SFDA program on account of their "small farms."

The main problem with the credit policies of cooperatives, land mortgage banks, or branches of nationalized banks is that credit continues to be given on the basis of land ownership as the primary collateral. Even when these credit institutions have very liberal lending policies, they usually insist that cultivators must be in a position to mortgage at least four to seven acres of land in order to obtain a large enough long-term or medium-term credit for the purchase of a tubewell or a pumpset. The majority of small farmers are left out. If as a result the small farmer does not have assured water supply, this in turn means that he cannot utilize short-term production credit for buying fertilizers, and so on, a phenomenon often interpreted by the cooperative bank officials as "lack of demand." Even when the farmer owns the requisite amount of land, as long as it is "encumbered" (i.e., mortgaged to some other credit institution or private moneylender), he cannot use it as collateral for any other loan negotiation. All these problems are, of course, much more acute for the large numbers of tenants and sharecroppers who do not own but only cultivate land and have, therefore, little creditworthiness. Since most of the small tenants are on oral lease, they do not in general have access even to short-term cooperative or bank credit for current production purposes, and have to fall back on the village moneylender's tender mercy. Attempts at introducing the crop loan system where credit is production oriented rather than security-oriented have been fragmentary and limited.

Education

Public investment in human capital formation, particularly through education, is often regarded as an important way of affecting the long-run distribution of income. Evidence on the distribution of benefits from such investment in India is scanty, but most studies of enrollment, wastage, and drop-out rates in school, as well as participation in higher education, suggest that the benefits of educational subsidies accrue disproportionately less to the lower income groups at each level of education. Even when one has access to education, the poor man with less "contacts" and mobility has a smaller opportunity to get jobs commensurate with his education (the government's policy of ensuring job quotas for some backward castes and groups is clearly inadequate and is sometimes misused).

Rural Investment and Employment Creation

The other area of redistributive public investment advocated in the Indian Plans, particularly since the late 1950s, is investment in rural works programs creating alternative employment for rural unskilled and underemployed labor and at the same time producing durable assets (in the form of roads, soil conservation, minor irrigation, afforestation, and so on) without involving much use of scarce inputs like steel or cement. But the actual expenditure incurred on this account has been extremely small, the programs have been badly administered and, whenever resource constraints have necessitated curtailing of plans midway, the axe has usually fallen first on programs like these. Very recently the government has adopted, somewhat more earnestly, a Crash Scheme for Rural Employment (CSRE) designed to provide in every district in the country employment for 1,000 persons for a period of ten months a year on public works at off-season market wage rates. This is only an experimental scheme and is not aimed at more than touching the bare fringe of the massive problem of unemployment and underemployment in rural India. Yet it is worth pointing to some of the major problems in the actual operation of CSRE. One such problem is that of organization. The rigidities of government departmental organization are well known. The district administrative machinery is often woefully inadequate in preparing technically sound projects suited to the specific problems of timing, location, skills, and other constraints of the local underemployed. Frequently, the task of organizing the works is entrusted to labor contractors. This immediately leads to a big cut in the wage share of the workers. Then, the contractor usually hires people from around the village of his own residence, and that may not be among the pockets of acute unemployment in the district. Since the contractor is usually paid according to the amount of work done, he is sometimes in a hurry to get the job done in bouts of intensive activity for a few weeks. Over this period, the official requirement of the Scheme to provide employment to those who belong to families where no adult member is employed is quite often ignored. For the same reason the Scheme, in spite of its intentions, does not provide continuity of employment. Second, in a private-ownership economy the benefits of public works (like construction of roads or land improvement) accrue differentially to different groups and this is limited with problems of mobilizing responsible local participation in terms of financial and organizational efforts involved in such programs, problems which the Chinese have successfully tackled through the institution of the commune. Third, because of the very nature of public works, there is relatively low participation by female members of poor households and by laborers attached to big farms who may not have much freedom in working outside even in off seasons. Finally, because of political pressures and regional pulls, programs like CSRE tend to be thinly spread over the country as a whole rather than concentrated in areas of severe incidence of poverty and underemployment.

Price, Incomes, and Tax-Subsidy Policy

Let us now turn to the more conventional arena of price, incomes, and tax-subsidy policies to help the poor. In agricultural prices, the government policy in the last decade or so has been to provide relatively high support prices for foodgrains and to try to distribute the procured grains at fair price shops with a large subsidy. Since the major part of marketable surplus of grains is controlled by big farmers, the high support prices mostly help them rather than small farmers (although the latter may have benefited to some extent from the reduction in interseason price fluctuations that high support prices may have brought about). The system of public distribution of grains is, however, very weak except in about four states. The poor, including the small farmers, are largely dependent on the open market for their grains consumption and have been directly hit by the steep price rises of recent years. The statutory stipulation of minimum wages in industry or agriculture has been virtually inoperative in the vast unorganized nonunionized sectors where the overwhelming majority of the poor work; nothing more could be expected in a situation of acute underemployment. Similarly inoperative has been the rent control legislation in protective tenancy reforms in agriculture, as can be expected in a situation of inexorable pressure on land.

In the Indian context there are only limited possibilities of substantial expansion of employment in the organized sector through price-induced changes in product pattern or techniques of production. The major use of price policy for increasing employment has therefore been to encourage and protect, at the expense of large subsidies and grants, traditional village industries, particularly hand-spinning and hand-weaving of cloth which involve nearly four million poor households. The Indian planning discussion has held long and unending debates on the wisdom of protecting what is quite often an admittedly inferior technology from the competition of a superior technology of mill production for the sake of helping—or at least not uprooting—large numbers of poor households. Other kinds of price policy which may have affected choice of technology relate to underpricing of capital and foreign exchange—in agriculture this has encouraged labor-displacing mechanization, particularly of harvesting and threshing operations in some regions; in the industrial sector this has reinforced or at least failed to counter the tendency of wholesale transfer of labor-saving technical progress of industrially advanced countries.

As for direct provision of public consumption and welfare measures for the poor in the form of health and sanitation, nutrition, drinking water, housing, education, transport, and communication and electricity, there has been some progress over the last two decades, but facilities in proportion to minimum needs remain apparently meagre. Apart from the problem of developing an adequate administrative delivery infrastructure, finance has been a major constraint: whenever the overall financial situation gets worse, these social welfare programs have been the first to be shelved in order to save the so-called core sectors in the Plan. There is also some evidence that the upper-income groups have been able to appropriate for themselves a disproportionate share of some of the expanding social services (particularly education, transport and communication facilities, and low-cost housing).

Conclusions

In sum, the problems of poverty in India remain intractable, not because redistributive objectives were inadequately considered in the planning models, nor because general policies of the kind prescribed in this volume were not attempted. Of course, on the micro level there were specific programs that were ill-conceived and uncoordinated and there were familiar problems of administrative rigidities on the part of an ex-colonial bureaucracy largely oriented to maintaining law and order and collecting revenue. But the major constraint is rooted in the power realities of a political system dominated by a complex constellation of forces representing rich farmers, big business, and the so-called petite bourgeoisie, including the unionized workers of the organized sector. In such a context it is touchingly naïve not to anticipate the failures of asset distribution policies or the appropriation by the rich of a disproportionate share of the benefits of public investment.

Two other kinds of constraints follow from the same primary political constraint. One has to do with the generation and mobilization of the surplus necessary to finance redistributive programs. With a vast network of deliberately designed exemptions and loopholes in the tax laws, all catering to the various pressure groups in the top deciles of the population, the system of income and wealth taxation is largely incapacitated to yield much extra surplus; already nearly three-fourths of total tax revenue come from indirect taxes which, apart from frequently stoking the fires of inflation, are not progressive in their overall incidence in spite of some stiff taxes on selected luxury items. With low rates of profits in public enterprises and huge subsidies in supporting prices paid to big farmers and wages and salary increases paid to white-collar workers, there is little surplus left to help the poor. Faced with a financial squeeze, the government immediately prunes social welfare programs for the poor, or resorts to deficit financing, or both; the inflationary consequences hit the poor hardest. It is paucity of surplus and the consequent fall in the rate of public investment which largely explain why in recent years India has had a miserable performance in overall growth as well as in mitigation of poverty.

The second set of constraints that follows from the ultimate political constraint mentioned above relates to the nature of the local bureaucracy which administers the poverty programs. More often than not the local administrative machinery is manned by people belonging to the families of the rural oligarchy and the urban elite. One does not have to believe in conspiracy

theories to note that good-intentioned redistributive programs are sometimes
negated by the local vested interests with at least tacit administrative con-
nivance. To quote a Bengali rural proverb, "if there are ghosts inside your
mustard seeds, how would you use them to exorcise the ghosts?"

CUBA–DUDLEY SEERS

In Cuba, the development strategy has put heavy emphasis on the elimination of poverty, through a sharp reduction in inequality.[2] The degree of
equality in Cuba is now probably unique. It is a case, therefore, highly perti-
nent to the issues of this report: if one could set up an experiment in the social
sciences, it might well look like Cuba.

Economic data on Cuba are scarce and it is impossible here to deal at all
fully with the results of the revolution. But it seems broadly that, although
there was a spurt forward in many productive sectors immediately after the
revolution, the national income rose only about in line with population from
1961 to 1968,[3] and then declined in the following three years.[4] The main
issue therefore appears to be whether redistribution has inhibited growth.

But this is misleading. Before trying to explain what has occurred, I would
like to point out that to discuss the "trade-off" in these terms is theoretically
mistaken when elimination of poverty is the central objective. Then the important question to pose about a country's performance is not, how much did
the nation's income grow? But rather, whose income grew? And what sort
of production increased? Increases in the income of the top 20 percent have
no direct impact on absolute poverty—they aggravate relative poverty (i.e.,
inequality). Besides, if the object is to change the existing distribution of
income, this implies the inappropriateness of prices produced by this distribution and used in estimates of growth.[5]

It is often argued that, however narrowly the benefits of growth are concentrated, poverty can be cured one day in the future by redistributing the
national product after it has increased. The political assumptions of this argument are questionable because growth makes those who benefit from it more
powerful. But in any case, the conclusion does not necessarily follow even in

---

[2]I would like to acknowledge the valuable assistance of Richard Stanton. Readers
should note that the argument in places has had to be compressed in order to fit within
the word limit set for each case study.

[3]See Dorticos (1972). It is not clear whether adjustment had been made for price
changes, but the most favorable assumption is that he was using a fixed-price comparison. Since wages and prices were frozen for much of this period, it would not matter
greatly. However, since the Marxist definition of income was presumably used, the
actual rise was somewhat higher; this definition excludes the social services, the most
dynamic sector.

[4]For figures from which the following can be inferred, see the unsigned "La Perspectivas Desarrollo de la Economia Cubana, 1971-75," *Economia y Desarrollo* no. 13
(September–October 1972), p. 194.

[5]There are additional problems of measuring, or even defining, the national income in
countries with large rural populations.

purely economic terms. Because of the specificity of assets, it depends on what types of production increased—one cannot cure poverty by redistributing cosmetics or casino tickets.[6]

In the case of Cuba, there is indeed a question about the consistency of objectives, but it cannot be posed in such naïve terms. The movement of an aggregate has particularly little meaning when far-reaching changes take place in the structure of production and income, including the emigration of a large fraction of those who were formerly rich. The question which *is* raised is the slowness in improving the lot of the poor. In the first few years after the revolution, dire poverty and unemployment were virtually eliminated.[7] But further progress in the production of necessities, especially food, or of goods which could be exported, was slow. Sugar output in the 1970s (except for the special effort which produced 8.5 million tons in 1969/70) has not exceeded typical prerevolutionary levels. From 1962 to 1968/69 nonsugar agricultural output fell by 18 percent[8] and supplies of consumer goods, including necessities such as food, grew tighter.[9] Progress in rehousing those in slum or overcrowded dwellings was slow. It is true that teaching and medical services, which are essential to the elimination of poverty, expanded rapidly. But the infant mortality rate obstinately remained around 40 per 1,000.[10]

The key question is not whether the redistribution and the associated use of moral rather than material incentives caused the per capita incomes to rise little if at all between 1958 and 1971, but whether they contributed to the failure to make further substantial inroads into poverty after 1961.

The Pre-revolutionary Situation

This issue should be looked at in historical perspective. In the 1950s, Cuba was beset by serious social problems. Open unemployment was some 16 percent in 1956/57,[11] poverty was widespread, with a large fraction of the population illiterate and undernourished (especially those in large rural families).[12] This was not, however, due to inadequate national income,

---

[6]It could be argued that casinos, if not croupiers, can be converted to productive use—but this is expensive.

[7]A comparison of nutritional surveys in 1967 with those made a decade earlier showed "a definite improvement" in the state of nutrition. See Navarro (1972).

[8]Acosta (1972).

[9]In 1969, despite the improvement in nutrition of the lowest-income groups, there was an important increase from ½ liter to 1 liter a day in the milk ration for children under seven and other special categories, but this may not have been fully reflected in actual consumption.

[10]In fact this rate had been 35 in 1953. It is possible to ascribe the rise to 38 in 1966 to improvements in statistical collection. JUCEPLAN (1967) estimates that the correct figure should have been 39 in both years. But the further increase to 41 in 1968 suggests that poverty was proving an intractable problem. However, the rate fell back to 36 (a provisional figure) in 1971, according to United Nations (1973).

[11]Consejo Nacional de Economia (1958).

[12]The sample surveys of rural workers carried out by the Catholic University Group (ACU) demonstrates this. For example, less than 10 percent of homes had running water.

which at about $500 a head[13] was quite high enough to make acute poverty unnecessary.

The distribution of this income was however highly concentrated, and so was access to medical and educational facilities. Although no coefficient of concentration can be estimated, Cuba must have been among those countries in which it was "relatively high" (i.e., >0.5). (See Chapter I.) At its roots lay a highly concentrated distribution of property, especially of land, 9 percent of the landowners holding 73 percent of the land.[14] Many factories and much land belonged to foreign companies. Contrasts between incomes, housing, health, and educational levels in Havana and the rural areas were particularly marked.

There seemed little prospect of the chronic poverty being alleviated. Up to the 1920s, the Cuban economy had advanced rapidly—with sugar output reaching 5 million tons in the mid-1920s—but it developed severe inequalities in the process. In the following three decades, progress was slow. Increased sugar output was restrained by quotas and industrialization was hindered by the Reciprocal Trade Agreement (1934) with United States.[15] Apart from tourism (the benefits of which largely accrued either to foreigners or to groups and areas already rich) there was little dynamic in the economy, which had considerable surplus capacity in capital as well as labor. A succession of dictatorships notorious for their inefficiency and corruption[16] repressed the political forces that favored the redistribution of income.

Steps after the Revolution to Redistribute Income

Most of the implements of redistribution mentioned in Chapter II were used after the revolution. (a) *Assets were redistributed.* Tenants of smallholdings and houses became their owners.[17] In addition, nationalization, starting with foreign-owned companies and landholdings, spread to all productive assets. There was no compensation for U.S. asset-holders and, though most local property-owners were paid annuities, these involved a degree of expropriation. Much property (especially housing) was abandoned by emigrants. (b) *Public investment and consumption were concentrated on the poor,* especially health and educational services. Particular attention was paid to the reduction of illiteracy, and there was a very big increase in adult education at all levels, including technical training. The expansion of public

---

[13]Oshima (1961). His reference is to the position in 1957.

[14]Estimates of INRA before the land reform.

[15]The prerevolutionary period is analyzed in Seers (1964).

[16]Truslow (1951) was particularly scathing, describing the Ministry of Education as "a principal focus of political patronage and graft . . . a cave of entrenched bandits and of gunmen and an asylum of professional highway robbers" (p. 425). These unusually strong words, for a report published under World Bank auspices, speak for the international reputation of Cuba in that period.

[17]After the second stage of the agrarian reform in 1963, 24 percent of the land remained in private hands; much of this was incorporated in the state sector after the Third Reform of 1968/69. See Acosta (1972).

expenditure made big inroads into unemployment, and by being concentrated in rural areas it helped reduce the urban-rural imbalance. (c) *Income was redistributed* in three ways. (i) Wages were increased, especially at lower levels, the effective minimum becoming nearly 100 pesos a month by 1971 for both agriculture and industry.[18] Pensions were made universal and raised to levels near or at the corresponding wage levels. At the other end of the scale, salary rates for managerial jobs were reduced, few being left above 300 pesos, so that a span of about 3-to-1 covered the great majority of wage and salary rates.[19] (ii) Piece rates and other incentive payments were abolished, and claims for overtime discouraged.[20] Stress was laid, especially in education, on moral incentives, made concrete in medals, titles, and the like, to take the place of financial acquisitiveness. (iii) Charges for medical attention, schooling, and some other services (e.g., water, school meals, entrance to sporting events, local telephone calls) were eliminated, as were loan obligations of smallholders. Basic foodstuffs were put on ration and their prices were kept low, and so were the prices of other basic goods and services such as bus journeys. Consequently the range of real incomes became even less than that of money incomes.

A feature of this report is attention to the political conditions for a poverty-oriented strategy (see Chapter III). In Cuba the government was strong enough after revolution to put the redistributive measures into effect. The political power both of the poor rural areas (where the revolution originated) and also of many urban dwellers had been mobilized. The military and police forces, which had been an integral part of the former régime, and might have attempted to overthrow the new one, were disbanded and replaced, and many of the rich started to emigrate.

Causes of Production Problems

These measures had an impact on poverty.[21] Why was the improvement not sustained? Of course, at this stage, fifteen years after the revolution, a thoroughgoing evaluation would be premature. Evaluations of the social progress of the Soviet or Chinese revolutions after only fifteen years would have proved misleading. Nevertheless it is possible to indicate some elements in the explanation.

---

[18]At the time of the revolution, 1 peso officially equalled US$1; they were perhaps also roughly equal in purchasing power. Since then, the price structure has changed so much in Cuba that comparisons are now difficult, if not meaningless.

[19]An official currently in a senior post was allowed a personal supplement to maintain his income level.

[20]However, workers in establishments with good records of attendance and voluntary work were allowed higher pensions when they retired.

[21]In terms of the concepts of Chapter II, a "poverty-weighted" national income would show a sharp rise in the first few years after the revolution, though perhaps an index giving all the weight to the bottom 40 percent would be more meaningful—at least in Cuba. Such an index would not allow, of course, for the rise in the welfare of the poor due to public services (especially education and health) and to changes in the price structure (especially reduction of prices for necessities).

In other contexts, it might have been expected that the reduced concentration of income would lead to a fall in investment. However, this has not happened in Cuba. Investment has been almost completely under public control,
and has been supported by heavy aid, especially from the Soviet Union. It has
been more than 20 percent of the national income (though the precentage
might have been lower if growth had been faster).

Part of the explanation of production difficulties lay in the international
context. The loss of professional and skilled manpower through emigration
to the United States aggravated production problems. So did the switch to
Soviet and East European sources of supply for intermediate products and
equipment—especially spare parts, as a result of a trade embargo—and to the
same sources of technical expertise. (Cuba was neglected by many aid
agencies, even multilateral ones.) Moreover, part of the country's resources
were tied up in military preparations to deal with possible invasions, especially after the Bay of Pigs.[22]

Yet by the early 1970s these problems had been eased. In many sectors,
the loss of qualified personnel had been offset by the results of the big
increase in education and training programs; the conversion to COMECON
sources of inputs had been very largely completed; and the threat of invasion
had dwindled. Indeed the trade embargo and military intervention were in
some respects economic assets. They provided an excuse for shortages; by
stimulating nationalism, they also encouraged voluntary labor, which was
extensively used to break production bottlenecks. The cutting of trade and
other links with countries in the Western Hemisphere reduced the "demon-
stration effect" of standards of consumption which could not be afforded by
the population as a whole as well as the influence of technical assistance
which would doubtless have been inappropriate for Cuba's development
strategy.

A main cause of production problems has to be sought in economic management. The economy has lacked the central rationale of either a price
system or an overall development plan,[23] which was a contributory factor in
policy mistakes[24] (e.g., reversals of sugar policy). Moreover, financial
accounting was abandoned for both individual enterprises and the economy
as a whole.

Managers of factories and farms ceased to keep accounts, or even to know
their costs of production (the economy being in effect treated as one big

---

[22]It is interesting to speculate what the production experience of Cuba would have
been—and whether less egalitarian policies would have been followed—if instead of
embargo, blockade, and invasion, Cuba had received external support from capitalist
countries in the early years of the revolution.

[23]There *have* been, however, medium-term physical plans for particular sectors, and
annual plans for foreign exchange, labor use, and key products.

[24]For example, several reversals of sugar policy, most notably the early decision to
uproot 15 percent of the acreage given to sugar on the grounds that planned "industrialization and diversification" would make it necessary. Replanning took place in the mid-
1960s. For a highly critical account of Cuban agricultural policies see Dumont (1970),
especially Chapter V; also, "El Sector Agropecuario en la década 1959-69," Instituto
de Economía, Universidad de la Habana. Mimeographed. Havana, 1971.

enterprise without interdepartmental invoices). This not only caused inefficiency (including hoarding of labor); project evaluation also became practically impossible.

No attempt was made to match rises in wages, pensions, public services, or investment (or reductions in prices) by measures to absorb the consequent increases of purchasing power, and the government has persistently rejected a currency reform (apart from a confiscation of large notes soon after the revolution). So cash in the hands of the public rose to very high levels:[25] retail inventories virtually disappeared (except for reading matter and pharmaceuticals); and long queues had become a familiar sight. There appears also to have been a considerable black market.[26]

The market imbalance had results somewhat inconsistent with social objectives. A family's consumption level came to depend partly on whether its members had between them the time and stamina needed for queuing, which penalized the elderly and those with children under school age, and partly on access to official transport, canteens, and so forth.

The market imbalance also meant a vicious circle: queuing led to absenteeism and production difficulties, which in turn aggravated the shortages. Moreover, since many families could not spend the wages of their employed males, the government made little progress in its attempt to mobilize the female labor reserve of 1.5 million. In addition, the prevalance of absenteeism and black market operations impaired the appeal to moral incentives.

Cuban experience in the 1960s, therefore, turns out not to have been a proper test of an egalitarian policy, which does not necessarily entail the abandonment of financial controls or complete abolition of material incentives. It is possible, however, that all these policies had their roots in the years of guerrilla warfare, when there was, of course, no need for accountancy or an appeal to material incentives.[27]

The Recent Change in Strategy

In 1970 this complex of problems grew worse, partly because of the diversion of labor to the attempted sugar crop of 10 million tons. A sweeping change of policy took place, designed to increase material incentives as well as to restore financial balance, both overall and for production units.[28] Prices of "nonessential" goods were raised sharply, those of restaurant meals being

---

[25]About 3.3 billion pesos at the end of 1970, or more than the total annual wage bill. See Dorticos (1972).

[26]According to the Prime Minister's May 1, 1971, speech, the highly specific nature of the rationing system encouraged ration-swapping (which is the starting point of a black market).

[27]Another contributing factor may have been the euphoria which followed the successful repulsion of the Bay of Pigs invasion.

[28]A recent policy statement by Fidel Castro [November 25, 1973, before the 13th Congress of the CTC] admitted implicitly that the distribution of income had not been closely enough geared to productive contribution. Before reaching communism, which implied distribution according to need, it was necessary first to apply "the inexorable law" of socialism, that each should be paid according to his labor.

at least doubled and of rum trebled. New production norms were introduced. An "antiloafing" law was passed. Television sets, refrigerators, and even apartments started to be offered as prizes for good records of attendance and production. It was decided to make cars available to technicians and union officials. Wage increases were linked to productivity. Some pension rates were lowered (for those yet to retire). Accounting was reintroduced and a standard system adopted in 1973. Government statements stressed the importance of saving materials and electricity.

A development plan for the period 1971-75 was also prepared. Although this plan focuses conventionally on a high growth rate (11 percent),[29] it could be argued that aggregates have more significance now that income is distributed more equitably, poverty has been reduced, and production is concentrated on necessities.

It is far too early to see the impact of the new policies on equality, production, or poverty. However, cash in the public's hands has fallen;[30] queues have shortened; absenteeism has declined; and the national income is reported to have risen by 9 percent in 1972, despite a poor sugar crop, and 13 percent (very provisionally) in 1973.[31] The quantity of underutilized capital and human resources in 1971 certainly permitted a surge forward in output, including foodstuffs. However, the new policies may well cause some of what was previously disguised unemployment (because of the hoarding of labor) to emerge into the open. Additionally, the distribution of consumption is becoming rather less equal. The growth in production, therefore, may not mean a comparable rise in consumption at the lowest levels.

While interpretation of Cuban experience is complicated by the temporary abolition of financial controls, it suggests that very drastic redistribution, especially if it takes the form of abolishing incentives, may interfere with the reduction of poverty (at least in a society which has been conditioned to expect personal rewards). Now that financial controls are being introduced, it will be easier to assess whether what is still a highly egalitarian society has the dynamic potential to complete the task of eliminating poverty.

TANZANIA–REGINALD H. GREEN

Since Independence, Tanzania has attained a moderate but fairly steady growth rate. Between 1964 and 1972 the country has averaged about 5 percent a year in real terms, compared to 3 percent over the 1961-64 period and somewhat less over the previous decade. The relevant policy-change dates were Independence in 1961, the first comprehensive planning exercise in 1964, and serious priority to asset and income redistribution in 1967. Independence was followed by planning and growth, but no correlation between

---

[29]See "La Perspectivas Desarrollo de la Economia Cubana, 1971-75," p. 194, loc. cit. The growth rate of agriculture, apart from sugar, is put at the very high rate of 16.4 percent.

[30]Castro, loc. cit. The reduction had been 1.23 billion pesos in two and a half years.

[31]Ibid.

egalitarianism and growth in the short run is evident. External factors—weather, rundown of diamond production, export prices—have been moderately worse since 1967 (albeit aid levels have been higher), giving credit to the tentative conclusion that concentration on egalitarian and socialist measures has been at least neutral in its impact on growth.

The shift to a more radical policy initially arose from a realization that the 1961-67 period had seen the first steps toward the emergence of elites in a form likely to "nationalize" the colonial structure rather than lead to egalitarian socialism. These elites included Tanzanian large farmers, small businessmen, intellectuals, managers of the parastatals and the private sector, senior civil servants, and political leaders. As these were at most weak proto-elites in 1967, the 1967-73 strategy has been largely prophylactic, freezing the citizen tap, squeezing the small private sector modestly, nationalizing the large private sector, and seeking to build up the economic and political power of the poor through asset creation, expenditure redirection, and participation.

In 1972, average output was about $100. The poorest 40 percent of the population had per capita incomes below $50 and about one-sixth of total income while the richest 20 percent had per capita incomes over $190 and slightly over half of total income. This probably represents a shift of about 8 percent away from the top quintiles since 1967, a gain of about 2.5 percent to the bottom two quintiles and a gain of 5.5 percent to the middle two quintiles. Public consumption was about 10 percent of GDP; investment was of the order of 24 percent. The impact of direct and indirect taxes and use of public services would probably raise the bottom two quintiles' share to about one-fifth of total income and reduce the top quintile's to somewhat under half. The very top end of the income distribution is dominated by some 5,000 expatriates who provide high-level skills. The lowest two quintiles are predominantly rural. The urban unemployed and informal sectors are relatively small absolutely and in comparison with other African countries. Nonagricultural recorded wage employment has grown over 6 percent a year for half a decade, tending to match the rate of urbanization.

The public sector citizen wage/salary range runs from Sh 3,600 to Sh 58,000 per year. As three-quarters of large- and medium-scale economic activity is in this sector, and the share is rising, this set of scales is increasingly dominant. Medium-size citizen private business and professional incomes are —in perhaps 3,000 to 5,000 cases—near or above the top of this range, but unlikely to grow absolutely in levels or numbers. With all land state-owned, and the rural emphasis on *ujàmaa* (cooperative) villages, there now is virtually no chance that the 10,000 or so citizen-farm families with incomes (cash and kind) above Sh 10,000 will expand individually or as a class to dominate the agricultural sector.

From 1967 to 1973, urban wage/salary inequality sharply fell, large-scale landlord holdings experienced a total takeover (with very limited compensation), the retailer profit margin growth reversed, and a broadening of the rural/urban gap halted. While the actual distribution of income was only marginally better in 1973 than in 1967, the trend appears to be positive and built on programs which should sustain it and allow the growth needed to finance it.

Instruments of Redistribution

Asset redistribution has centered on nationalization and directly productive public investment, rural infrastructure creation, and *ujàmaa* village promotion and support.

By 1972, three-quarters of large- and medium-scale economic activity were in the public sector, compared with perhaps one-fifth in 1966. The contribution of national parastatals and cooperatives to monetary GDP was estimated to be about 23 percent, and to monetary fixed investment, 57 percent, while their net cash flow (before tax and depreciation) was almost 40 percent of domestic savings. Although under one-third of parastatal assets were nationalized—as opposed to created by public investment—the 1967-71 nationalizations shifted the actual balance and planning outlook radically.

Decentralization and institutional reform have raised the share of recurrent and public investment expenditure directed to rural areas and altered the balance significantly toward poorer farmers. Probably half of public capital and recurrent annual expenditure from 1967 to 1972 has been shifted to the bottom two quintiles. This includes expenditure on selective input subsidies, rural adult and rural skill education, initial materials and food-*cum*-feeder roads, seeds, cattle for *ujàmaa* villages, water and health expenditure directed toward *ujàmaa* villages, and additional expenditure on rural roads and services. Given that this capital formation, enhancing human skills and creating public assets, amounted to about 3 percent of GDP, it formed a major redistribution effort in favor of the rural poor.

Ujàmaa (cooperative or communal) villages now number about 7,000, with about 3 million participants or over a quarter of rural Tanzanians. There is a clear geographic and income group correlation between poverty and *ujàmaa* village membership. Priority for rural capital and recurrent services plus provision of training for internal technical and farm management strengthening is designed to provide both immediate increases in living standards and medium-term increases in productive capacity. The rapid growth of the villages and the relatively low rate of members leaving suggest that the former goal is being attained; results in increasing productivity are unclear or mixed (as would be expected in a program only in its fourth year, with most villages under two years old). Some major achievements, e.g., regionally with maize at Dodoma, have been recorded.

Price changes have included an income policy which has narrowed the pretax range between the highest to the lowest paid public sector (including parastatal) worker from over 70-to-1 at Independence to about 18-to-1 today. Taking account of direct and indirect taxation, and the greater increases in prices affecting the higher-income groups, the effective differential in terms of consumption standards has fallen from about 60-to-1 to perhaps 13-to-1, including fringe benefits and access to public services. This policy has included absolute cuts followed by a six-year freeze at the top and a threefold increase at the bottom. Price controls have been used to raise rural prices—though not necessarily above import parity given recent world price increases—and to squeeze distributive sector margins. The latter had more than doubled (in percentage terms) over the 1970-73 period so that the measures seem to have aided income distribution with fairly minimal effects on production or investible surplus. Individual cases of serious allocative inefficiency have arisen, e.g., in rice and meat where urban land interests and rural producer or public investible surplus interests clashed. Viable compromise solutions mediating among the goals have usually been reached, though sometimes with severe delays.

Similarly, credit planning has been used to force both more effective purchasing use of commercial credit and more effective bill collection. Domestic credit formation growth has been cut from over 20 percent in between 1969 and 1971 to under 10 percent in 1971/72 and 1972/73, with little evident loss in output growth.

In the productive sector, nonagricultural employment has grown on average by 6.5 percent per year. This suggests that the incomes policy has led to improved use of labor (organizational rather than capital-intensive in nature) and that demand increases in the mass market have more than offset any tendency for modern sector expansion to lag.

Government expenditure, while still urban biased, has risen rapidly and is less urban biased than personal income; it has been steadily pushed toward such areas as rural water, rural health centers, primary and mass adult education, agricultural services, and feeder roads. The taxation system is fairly progressive, with incidence ranging from perhaps 3 percent to 5 percent on the bottom two quintiles, to 17.5 percent on urban minimum wages, and 30 percent to 40 percent at $3,000.

An important regulation is the rule forbidding leaders of the party,[32] middle and senior civil servants, and middle and senior public productive sector employees from having second jobs, earning rental or share incomes, or running any business except a small farm without permanent (as opposed to seasonal) paid labor. Spouses of these individuals face similar restrictions. This code is enforced with relative strictness even at the rural level, although its impact there is less.

Government Objectives

In the case of Tanzania, the direction of change clearly flows from the government's commitments to egalitarian, participatory, self-reliant socialism and to the increasingly clear articulation of these commitments since the Arusha declaration of 1967.

Rural priority has led directly to support of *ujàmaa* villages, rural credit and services, reconstruction and expansion, tax revision, and decentralization. Seventy percent to 75 percent of the population is dependent on small individual or communal agricultural holdings (*not* 95 percent, as sometimes

---

[32]Tanzania is a single-party state with a relatively well-articulated party from the ten-family-cell level up and perhaps a million active members.

stated) and the implications of this fact for egalitarianism are clearly grasped.

The alleviation of poverty is usually formulated in terms of creating conditions allowing every able-bodied Tanzanian to earn enough to meet a minimally acceptable standard of personal consumption and have free access to education (including adult literacy and vocational training), health, pure water, and information. Minimum wages, rural services and investment programs, and abolition of all school fees and all direct taxes on increases below the minimum wage flow from this objective.

The reduction of inequality has been viewed as calling for the concentration of all gains on households at or below income levels of Sh 12,000 per year in the urban areas and Sh 6,000 per year in the rural areas. Greatest emphasis has been on households at or below Sh 3,000 per year. This concentration has led to public sector salary cuts in 1961 and 1966 and freezes since; reconstruction of parastatal scales to parallel civil service ones; increased taxation (direct and indirect) on the top two quintiles; steady reduction of the role of private business especially new, large, domestic private business; and the extinction of the large-scale private landlord class.

The active participation of Tanzanians in decisions directly affecting themselves has been regarded as a positive end in itself. This has led to decentralization of regional and district government, broad controls of budget and other activities being allotted to regional and district development councils. Greater participation of workers is being introduced in parastatal management as well as in *ujàmaa* village organization. There has also been a tendency toward more regional, district, and cooperative activity on the small business level where it is not well handled (or not handleable) by the national parastatals.

Socialism is seen as necessary for participation, national self-determination, and egalitarianism. Tanzanian objectives emphasize these as well as the extension of the public sector in production. With 75 percent of large-scale economic activity and about 80 percent of monetary fixed capital formation in the public sector, the results of this objective in terms of the mode of production are clear at the macro level. The decentralization thrust into small-scale activity is less clear.

Self-reliance, or national self-determination, is seen as requiring the dominance of Tanzanian ownership, management, investment, savings, and decision-making in the economic as well as social and political spheres. This national posture has led to a stress on raising domestic surplus generation and broadening Tanzanian participation in decisions as well as to a more mass-oriented demand and capacity-oriented approach to production and service development.

The generation of an investible surplus has been seen as critical to achieving all other objectives, even if on occasion conflicting in detail with some of them. From the surplus has flowed a high ratio of tax to monetary GDP (about 40 percent) and the large cash flow (pretax profit plus depreciation) surpluses of Tanzanian parastatals, Tanzanian share of multinational parastatals, cooperatives, and *ujàmaa* villages.

Problems

Three very evident problems are: containing inflation (largely imported) without damaging egalitarianism or the generation of investible surplus, maintaining incentives and morale at both the bottom and the top, and sustaining the growth in management capacity necessary to operate coordinated, decentralized planning involving multiple instruments.

In the context of an open economy with limited and late data, rapid changes in world prices greatly hamper effective planning. Because there is no desire to erode the purchasing power of the minimum wage, the effective rural consumption power, or public sector investible surplus, price management poses technical and political conflicts. At best these result in pressures for greater efficiency or in trade margins going to upper income (proprietor or employee) consumption; at worst to serious delays and some internal inconsistencies.

Morale and incentives pose problems at the top and bottom. With the slower pace of citizen promotion, increasing numbers of senior citizen managers and civil servants face falling real incomes. Managerial and civil service salary scales in the three neighboring countries and in the joint East African services may be 50 percent to 200 percent higher, and Tanzanians are acutely aware of this fact. As well, Tanzanians face the special strains of a more participatory and decentralized system. However, morale is in fact probably better than five years ago and at least as good as in Kenya or Zambia. At bottom the problems are low absolute gains and the time lag in attaining them, particularly for the very poor now farming, or having in the past three years farmed, *ujàmaa* villages. In some cases rural asset creation (largely government but significantly self-help) has provided tangible gains, and in others initial output expansion has been significant, but real problems exist for many villages in maintaining momentum.

Management efficiency is needed because the margins for waste are low, especially with large-scale economic activity dominated by the public sector and public expenditure significant and rising. Efficiency is hard to achieve because decentralization and use of multiple institutions and instruments in the context of poor communications, patchy and often unreliable data, and scarce manpower pose very taxing demands. Equally radical change is harder to manage effectively than incremental growth within a fixed structure.

SRI LANKA–LAL JAYAWARDENA

Income distribution over the last two decades in Sri Lanka has moved markedly towards greater equality, both by reductions in the shares received by the top decile of households and by significant if small increases among the poorer deciles.[33] A major cause of this greater equality has been the generation of incomes among small-scale producers in both agriculture

---

[33]This essay owes a great deal to discussions with and statistical assistance from S. Narapalasingam and P. N. Radhakrisiman.

and industry, supplemented by legislation of varying degrees of effectiveness to ensure that a higher share of this income accrues to the small-scale producer himself; indeed policy initiatives undertaken since 1970 by the United Front government can be expected to accentuate this egalitarian trend in the future. In addition, greater equality in income from production has been reinforced by a level of welfare-state policies including subsidized food and transport, exceptional in a developing country.

Between 1953 and 1969/70, as shown in Annex Table 2, the share of income received by the top decile of households in Sri Lanka fell by nearly 11 percent—from about 41 percent to 30 percent—while over this same period, the share of the bottom quintile has increased by 2 percentage points. The share in income of the poorest 40 percent of households—which we may term "the poverty sector"—has risen between 1963 and 1969/70 from under 15 percent to nearly 19 percent. In 1969/70 this poorest 40 percent earned incomes of below Rs 200 per month. In 1963, some 72 percent of households had incomes below this cutoff point, again indicative of the improvement since then.

Annex Table 2: Percentage of Total Income Received by Decile Groups of Spending Units or Households in Sri Lanka, 1953, 1963, and 1973

Deciles	Percentage of Income: Spending Units or Households		
	1953	1963	1970
Lowest	1.9	1.5	3.3
Second	3.3	3.0	3.9
Third	4.1	4.0	5.0
Fourth	5.2	5.2	5.0
Fifth	6.4	6.3	6.5
Sixth	6.9	7.5	7.9
Seventh	8.3	9.0	10.0
Eighth	10.1	11.2	12.0
Ninth	13.2	15.5	15.0
Highest	40.6	36.8	30.0
Total	100.0	100.0	100.0
Concentration ratio	0.46	0.45	0.35

Sources: (1) *Ceylon Consumer Finance Survey conducted in 1953 by the Central Bank of Ceylon;* (2) *Ceylon Consumer Finance Survey conducted in 1963 by the Central Bank of Ceylon;* (3) *the Socio-Economic Survey conducted in 1969/70 by the Department of Census and Statistics.*

Production Policies

What factors explain these changes? Although these changes date back to the mid-1950s, the quantitative answer must in part concentrate on the period 1963 to 1969/70 because of the absence of comparable GDP data for the earlier period. The resulting conclusions therefore can be safely extended in a more qualitative way to the earlier period as well—and indeed, also to the subsequent period. In the first place, there was a link between the changes in income distribution in the 1963-1969/70 period and the pattern of GDP growth. Gross domestic product at constant prices increased at a compound rate of 5 percent per annum during the seven-year period 1963-70, sustained by high growth in sectors which generate income for the small-scale producer and the unskilled worker. Particularly important among the commodity-producing sectors contributing to this growth were paddy (6.6 percent), subsidiary crops (6.5 percent), small scale industry (8 percent), construction (12 percent), and organized manufacturing (7 percent). These sectors accounted for a little less than a third of GDP in 1970.

The impact of high growth rates in these sectors on the pattern of income distribution is indicated by the pattern of factor rewards characterizing each sector. Rural landholding in Sri Lanka has *always* been relatively egalitarian. Paddy holdings below 5 acres account for 95 percent of the total number of holdings and 85 percent of the cultivated area. Most paddy incomes accrue to households in the income range of the bottom 40 percent of the population, as does most income from subsidiary crops and small industries.

In the case of construction, wages accruing to unskilled and semiskilled labor have generally benefited the poorer segment of the population. On the other hand, output increases in organized industry may not have contributed to any significant reduction in inequalities, since skilled employment incomes generally accrue to the top 40 percent of the households.

There is some evidence also that this pattern of GDP growth has been associated with an increase in the income from property accruing to the lower income groups. The data[34] suggest a trend towards increasing access to property among the poorer income groups; nonmonetary income per capita increases by upwards of 30 percent in the poorer deciles while decreasing significantly in the richer deciles.

The reasons underlying this pattern of sectoral production growth—and contributing to the better distribution of *earned* income in the past—are to be found in various aspects of government policy. First, and perhaps the most important of these aspects in a quantitative sense, has been the encouragement given by successive governments to import substitution programs for both paddy and subsidiary crops. The impetus for these programs came not so much from an awareness of the income distribution benefits that would result, but from the need to grapple with the persistent foreign exchange imbalance that has characterized Sri Lanka virtually since independence in 1948. This program involved a mixture of policies: guaranteed producer prices for paddy, the provision of credit and its collection under

---

[34]In the absence of data bearing directly on this question, it has been necessary to find a proxy for property income in the form of nonmonetary income—that is, mainly the value of home grown produce and the net rental value of owner-occupied housing units. The assumption implicit in this procedure is that, any increases in nonmonetary income so defined are linked to net accretions to poverty.

supervision and, more recently, a policy of successively curtailing the rice subsidy, which by raising the domestic price level made production more remunerative, shifting the cost to the urban purchasing families. These measures were complemented, of course, by the purely technological aspects of the "Green Revolution" and the resulting increase in yields per acre through the introduction of new varieties of seed.

Second, these particular import substitution policies have been supplemented by the Paddy Lands Act, designed to ensure that production gains seep down to the tenant and are not trapped in the hands of the wealthy farmer. The Act, introduced in 1958, seeks to safeguard the rights of the tenant cultivator of paddy lands, protect him against eviction, and limit the share of crops he would be required to surrender to his landlord to a quarter (compared to the traditional half). The effectiveness of this piece of legislation is still a matter of controversy, but its potential importance is not doubted: 30 percent of paddy operators are tenants, as opposed to owner-operators, and they cultivate around a quarter of all lands under paddy.

Third, the focus of government investment on irrigation programs was largely designed to benefit the small farmer and the associated transfer of peasants to the drier areas of the country under so-called colonization schemes. The quantitative impact of the latter is not of major importance, however, since only a relatively small number of families were settled under new schemes over the period 1953 to 1970.

Furthermore, there is every reason to expect this favorable trend in the distribution of *earned* income to continue as a result of policies introduced since 1970. A more explicitly poverty-focused strategy has been adopted, including particularly a decentralized program of village-level development. Guidelines for the program envisage that investment should be concentrated on quick yielding production investment, roughly a third in agriculture, a quarter in industry, a fifth on roads, and only a fifth on irrigation and minor water supply and housing and civic building. A modest village-level target for employment creation was also included.

The land reform program, in force since August 1972, seeks to establish a ceiling for landholding by any person of twenty-five acres in the case of paddy land, and fifty acres in the case of other agricultural land. The program provides for a Land Commission in order to ensure that land in excess of these ceiling amounts is demarcated and vested in the hands of the state for development in a suitable manner. With the fifty-acre ceiling envisaged in the law, the Land Reform Commission has estimated very roughly that 330,000 acres of excess land in tea, rubber, and coconut will be vested in the state. The distinguishing characteristic of this reform is that this "excess" land is available for distribution not so much to a previously *resident* labor force (due to low man/land ratios on the relevant crops) but to landless labor from outside the plantation areas.

The class of landowner principally affected by the Act is the private proprietor of land—to a large extent under coconut and to a lesser extent in tea and rubber. In this sense the law seeks to cut into the economic base of the indigenous Ceylonese landed elite.[35] Valuable though the law is as a first step in this direction, its provisions reflect the intrinsic political difficulties of carrying through reform measures of this kind on a sufficiently far-reaching scale. The ceilings provisions, for instance, are considerably more generous than those proposed by the ILO Employment Mission strategy, which argued that any worthwhile reform ought to proceed on the basis of seeking to achieve minimum and maximum (or ceiling) incomes per family in the agricultural sector.[36] Its proposals envisaged that the rural family's ceiling income would be translated into varying land *ceilings* depending on the crop. In the case of paddy, this ceiling would have amounted on average to around five acres per family and, in the case of coconuts to no more than twenty-five acres. The corresponding ceilings in the present land reform law are twenty-five acres and fifty acres respectively. These ceilings apply not to a "family" as such, but to "persons" aged 18 years and over within a family group. In other words, once these other dependents are taken account of, the effective ceiling per "family" could be more than double the fifty-acre limit of the law. Despite this and other limitations, it has to be mentioned nevertheless that the present law represents a major departure in approach to the indigenously owned plantation sector, compared to anything which has gone before it and is widely conceived as only an initial step toward a more fundamental reform.

Social Welfare Policies

The redistributive impact of production policy on *earned* income was reinforced by a commitment to social policy in Sri Lanka, to a degree exceptional for developing countries with low per capita income. In the 1960s, roughly *half* of current government expenditure was directed towards social welfare of one kind or another, primarily free education, health services, and subsidized food and transportation. It becomes necessary, therefore, to adjust the data in Annex Table 2 for the various "Social Benefits" provided by government by allocating these among the deciles of the population on the basis of the incidence of the subsidy involved in each case.[37]

---

[35]Public companies, and to that extent the majority of well-managed foreign owned plantations under tea and rubber, along with land belonging to religious and charitable institutions are exempted.

[36]ILO (1971*a*), pp. 92-95.

[37]The following procedure was adopted: the total of factor incomes estimated for 1973 was broken down on the basis of the 1970 pattern of income distribution. To the resulting magnitudes were added estimates of "social benefits" accruing to different income groups. For example, in 1973, as a result of budgetary measures announced in the previous year, only those not paying income tax were entitled to the weekly free measure (2 pounds) of rice. Accordingly, this was valued at the price charged by government from income taxpayers and their dependents, in the case of households earning less than Rs 660 per month, the cutoff point for the levying of income tax. In the absence of firm data regarding other forms of subsidy, their incidence has been approximated by distributing the amounts in proportion to the number of persons in each income group of households. If these subsidies are distributed among different income groups strictly according to their incidence, the lower- and middle-income groups would have accounted for a greater share of the subsidies than received by them on the basis of the straight pro rata distribution used in the present calculations. This would have increased the concentration ratio still further.

Annex Table 3: Percentage of Total Income and Social Benefits* Received by Decile Groups in Sri Lanka, 1963 and 1973

Deciles	Percentage of income in Households/Spending Units		Percentage of income per person† in Households/Spending Units Groups		Adjusted percentage increase in real income, 1963-1973
	1963	1973	1963	1973	
Lowest	2.0	3.8	3.5	6.1	+105.3
Second	3.8	5.0	4.6	6.3	+ 61.3
Third	2.7	6.1	5.9	6.8	+ 35.7
Fourth	7.5	6.6	6.7	7.4	+ 30.1
Fifth	6.8	7.5	7.3	8.0	+ 29.1
Sixth	7.6	8.2	8.2	8.7	+ 25.0
Seventh	9.5	9.9	8.7	10.4	+ 40.8
Eighth	11.1	11.9	10.7	11.3	+ 24.4
Ninth	15.0	14.9	13.4	13.2	+ 16.0
Highest	34.0	26.1	31.0	21.8	− 17.2
Concentration Ratio	0.40	0.29	0.34	0.21	

*These consist of subsidy on rice, losses incurred by public transport, free education, and health services.
†In this case, the decile groups are obtained by persons distributed according to the number of persons in the different income groups of spending units (1963)/households (1973).

Annex Table 3 presents the data on income distribution after making these adjustments and, as expected, the distribution of incomes in terms of households/spending units became considerably more egalitarian in *both* 1963 and 1973. As compared with Annex Table 2, the concentration ratio falls from .45 to .40 in 1963 and from .35 to .29 in 1973.

If allowance is made for variations in the size of households/spending units between 1963 and 1973, and the data presented in terms of *persons* per decile, the concentration ratio is reduced still more to .34 in 1963 and .21 in 1973. This follows from the relatively smaller size of households in the poorer deciles. With this adjustment, the poorest 40 percent of the population received 27 percent of income in 1973 as compared with 21 percent in 1963. On the other hand, the share of the top 10 percent of population in total income fell during this period from 31 percent to 22 percent.

Even more dramatic evidence of the shift to a more egalitarian distribution during this decade can be provided by making the comparison in terms of average per capita *real* income (inclusive of social benefits) in each decile.[38] The data in Annex Table 3 indicate that while in *real* terms the per capita income of the *poorest decile* has more than *doubled* over the decade, that of the richest has fallen by 17 percent. This, in fact, underestimates the real income decline of the rich since the data has not allowed for tax payments by them.[39] Moreover, under the present government the introduction of "compulsory savings" has aimed at limiting monthly *expenditures* to a ceiling level—initially of around Rs 3,500 and subsequently of Rs 2,000.

One final area of inquiry remains. In considering the impact of social welfare policy on income distribution in Sri Lanka over this decade, it is important to ask what the outcome might have been if the amounts directly transferred as consumer purchasing power to the poorer groups in society had been spent instead in adding to the capital stock of these groups. An illustrative calculation has been made of the hypothetical impact on income distribution of eliminating the food subsidy alone from the 1963-69 period— consistently around 5 percent to 6 percent of GDP—and devoting the resources saved to "poverty-focused" capital formation.[40] On various simplifying assumptions, the calculation shows that the poorest 40 percent would lose over the first six years, but after that the addition to income resulting from the investment would outweigh the subsidy foregone in that year.

---

[38]The deflator used to calculate real incomes is the same for all deciles and is the implicit price index derived from the Central Bank's estimate of GDP at current and constant prices for the years 1963 and 1973.

[39]Income tax rates in Sri Lanka operate on a progressive scale ranging from 7.5 percent to 65 percent. If the Assessable Income of the family does not exceed Rs 6,000, then the family is not liable to pay income tax.

[40]Following the model outlined in Chapter III, it has been assumed that the output capital ratio for the hypothetical "poverty-focused" investment would have been less favorable than for the economy as a whole; accordingly a ratio of .25 as compared to the national average of .31 was assumed together with an investment-output lag of two years.

South Korea–Irma Adelman

In the post-World War II economic history of South Korea may be seen a development process that benefited not only the upper- and middle-income groups, but also the poorest members of society, whose welfare was substantially raised. This process had three distinct phases.[41] First came a phase lasting from 1945 to 1952, in which assets were redistributed but there were no major dynamic changes; second was a dynamic asset redistribution phase, from 1953 to 1963; and the third phase, from 1964 onwards, was a redistribution-*cum*-asset-value-realization phase, that still continues.

The Static Asset Redistribution Phase

A major redistribution of Korean wealth was an unintended yet almost inevitable result of the end of Japanese rule by World War II and the subsequent dislocations due to partition and the Korean War. This static asset redistribution phase is the first of those mentioned above, occurring between 1945 and 1952. Changes included substantial land reform and a significant leveling of inequalities in the ownership of other forms of physical capital.

At independence and partition in 1945, South Korea was primarily an agricultural country, with three-quarters of its working population engaged in farming.[42] More than two-thirds of the farm families were full-time tenants, and most of the others were part-time tenants.[43] The tenant-landlord relationship was harsh[44] with rents varying from 50 percent to 90 percent of the crop.[45] There was extreme rural poverty.

Land reform proceeded in two stages. Under American auspices in 1947, land once held by Japan was redistributed, reducing the full-time tenancy rate from 70 percent to 33 percent within one year and improving tenancy conditions with a 33-percent ceiling on rents.[46] A second, purely domestic land reform in 1950 redistributed Korean landlord holdings, with nominal compensation, and virtually eliminated tenancy. The 1950 redistribution established a structure of very small owner-operated farms.

The second reform also imposed a limit of one hectare of paddy land, but this was actually reached by less than one percent of the households. The proportion of submarginal households (those with less than one hectare) rose to approximately 72 percent of the total, and has since been increasing (to 79 percent in 1970). While the 1950 land reform set the socio-political conditions for equalitarian growth of rural incomes, it exacerbated the prob-

---

[41]For further discussion of these points, see Adelman (1974).

[42]Henderson (1968), p. 75. In 1939, overall Korean industrial output has been 39 percent of the total; however, virtually all of the industrial activity was centered in the North.

[43]Hatada (1969), p. 127.

[44]In 1947, 60 percent of civil cases in one district concerned tenant-landlord relationships. See Henderson (1968), p. 278.

[45]Ibid., p. 156.

[46]Pak (1966), pp. 94-95, and Henderson (1968), p. 156.

lems of low income and low productivity on the farm by drastically increasing the number of submarginal farms.

At independence, Korea was not characterized by great inequalities of wealth since Japan had monopolized virtually all entrepreneurial activity during the colonial period. What Korean fortunes there were in the South in 1945 were rapidly eroded by the economic chaos caused by the partition; the disruption of commercial and other economic networks; the loss to the North of all heavy industry, major coal deposits, and almost all electric power generating capacity; rampant inflation; a major wave of crimes against property; and the flood of over 1.5 million refugees from the North.[47]

The Korean War repeated the process of wholesale redistribution of capital and leveling of wealth. Over 1.3 million Koreans were killed and property damage resulting from the fighting has been estimated at $2 billion.[48] Agricultural output dropped by 27 percent between 1949 and 1952, and real GNP by 16 percent. Prices rose 500 percent in 1951 and another 100 percent in 1952. In addition, the Korean War had a profound social impact obliterating social distinctions and disrupting social networks.[49] The estimate that 25 percent of the population roamed the countryside as refugees for about two years suggests the magnitude of the disruption.

The Dynamic Redistribution Phase

The 1953-63 dynamic redistribution phase was essentially an educational explosion of major proportions. Economically, there were three subphases: reconstruction (1953-1958), import substitution and stagnation (1958-1962), and a good harvest (1963). Politically, the period was one of high centralization, coupled with unusually high corruption and a significant degree of student-triggered political instability.

From 1953 to 1963, the literacy rate rose from 30 percent to over 80 percent. Universal primary education became the rule in the countryside as well as in cities; and secondary and higher education also grew extremely rapidly. Thus, by 1964, Korea had a per capita income of about $100 and one out of every 280 Koreans were in college. By 1965, Korea's human resource development had exceeded the norm for a country with *three* times[50] its median per capita GNP.

At the same time, in 1964 the unemployment rate among college graduates was approximately 50 percent, according to official estimates.[51] The rate of employment in suitable (i.e., white collar) jobs was estimated at only between 5 percent and 10 percent.[52] Despite a tradition against manual labor, in 1964

---

[47]Henderson (1968), p. 139.

[48]Cole and Lyman (1971), p. 22.

[49]Lee (1968), p. 55.

[50]Harbison and Myers (1964), pp. 31-48.

[51]These are Ministry of Education Statistics, based on school records. They are of dubious validity, but were generally believed to be correct, which, psychologically is what matters.

[52]Henderson (1968), p. 223.

college graduates were competing for jobs as municipal street sweepers in Seoul and some even signed up to mine coal in the Ruhr. It is therefore not surprising that students were in the vanguard of political protest.

The first part of this period was one of economic recovery,[53] with an annual growth rate of GNP of approximately 5.5 percent and major investment in manufacturing and social overhead, financed by U.S. foreign assistance. The industrialization effort was one of import substitution centered on the development of nondurable consumer goods industries and their intermediate inputs. Following the plan of growth was a period of stagnation from 1958 to 1962, during which per capita income was essentially constant—the result of exhausting the opportunities for further import substitution, of a tight monetary and fiscal policy to curb rapid inflation, and of a decline in foreign assistance.

The choices facing Korea by 1964 were (i) to carry import substitution further especially in intermediate and heavy industries (the capital-intensive path adopted by most other economies) or (ii) to emphasize export expansion in labor-intensive consumer nondurables. Korea chose the latter strategy, as it offered the most rapid growth prospects consistent with Korea's comparative advantages in labor skills.

The Redistribution-cum-Asset-Value-Realization Phase

The first two phases of Korean post-World War II development, by redistributing assets and opportunities for asset accumulation, set the stage not only for economic growth, but, if desired, for egalitarian economic growth as well. What was required next, to achieve equitable growth, was a set of policies which would create favorable markets for the redistributed assets, or for their services, or both—in other words, a set of policies which would lead to rapid labor- and skill-intensive growth.[54]

Such a set of policies was initiated during the redistributed-asset-value-realization phase in 1964 by applying standard economic tools to create an appropriate system of incentives and by reorienting the overall development strategy from one of import substitution to one of export expansion. Korean development strategy was chosen primarily on purely economic growth considerations; the favorable equity consequences, while now welcomed, were not recognized at the time.

The politico-economic climate leading to these policies included a strong commitment by the President to "a political strategy emphasizing economic performance"[55] and an unusual degree of control over the economy by the Korean government, both in directly implementing economic decisions and in forcing the private sector to comply. Moreover the Korean people, frustrated by long years of colonial exploitation, two wars, and a wardship status, displayed an ambition and a drive which must not be underestimated.

[53]The discussion in this section draws upon Cole and Lyman (1971), pp. 123-129 and Balassa (1970).

[54]The discussion in this section draws upon Adelman (1967), Cole and Lyman (1971), chapters 7 and 8, Balassa (1970), and Brown (1973).

[55]Cole and Lyman (1971), p. 86.

Annex Table 4: Korean Distribution of Categories of Revenue, 1970
(in percentage points)

Deciles	Wages and* salary	Self-employment† agriculture	Self-employment‡ nonagriculture	Property‡ income	All income
1	2	5	4	1	3
2	3.5	5.5	4.5	2	4
3	4.5	6	5	3	5
4	6	7	5.5	4	6
5	7	8	6	5	7
6	9	10	7	7	8
7	11	11	8	8	11
8	13	12.5	12	10	12
9	16	15	14	15	15
10	28	20	34	45	29

*Calculated from wage distribution data given in 1970 *Report on Wage Survey*, Vol. 1 *Summary*, p. 122; Vol. 2 *Summary*, p. 220; and *Report on the Wage Survey*, p. 43 (1967).

†Based on data on distribution of agricultural income in *Yearbook of Agriculture and Forestry Statistics*, (1971) and (1968), Tables 122 and 16.

‡Distributed according to curve suggested by C. Morrison, IBRD Consultant Report on Korea, August 1973.

Two important changes in economic incentives were introduced in late 1964 and early 1965. The first (the interest rate reform) had the effect of altering the wage-to-capital rental ratio dramatically; the second (the package of trade measures) enabled the economy to follow an outward-looking trade policy. Together these changes permitted the economy to pursue a growth strategy more nearly in line with its true comparative advantage.

By the reform the commercial bank interest rate for both savings accounts and deposits was *doubled,* to a nominal level of almost 30 percent (which, allowing for a reduced rate of inflation, resulted in about a 20 percent real rate).[56] This meant a sharp increase in the relative rental price of capital. While there is little evidence that this increase led to the adoption of more labor-intensive technology in existing industries, the labor-intensiveness of overall production increased substantially by the resultant emphasis on the expansion of the relatively labor-using sectors.[57] The interest rate reform also resulted in an increase of savings, making larger domestic sources available for investment.

Under the trade incentives reform,[58] the won was devalued by 50 percent, and a battery of export incentives and export promotion mechanisms was

---

[56]Brown (1973) discusses the effects more fully.

[57]For six out of eight sectors with less than the median capital-output ratio, the ratio of exports to imports increased between 1960 and 1968. The same ratio decreased for all but one sector with above average capital-output ratio. See Norton (1971b).

[58]Before 1960, Korea's system of trade incentives had favored import substitution; tariffs and quantitative restrictions afforded substantial protection to domestic import-substitute industries, and in the absence of export subsidies, the over-valued exchange

introduced.[59] Import restrictions were also liberalized.[60] At the same time, successful monetary and fiscal policies were undertaken to reduce the rate of inflation.

The major results of policy changes were (i) a phenomenally rapid expansion of exports and GNP (at average annual rates of 38 and 11 percent in constant prices respectively, between 1964 and 1970) and (ii) a rise in nonfarm employment of 1.6 million accompanied by a drop in unemployment from 7.7 percent to 4.5 percent of the labor force (over the same period). The increases in exports were almost exclusively in labor-intensive industries.[61] Indeed, between 1966 and 1970 nearly one-half (320,000) of the overall increase in the labor force was absorbed *directly*[62] into export-related employment. This large labor absorption occurred despite some evidence that, between 1968 and 1970 overall production became more efficient in its use of labor.[63]

Effect on the Distribution of Income

The effects of the Korean "redistribution-*cum*-growth" strategy can only be inferred by piecing together the relevant fragmentary evidence, since there are no acceptable annual data for the size distribution of income in Korea. Available data can be used however to construct estimates of the size distribution in 1964 and 1970.[64]

By 1964, the distribution of income in Korea was among the best in the developing world, and remained so in 1970. (Compare Annex Table 4 with Table I.1.) Although there was little change in the overall size distribution of income between 1964 and 1970, there were changes in composition. (i) The distribution of both agriculture incomes and wage and salary incomes became somewhat more even between the two dates. (ii) The gap between average income in agriculture and industry increased between the two dates (from a ratio of 1.4 to a ratio of 2). (iii) The relative share of the most unequally

---

rate imparted a bias against exports. An attempt to rectify this situation was made in 1961, with a 50 percent devaluation and an easing of import restrictions, but the subsequent inflation during 1962-63 substantially nullified its effects. The concurrent balance of payments crisis led to the reimposition of import controls and the reintroduction of multiple exchange rates.

[59]See Balassa (1970), p. 9 for details.

[60]Ibid.

[61]Eighty-six percent of the increase in exports came from five commodities. These ranked 1-3 and 5-6 in terms of the magnitude of their direct labor-output coefficients in the 1970 ILO Table.

[62]The direct and indirect labor absorption was naturally greater.

[63]1970 direct labor-output coefficients applied to 1968 production understate 1968 employment by nearly 20 percent.

[64]The techniques used are explained in detail in Morrison (1972). Essentially two size distributions of income were reconstructed, by using information on distributive shares for 1970 and 1964 together with data on the distribution of wages and salary incomes and agricultural incomes for both dates. The results were cross checked with information from urban and rural household budget surveys, and with data on the distribution of employment. They were also subjected to sensitivity analyses concerning reasonable, data-consistent, alternative assumptions, and proved largely insensitive to them.

distributed component of overall income, property income, rose by 33 percent. At the same time, however, the share of wage and salary income increased by 40 percent and that of agricultural income dropped by 32 percent.

Since the relative distribution of income changed little during the rapid growth phase of the Korean economy, one can infer that the real incomes of the poorest 20 percent more than doubled. Between 1964 and 1970, real wage rates of production workers in manufacturing rose by over 85 percent and those of wage earners in agriculture doubled. The real incomes of the poorest quintile of farm households increased by 15 percent. These wage changes were the result of market forces, since unionization of labor played no role. Agricultural incomes rose, however, aided by the government's fixing of a high price for rice.

The processes implicit in all these changes are consistent with the U-shaped hypothesis concerning the relation between the equality of the distribution of income and the development process. They are indicative of how the upturn in the U-shape can take place during the last phases of the development process, provided that the appropriate economic strategies are followed and the right preconditions established.

TAIWAN—GUSTAV RANIS

The record of the Taiwanese economy between 1950 and 1970[65] indicates the coexistence of high and rising growth rates, the gradual elimination of underemployment, and an apparent improvement in the size distribution of income. Taiwan thus may constitute one of the very few exceptions to the somber findings of Kuznets and Adelman who, on the basis of time series and cross-sectional evidence, found a prevailing U-shaped relationship between growth and distribution over time. Taiwan thus points to the possibility that there may be no necessary conflict in other countries, even in the short term, between growth and income distribution. The generally observed U-shaped relationship must be viewed as not inevitable in nature, but subject to control by man.

Taiwan may be classified as a labor surplus open dualistic economy with a relatively poor natural resources base. Since the change in income distribution can only be analyzed successfully in the context of how growth took place, a multisectored analysis over time is needed. For this, Taiwan's 1950-70 transition period may be conveniently divided into an import substitution subphase in the 1950s and an export substitution subphase in the 1960s.

Even at the outset—in the early 1950s—the initial conditions in Taiwan were unusually favorable for a phase of import substitution, sustained for sufficient time to allow for two critical later developments: the maturation of indigenous entrepreneurial capacity to permit successful export orientation afterwards, and adequate agricultural infrastructure to permit full rural mobilization. On the one hand there had been a substantial influx of talented entrepreneurs from the mainland; on the other, the Japanese colonial policy

---

[65]See also Fei and Ranis (in press).

had left behind an unusually strong agricultural infrastructure, in terms of both such institutional features as land reform and farmers' associations and such economic features as investments in irrigation and research. As a consequence, even during the 1950s, Taiwan's overall annual growth rate at more than 7 percent was very respectable indeed, with agriculture doing unusually well in the context of a vigorous import substitution industrialization drive[66] (see Annex Table 5). Early substantial increases in agricultural labor productivity were made possible in this fashion—i.e., through the high receptivity, via equitable asset distribution and infrastructure, to the introduction and even spread of the seed-fertilizer type of technology change, including a substantial volume of double cropping. This, in turn, meant not only a good growth rate *and* a fairly equitable distribution of income within agriculture, but also encouragement for the rapid growth of nonagriculture during this period—indirectly via the export of agricultural goods (first sugar, then asparagus, mushrooms, and so forth) and directly via the generation of an agricultural surplus in the form of food and domestically used raw materials. The resulting rapid growth of nonagricultural output (8.7 percent annually) during this period is shown in Annex Table 5.

Annex Table 5: Growth of Output, Employment, Productivity, and Wages in Taiwan

(average annual percentage growth rates)

	1952-60	1960-69	1952-69
Real GDP	7.2	9.9	8.6
Real GDP per Capita	3.6	6.7	5.2
Agricultural Output	5.5	7.0	6.3
Nonagricultural Output	8.7	12.5	10.7
Agricultural Employment	.6	.4	.5
Nonagricultural Employment	3.1	6.6	4.9
Agricultural Labor Productivity	4.9	6.6	5.8
Agricultural Real Wage	2.5	5.1	3.8
Nonagricultural Labor Productivity	5.6	5.9	5.8
Nonagricultural Real Wage	4.4	4.2	4.3

Sources: National Income of the Republic of China, 1951-71; *Taiwan Statistical Data Book*, 1970, 1971, 1972; *Taiwan Agricultural Yearbooks; Input-Output Tables of Taiwan*, 1961, 1964, 1966.

The import substitution subphase terminated roughly at the end of the 1950s. It had been characterized by the increasing allocation of foreign exchange to capital goods and away from consumer good imports, the decline of imported consumer goods as a proportion of total supply, the increasingly internal orientation of the economy as measured by the decline of foreign trade in GNP, and the continued use of traditional exports (80 percent of

[66]In the absence of such favorable conditions, import-substitution policies normally discriminate so much against agriculture as to lead to near stagnation in that sector during this period.

the total) to help the total process. The turn to a more outward or export-oriented growth phase can be seen clearly in major changes in the policy mix (stabilization instead of inflation, realistic instead of overvalued exchange rates, tariffs instead of quota restrictions, higher interest rates instead of credit rationing, and so on). Associated with these changes in policy were major changes in the structure of the economy, such as land reform.

The overall growth rate of this small open economy, quite respectable during import substitution, accelerated further to almost 10 percent during this export-oriented subphase (see Annex Table 5). Underlying this excellent aggregative performance was the continued and enhanced expansion of agricultural productivity, accompanied by now much more, and more labor-intensive, nonagricultural growth. After 1963, there was an absolute as well as a relative decline in the agricultural population. A high level of entrepreneurial maturity combined with a large surplus of unskilled labor enabled Taiwanese industrial goods to penetrate international markets on a competitive basis. The consequence was a radical change from land to labor-intensive exports, with the industrial sector itself providing an ever larger share of the fuel (in terms of exports provided) for its own future growth. By the end of the decade the share of nontraditional exports had reached 80 percent of a total which was itself growing at rates in excess of 30 percent and substantially enhancing the external orientation of the economy. Industrial labor absorption rates were twice as high in the 1960s as in the 1950s (jumping from 3 percent to 6-plus percent annually). By the end of the decade, and in spite of substantial population growth (in excess of 2.5 percent annually), the labor supply reserve had thus gradually been exhausted, and a post-transition phase of unskilled labor shortage accompanied by rapidly rising real wages in both sectors made its appearance.

This all too brief analysis of the nature of the accelerated growth performance of Taiwan also explains why income distribution improved over the same period. Of course, it would not be surprising if income distribution improved after 1970, when labor shortage first displaced labor surplus conditions. Consistent with Arthur Lewis as well as the Kuznets and Adelman findings, this would mean that stagnant wages accompanied by a rapid increase in property incomes gave way to a reversal once real wages in the whole system increased in a sustained fashion, as in the mature economy case. But most less developed countries are not in sight of that turning point, and would take little comfort from the conclusion that distributional outcomes cannot be improved until it has been reached—which is in any case the main objective of their transition efforts. What is much more interesting and to the point in the Taiwanese case, therefore, is that the size distribution of income apparently improved between the mid-1950s and mid-1960s, long before the economy's basic labor surplus conditions came to an end.

Our statistical evidence on this point is admittedly less than perfect. The two direct sources are 1953 and 1964 surveys reported by Chang and Hinrichs[67] indicating a rather dramatic improvement in the Gini coefficient, from

[67]Chang and Hinrichs (1968), p. 135.

.56 in 1953 to .33 in 1964. There is much less detail available for the 1953 survey; nevertheless the crucial finding concerning an improvement in equity is very likely to stand up.[68]

While we are not yet ready to be definitive on the precise reasons for this unusual outcome,[69] we attribute it to a number of the features attending the nature of the Taiwanese transition growth path. First, the expansion path in both agriculture and nonagriculture was extremely labor-intensive, especially during the second or export-oriented subphase when the policy setting became more market oriented. Thus, in spite of the fact that wages lagged behind productivity increase—as we would expect under conditions of labor surplus—technological change was sufficiently labor-using in character for the wage bill within each sector not to decline but to rise substantially.

Second, within the industrial sector income distribution was apparently more equal than within the preponderant agricultural sector. Here, income distribution resulted mainly from the fact that, unlike the more typical case, the ownership of industrial assets was widely distributed from the start. Instead of a large-scale indigenous industrial class, the immigration of large numbers of medium- and small-scale entrepreneurs in 1948/49 filled a vacuum left after the Japanese departure. Moreover, over time, this industrial structure was maintained; in combination with high labor intensity and a good deal of social mobility from worker to entrepreneurial status, the industrial sector thus held an advantage which is contrary to most lesser developed country experience as summarized by Kuznets; this helped rather than hurt distribution as reallocation proceeded.

Third, there was an unusually low wage or income differential between the agricultural and nonagricultural sectors throughout the period. As late as 1964, the average industrial family had an income only 15 percent above that of the average agricultural family. The upward "pull" on wages of such exogenous forces as multinational corporations and union pressures, reinforced by government salary increases, was apparently much weaker in Taiwan than in most contemporary less developed countries. These factors, in combination, meant that the rapid reallocation of population from one sector to another was not accompanied by a worsening of the overall distribution resulting simply from the intersectoral shift.[70]

Finally, there are a number of factors at work *within* each sector consistent with an improvement in the overall size distribution during the entire

---

[68]Approximately 20 percent of the 1953 household income is apparently not reported. This is one reason the results must be viewed with considerable caution. But it is important to note that the Lorenz curve for 1964 would *still* lie "above" the Lorenz curve for 1953, even if we allocated all the missing 20 percent of income to the high income groups. Thus we have fairly definite evidence that the income distribution did become more equal even if we can't be precise on how much more equal. For our purposes here, this is sufficient.

[69]Research is currently underway on this very question.

[70]Swamy (1967), pp. 155-174, for example, estimates that the movement between sectors along with an increase in the intersectoral differential has accounted for 85 percent of the change in income disparities in India during the 1951-68 period.

period under observation. Although the share of rents increased in agriculture and profits in industry, this may have been combined with an improved income distribution *within* each sector, contrary to what might be expected. This is partly due to the aforementioned increased labor intensity and partly to substantial class mobility, with small farmers and entrepreneurs emerging from tenant and worker status, especially during the second subphase. More precisely, we know that real agricultural wage or farm family income, while lagging behind productivity, crept up substantially—increasing by 3.8 percent annually between 1952 and 1969 (see Annex Table 5). This, coupled with a fairly even initial distribution of agricultural assets, due to land reform (both pre- and postindependence), means that the increases of productivity took place mainly on owner-operated small farms, with both wage and rental incomes fairly evenly distributed. In nonagriculture, similarly, wages increased gradually and with some lag behind industrial labor productivity (Annex Table 5); here also initial asset distribution was fairly equal, with no major industrial concentration and most of the assets in the hands of relatively small- and medium-scale entrepreneurs, mainly migrants from the mainland. To this must be added the aforementioned phenomenon of marked class mobility, especially during the second and more market-oriented subphase, with substantial numbers of both industrial and agricultural workers taking advantage of resource access to become small entrepreneurs. This relatively equitable initial distribution of real assets and relatively fair access, at a price, to foreign exchange, credits, and so forth, was given further support by the unusually high and well-distributed level of literacy and education generally.

Underlying all this economic reasoning, of course, is the question of the underlying political basis for making the "right" policy decisions at the "right" time to permit the adjustment of the economy to its changing opportunities in the ways indicated. Most critical is the question of how the transition from the hothouse import-substitution conditions of the 1950s to the competitive export orientation of the 1960s was effected without running up against the vested interests which inevitably spring up—especially within the industrial sector and the bureaucracy itself.

One explanation is that you need a fairly strong government which knows what it wants and needs and which, even though closely allied with certain industrial and other interest groups, can persuade them of the necessity of change. At another level, "necessity is the mother of invention," i.e., a labor-surplus, natural resources-poor country like Taiwan sooner or later has no choice but to shift out of land and into labor-intensive production and export lines. This "necessity" translated itself into declining rates of return, social and private, as "easy" consumer goods import substitution markets became gradually exhausted and backward linkage import substitution too difficult and expensive; thus the task of persuasion was made easier.

Finally, the role of U.S. foreign aid has been very helpful in this regard— much more so than in terms of its quantitative or simple resources impact.

The timely arrival of large quantities of program (nonproject) aid at the end of the 1950s and early 1960s was doubtless largely responsible for providing the little extra buffering and reassurance for a system which had to be persuaded to head out on new uncharted import liberalization tracks. Finance ministers and central bankers welcome a substantial "ballooning" of aid, especially at a time when major change from direct to indirect controls seems to threaten revenues and foreign exchange reserves. Undoubtedly aid inflows were helpful also in the general resources augmentation sense and in providing some valuable specific inputs, e.g., into the rural sector, but we firmly reject the notion that aid was "responsible" for Taiwan's good performance. Rather, aid facilitated the policy changes required for the restructuring which could take place once the necessary local decisions had been made.

In summary, a full and integrated explanation of the Taiwan pattern over the past two decades will clearly have to await further work examining the distribution of income within a growth-theoretic framework. But there are a number of factors which, on the basis of our present understanding, seem to have contributed most to the favorable outcome of an improved distribution of income, side by side with rapid growth in Taiwan. The combination of a fairly even initial distribution of assets, with the timely shift from an import substitution to a market- and export-oriented policy package, is undoubtedly the key ingredient of any explanation. It permitted the growth path to be endowment or labor-intensive and the functional distribution of income not to turn against labor even under labor surplus conditions. With real wages creeping up even before labor scarcity was reached and changes in the technology-*cum*-output mix heavily labor-using, increases in rent and profits are consistent with increases in wage shares. Even if the wage share should fall under such circumstances, it is still possible for income distribution to improve with substantial mobility from worker to self-employed entrepreneurial status and the shift from the top to the middle group of profit recipients (or from windfall to earned profits). If within-sector distribution, moreover, is more equal in industry, a rapid intersectoral reallocation should help the aggregate distribution index. The initially small intersectoral wage gap and its maintenance over time—through the absence of such exogenous forces as union and government salary pressures pulling up industrial wages —represent a third component of this (admittedly still tentative) explanation.

BIBLIOGRAPHY

Acharya, S. 1974. Fiscal/Financial Intervention, Factor Prices and Factor Proportions: A Review of Issues. Paper prepared for the Development Economics Department of the World Bank. Washington, D.C.

Acosta, J. 1972. Land Reform Laws in Cuba and the Peasants Private Sector. *Economía y Desarrollo* no. 12 (July–August): 84-115.

———. 1973. La Revolución Agraria en Cuba: El Desarrollo Económico. *Economía y Desarrollo* no. 17 (May–June).

Adelman, I. 1967. *Practical Approaches to Development Planning—The Case of Korea.* Baltimore: Johns Hopkins Univ. Press.

———. 1974. Reflections on Strategies for Distribution Oriented Growth (in press).

Adelman, I. and Morris, C. T. 1967. *Society, Politics and Economic Development.* Baltimore: Johns Hopkins Univ. Press.

———. 1971. An Anatomy of Patterns of Income Distribution in Developing Nations. Paper prepared for USAID, mimeographed. Washington, D.C.

———. 1972. Who Benefits from Economic Development? Paper prepared for the World Bank, mimeographed. Washington, D.C.

———. 1973. *Economic Growth and Social Equity in Developing Countries.* Stanford, Calif.: Stanford Univ. Press.

Adelman, I. and Robinson, S. 1973. *A Non-linear, Dynamic Microeconomic Model of Korea—Factors Affecting the Distribution of Income in the Short Run.* Woodrow Wilson School Research Program in Economic Development Discussion Paper no. 36. Princeton, N.J.: Princeton Univ.

Adelman, I. and Tyson, L. D. 1973. A Regional Microeconomic Model of Yugoslavia—Factors Affecting the Distribution of Income in the Short Run. Paper prepared for the Development Research Center of the World Bank, mimeographed. Washington, D.C.

Ahluwalia, M. S. 1973. Taxes, Subsidies and Employment. *Quarterly Journal of Economics* 88 (August): 393-409.

Anand, S. 1974. The Size Distribution of Income in Malaysia. Paper prepared for the Development Research Center of the World Bank, mimeographed. Washington, D.C.

Andic, S. and Peacock, A. T. 1961. The International Distribution of Income, 1949 and 1957. *Journal of the Royal Statistical Society* (General Series) 124: 206-218.

Atkinson, A. B. 1970. On the Measurement of Inequality. *Journal of Economic Theory* 2 (September): 244-263.

Bairoch, P. 1973. *Urban Unemployment in Developing Countries.* Geneva: International Labour Organization.

Balassa, B. 1970. Industrial Policies in Taiwan and Korea. World Bank Working Paper no. 68, mimeographed. Washington, D.C.: World Bank.

Banco de México, Oficina de Proyecciones Agrícolas. 1966. *Encuesta Sobre Ingresos y Gastos Familiares.* Mexico City.

Bandyopadhyay, D. 1972. Bargardars of Saliham. Paper presented to the Public Administration Case Workshop, Administrative Staff College of India, mimeographed. New Delhi.

Bardhan, P. K. 1970. On the Minimum Level of Living and the Rural Poor. *Indian Economic Review* 5 (April): 129-136.

———. 1973*a.* On the Incidence of Poverty in Rural India in the Sixties. *Economic and Political Weekly* 8 (February special number): 245-254.

———. 1973*b.* The Pattern of Income Distribution in India: A Review. Paper prepared for the Development Research Center of the World Bank, mimeographed. Washington, D.C.

———. 1973*c.* Planning Models and Income Distribution with Special Reference to India. Paper prepared for the Bellagio Working Party on Planning Models for Income Distribution and Employment.

———. 1973*d.* Variations in Agricultural Wages. *Economic and Political Weekly* 8 (May 26): 947-950.

Bardhan, P.K. and Srinivasan, T. N. 1971. Cropsharing Tenancy in Agriculture: A Theoretical and Empirical Analysis. *American Economic Review* 61 (March): 48-64.

Barlow, R. 1974. Applications of a Health Planning Model in Morocco (in press).

Barraclough, S. L. and Danike, A. L. 1970. Agrarian Structure in Seven Latin American Countries. In *Agrarian and Peasant Movements in Latin America,* ed. R. Stavenhager. New York: Doubleday.

Basta, S. S. and Churchill, A. 1974. Iron Deficiency Anemia and the Productivity of Adult Males in Indonesia. World Bank Staff Working Paper no. 175, mimeographed. Washington, D.C.: World Bank.

Beckerman, W., and Bacon, R. 1970. The International Distribution of Income. In *Unfashionable Economics, Essays in Honour of Lord Balogh,* ed. P. Streeten. London: Weidenfeld and Nicholson.

Bell, C. 1972. The Acquisition of Agricultural Technology: Its Determinants and Effects. *Journal of Development Studies* 9 (October): 123-159.

———. 1974. Ideology and Economic Interests in Indian Land Reform. In *Agrarian Reform and Agrarian Reformism,* ed. A. D. Lehmann. London: Faber.

Bell, L. C. and Prasad, P. K. 1972. The Share Croppers of Punea District. Paper prepared for the Land Reforms Commissioner, mimeographed, n.p.

Berelson, B. 1974. An Evaluation of the Effects of Population Control Programs. *Studies in Family Planning* 5 (January): 2-12.

Bergan, A. 1967. Personal Income Distribution and Personal Savings in Pakistan: 1963/1969. *Pakistan Development Review* 7 (Summer): 160-212.

Berry, A. 1972*a. The Relevance and Prospects of Small Scale Industry in Colombia.* Economic Growth Center Discussion Paper no. 142. New Haven, Conn.: Yale Univ.

————. 1972*b*. *Unemployment as a Social Problem in Urban Colombia*. Economic Growth Center Discussion Paper no. 145. New Haven, Conn.: Yale Univ.

Bhagwati, S. 1973. Education, Class Structure and Income Inequality. *World Development* 1 (May): 21-36.

Bhattacharya, N. and Chatterjee, A. K. Some Characteristics of Jute Industry Workers. *Economic and Political Weekly* 8 (February special number): 297-308.

Blaug, M. 1967. El Método de Análisis de Gastos para el Planeamiento de la Educación en los Países de Desarrollos. Economics Department Informe EC-157. Paper prepared for the World Bank, mimeographed. Washington, D.C.

————. 1970. *The Economics of Education—An Annotated Bibliography*. 2nd ed. Oxford: Pergamon.

Blaug, M., Lydall, R. and Woodhall, M. 1969. *The Causes of Graduate Unemployment in India*. London: Penguin.

Blitzer, C., Clark, P. B. and Taylor, L., eds. *Economy-wide Models and Development Planning* (forthcoming).

Bos, H. C. 1965. *Spatial Dispersion of Economic Activity*. Rotterdam: Rotterdam Univ. Press.

Bourque, P. J. and Cox, M. 1970. *An Inventory of Regional Input-Output Studies in U.S.* Seattle: Graduate School of Business Administration, University of Washington.

Bowles, S. 1969. *Planning Educational Systems for Economic Growth*. Harvard Economic Studies vol. 133. Cambridge, Mass.: Harvard Univ. Press.

Bronfenbrenner, M. 1971. *Income Distribution Theory*. Chicago: Aldine Atherton.

Brown, G. 1973. *Korean Pricing Policies and Development in the 1960s*. Baltimore: Johns Hopkins Univ. Press.

Bruno, M. 1967. Optional Patterns of Trade and Development. *Review of Economics and Statistics* 49 (November): 545-554.

Byres, T. 1974. Land Reform, Industrialization and the Marketed Surplus in India: An Essay on the Power of Rural Bias. In *Agrarian Reform and Agrarian Reformism*, ed. A. D. Lehmann. London: Faber.

Cassen, R. H. 1973. Economic-Demographic Interrelationships in Developing Countries. Paper read to the Conference on Population Size and Its Determinants, March 1973, Oxford.

Centro de Investigaciones Agrarias. 1970. *Estructura Agraria y Desarrollo Agricola en México*, vols. 1-3, Mexico City.

Chang, K. 1968. Distribution of Personal Income in Taiwan in 1953 and 1964. In *Economic Development in Taiwan*, ed. K. Chang. Taipei: Chengchung.

Chaudri, D. P. 1974. New Technologies and Income Distribution in Agriculture. In *Agrarian Reform and Agrarian Reformism*, ed. A. D. Lehmann. London: Faber.

Chelliah, R. J. 1971. Trends in Taxation in Developing Countries. *IMF Staff Papers* 18 (July): 254-331.

Chenery, H. B. 1962a. *Approaches to Development Planning,* U.S. Agency for International Development, Office of Program Coordination Policy, Discussion Paper no. 5, mimeographed. Washington, D.C.

————. 1962b. Development Policies for Southern Italy. *Quarterly Journal of Economics* 76 (November): 515-547.

————. 1970. Research on Economic Development. In *Economics,* ed. N. Ruggles. Englewood Cliffs, N.J.: Prentice Hall.

————. 1971. Targets for Development. In *The Widening Gap,* ed. B. Ward. New York: Columbia Univ. Press.

Chenery, H. B. and Clark, P. 1959. *Interindustry Economics.* New York: John Wiley.

Chenery, H. B. and Eckstein P. 1970. Development Alternatives for Latin America. *Journal of Political Economy* 78 (July–August): 966-1006.

Chenery, H. B. and Raduchel, W. 1971. Substitution in Planning Models. In *Studies in Development Planning,* ed. H. B. Chenery. Cambridge, Mass.: Harvard Univ. Press.

Chenery, H. B. and Syrquin, M. *Patterns of Development, 1950-1970* (forthcoming).

Chenery, H. B. and Taylor, L. 1968. Development Patterns Among Countries and Over Time. *Review of Economics and Statistics* 50 (November): 391-416.

Cheung, S.N.S. 1968. Private Property Rights and Sharecropping. *Journal of Political Economy* 76 (November–December): 1107-1122.

Cline, W. R. 1972. *Potential Effects of Income Redistribution on Economic Growth.* New York: Praeger.

————. 1973. Income Distribution and Economic Development: A Survey and Tests for Selected Latin American Cities. Paper prepared for ECIEL and read to the International Conference on Consumption, Income and Prices, October 1-3, 1973, Hamburg.

Coale, J. J. 1958. *Population Growth and Economic Development in Low Income Countries.* Princeton, N.J.: Princeton Univ. Press.

Cole, D. C. and Lyman, P. N. 1971. *Korean Development: The Interplay of Politics and Economics.* Cambridge, Mass.: Harvard Univ. Press.

Consejo Nacional de Economía. 1958. *Simposia de Recursos Naturales.* Havana.

Cruise O'Brien, D. 1972. Modernization, Order and the Erosion of a Democratic Ideal: American Political Science 1960-70. *Journal of Development Studies* 8 (April): 351-378.

Dandekar, V. M. and Rath, N. R. 1971. Poverty in India. *Economic and Political Weekly* 6 (January 2): 25-48, (January 9): 106-146.

Dantzing, G. B. and Wolfe, P. 1961. Decomposition Principle for Linear Programs. *Econometrica* 29 (October): 767-778.

Dasgupta, B. 1973. Calcutta's Informal Sector. *Bulletin of the Institute of Development Studies* 5 (October): 53-75.

Day, R. H. and Heidhues, T. 1966. Towards a Macroeconomic Model of Agricultural Production and Development. Farm and Market Workshop Paper no. 6072. Madison: University of Wisconsin Social Systems Research Institute.

Delagarza, F. and Manne, A. 1973. Energeticos, A Process Analysis of the Energy Sectors. In *Multi-Level Planning—Case Studies in Mexico,* ed. L. M. Goreux and A. Manne. Amsterdam: North-Holland.

Dirección General de Estadística y Censos. 1969. *Encuesta Nacional Sobre Ingresos Familiares,* Serie de Investigaciones Muestrales. Santiago.

Dorticos, O. 1972. Development of Cuban Economy: Analysis and Perspectives. *Economía y Desarrollo* no. 12 (July–August): 28-62.

Dougherty, C.R.S. 1972. Substitution and Structure of the Labor Force. *Economic Journal* 82 (March): 170-182.

Doving, F. 1959. The Share of Agriculture in a Growing Population. *[FAO] Monthly Bulletin of Agricultural Economics and Statistics* (August–September): 1-9.

Duloy, J. H. and Hazell, P. B. Substitution and Nonlinearities in Planning Models. In *Economy-wide Models and Development Planning,* ed. C. Blitzer, et al. (forthcoming).

Duloy, J. H. and Norton, R. D. 1973a. CHAC, A Programming Model of Mexican Agriculture. In *Multi-Level Planning—Case Studies in Mexico,* ed. L. M. Goreux and A. Manne. Amsterdam: North-Holland.

———. 1973b. CHAC Results: Economic Alternatives for Mexican Agriculture. In *Multi-Level Planning—Case Studies in Mexico,* ed. L. M. Goreux and A. Manne. Amsterdam: North Holland.

Dumont, R. 1970. *Cuba: Est-il Socialiste?* Paris: Edition du Seuil.

Economic Commission for Asia and the Far East. 1971. *Economic Survey of Asia and the Far East* (E/CN.11/1047). Bangkok.

Ellman, J. 1968. The Use of Input-Output in Regional Economic Planning: The Soviet Experience. *Economic Journal* 83 (December): 855-867.

Enos, J. 1970. *Modelling the Economic Development of a Poorly Endowed Region: The Northeast of Thailand.* Santa Monica, Calif.: Rand Corporation.

Fei, J.C.H. and Ranis, G. 1964. *Development of the Labour-Surplus Economy: Theory and Policy.* Homewood, Ill.: Richard D. Irwin.

———. 1974. A Model of Growth and Employment in the Open Dualistic Economy: The Cases of Korea and Taiwan (in press).

Feldstein, M.A., Piot, M. A. and Sunderasan, T. K. 1973. *Resource Allocation Model for Public Health Planning: A Case Study of Tuberculosis Control.* Geneva: World Health Organization.

Ferguson, C. E. and Nell, E. J. 1972. Two Review Articles on Two Books on the Theory of Income Distribution. *Journal of Economic Literature* 10 (June): 437-453.

Figueroa, A. and Weisskoff, R. 1974. Viewing Social Pyramids: Income Distribution in Latin America. Paper read to the Second Latin American

Conference of the International Association for Research in Income and Wealth, July 10, 1974, Rio de Janeiro.

Fishlow, A. 1972. Brazilian Size Distribution of Income. *Papers and Proceedings of the American Economic Association* 62 (May): 391-402.

———. 1973a. Brazilian Income Size Distribution—Another Look. Mimeographed.

———. 1973b. The Introduction of Distributional Aspects into Planning Models and Procedures. Paper prepared for the Bellagio Working Party on Planning Models for Income Distribution and Employment.

Food and Agriculture Organization. 1971 *Report on the 1960 World Census of Agriculture,* vol. 5. Rome.

Fox, D. J. 1972. Patterns of Morbidity and Mortality in Mexico City. *Geographical Review* 2 (April): 151-185.

Foxley, A. and Muñoz, O. 1973. Redistribución del Ingreso, Crecimiento Económico y Estructura Social: el Caso Chileño. *El Trimestre Económico* 40 (October–December): 905-936.

Frank, C. R. 1971. The Problem of Urban Unemployment in Africa. In *Employment and Unemployment Problems of the Near East and South Asia,* ed. R. C. Ridker and H. Lubell. New Delhi: Vikas.

Friedman, J. and Alonso, W., eds. 1966. *Regional Development and Planning—A Reading.* Cambridge, Mass.: MIT Press.

Geoffrion, A. 1970. Elements of Large Scale Mathematical Programming, Parts I and II. *Management Science* 16 (July): 652-691.

Griffin, K. 1974. The International Transmission of Inequality (in press).

Hanssen, J. S. 1970. *Optimal Patterns of Location.* Amsterdam: North-Holland.

Harbison, F. and Myers, C. A. 1964. *Education, Manpower, and Economic Growth.* New York: McGraw-Hill.

Harral, C. G. et al. 1974. Study of the Substitution of Labor and Equipment in Civil Construction: Phase II Final Report. World Bank Staff Working Paper no. 172, mimeographed. Washington, D.C.: World Bank.

Harris, J. R. and Todaro, M. P. 1970. Migration, Unemployment and Development: A Two Sector Analysis. *American Economic Review* 60 (March): 126-142.

Hart, K. 1973. Informal Income Opportunities and the Structure of Urban Employment in Ghana. *Journal of Modern African Studies* 11 (March): 61-89.

Hatada, T. 1969. *A History of Korea.* New York: Clio Press.

[U.S. Department of] Health, Education and Welfare. 1972. *Syncrisis: The Dynamics of Health, Vol. I, Panama.* Washington, D.C.: U.S. Government Printing Office.

Henderson, G. 1968. *Korea, the Politics of the Vortex.* Cambridge, Mass.: Harvard Univ. Press.

Herdt, R. W. and Baker, E. A. 1972. Agricultural Wages, Production and the High-Yielding Varieties. *Economic and Political Weekly* 7 (March 25): A-23 to A-30.

Hirschman, A. O. 1963. *A Journey Toward Progress: Studies of Economic Policy Making in Latin America.* New York: 20th Century Fund.

———. 1969. *How to Divest in Latin America and Why.* Essays in International Finance no. 76. Princeton, N.J.: Princeton Univ. Press.

Ho, Y. M. and Huddle, D. 1972. The Contribution of Traditional and Smaller-Scale Culture Goods in International Trade and Employment. Rice Univ. Discussion Paper no. 35, mimeographed. Houston.

Hobsbawn, E. 1973. Peasants and Politics. *Journal of Peasant Studies* 1 (October): 3-22.

Hofmeister, R. 1971. Growth with Unemployment in Latin America: Some Implications for Asia. In *Employment and Unemployment Problems in the Near East and South Asia,* ed. R. G. Ridker and H. Lubell, vol. 2. New Delhi: Vikas.

———. 1974. Economic Situation and Prospects of Pakistan 1974 Annex D. Document of the World Bank forthcoming.

———. [1974.] Notes from a World Bank economic mission to Pakistan, unpublished.

Huntington, S. P. 1968. *Political Order in Changing Societies.* New Haven, Conn.: Yale Univ. Press.

Illich, I. 1971. *De-Schooling Society.* World Perspective Series. New York: Harper & Row.

India, Banking Commission. 1971. *Report of the Study Group on Non-Banking Financial Intermediaries.* Bombay.

India, Directorate of Economics and Statistics. 1968. *India, Growth Rates in Agriculture 1949-50 and 1964-65.* New Delhi

India, Planning Commission. 1973. *Approach to the Fifth Five-Year Plan.* New Delhi.

Instituto Brasileiro de Geografia e Estadística, Servico Nacional de Recenseamento. 1965. *VII Recenseamento Geral do Brasil, 1960, Censo Demografico: Resultados Preliminares.* Riò de Janeiro.

International Labour Organization. 1970. *Towards Full Employment: A Programme for Colombia.* Prepared by an interagency team organized by the ILO. Geneva.

———. 1971a. *Matching Employment Opportunities and Expectations: A Programme of Action for Ceylon.* The report of an interagency team organized by the ILO. Geneva.

———. 1971b. *Projection Model for a Full Employment Strategy.* (Technical Paper no. 9). Geneva.

———. 1972. *Employment, Incomes and Equality, A Strategy for Increasing Productive Employment in Kenya.* Report of an interagency team organized by the ILO. Geneva.

———. 1973. *Sharing in Development: A Programme of Development, Equity and Growth for the Philippines.* Vol. 1, Main Report. Geneva.

Jain, S. and Tiemann, A. 1973. Size Distribution of Income: A Compilation of Data. Development Research Center Discussion Paper no. 4, mimeographed. Washington, D.C.: World Bank.

Jallade, J-P. 1974. *Public Expenditure on Education and Income Distribution in Colombia.* World Bank Staff Occasional Paper no. 18. Baltimore: Johns Hopkins Univ. Press.

Jodha, N. S. 1973. Special Programmes for the Rural Poor: the Constraining Framework. *Economic and Political Weekly* 8 (March 31): 633-639.

Juntas Central de Planificación, Dirección Central de Estadística. 1967. *Resumen de Estadísticas de Población,* no. 3. Havana.

Kaldor, N. 1956. Alternative Theories of Distribution. *Review of Economic Studies* 23: 83-100.

Kalecki, M. 1954. *Theory of Economic Dynamics: An Essay on Cyclical and Long Run Changes in Capitalistic Economy.* London: Allen and Unwin.

Kaser, M. C., ed. 1968. *Economic Development for Eastern Europe.* London: Macmillan.

Kocher, J. E. 1973. *Rural Development, Income Distribution and Fertility Decline.* New York: Population Council.

Korean Development Association. 1967. *A Study of Regional Planning by Using Regional Input-Output Model.* Seoul.

Kornai, J. 1969a. Multi-Level Programming—A First Report on the Model and on the Experimental Computation. *European Economic Review* 1 (Fall): 134-191.

———. 1969b. Man Machine Planning. *Economics of Planning* 9: 209-234.

Kornai, J. and Lipthak, T. H. 1965. Two Levels of Planning. *Econometrica* 33 (January): 141-169.

Krishna, R. 1973. Unemployment in India. *Indian Journal of Agricultural Economics* 28 (January–March): 1-23.

Kuhn, T. S. 1962. *Structure of Scientific Revolutions.* Chicago: Univ. of Chicago Press.

Kuznets, S. 1955. Economic Growth and Income Inequality. *American Economic Review* 45 (March): 1-28.

———. 1963. Quantitative Aspects of Economic Growth of Nations: III, Distribution of Income by Size. *Economic Development and Cultural Change* 11 (January): 1-80.

———. 1972. The Gap: Concepts, Measurement and Trends. In *The Gap Between Rich and Poor Nations,* ed. G. Ranis. London: Macmillan.

Lamb, G. 1973. The Definition and Determination of the Objective Function. Paper prepared for the Bellagio Working Party on Planning Models for Income Distribution and Employment.

Landau, L. 1971. Determinants of Savings in Latin America. In *Studies in Development Planning,* ed. H. B. Chenery, et al. Cambridge, Mass.: Harvard Univ. Press.

Lee, H. 1968. *Time, Change, and Administration: Korea's Search for Modernization.* Honolulu: East-West Centre.

Lehmann, A. D. 1971. Political Incorporation versus Political Stability: The Case of the Chilean Agrarian Reform, 1965-70. *Journal of Development Studies* 7 (July): 365-395.

————., ed. 1974. *Agrarian Reform and Agrarian Reformism.* London: Faber.

Lele, U. J. 1972. Role of Credit and Marketing Functions in Agricultural Development. Paper read to the International Economic Association Conference on the Place of Agriculture in the Development of Underdeveloped Countries, August–September 1972, Bad Godesberg.

————. 1974. Phase I Report of the African Rural Development Study, Parts I and II. Paper prepared for Development Economics Department of the World Bank, mimeographed. Washington, D.C.

Lewis, W. A. 1954. Economic Development with Unlimited Supplies of Labor. *Manchester School* 22 (May): 139-191.

————. 1955. *A Theory of Economic Growth.* London: Allen and Unwin.

Leys, C. T. 1969. The Analysis of Planning. In *Politics and Change in Developing Countries,* ed. C. T. Leys. Cambridge: At the University Press.

Lindblom, C. E. and Braybroke, D. 1963. *A Strategy of Decision.* Glencoe, Ill.: Free Press.

Lipton, M. Strategy for Agriculture: Urban Bias and Rural Planning. In *The Crisis of Indian Planning: Economic Planning in the 1960s,* ed. P. Streeten and M. Lipton. London: Oxford Univ. Press.

————. 1974. Towards a Theory of Land Reform. In *Agrarian Reform and Agrarian Reformism,* ed. A. D. Lehmann. London: Faber.

Lopes, F. L. 1972. Inequality Planning in the Developing Economy. Ph.D. dissertation, Harvard Univ.

MacEwan, A. 1971. *Development Alternatives in Pakistan—A Multisectoral and Regional Analysis of Planning Problems.* Harvard Economic Studies, vol. 134. Cambridge, Mass.: Harvard Univ. Press.

Malenbaum, W. 1970. Health and Productivity in Poor Areas. In *Empirical Studies in Health Economics: Proceedings,* ed. H. E. Klarman. Baltimore: Johns Hopkins Univ. Press.

————. 1973. Health and Economic Expansion in Poor Lands. *International Journal of Health Services* 3: 161-176.

Marsden, K. 1969. Toward a Synthesis of Economic Growth and Social Justice. *International Labour Review* 100 (November): 389-418.

————. 1970. Progressive Technologies for Developing Countries. *International Labour Review,* 101 (May): 475-502.

Marshall, A. 1890. *Principles of Economics.* London: Macmillan.

Martin, R. C., ed. 1956. *T.V.A. — The First 20 Years: A Staff Report.* [University, Ala.:] Univ. of Alabama Press.

Maruhnic, J. 1973. Statistical Appendix to *Education and Income Distribution* by F. H. Harbison. Princeton University Policy Research Workshop, USAID, Brookings Institution, and Princeton Univ., mimeographed.

Mazumdar, D. 1973. Theory of Urban Underemployment in LDC's. Paper prepared for the World Bank, mimeographed. Washington, D.C.

————. 1974. The Problem of Unemployment in Peninsular Malaysia. Draft report prepared for the World Bank.

Medholm, C. 1973. *Research on Employment in the Rural Nonfarm Sector in*

Africa. Africa Rural Employment Paper no. 4. East Lansing: Michigan State Univ.

Mennes, L. M. and Tinbergen, J. G. 1969. *The Element of Space in Development Planning.* Amsterdam: North-Holland.

Mikesell, R. F. and Chenery, H. B. 1949. *Arabian Oil: America's Stake in the Middle East.* Chapel Hill: Univ. of North Carolina Press.

Mikesell, R. F. and Zinser, J. E. 1973. The Nature of Savings Function in Developing Countries: A Survey of the Theoretical and Empirical Literature. *Journal of Economic Literature* 11 (March): 1-26.

Minhas, B. S. 1970. Rural Poverty, Land Redistribution and Economic Strategy. *Indian Economic Review* 5 (April): 97-128.

———. 1971. Man, Poverty and Strategy of Rural Development in India. Paper prepared for the Economic Development Institute, World Bank, mimeographed. Washington, D.C.

Moore, B., Jr., 1966. *Social Origins of Dictatorship and Democracy: Lord and Peasant in the Making of the Modern World.* Boston: Beacon Press.

Morawetz, D. 1974. Employment Implications of Industrialization in Developing Countries: A Survey. World Bank Staff Working Paper no. 170, mimeographed. Washington, D.C.: World Bank.

Morrisson, C. 1972. Korea. Paper prepared for Development Research Center of the World Bank, mimeographed. Washington, D.C.

Myrdal, G. 1968. *Asian Drama—An Inquiry into the Poverty of Nations.* New York: 20th Century Fund.

National Bureau of Economic Research. 1957. *Problems in the Anthology for the International Comparison of Economic Accounts.* Studies in Income and Wealth, vol. 20. Princeton, N.J.: Princeton Univ. Press.

National Council of Applied Economic Research. 1962. *Urban Income and Saving.* New Delhi.

———. 1965. *All India Rural Household Survey, Vol. II.* New Delhi.

Navarette, I. 1960. *La Distribución del Ingreso y el Desarrollo Económico México.* Universidad Nacional Autonomía de México Instituto de Investigaciones Económicas, Escuela Nacional de Económica. Mexico City.

Navarro, V. 1972. Health, Health Service and Health Planning in Cuba. *International Journal of Health Services* 2 (August): 406.

———. 1973. The Underdevelopment of Health or the Health of Underdevelopment. Paper read to the Pan American Conference on Health Manpower Planning, September 1973, Ottawa.

Nelson, J. 1973. *Public Housing Illegal Settlements and the Growth of Colombian Cities.* Report to the Urban and Regional Development Division of USAID, Bogota.

Newbery, D.M.G. 1973. The Choice of Contract in Peasant Agriculture. Paper read to the Conference on Agriculture in Development Theory, May [revised version dated August] 1973, mimeographed. Bellagio.

Norton, R. 1971*a*. A Linear Programming Model of Regional Investment Allocation. Ph.D. dissertation, Johns Hopkins Univ.

————. 1971*b*. The South Korean Economy in the 1960s. Paper read to the Association for Asian Studies, March 29, 1971, Washington, D.C.

Nuti, D. M. 1970. Vulgar Economy in the Theory of Income Distribution. *De Economist* 118:363-9.

Organization for Economic Cooperation and Development. [Little, I.M.D. and Mirrlees, J. A.] 1969. *Manual of Industrial Project Analysis in Developing Countries.* Paris: OECD Development Center.

Organization for Economic Cooperation and Development. 1970. *Gaps in Technology, Analytical Report.* Paris.

Oshima, H. 1961. The National Income and Production of Cuba in 1953. *Food Research Institute Studies* 2 (November): 213-227.

————. 1962. The International Comparison of Size Distribution of Family Incomes with Specific Reference to Asia. *Review of Economics and Statistics* 44 (November): 439-445.

Pak, K. 1966. *A Study of Land Tenure in Korea.* Seoul: Korea Land Economics Research Center.

Pasinetti, L. L. 1962. The Role of Profit and Income Distribution in Relation to the Role of Economic Growth. *Review of Economic Studies* 2 (October): 267-279.

Patel, S. J. 1964. The Economic Distance Between Nations: Its Origin, Measurement and Outlook. *Economic Journal* 74 (March): 122-129.

Pen, J. 1971. *Income Distribution Facts, Theories and Policies,* trans. T. S. Preston. New York: Praeger.

Psachropoulus, G. 1972. *The Economic Return to Education: International Comparison.* Amsterdam: Elsevier.

Pyatt, G., et al. 1972. Comprehensive Employment Planning Applied to Iran. Paper prepared for the ILO World Employment Program, mimeographed. Warwick.

Pyatt, G. and Thorbecke, E. Outline for *Planning for Growth, Redistribution and Employment.* Mimeographed. [Warwick?].

Raj, K. N. 1973. The Politics and Economics of "Intermediate Regimes." *Economic and Political Weekly* 8 (July 7): 1189-1198.

Rampel, H. and Harris, J. R. *Rural-Urban Migration and Urban Unemployment in Kenya* (forthcoming).

Ranis, G. 1961. Industrial Efficiency and Economic Growth: A Case Study of Karachi. Monographs in Tile Economics of Development no. 5, Institute of Development Economics. Karachi.

Reid, E. 1973. *Strengthening the World Bank.* Chicago: Adlai Stevenson Institute.

Reuber, G. L. 1973. *Private Foreign Investment in Development.* New York: Oxford Univ. Press.

Rich, W. 1973. *Smaller Families through Social and Economic Progress.* Overseas Development Council Monograph Series no. 7. Washington, D.C.

Riggs, F. W. 1964. *Administration in Developing Countries.* Boston: Houghton Mifflin.

Robinson, J. 1972. The Second Crisis of Economic Theory. *American Economic Review* 62 (May): 1-10.

Samuelson, P.A. 1952. Spatial Price Equilibrium and Linear Programming. *American Economic Review* 42 (June): 283-303.

Schaffer, B. B. 1969. The Deadlock in Development Administration. In *Politics and Change in Developing Countries,* ed. C. T. Leys. Cambridge: At the University Press.

Seers, D., ed. 1964. *Cuba: The Economic and Social Revolution.* Chapel Hill: Univ. of North Carolina Press.

————. 1973. The Planning Context and the Forms of Planning. Paper prepared for the Bellagio Working Party on Planning Models for Income Distribution and Employment.

Selowsky, M. and Taylor, L. 1973. The Economics of Malnourished Children: An Example of Disinvestment in Human Capital. *Economic Development and Cultural Change* 22 (October): 12-39.

Selznick, P. 1949. *T.V.A. and the Grass Root: A Study in the Sociology of Formal Organization.* Berkeley: Univ. of California Press.

Sen, A. K. 1973a. *Employment Policy and Technological Choice.* Geneva: International Labour Organization.

————. 1973b. Poverty, Inequality and Unemployment: Some Conceptual Issues in Measurement. *Economic Political Weekly* 8 (August special number): 1457-1464.

Serck-Hanssen, J. 1970. *Optimal Patterns of Location.* Amsterdam: North-Holland.

Singer, H. W. et al. 1973. *Trade Liberalization, Employment and Income Distribution, A First Approach.* Institute of Development Studies Discussion Paper no. 31. Sussex.

Singer, H. W. and Reynolds, S. 1973. Aspects of the Distribution of Income and Wealth in Kenya. Paper read to the Unesco Conference on the Social Science Project on Human Resources Indicators, November 1973, Institute of Development Studies, Sussex.

Stewart, F. 1972. Trade and Technology. Paper read to the Cambridge Conference on Development, Cambridge.

Stiglitz, J. 1969. Distributions of Income and Wealth Among Individuals. *Econometrica* 37 (July): 382-397.

————. 1973. *Alternative Theories of Wage Determination and Unemployment in LDC's.* Cowles Foundation Discussion Paper. New Haven, Conn.: Yale Univ.

Suh, S. M. 1974. Size, Technology and Other Economic Characteristics in Malaysian Industry. Paper prepared for the Development Research Center, World Bank, mimeographed. Washington, D.C.

Swamy, S. 1967. Structural Changes and the Distribution of Income by Size: The Case of India. *Review of Income and Wealth* 13 (June): 155-174.

Takayama, T. and Judge, G. 1971. *Spatial and Temporal Price and Allocation Models.* Amsterdam: North-Holland.

Taylor, L. 1973. *Multi-sectoral Models in Development Planning: A Survey.*

Economic Development Report no. 230, Development Research Group, Harvard Univ. Center for International Affairs. Cambridge, Mass.

———. Theoretical Foundations and Technical Implications. In *Economy-wide Models and Development Planning,* ed. C. Blitzer et al. (forthcoming).

Theil, H. 1967. *Economics and Information Theory.* Amsterdam: North-Holland.

Thorbecke, E. 1973. The Employment Problem: A Critical Evaluation of Four ILO Comprehensive Country Reports. *International Labor Review* 107 (May): 393-423.

Thorbecke, E. and Sengupta, J. K. 1972. A Consistency Framework for Employment Output and Income Distribution: Projections Applied to Colombia. Paper prepared for Development Research Center, World Bank, mimeographed. Washington, D.C.

Tims, W. 1968. A Growth Model and its Applications—Pakistan. In *Development Policy—Theory and Practice,* ed. G. F. Papanek. Cambridge, Mass.: Harvard Univ. Press.

Tinbergen, J. 1958. *The Design of Development.* Baltimore: Johns Hopkins Univ. Press.

———. 1964. *Economic Policy: Principles and Design.* Amsterdam: North-Holland.

Tinbergen, J. et al. 1969. Econometric Models for Education. In *Economics of Education 2,* ed. M. Blaug. Harmondsworths and Baltimore: Penguin.

Todaro, M. P. 1969. A Model of Labor Migration and Urban Unemployment. *American Economic Review* 59 (March): 138-148.

Tokman, V. 1972. Tecnología y Empleo en el Sector Industrial del Perú. Mimeographed. Santiago: O.E.A.-Ilpes.

Truslow, F. A. et al. 1951. *Report on Cuba.* World Bank Economic and Technical Mission Report. Washington, D.C.

Turnham, D. (assisted by Jaeger, I.) 1971. *The Employment Problem in Less Developed Countries: A Review of Evidence.* Development Centre Studies Employment Series no. 1. Paris: Organization for Economic Cooperation and Development.

United Nations Statistical Office. 1968. *A System of National Accounts.* Department of Economic and Social Affairs, Studies in Methods Series F, no. 2, Rev. 3 (St/Stat/Ser F/2 Rev. 3). New York.

United Nations. 1970a. *An Integrated System of Demographic Manpower and Social Statistics, and its Links with the System of National Economic Accounts.* Economic and Social Council Statistical Commission (3/CN.3/384). New York.

———. 1970b. *Science and Technology for Development: Proposals for the Second United Nations Development Decade.* New York.

United Nations Statistical Office. 1971. *Demographic Yearbook.* Population and Vital Statistics Report. Department of Economic and Social Affairs. New York.

United Nations. 1973. *Multi-National Corporations in World Development.* New York.

United Nations Industrial Development Organization. 1972. *Guidelines for Project Evaluation.* New York: United Nations.

Uphoff, N. 1972. The Expansion of Employment Associated with Growth of GNP: A Projecture Model and its Implications for Ghana. *The Economic Bulletin of Ghana* 2: 3-15.

———. 1973. *Political Constraints and Benefits.* Paper prepared for the Bellagio Working Party on Planning Models for Income Distribution and Employment.

USAID. 1970a. *Spring Review of Land Reform, Country Papers,* 2nd. ed., Vol. 5, June (SR/LR/C-4). Washington, D.C.

———. 1970b. *Spring Review of Land Reform, Country Papers,* 2nd ed., Vol. 9, June (SR/LR/C-15, 16). Washington, D.C.

Vaitsos, C. 1973. The Changing Policies of Latin American Governments Towards Economic Development and Direct Foreign Investment. Paper read to the Conference on Latin American Economic Interactions, March 1973, University of Texas, Austin. [IDS Communication 106.]

Visaria, P. and Visaria, L. 1973. Employment Planning for the Weaker Sections in Rural India. *Economic and Political Weekly* 8 (February special number): 269-276A.

Webb, R. 1972. *The Distribution of Income in Peru.* Woodrow Wilson School Research Program in Economic Development Discussion Paper no. 26. Princeton, N.J.: Princeton Univ.

Weeks, J. 1973. Uneven Sectoral Development and the Role of the State. *Bulletin of the Institute of Development Studies* 5 (October): 76-82.

Weisskoff, R. 1970. Income Distribution and Economic Growth in Puerto Rico, Argentina and Mexico. *Review of Income and Wealth* 16 (December): 303-332.

———. 1973. A Multi-Sector Simulation Model of Employment, Growth, and Income Distribution in Puerto Rico: A Reevaluation of "Successful" Development Strategy. Paper prepared for the Yale Concilium of International Affairs and U.S. Dept. of Labor Manpower Administration, mimeographed. New Haven.

World Bank. 1972. *Atlas.* Washington, D.C.

———. 1973a. *Trends in Developing Countries.* Washington, D.C.

———. 1973b. World Economy and Developing Countries. Mimeographed. Washington, D.C.

Zagoria, D. S. 1972. A Note on Landlessness, Literacy and Agrarian Communism in India. *Archives Européennes de Sociologie* 13.

Zaldivar, R. 1974. Agrarian Reform and Military Reformism in Peru. In *Agrarian Reform and Agrarian Reformism,* ed. A. D. Lehmann. London: Faber.

Zymelman, M. 1973. Cost Effectiveness of Alternative Learning Technologies Industrial Training—A Study of In-Plant Training and Vocational Schools. World Bank Staff Working Paper no. 169. Washington, D.C.: World Bank.